Theoretical and Empirical Exercises in ECONOMETRICS

Theoretical and Empirical Exercises in ECONOMETRICS

Nlandu Mamingi

University of the West Indies Press
Jamaica • Barbados • Trinidad and Tobago

The University of the West Indies Press
1A Aqueduct Flats Mona
Kingston 7 Jamaica
www.uwipress.com

09 08 07 06 05 5 4 3 2 1

CATALOGUING IN PUBLICATION DATA

Mamingi, Nlandu.
Theoretical and empirical exercises in econometrics / Nlandu Mamingi.
p. cm.
Includes bibliographical references.
ISBN: 976-640-176-4

1. Econometrics. I. Title.

HB139.M38 2005 300.01'5195

Book design by Roy Barnhill.
Cover design by Robert Harris.

Printed in the United States of America.

To Nsona Levo
Matumuene Nlandu
Zola Nlandu
Mundayi Nlandu

Contents

List of Tables

List of Figures

Foreword

I am greatly honoured and happy to write the foreword to this econometrics book, written by one of my most beloved and trusted students, Dr Nlandu Mamingi, who is now a faculty member of the Department of Economics at the University of the West Indies, Cave Hill campus, Barbados. When Nlandu walked into my advanced econometrics class in the late 1980s, it did not take me long to recognize him as a scholar-in-the-making. His drive for knowledge and determination to push the frontiers of econometrics forward kept him free of the immediate problems and frustrations of a lonely graduate student facing the unfriendly winters of upstate New York. Nlandu was always happy and cordial. His doctoral thesis, entitled "Essays on the Effects of Misspecified Dynamics and Temporal Aggregation on Cointegrated Relationships", is a masterpiece that was way ahead of its time. Researchers around the world are still working on some of the issues raised by Nlandu in his 1992 dissertation.

This book of exercises that Nlandu has put together will be extremely valuable as supplemental material that can help both undergraduate and postgraduate students, as well as their teachers, worldwide. The coverage of the book, beginning with simple regression models and continuing with generalized regression, dummy variables, limited dependent variables, simultaneous equations, dynamic regressions, unit roots, vector autoregressions, cointegration and error correction models, aggregation problems, forecasting and panel data models, is now standard in most countries and, thus, would help numerous students. The exercises are well planned, and the solutions are given clearly. The purpose and scope of the book is unique; that is, it has no competitor. Accordingly, I expect the book to do well. Certainly, I would like to have a copy on my desk.

By writing this book on such a useful but technical topic Nlandu has delighted all his past teachers, colleagues and students. On behalf of all, I congratulate him and wish him the best.

Kajal Lahiri
Albany, New York

Preface

This book is a result of more than twenty years of involvement with econometrics in various capacities (student and/or teacher and/or researcher) at the University of Kinshasa (The Democratic Republic of Congo), the Institute of Social Studies (The Hague, The Netherlands), the State University of New York (Albany, New York), the World Bank (Washington, D.C.) and the University of the West Indies (Cave Hill campus, Barbados).

The book, which is written in the same vein as Phillips and Wickens (1978 a,b), does not attempt to duplicate the many econometrics books in use, some of which have become standards. Rather, it tries to supplement them by focusing exclusively on theoretical and empirical exercises, in a systematic way. Put differently, this book helps the reader verify his or her knowledge of econometrics acquired elsewhere.

This book is intended for use mainly by undergraduate economics students, although some graduate beginners as well as econometrics practitioners may also find the text useful. Many exercises were taken from tutorials and examinations from my Econometrics I and Econometrics II classes at the University of the West Indies, Cave Hill campus. Where exercises were knowingly borrowed from other sources, these have been acknowledged.

There are three novel approaches in the book. First, acknowledging this as a computer era, the book reemphasizes theoretical exercises that can be useful in interpreting empirical results. It is known, for example, that the *Durbin-Watson* (DW) statistic is not valid in the presence of a lagged dependent variable. However, most computer software returns the DW statistic even in the presence of a lagged dependent variable. It is thus up to the user to know that the statistic is invalid in this situation. Second, the book contains very useful essay questions that deal with important econometric issues. It is my experience that the inability of many students to summarize, in a coherent way, econometric issues learned, as well as to build possible links between or among issues (e.g., issues in simultaneous equations models, vector autoregressions models and error correction models), presents a knowledge gap that needs to be addressed. Third, the book is bold enough to present a number of exercises that do not have clear-cut answers, acknowledging that from time to time gaps may exist between theory and practice (for example, in a Box–Jenkins environment, one may have a gap between the theoretical correlogram and the empirical correlogram for one reason or another; in an aggregation over time environment, one may also have a gap between theoretical and empirical results). *Note that the answers to questions are as detailed as possible. Those answers are not, however, necessary reference answers to examination questions but rather a learning tool.*

The book is divided into four parts, each of which contains at least one chapter. Each chapter has an introduction, a question section divided into theoretical and empirical questions, an answer section and a section on supplementary exercises. Some questions have been used in econometrics courses (EC36C and EC36D) at the University of the West Indies, and these have been identified in the text.

Part One deals with single equation regression models and has three chapters. Chapter 1 is concerned with exercises related to the conceptual framework of regression, the properties of estimators and hypothesis testing. Chapter 2 develops exercises concerned with the relaxation of assumptions of the classical linear model. Chapter 3 consists of exercises dealing with dummy variables as explanatory variables as well as endogenous variables.

Part Two focuses on simultaneous equations models and only has one chapter. Chapter 4 centres on exercises related to the main issues in simultaneous equations models.

Part Three is concerned with dynamic regression models. It has three chapters. Chapter 5 develops exercises in the context of dynamic regressions in the classical sense: distributed lag models, autoregressive distributed lag models and expectation models. Chapter 6 deals with a more modern approach to dynamic regressions: unit root, cointegration, vector autoregressions and error correction models. Chapter 7 concentrates on aggregation over time, which is seriously overlooked in most econometrics books.

Part Four deals with forecasting and panel data models. Chapter 8 tackles forecasting by emphasizing the main issues involved in forecasting, as well as forecast comparison. Chapter 9 deals with panel data models at the elementary level.

Acknowledgments

It is a privilege to record my appreciation to those who have influenced my thinking on econometrics and subsequently, directly or indirectly, have had an impact upon this book. Professor Frank Alleyne, dean of the Faculty of Social Sciences at the Cave Hill campus of the University of the West Indies, has been instrumental in supporting this project in various ways. I sincerely thank him. I also acknowledge my teachers at the University of Kinshasa, Professors David Wheeler (now Lead Economist at the World Bank), Kalonji Ntalaja and Kintambu Mafuku, who initiated me into econometrics. At the Institute of Social Studies I had the privilege to be taught and supervised by a great teacher and researcher, Professor Marc Wuyts. From him, I learned the sense of questioning concepts. Professor, I salute you. My teacher and PhD advisor at the State University of New York at Albany, Professor Kajal Lahiri, taught me to be independent. Professor, I am deeply grateful to you. The World Bank environment helped me realize the gap that can exist between theory and practice. My colleagues in the Department of Economics of the University of the West Indies, Cave Hill campus, have created an environment conducive to good work. I thank you all: Professor Michael Howard, Professor Andrew Downes, Dr Sunday Osaretin Iyare, Dr Stephen Harewood, Dr Arindam Banik and Dr Judy Whitehead. My several times co-authors, Dr Susmita Dasgupta and Dr Benoît Laplante, are also acknowledged for giving me the opportunity to apply econometric theory to concrete problems. The numerous students I have had at the University of Kinshasa and the University of the West Indies are acknowledged for asking provocative questions.

Thanks are due to the following publishers for granting me permission to use material for which they hold copyright: the Sir Arthur Lewis Institute of Social and Economic Research, World Scientific Publishing Company, and Elsevier.

Mrs Annette Greene, my assistant, is recognized for diligently typing a great deal of the text. Miss Jennifer Hurley, who ably edited the text, is also thanked. Two anonymous reviewers are acknowledged for carefully reading the manuscript and making very useful remarks. For understanding the importance of the work and acting accordingly, my wife, Nsona Levo, and my children, Matumuene Nlandu, Zola Nlandu and Mundayi Nlandu, are sincerely thanked.

Abbreviations and Symbols

2SLS or TSLS	Two stage least squares
3SLS	Three stage least squares
ACF	Autocorrelation function or correlogram
ADF	Augmented Dickey–Fuller
ADL	Autoregressive distributed lag
AEG	Augmented Engle–Granger
AIC	Akaike information criterion
AR	Autoregressive
ARMA	Autoregressive moving average
ARIMA	Autoregressive integrated moving average
BOP	Balance of payments
CLM	Classical linear model
CPI	Consumer price index
DGP	Data generation process
DL	Distributed lag
DW	Durbin–Watson
ECM	Error correction model
ESS	Explained sum of squares
FE	Fixed effects
FIML	Full information maximum likelihood
GDP	Gross domestic product
GLS	Generalized least squares
GMM	Generalized method of moments
ILS	Indirect least squares
IRF	Impulse response function
IV	Instrumental variable
LIML	Limited information maximum likelihood
LM	Lagrange multiplier
LR	Likelihood ratio
LS	Least squares
LSDV	Least square dummy variables
MA	Moving average
MAE	Mean absolute error
MAPE	Mean absolute percent error
ML	Maximum likelihood
MLE	Maximum likelihood estimation (or estimate)

MSE	Mean square error
Newey–West HAC	Newey-West heteroscedasticity autocorrelation consistent covariance estimate
OLS	Ordinary least squares
PACF	Partial autocorrelation function or partial correlogram
r^2	Coefficient of determination (simple regression model)
R^2	Coefficient of determination (multiple regression model)
$\bar{R}^2$	Adjusted coefficient of determination
RMSE	Root mean square error
RSS	Residual sum of squares
RRSS	Restricted residual sum of squares
SC	Schwarz criterion
SEM	Simultaneous equations model
SUR	Seemingly unrelated regressions
TSP	Time Series Processor
TSS	Total sum of squares
URSS	Unrestricted residual sum of squares
VAR	Vector autoregression
W	Wald
White HCC	White heteroscedasticity consistent standard errors and covariance
WLS	Weighted least squares
WTP	Willingness to pay
$\otimes$	Kronecker product
Φ	Cumulative normal distribution function
ϕ	Normal density function
$\sum$	$\sum_i$ or $\sum_t$

Part One

Single Equation Regression Models

Part One of this book focuses on exercises related to single equation regression models. Chapter 1 deals with exercises in the context of the classical linear regression model, supposing that the assumptions of the model are fulfilled. Chapter 2 concentrates on exercises related to issues resulting from relaxation of the assumptions of the classical linear regression model. Chapter 3 is concerned with exercises dealing with dummy variables as explanatory variables as well as dependent variables.

CHAPTER 1

The Classical Linear Regression Model

1.1 INTRODUCTION

One of the most important tools of econometrics is regression. Regression models attempt to evaluate the average relationship between one variable, called the dependent variable, and another variable (or variables) called the independent variable(s). The ultimate objectives of the regression are the following:

(a) To obtain the estimates of parameters;
(b) To examine the impact of independent variables on the dependent variable (e.g., the impact of income on consumption in the Keynesian consumption theory);
(c) To verify economic theory (e.g., the Keynesian consumption theory);
(d) To conduct policy analysis (e.g., how changes in income policy affect consumption patterns);
(e) To forecast or predict the dependent variable (e.g., what will the consumption level be in the future?).

An appropriate methodology is required to accomplish these goals. Consider the following:

$$Y = X\beta + u \tag{1.1}$$

where Y is an $\mathbf{n} \times \mathbf{1}$ vector of observations on the dependent variable, X is an $n \times k$ matrix of explanatory variables, including the column vector of ones, β is a $\mathbf{k} \times \mathbf{1}$ vector of parameters and u is an $\mathbf{n} \times \mathbf{1}$ vector of errors or disturbances. Equation (1.1) is a multiple regression as X contains more than one explanatory variable. If X reduces to a column vector of ones and one explanatory variable then Equation (1.1) becomes a simple regression model. Equation (1.1) is linear in parameters. Moreover, it is a single equation model as opposed to a simultaneous equations model. The equation becomes fully an econometric model if some assumptions about the disturbances are made.

After formulating the model and acquiring the data, the task is to estimate β, the vector of parameters. This requires knowledge of the methods of estimation as well as the assumptions for the validity of these methods. The most popular methods are the method of moments, or, more recently the generalized method of moments (GMM), the method of least squares (LS) and the method of maximum likelihood (ML). In the method of moments, sample moments are equated to population moments to obtain estimators. In the method of least squares, minimization of some residual sum of squares is required to derive the estimators. In the method of maximum likelihood, some likelihood function (density function of parameters) is maximized to obtain estimators. After obtaining the estimates of parameters, the question of the characteristics of the associated estimators arises. Here, small sample (finite) properties can be distinguished from large sample (asymptotic) properties of estimators. The most important properties are *unbiasedness*, *minimum variance* (best) and *efficiency*, in the context of finite samples, and *consistency* in the context of large samples.

A second task is to test a certain number of hypotheses. In the linear framework and in small samples, the most common tests are the t test and the F test. In large samples as well as the nonlinear context, the Wald (W), the likelihood ratio (LR) and the Lagrange multiplier (LM) tests are the main tools for testing. The latter tests are also useful in the search for a workable model. In fact, before testing hypotheses, specification and diagnostic checking need to be conducted.

The pursuit of the major objectives of econometrics – policy analysis, economic theory verification and forecasting – makes sense only if the model is adequate, that is, if it passes the main diagnostic tests; otherwise, the model should be revisited. Similarly, some measures of goodness of fit – in-sample and/or out-of-sample – are an important ingredient of regression analysis or econometric methodology.

Although regression models can take the form of single equation models or simultaneous equations models, Part One deals only with single equation models. The exercises of this chapter are related to the conceptual framework of regression, the properties of estimators and hypothesis testing.

1.2 QUESTIONS

1.2.1 Theoretical Exercises

Question 1.1 State the assumptions of the classical linear regression model and carefully explain the importance of each assumption (UWI, EC36C, term tests 1997, 1999, 2001).

Question 1.2 Write an essay on the sample properties of estimators.

Question 1.3 Explain the relationship between the standard normal distribution, chi-square, Student's t and Fisher's F distributions (UWI, EC36C, tutorial 2002).

Question 1.4 In the context of a linear regression model, compare and contrast the following two methods of estimation: least squares and maximum likelihood (no abusive use of formulas) (UWI, EC36C, term test 1996).

Question 1.5 Write a concise note on the relationship between $R^2, \bar{R}^2$ and the F statistic (including their role in modelling) in a linear regression model (UWI, EC36C, term tests 1996, 2003).

Question 1.6 Discuss the following statement: "Multiple regression is more useful than simple regression in quantifying economic relationships" (UWI, EC36C, tutorial 2002).

Question 1.7 What do econometricians mean by "too-large sample problem"?

Question 1.8 Explain in detail the meanings of the constant term in a linear regression model.

Question 1.9 Consider the following regression $Y = X\beta + u$ where Y is an $\mathbf{n} \times \mathbf{1}$ vector of observations, X is an $n \times k$ matrix of explanatory variables including the column vector of ones, β is a $\mathbf{k} \times \mathbf{1}$ vector of parameters and u is an $\mathbf{n} \times \mathbf{1}$ vector of disturbances.

a) Prove that the coefficient of determination R^2 is the square of the single correlation between Y and its fitted value $\hat{Y}$.
b) Show that while the ordinary least squares (OLS) estimator of β attains the Cramer-Rao MVB (minimum variance bound), that of the variance σ^2 does not.
c) Show that the OLS estimator S^2 and the ML estimator $\tilde{\sigma}^2$ of σ^2 are both consistent (UWI, EC36C, term test 2001).

Question 1.10 Consider the regression $Y = X\beta + U$ where Y is an $\mathbf{n} \times \mathbf{1}$ vector of observations, X is an $n \times k$ matrix of explanatory variables including the column vector of ones, β is a $\mathbf{k} \times \mathbf{1}$ vector of parameters and U is an $\mathbf{n} \times \mathbf{1}$ vector of disturbances. Show that:

a) The sum of residuals needs not be zero if the constant term is not present.
b) $\bar{Y} \neq \bar{\hat{Y}}$ if (a) holds.

Question 1.11 Write a note on LM, LR and Wald tests.

Question 1.12 Consider the following regression model:

$$Y = X\beta + U$$

where Y is an $\mathbf{n} \times \mathbf{1}$ vector of observations on the dependent variable, X is an $n \times k$ matrix of explanatory variables including the column vector of ones, β is a $\mathbf{k} \times \mathbf{1}$ vector of parameters and U is an $\mathbf{n} \times \mathbf{1}$ vector of disturbances. Moreover, the number of observations, n, is equal to the number of parameters, k.

a) What is the implication of $n = k$ in terms of X?
b) Derive $\hat{\beta}$, the OLS estimator of β.
c) Derive $\hat{Y}$, the predicted values of Y. Comment on the result.
d) Derive R^2. Comment on the result.
e) Derive the F statistic. Comment on the result.
f) What econometric issue does this regression give rise to? (UWI, EC36C, term test 2003)

Question 1.13 A Cobb–Douglas production function is specified as

$$Log\,Q_i = C + \beta_1\,Log\,K_i + \beta_2\,Log\,L_i + u_i \qquad \text{(Q1.13.1)}$$

where Log = logarithm, Q_i = output, K_i = capital (machine-hours), L_i = labour (worker hours), i stands for the firm and u_i is the usual error term. Assume that $u_i \sim IN(0,\sigma^2)$.

a) Rewrite the model in nonlinear form.
b) Show that $E(Q_i) \neq e^C K_i^{\beta_1} L_i^{\beta_2}$.
c) Obtain a consistent estimator of Q_i.

1.2.2 Empirical Exercises

Question 1.14 Using the information in Table 1.1 for Jamaica, do the following:

a) Estimate the linear regression equation

$$CPI_t = \alpha + \beta IM_t + u_t$$

where CPI_t is the consumer price index, IM_t is the import price index and u_t is the error term.
b) Test the significance of α and β. Use 5 percent level of significance throughout.
c) Compute r^2 using the results derived in (b) and test for its significance.
d) Comment on the overall relevance of the regression.
e) Test whether there is a structural change in the year 1985. (UWI, EC36C, tutorial 2003)

TABLE 1.1
Price Statistics: Jamaica 1972–1997

Year	IM	CPI	Year	IM	CPI
1972	0.8	1.0	1985	9.0	10.2
1973	1.0	1.2	1986	8.7	11.7
1974	1.5	1.5	1987	10.1	12.5
1975	1.7	1.7	1988	10.9	13.5
1976	1.8	1.9	1989	12.2	15.5
1977	2.1	2.1	1990	16.7	18.9
1978	2.1	2.9	1991	27.2	28.5
1979	2.4	3.7	1992	54.8	50.6
1980	3.0	4.7	1993	59.6	61.7
1981	3.3	5.3	1994	84.6	83.4
1982	3.1	5.7	1995	100.0	100.0
1983	3.7	6.3	1996	119.8	126.4
1984	6.8	8.1	1997	115.9	138.6

Note: IM: import price index (1995=100); CPI: consumer price index (1995=100).

Source: Statistical Institute of Jamaica, *Statistical Abstract* (various issues).

Question 1.15 Table 1.2 presents the data for money supply (x_t) and retail price index (y_t) for Barbados from 1972 to 2001.

a) Fitting the data to the following model using ordinary least squares (OLS)

$$y_t = \alpha + \beta x_t + u_t \qquad t = 1,2,3,...,30$$

obtain the estimated coefficients, residual sum of squares (RSS), standard errors, t and F statistics. (State the method you use to obtain the statistics and any assumptions of interest.) Use any appropriate computer software programme.

b) By how much does the retail price index increase as a result of a one-unit increase in the money supply?

c) Compute and interpret the corresponding elasticity from (b).

d) Suppose that the above linear model is replaced by the following log-log model:

$$Ln\ y_t = \alpha + \beta\ Ln\ x_t + u_t \qquad t = 1,2,3,...,30$$

Compute the slope or marginal effect (dy_t/dx_t) and the elasticity. Comment on the difference between the latter elasticity and that obtained in (c).

e) Compute and interpret the slope and the elasticity in each of the following:

Log-lin: $Ln\ y_t = \alpha + \beta\, x_t + u_t$

Lin-log: $y_t = \alpha + \beta\, Ln\, x_t + u_t$

Reciprocal: $y_t = \alpha + \beta(1/x_t) + u_t$

TABLE 1.2
Money Supply and Price Index in Barbados 1972–2001

Year	Money Supply (Bds$ '000)	Retail Price Index (1994=100)	Year	Money Supply (Bds$ '000)	Retail Price Index (1994=100)
1972	79,709	16.2	1987	477,672	77.3
1973	76,123	18.9	1988	574,608	80.9
1974	90,507	26.3	1989	514,646	86.0
1975	105,158	31.6	1990	624,738	88.6
1976	118,009	33.2	1991	549,915	94.2
1977	134,873	35.9	1992	610,797	99.9
1978	164,182	39.4	1993	624,738	101.1
1979	229,216	44.5	1994	795,638	101.1
1980	255,440	51.0	1995	899,305	103.0
1981	269,679	58.4	1996	1,036,746	105.5
1982	266,099	64.4	1997	1,263,776	113.6
1983	309,108	67.8	1998	1,317,556	112.2
1984	301,392	71.0	1999	1,399,669	113.9
1985	345,208	73.8	2000	1,519,773	116.7
1986	403,039	74.7	2001	1,584,835	119.7

Source: Central Bank of Barbados, *Annual Statistical Digest*, 2002.

TABLE 1.3
Saving and Income Relationship: OLS Results, 1970–2000

Variable	Coefficient	Standard Error	t Statistic	Prob.
Constant	–648.1236	118.1625	–5.485018	0.0000
Y	0.084665	0.004882	17.34164	0.0000
R^2	0.912050	Mean dependent variable		1250.323
Adjusted R^2	0.909017	F statistic		300.7324
RSS	1778203.	Prob(F statistic)		0.000000

Note: Variables are in \$000. Y = income.

f) Compute and interpret the following:
   i) instantaneous rate of growth of money supply;
   ii) compound rate of growth of money supply;
   iii) absolute rate of increase of money supply. (UWI, EC36C, tutorial 2003)

Question 1.16 Consider the following saving model:

$$S_t = \alpha + \beta Y_t + u_t \tag{Q1.16.1}$$

where S_t is saving, Y_t stands for income, u_t is the error term and t is the time index. Fitting data to the above saving model using OLS gives the results shown in Table 1.3.

a) Interpret the results, supposing all the assumptions of the classical linear model (CLM) hold.
b) Derive the estimated consumption function.
c) Show that the residual sum of squares (RSS) remains the same.
d) Show that the corresponding standard errors of estimators are the same in both models.
e) Compare the values of R^2 from the two models.

Question 1.17 Howard and Mamingi (2001) used, among others, the following version of the standard reserve flow equation to see whether or not the monetary approach to the balance of payments holds for Barbados:

$$\frac{\Delta R_t}{(R+D)_t} = \gamma_1 + \gamma_2 \frac{\Delta P_t}{P_t} + \gamma_3 \frac{\Delta Y_t}{Y_t} + \gamma_4 \frac{\Delta i_t}{i_t} + \gamma_5 \frac{\Delta m_t}{m_t} + \gamma_6 \frac{\Delta D_t}{(R+D)_t} + u_t$$

where
R_t = international reserves in Barbados \$million;
i_t = nominal interest rate in %;
P_t = consumer price index;
Y_t = real income in Barbados \$million;
m_t = money multiplier;

D_t = domestic credit in Barbados \$million;
Δ = first difference operator;
u_t = error term;
t = time index.

Using data for Barbados in the period 1973–1998 and OLS, they obtained the following results:

$$\widehat{\frac{\Delta R_t}{(R+D)_t}} = 0.058 + 0.158\frac{\Delta P_t}{P_t} + 1.097\frac{\Delta Y_t}{Y_t} - 0.152\frac{\Delta i_t}{i_t} - 0.685\frac{\Delta m_t}{m_t} - 1.007\frac{\Delta D_t}{(R+D)_t}$$

$$\text{RSS} = 0.181067$$

$$\begin{bmatrix} 0.000657 & -0.001967 & -0.00742 & 0.000552 & -0.000954 & -0.000535 \\ & 0.026738 & 0.022712 & 0.001820 & 0.009637 & 0.002804 \\ & & 0.350372 & -0.015812 & -0.001509 & 0.006431 \\ & & & 0.008131 & 0.005216 & 6.55E-5 \\ & & & & 0.048476 & 0.011609 \\ & & & & & 0.012637 \end{bmatrix}$$

where RSS = residual sum of squares and [...] = variance-covariance matrix of estimates. Use $\alpha = 0.05$.

a) Test the significance of each parameter except the constant term.
b) The monetary approach predicts that $\gamma_6 = -1$. Test the latter hypothesis.
c) Test the hypothesis $\gamma_5 = \gamma_6$.
d) Two further regressions, based on the original specification, were computed for the periods 1973–1985 and 1986–1998, yielding residual sum of squares of 0.100101 and 0.050142, respectively. Test the hypothesis that the parameters are identical in the two periods.
e) Write a concise report on the results of the exercise.

1.3 ANSWERS

Answer 1.1

Consider the following model:

$$Y = X\beta + U$$

where Y is an $\mathbf{n} \times \mathbf{1}$ vector of observations on the dependent variable, X is an $n \times k$ matrix of explanatory variables including the column vector of ones, β is a $\mathbf{k} \times \mathbf{1}$ vector of unknown parameters, and U is an $\mathbf{n} \times \mathbf{1}$ vector of errors. The assumptions of the classical linear model are the following:

Assumption 1: The model is linear in the parameters and subsequently can be written as a linear function of a dependent variable on a set of known independent variables (after transformation or not) and the error term. Beyond linearity per se, this assumption emphasizes the correctness of the specification; that is, basically there are no problems of omitted variables, functional form, measurement error and parameter variability. The violation of this assumption leads to some specification biases.

Assumption 2: $E(U) = E(U/X) = 0$. There are two statements here. First, the equality means that X and U are independent (see also assumption 4). That is, X cannot help forecast U. Second, and more importantly, the mean value of errors, conditional upon the given X, is zero. That is, on average there are no errors; or better, the errors average out. Put another way, this assumption states that the factors not explicitly included in the model, and therefore subsumed in U, do not systematically affect the mean value of Y; the positive error values cancel out the negative error values so that their average or mean effect is zero. The violation of this assumption leads to a biased intercept (for more details, see Kennedy, 1992, 110–112).

Assumption 3: Errors are spherical; that is, $E(UU') = \sigma^2 I$ where I is an $n \times n$ identity matrix. This assumption can be broken down into two assumptions: homoscedasticity or absence of heteroscedasticity; and absence of autocorrelation. Homoscedasticity is the situation for which the variance of the errors remains constant along observations. The violation of this assumption gives rise to heteroscedasticity, which in this context brings about inefficiency of estimators and forecasts, as well as wider confidence intervals and invalidation of the usual test statistics. Elsewhere, as in the case of the limited dependent variable model, it also brings about inconsistency of estimators. The second assumption is that of absence of autocorrelation, meaning that errors in different points in time or space are not linked to one another. When this assumption is violated, the errors are said to be autocorrelated or serially correlated. Autocorrelation of errors results in inefficiency of estimators as well as invalidation of the usual test statistics. In the presence of a lagged dependent variable, autocorrelation of errors also gives rise to biased and inconsistent estimators. Note that the violation of at least one of these assumptions (either homoscedasticity or absence of autocorrelation) gives rise to errors that are nonspherical. Assumptions 2 and 3 combined mean that the errors are white noise.

Assumption 4: X is nonstochastic or fixed. This means that the explanatory variables are fixed from experiment to experiment. This assumption implies an absence of correlation between the explanatory variables and the error term, $E(X'U) = 0$. This assumption helps disentangle the respective impact of X and U on Y. Note that a stochastic X plays the same role as a nonstochastic X provided that $E(X'U) = 0$. The violation of this assumption brings about bias (e.g., simultaneity bias and/or inconsistency).

Assumption 5: X is of full-rank; that is, $r(X) = k < n$. This assumption implies a lack of dependence between or among explanatory variables of the model. This condition is known as absence of perfect (exact) multicollinearity. The violation of this assumption leads to the impossibility of estimating all the parameters of models (though there is the possibility of estimating some linear combinations of the parameters).

Note that although normality is not an assumption of the CLM, it is needed to derive estimators in the case of maximum likelihood estimation and to build confidence intervals, as well as to conduct hypothesis testing in the case of least squares estimation.

Answer 1.2

Estimators can be obtained in several ways. The question of whether the estimators so obtained are good is of interest to econometricians.

There are two sets of sample properties distinguished by the size of the samples: finite sample properties and asymptotic properties. Finite sample properties of estimators are properties of estimators related to fixed samples. Asymptotic properties are those estimator properties derived under the condition that the samples are getting larger and larger.

Among the most important finite sample properties are unbiasedness, minimum variance (best), and efficiency. Unbiasedness means that in repeated samples, on average the estimate equals the value of the parameter. In plain English, it means that if we draw samples of the same size (finite sample size) and compute the estimate each time, the average of those estimates is equal to the value of the parameter.

It is known in statistics that measures of central tendency alone are not good enough to characterize a distribution; there is a need to supplement them with measurements of spread (e.g., variance), hence, the existence of the minimum variance (or best) property related to spread. An estimator is best if its variance is less than that of another estimator.

The unbiasedness and minimum variance properties combined give rise to efficiency. That is, an estimator is said to be relatively more efficient than another if both are unbiased and the former has smaller variance than the second. This means that an efficient estimator may be simply the better of two inefficient estimators. To solve this problem one introduces full efficiency. An estimator is fully efficient if it is unbiased and attains the Cramer-Rao minimum variance bound (MVB). Note that in the class of linear estimators, the one that is unbiased and best is called BLUE (best linear unbiased estimator).

Most estimators do not have good small sample properties or they have good small sample properties under stringent conditions, hence the need to consider large sample properties, which are asymptotic unbiasedness, consistency and asymptotic efficiency. Asymptotic unbiasedness means that at the limit the estimator is unbiased. In particular, an estimator can be biased in small samples and unbiased in large samples. Perhaps the most important large sample property of estimators is consistency. An estimator is consistent if its probability limit is equal to the parameter. In other words, the estimator approaches the true value of the parameter in probability as the sample size goes to infinity. A sufficient condition is that the estimator must be asymptotically unbiased and its asymptotic variance must go to zero. Another property is asymptotic efficiency. An estimator is asymptotically efficient if it is consistent, asymptotically normally distributed and its asymptotic variance is smaller than the asymptotic variance of another consistent estimator (its asymptotic variance goes to zero faster than that of another consistent estimator). (For algebraic derivation of properties, see, for example, Answer 1.9 [b] and [c], 2.6 [b], 2.8 [b] and [c], and 2.14 [b].)

Answer 1.3

Let Z follow the standard normal distribution. To recall, it is a bell-shaped (symmetric) curve with the following features. Its mean is 0 and its variance 1. Moreover, 68.26 percent of values of the distribution lie within one standard deviation from the mean; 95.44 percent of values of the distribution are concentrated within two standard deviations from the mean and 99.74 percent are within three standard deviations from the mean.

Raising Z to power two gives rise to a new distribution called the chi-square distribution, denoted χ^2_{df}; that is,

$$Y = \chi^2_{df} = Z^2$$

The χ^2_{df} is characterized by the parameter called degree of freedom (df). In this particular case, the degree of freedom is equal to one. The distribution is skewed; its mean is equal to the degrees of freedom and its variance is twice the degrees of freedom. Note that as the degrees of freedom go to infinity, the χ^2 distribution goes to the standard normal distribution.

The t distribution combines the standard normal and χ^2_{df} distributions. It is the ratio of some standard normal distribution and the square root of some χ^2_{df} divided by its degrees of freedom; that is,

$$X = t = \frac{Z}{\sqrt{\chi^2 / df}}$$

The t distribution looks like the normal distribution except that it is fatter at the tails than the normal distribution. Its mean exists only if the degrees of freedom are greater than one, in which case the mean is zero (why?). Its variance is equal to the degrees of freedom divided by the degrees of freedom minus two if the degrees of freedom are greater than two.

The last distribution, F, is a ratio of two independent χ^2_{df} values, weighted each by the inverse of its degrees of freedom; that is,

$$F = \chi^2_{s1} / s1 \big/ \chi^2_{s2} / s2$$

where s1 and s2 are degrees of freedom. The distribution is skewed to the right and looks like a χ^2 distribution.

Answer 1.4

The major objective of these methods is to obtain estimators or estimates of the parameters in a given relationship. Whereas in the LS method one minimizes some residual sum of squares to derive estimators, in the ML method one maximizes some likelihood function (joint density function of parameters). In the ML method, normality is required to obtain estimators; in the LS method, it is only used to derive confidence intervals for parameters and/or to conduct hypothesis testing. Moreover, while the two methods give rise to the same estimator of the β parameter, their residual variances are different. Indeed, the estimator of the true variance of error is unbiased in the case of LS and biased in the case of ML. Nevertheless, in the latter case, the bias vanishes in large samples.

Answer 1.5

Let us first explain R^2. Consider the following:

$$Y = X\boldsymbol{\beta} + U$$

where Y is an $\mathbf{n} \times \mathbf{1}$ vector of observations on the dependent variable, X is an $n \times k$ matrix of explanatory variables including the column vector of ones, β is a $\mathbf{k} \times \mathbf{1}$ vector of parameters and U is an $n \times 1$ error term. In this context, R^2, known as the coefficient of determination, indicates the proportion (or percentage) of the variation in the dependent variable (here Y) explained by the regression or the independent variables (here X). Thus, it is a measure of goodness of fit of the regression line to the data. This can easily be seen from the formula:

$$R^2 = \frac{\text{ESS}}{\text{TSS}} = 1 - \frac{\text{RSS}}{\text{TSS}}$$

where
ESS stands for the explained sum of squares $(\hat{Y}'\hat{Y} - n\bar{Y}^2)$
TSS is the total sum of squares $(Y'Y - n\bar{Y}^2)$
RSS is the residual sum of squares $(\hat{U}'\hat{U})$.

In the presence of a constant term, the statistic takes on values between 0 and 1. A value of 1 indicates a perfect fit and that of 0 an absence of fit.

R^2 can also be used as a measure of accuracy of prediction of movements in the dependent variable. That is,

$$R^2 = \frac{\left[(Y'\hat{Y} - n\bar{Y}^2)\right]^2}{(Y'Y - n\bar{Y}^2)(\hat{Y}'\hat{Y} - n\bar{Y}^2)} = \frac{\left[\sum_i (Y_i - \bar{Y})(\hat{Y}_i - \bar{Y})\right]^2}{\sum_i (Y_i - \bar{Y})^2 \sum_i (\hat{Y}_i - \bar{Y})^2} = R^2_{Y\hat{Y}}$$

where $R^2_{Y\hat{Y}}$ is the squared correlation between the observation values of Y and the predictor $\hat{Y}$. Note, however, a model with a good in-sample R^2 does not necessarily translate into a good forecasting model (ex-post or ex-ante forecast of the dependent variable).

The question of whether R^2 (or more precisely its population equivalent) is significant or not allows us to build the link between R^2 and the F statistic. Indeed, the relevant test statistic to answer the above question is the F statistic, computed as follows:

$$F = \frac{\text{ESS}/(k-1)}{\text{RSS}/(n-k)} = \frac{R^2/(k-1)}{(1-R^2)/(n-k)}$$

where k is the number of parameters to estimate including the constant. If F calculated is less than the critical value, then the regression does not explain the variation in the dependent variable; otherwise, it does. To repeat, what is needed is a high R^2. How "high" depends on whether the data are of time series or cross section or panel types. Definitely there is no magic cut off point. R^2 from time series is generally higher than those from cross section and panel data models.

In any event, R^2 is useful for modelling. However, since adding a variable (or a set of variables) always increases (or at least does not decrease) R^2, the latter statistic becomes somewhat problematic as a guide for modelling. To solve the problem of tradeoff of increasing R^2 and decreasing degrees of freedom when one or several variables are added, one uses the so-called adjusted R^2, $\bar{R}^2$. Indeed, the latter takes the degrees of freedom into account and is linked to R^2 in the following manner:

$$\bar{R}^2 = 1 - \frac{\text{RSS}/(n-k)}{\text{TSS}/(n-1)} = 1 - (1 - R^2)\left(\frac{n-1}{n-k}\right)$$

This statistic can, however, be negative. This happens when $R^2 < (k-1)/(n-1)$. In fact, $\bar{R}^2$ is not really a quantity squared. The rule for modelling using this statistic is the following: a variable is added if the t statistic of its associated coefficient is greater than 1; for a set of variables, the condition is that the associated F ratio is greater than 1. In both situations, $\bar{R}^2$ does increase. Note, however, that the rule is not straightforward in the situation where many individual variables have associated coefficients with t ratios less than 1 but with an associated F ratio greater than 1 (see the problem of multicollinearity) or if all the t ratios are greater than 1 but the associated F ratio is less than 1 (see Maddala, 1992, 167). For comparable models, the chosen model is the one with the highest $\bar{R}^2$ (Theil's $\bar{R}^2$ or $\bar{R}^2$ rule) or with the minimum $\hat{\sigma}^2$.

Three remarks are in order. First, $\bar{R}^2$ will be unable to pick up the "true model" if some models contain irrelevant variables. Second, the comparison between the values of $\bar{R}^2$ holds if models are nested (see Chapter 2). Third, despite all the fuss about $\bar{R}^2$, to the best of our knowledge up to now, there is no test statistic attached to it. The F test statistic is linked to R^2 and not to $\bar{R}^2$ (see also Cameron, 1993; Wooldridge, 2000).

Answer 1.6

With the exception of a few well known or established bivariate relationships (e.g., short term interest rate and long term interest rate, money and price) multiple regression is more useful than simple regression, for basically two reasons. First, even if one was interested only in the impact of one explanatory variable on the explained variable, it would be wise to include other explanatory variables as in reality in most economic relationships the dependent variable is explained by more than one explanatory variable. Not taking this into account most likely introduces some misspecification bias (omitted variable bias). Second, multiple regression helps reduce stochastic error (hence the residual variance, $\hat{\sigma}^2$) better than simple regression. This makes confidence intervals more precise. Note, however, in the choice of variables we must be guided by economic theory. Indeed, throwing in unnecessary or irrelevant variables may well destroy the very foundation of multiple regression as this will result in larger variances of estimates.

Answer 1.7

It is well known that estimators in practice do not have good small sample properties. Moreover, most test statistics have low power in small samples. That is, the null hypothesis is rejected less frequently than it is not rejected in small samples. Most econometric practitioners have reacted to these shortcomings of small samples by resorting to large samples. Indeed, with a fixed level of significance, the bigger the sample size, the higher the probability of rejecting the null hypothesis, hence the presumption "use a large sample to confirm the research hypothesis". Seen from a different angle, this questions the habit of often using the preassigned levels of significance: 1%, 5% and 10%. In fact, the increase (decrease) in sample size should be matched by a decreasing (increasing) significance level (see Maddala, 1992, 502).

Answer 1.8

With the exceptions of Rao and Miller (1971), the issue of the meanings of the constant term in regression has not been forcefully emphasized in the econometrics literature. We follow Rao and Miller (1971, 1–4) to some extent to answer the question.

To adequately interpret the constant term we must fully understand the distinction between a mathematical interpretation of a mathematical model and an econometric interpretation of a mathematical model. The interpretation of an intercept in a mathematical model is straightforward: it is the value taken by the dependent variable when all independent variables are simultaneously equal to zero.

Does this interpretation carry over to econometric models? Sometimes, yes. For example, in the Keynesian consumption function the autonomous consumption is the level of consumption when income is set to zero.

This interpretation does not often hold in many instances for econometric models. For example, suppose Y represents the number of wild animals killed by a hunter and X is the number of guns he uses. That is, the equation regression explains the number of wild animals killed by a hunter during a specific period of time. In this context, a person who does not have a gun is not considered a hunter. That is, it does not make sense equating X to zero as $X = 0$ does not belong to the subpopulation under study.

There are situations where the constant term has a clear interpretation without setting all independent variables to zero. One of those situations goes back to the genesis of the constant term such as related to the error term. To elaborate, consider the following regression:

$$Y_t = \beta X_t + u_t + e_t + v_t \qquad \text{(A1.8.1)}$$

where u_t is a purely random error, e_t is the linear approximation error and v_t is the omitted variable error. If the two errors e_t and v_t can be rewritten as $e_t = E_t + \bar{e}$ and, $v_t = V_t + \bar{v}$, respectively, where the "bar" stands for "mean", then Equation (A1.8.1) can be rewritten as follows:

$$Y_t = \bar{e} + \bar{v} + \beta X_t + u_t + E_t + V_t \tag{A1.8.2}$$

or

$$Y_t = c + \beta X_t + \varepsilon_t \tag{A1.8.3}$$

where ε_t is the new random error term ($u_t + E_t + V_t$) and the constant term, $c = \bar{e} + \bar{v}$, is generally dominated by $\bar{v}$. Hence, the constant term represents the average effect of omitted variables. There is a role for economic theory to help discriminate between this interpretation of the constant term and that seen above.

A slightly different interpretation of the omitted variable approach can be found in the context of dummy variable regressor(s) (see Chapter 3). An example is illuminating. Suppose that the salary of teachers (Y_i) depends on the years of experience (X_i) and the gender (male or female):

$$Y_i = c + \beta X_i + \delta D_i + u_i \tag{A1.8.4}$$

where D_i is the dummy variable (categorical variable) with 1 = male and 0 = female (see Chapter 3 for details). Here, the constant term is the average salary of a female teacher, holding constant the number of years of experience. It happens to be that c is related to the missing category. In fact, in this model there are two constant terms: c (for female) and $c + \delta$ (for male). In any event both represent some average salary, holding the years of experience constant.

In a panel data model framework (see Chapter 9) the constant term can also have a clear interpretation. In a fixed effects model, such as

$$Y_{it} = \alpha_i + \gamma_t + \beta X_{it} + u_{it} \tag{A1.8.5}$$

where $i = 1,\ldots,N$ stands for units and $t = 1,\ldots, T$ is time, the constant terms represent unit specificity or unit specific effects (α_i) and time specific effects (γ_t). Put differently, the α_is are individual constants that differentiate the different units and the γ_ts are time constants that capture each period particularity. For example, in a panel production function, the α_is represent firm managerial ability.

Summing up, the meaning of the constant term needs to be examined on a case by case basis. It is, however, worth noting that economic theory and perhaps common sense have a significant bearing on the outcome.

Answer 1.9

a) We are asked to show that $R^2 = R^2_{Y\hat{Y}}$. We know that:

$$R^2 = \frac{\text{ESS}}{\text{TSS}} = \frac{\Sigma\left(\hat{Y}_i - \bar{Y}\right)^2}{\Sigma\left(Y_i - \bar{Y}\right)^2} \qquad \text{by definition}$$

$$R^2 = \frac{\left[\Sigma\left(\hat{Y}_i - \bar{Y}\right)^2\right]^2}{\Sigma\left(Y_i - \bar{Y}\right)^2 \Sigma\left(\hat{Y}_i - \bar{Y}\right)^2} \quad \text{multiply and divide by } \Sigma\left(\hat{Y}_i - \bar{Y}\right)^2 \neq 0$$

$$R^2 = \frac{\Sigma\left(\hat{Y}_i - \bar{Y}\right)^2 \Sigma\left(\hat{Y}_i - \bar{Y}\right)^2}{\Sigma\left(Y_i - \bar{Y}\right)^2 \Sigma\left(\hat{Y}_i - \bar{Y}\right)^2}$$

$$= \frac{\left[\Sigma\left(Y_i - \hat{u}_i - \bar{Y}\right)\left(\hat{Y}_i - \bar{Y}\right)\right]^2}{\Sigma\left(\hat{Y} - \bar{Y}\right)^2 \Sigma\left(\hat{Y}_i - \bar{Y}\right)^2} \quad \text{since } \hat{Y}_i = Y_i - \hat{u}_i$$

$$= \frac{\left[\Sigma\left\{\left(Y_i - \bar{Y}\right) - \hat{u}_i\right\}\left(\hat{Y}_i - \bar{Y}\right)\right]^2}{\Sigma\left(\hat{Y} - \bar{Y}\right)^2 \Sigma\left(\hat{Y}_i - \bar{Y}\right)^2}$$

$$= \frac{\left[\Sigma\left(Y_i - \bar{Y}\right)\left(\hat{Y}_i - \bar{Y}\right)\right]^2}{\Sigma\left(\hat{Y} - \bar{Y}\right)^2 \Sigma\left(\hat{Y}_i - \bar{Y}\right)^2} \quad \text{since } \Sigma \hat{u}_i \hat{Y}_i = 0 \text{ and } \bar{Y}\Sigma \hat{u}_i = 0$$

$$= R^2_{Y\hat{Y}} \quad \text{by definition.}$$

QED

b) Writing the log likelihood:

$$\ln L = -\frac{n}{2}\ln 2\pi - \frac{n}{2}\ln \sigma^2 - \frac{1}{2\sigma^2}\left(Y - X\beta\right)'\left(Y - X\beta\right)$$

Taking the second derivatives

$$\frac{\partial^2 \ln L}{\partial \beta \, \partial \beta'} = -\frac{1}{\sigma^2}\left(X'X\right)$$

$$\frac{\partial^2 \ln L}{\partial\left(\sigma^2\right)^2} = \frac{n}{2\sigma^4} - \frac{\left(Y - X\beta\right)'\left(Y - X\beta\right)}{\sigma^6}$$

$$\frac{\partial^2 \ln L}{\partial \beta \partial \sigma^2} = -\frac{1}{\sigma^4}\left(X'Y - X'X\beta\right)$$

Taking $-E(\ldots) = I(\theta)$ where $I(\theta)$ is the information matrix of parameters

$$-E\left(\frac{\partial^2 \ln L}{\partial\beta\partial\beta'}\right) = \frac{1}{\sigma^2}(X'X)$$

$$-E\left(\frac{\partial^2 \ln L}{\partial(\sigma^2)^2}\right) = \frac{-n}{2\sigma^4} + \frac{n\sigma^2}{\sigma^6} \qquad \text{since} \quad E(u'u) = n\sigma^2.$$

$$-E\left(\frac{\partial^2 \ln L}{\partial\beta\partial\sigma^2}\right) = 0 \qquad \text{since} \quad E(X'Y - X'X\beta) = 0$$

The Cramer-Rao (CR) lower bound is thus:

$$CR(\theta) = I^{-1}(\theta) = I^{-1}\begin{pmatrix}\beta \\ \sigma^2\end{pmatrix} = \begin{pmatrix}\sigma^2(X'X)^{-1} & 0 \\ 0 & \frac{2\sigma^4}{n}\end{pmatrix}$$

We know that

$$\hat{\beta} = (X'X)^{-1}X'Y \quad \text{and} \quad \text{var}(\hat{\beta}) = \sigma^2(X'X)^{-1}.$$

As can be seen, $\hat{\beta}$ attains the CR lower bound.

We know that

$$\text{var}(S^2) = \text{var}\left(\frac{\sigma^2\chi^2_{n-k}}{n-k}\right) \qquad \text{since} \quad \frac{(n-k)S^2}{\sigma^2} \sim \chi^2_{n-k}$$

Thus,

$$\text{var}(S^2) = \frac{\sigma^4}{(n-k)^2}2(n-k) = \frac{2\sigma^4}{n-k}$$

since $\text{var}(ax) = a^2\,\text{var}(x)$ and $\text{var}(\chi^2_{n-k}) = 2(n-k)$.

As can be seen

$$\frac{2\sigma^4}{n-k} > \frac{2\sigma^4}{n}$$

Thus, S^2 does not attain the bound.

c) Two approaches can help answer the question of consistency of estimators. In the first approach, a sufficient condition is of interest and in the second, the probability limit framework is appropriate.

First approach: An estimator $\hat{\beta}$ is a consistent estimator of β if the following two conditions (sufficient conditions) are satisfied: asymptotic unbiasedness and asymptotic variance going to zero.

For OLS, we know that

$$S^2 = \frac{\hat{u}'\hat{u}}{n-k}$$

Taking the expected value gives:

$$E\left(S^2\right) = E\left(\frac{\sigma^2\chi^2_{n-k}}{n-k}\right) \qquad \text{since} \quad \frac{\left(n-k\right)S^2}{\sigma^2} \sim \chi^2_{n-k}$$

$$= \frac{\sigma^2}{n-k}E\left(\chi^2_{n-k}\right) \qquad \text{since} \quad E\left(aX\right) = aE\left(X\right)$$

$$= \frac{(n-k)\sigma^2}{n-k} \qquad \text{since} \quad E\left(\chi^2_{n-k}\right) = n-k$$

$$= \sigma^2 \qquad \text{QED.}$$

Thus, S^2 is an unbiased estimator of σ^2. Consequently, it is also asymptotically unbiased.

We also know that

$$\text{var}\left(S^2\right) = \text{var}\left(\frac{\sigma^2\chi^2_{n-k}}{n-k}\right)$$

$$= \frac{\sigma^4}{\left(n-k\right)^2}\text{var}\left(\chi^2_{n-k}\right) \qquad \text{since} \quad \text{var}\left(aX\right) = a^2\,\text{var}\left(X\right)$$

$$= \frac{2\sigma^4}{n-k} \qquad \text{since} \quad \text{var}\left(\chi^2_{n-k}\right) = 2(n-k)$$

Evaluating the limit of the above expression gives:

$$\lim_{n\to\infty}\frac{2\sigma^4}{n-k} = 0$$

Since the two conditions for consistency are fulfilled, we conclude that S^2 is a consistent estimator of σ^2.

For the maximum likelihood estimator, we know that

$$\tilde{\sigma}^2 = \frac{\hat{u}'\hat{u}}{n}$$

We also know that

$$\frac{\hat{u}'\hat{u}}{\sigma^2} \sim \chi^2_{n-k} \rightarrow \frac{n(\hat{u}'\hat{u})/n}{\sigma^2} \sim \chi^2_{n-k}$$

Thus,

$$\frac{n\tilde{\sigma}^2}{\sigma^2} \sim \chi^2_{n-k}\,.$$

Using the above expression, the expected value of $\tilde{\sigma}^2$ gives:

$$E(\tilde{\sigma}^2) = \sigma^2 - \frac{k}{n}\sigma^2$$

where

$$-\frac{k}{n}\sigma^2$$

is the bias. In large samples, this bias disappears, since

$$\lim_{n \to \infty} -\frac{k}{n}\sigma^2 = 0$$

That is, the estimator is asymptotically unbiased.

The variance of the estimator can be computed as:

$$\mathrm{var}\left(\tilde{\sigma}^2\right) = \mathrm{var}\left(\frac{\sigma^2\chi^2_{n-k}}{n}\right) = 2\frac{(n-k)}{n^2}\sigma^4 = \frac{1}{n}2\sigma^4 - \frac{2k}{n^2}\sigma^4$$

As can be seen,

$$\lim_{n \to \infty} \mathrm{var}\left(\tilde{\sigma}^2\right) = 0$$

Thus, $\tilde{\sigma}^2$ is a consistent estimator of σ^2.

Second approach: For OLS, the question of interest is whether *plim* $S^2 = \sigma^2$. We know that

$$\text{plim } S^2 = \underset{n\to\infty}{\text{plim}} \frac{\hat{u}'\hat{u}}{n-k} = \underset{n\to\infty}{\text{plim}} \frac{\sigma^2(n-k)}{n-k} = \sigma^2 \qquad \text{QED}$$

For ML, the question of interest is whether $\text{plim } \tilde{\sigma}^2 = \sigma^2$. We know that

$$\text{plim } \tilde{\sigma}^2 = \underset{n\to\infty}{\text{plim}} \frac{\hat{u}'\hat{u}}{n} = \underset{n\to\infty}{\text{plim}} \frac{\sigma^2(n-k)}{n} = \sigma^2 \qquad \text{QED}$$

Answer 1.10

a) We know that the normal equation resulting from the minimization of the residual sum of squares (RSS) is given by

$$X'Y = X'X\hat{\beta}$$

Replacing Y by its value in the above leads to

$$X'(\hat{Y} + \hat{U}) = X'X\hat{\beta}$$

Since $\hat{Y} = X\hat{\beta}$, the above expression can be written as:

$$X'(X\hat{\beta} + \hat{U}) = X'X\hat{\beta}$$

The above equality only holds if and only if

$$X'\hat{U} = \begin{bmatrix} X_1'\hat{U} \\ X_2'\hat{U} \\ \vdots \\ \vdots \\ X_k'\hat{U} \end{bmatrix} = \begin{bmatrix} 0 \\ 0 \\ \vdots \\ \vdots \\ 0 \end{bmatrix} = 0$$

Since X_1' is the row vector of ones, the first entry states that the sum of residuals is equal to zero. Put differently, there is no guarantee that the sum of residuals is zero if the constant term is not included in the regression.

b) We know

$$Y = \hat{Y} + \hat{U}$$

Multiplying the expression by X_1' and dividing by n, the sample size, leads to:

$$\frac{X_1'Y}{n} = \frac{X_1'\hat{Y}}{n} + \frac{X_1'\hat{U}}{n}$$

or

$$\overline{Y} = \overline{\hat{Y}} + \overline{\hat{U}}$$

Since there is no guarantee that the sum of residuals is zero in the case of a missing constant term, we can infer that:

$$\overline{Y} \neq \overline{\hat{Y}}$$

Answer 1.11

The LM, LR and Wald (W) tests are used to replace the F test statistic when the restrictions to be tested are nonlinear or the errors are not normally distributed. Moreover, they are large sample tests. In large samples, all three tests are distributed as a chi-square with the number of restrictions as the degrees of freedom. The three tests are equivalent in that context. In small samples, the tests have unknown sampling distributions. Furthermore, they can be different, with W ≥ LR ≥ LM.

To explain the three tests, consider the following regression:

$$Y = X\beta + u \tag{A1.11.1}$$

The log likelihood of (A1.11.1) is given by:

$$Log\,L = -\frac{n}{2}Log\,2\pi - \frac{n}{2}Log\,\sigma^2 - \frac{1}{2\sigma^2}(Y - X\beta)'(Y - X\beta) \tag{A1.11.2}$$

Maximization of (A1.11.2) leads to:

$$\tilde{\beta} = (X'X)^{-1}X'Y \quad \text{and} \quad \tilde{\sigma}^2 = \frac{\hat{u}'\hat{u}}{n} \tag{A1.11.3}$$

where $\hat{u}'\hat{u}$ stands for the unrestricted residual sum of squares. Now suppose we have some testable linear restriction (q):

$$R\beta = r \quad \text{or} \quad R\beta - r = 0 \tag{A1.11.4}$$

where R is $q \times k$, β is $k \times 1$ and r is $q \times 1$ (with $q < k$) (see any good econometrics textbook). This means that (A1.11.2) can be maximized subject to the constraint

(A1.11.4). This yields a new set of estimators: $\hat{u}_r'\hat{u}_r$ (the restricted residual sum of squares), $\tilde{\beta}_r$ and $\tilde{\sigma}_r^2$.

The LR test:

The LR test states that, if the restriction (A1.11.4) is true, then the value of the log maximum likelihood under no restriction will not be too different from that with restriction. The ratio of the two likelihoods is

$$\lambda = \frac{L(\tilde{\beta}_r, \tilde{\sigma}_r^2)}{L(\tilde{\beta}, \tilde{\sigma}^2)} \qquad \text{(A1.11.5)}$$

and the test statistic is

$$LR = -2Log\lambda = 2[Log\,L(\tilde{\beta}, \tilde{\sigma}^2) - Log\,L(\tilde{\beta}_r, \tilde{\sigma}_r^2)] \sim \chi_q^2 \qquad \text{(A1.11.6)}$$

Equation (A1.11.6) can be rewritten as:

$$LR = nLog(\hat{u}_r'\,\hat{u}_r - \hat{u}'\,\hat{u}) \qquad \text{(A1.11.7)}$$

A large value of the statistic leads to the rejection of the null hypothesis that the restriction is true. Note that the computation of the test statistic requires knowledge of both restricted and unrestricted estimators.

The Wald Test:

The question asked by this test is whether the unrestricted ML estimate fits the null hypothesis, that is, whether $R\tilde{\beta} - r = 0$. The test statistic is given by:

$$W = \frac{(R\tilde{\beta} - r)'[R(X'X)^{-1}R']^{-1}(R\tilde{\beta} - r)}{\tilde{\sigma}^2} \sim \chi_q^2 \qquad \text{(A1.11.8)}$$

where the components of the statistic are defined as above. Equation (A1.11.8) indicates that knowledge of the unrestricted estimate is enough to obtain the test statistic. Note that an alternative to Equation (A1.11.8) is given by:

$$W = \frac{n(\hat{u}_r'\,\hat{u}_r - \hat{u}'\,\hat{u})}{\hat{u}'\,\hat{u}} \sim \chi_q^2 \qquad \text{(A1.11.9)}$$

If the null is not rejected (p value greater than the level of significance) then the restriction is not rejected; otherwise, it is rejected.

The LM test:

The LM test requires only the estimation of the restricted model. Let the score statistic be

$$S(\beta_r) = \frac{\partial L}{\partial \beta_r}$$

where L stands for the likelihood function and β_r is the parameter of interest from the restricted model. The related test statistic is

$$LM = S'(\tilde{\beta}_r) I^{-1}(\tilde{\beta}) S(\tilde{\beta}_r) \sim \chi_q^2 \quad \text{(A1.11.10)}$$

where $I^{-1}(\tilde{\beta})$ is the inverse of the information matrix (Cramer–Rao lower bound) and $\tilde{\beta}_r$ is the maximum likelihood estimator of β_r. Equivalently, Equation (A1.11.10) can be written as:

$$LM = \frac{n(\hat{u}_r'\hat{u}_r - \hat{u}'\hat{u})}{\hat{u}_r'\hat{u}_r} \sim \chi_q^2 \quad \text{(A1.11.11)}$$

or

$$LM = nR^2 \quad \text{(A1.11.12)}$$

where R^2 is the R-squared from the regression of u_r on X. Greater values of the statistic result in the rejection of the null hypothesis that the restriction is true.

Answer 1.12

a) The implication is that X is a square matrix.
b) Minimization of

$$\hat{U}'\hat{U} = (Y - X\hat{\beta})'(Y - X\hat{\beta}) = Y'Y - 2\hat{\beta}'X'Y + \hat{\beta}'X'X\hat{\beta}$$

leads, through the first-order condition, to:

$$\hat{\beta} = (X'X)^{-1}X'Y$$

However, since X is square

$$\hat{\beta} = X^{-1}Y \quad \text{since} \quad (X'X)^{-1} = X^{-1}X'^{-1}.$$

c) We know that $\hat{Y} = X\hat{\beta}$. Replacing $\hat{\beta}$ by its value gives $\hat{Y} = X X^{-1}Y$, hence $\hat{Y} = Y$. This implies that at each instant in time or space the residual is zero. This means that the fit is perfect.

d) We know that:

$$R^2 = \frac{\hat{Y}'\hat{Y} - n\bar{Y}^2}{Y'Y - n\bar{Y}^2}$$

Using the result in (c),

$$R^2 = \frac{Y'Y - n\bar{Y}^2}{Y'Y - n\bar{Y}^2} = 1$$

The fit is perfect. This is an artifact due to $n = k$.

e) We know that

$$F = \frac{R^2 / (k-1)}{(1-R^2)/(n-k)}.$$

With $R^2 = 1$ and $n = k$, $F = 0/0$. The F statistic is indeterminate.

f) This is the issue of lack of degrees of freedom (here, zero).

Answer 1.13

a) The nonlinear form of the production function is

$$Q_i = AK_i^{\beta_1}L_i^{\beta_2}e^{u_i}$$

where $A = e^c$.

b) $E(Q_i) = AK_i^{\beta_1}L_i^{\beta_2}E(e^{u_i}) \neq AK_i^{\beta_1}L_i^{\beta_2}$
since $E(u_i) = 0$ does not imply that $E(e^{u_i}) = 1$.

c) We know that if

$$u_i \sim N(0,\sigma^2) \text{ then } E(e^{u_i}) = e^{\sigma^2/2}$$

Using the estimator of σ^2 and those of other parameters, we can write

$$\hat{Q}_i = \hat{A}K_i^{\hat{\beta}_1}L_i^{\hat{\beta}_2}e^{\hat{\sigma}^2/2}$$

This estimator of Q_i is biased but consistent. In fact, an unbiased estimator of Q_i does not exist (see also Wooldridge, 2000, 202–203).

Answer 1.14

a) OLS estimation leads to:

$$CPI_t = \underset{(0.987)}{0.657} + \underset{(0.022)}{1.057}\, IM_t$$

where standard errors are in parentheses.

b) For the constant term, the null and alternative hypotheses are, respectively, $H_0 : \alpha = 0$ and $H_i : \alpha > 0$. The distribution of interest is the t with the following critical value: $t_{24,0.05} = 1.711$. The t calculated is given by:

$$t = \frac{0.657 - 0}{0.987} = 0.666$$

Since t calculated is less than the critical value, that is, $0.666 < 1.711$, we do not reject the null hypothesis.

For the slope, $H_0 : \beta = 0$ and $H_1 : \beta > 0$. Distribution and critical value are the same as above. The t calculated is

$$t = \frac{1.057}{0.022} = 48.045$$

Since the calculated value is greater than the critical value we reject H_0. That is, the import price index positively affects the consumer price index.

c) The coefficient of determination is given by:

$$r^2 = \frac{\text{ESS}}{\text{TSS}} = 1 - \frac{\text{RSS}}{\text{TSS}} = 0.9899$$

The significance of r^2 is tested with an F test:

$$F = \frac{r^2/(k-1)}{\left(1-r^2\right)/(n-k)} = \frac{0.9899}{(1-0.9899)/24} = 2352.24$$

Since $2352.24 > F_{24}^{1} = 4.26$, we reject H_0. That is, we accept that 99% of the variation in CPI is explained by the regression (the import price index).

d) If all assumptions of the classical linear model are fulfilled, it can be said that the CPI is explained by the import price index, and a one-unit increase in the import price index brings about a 1.057 increase in the CPI. Moreover, 99% of the variation in CPI is explained by the regression.

e) We use the Chow test to see whether there is a structural change. To recall, the Chow test is given by:

TABLE 1.4
OLS Results: Price and Money Relationship, Barbados 1972–2001

Variable	Coefficient	Standard Error	*t* Statistic	Prob.
C	38.93365	4.299353	9.055699	0.0000
X	6.21E-05	5.94E-06	10.46560	0.0000
R^2	0.796406	Mean dependent variable		74.02667
$\bar{R}^2$	0.789135	*F* statistic		109.5287
RSS	6082.123	Prob(*F* statistic)		0.000000

Note: *Y* is price and *X* is money supply.

$$F = \frac{(\text{RRSS} - \text{URSS})/q}{\text{URSS}/(n-2k)}$$

where q is the number of constraints, RRSS is the restricted residual sum of squares from the basic regression and URSS stands for the unrestricted residual sum of squares, which is the sum of RSS from the 1972–1984 regression and RSS from the 1985–1997 regression. Using the results of the regression:

$$F = \frac{(414.3066 - 410.103457)/2}{410.103457/(26-4)} = 0.112739$$

The associated p value being 0.833896, we do not reject the null hypothesis that there is no structural change in the year 1985. (Under which conditions is the test valid?)

Answer 1.15

a) We use OLS. We suppose that all assumptions of the classical linear regression model are fulfilled. We also assume that errors are normally distributed. Results are shown in Table 1.4.
b) A one-unit (Bds \$1,000) increase in the money supply brings about a 0.0000621 increase in the retail price index.
c) Following the general definition of elasticity, we compute the latter from (b) as:

$$E_m = \frac{dY}{dX} \cdot \frac{\bar{X}}{\bar{Y}} = 0.0000621 \, \frac{564738.5}{74.02667} = 0.474$$

A 1 percent increase in the money supply brings about a 0.474 percent increase in the retail price index.

TABLE 1.5
OLS Results: Log Price and Log Money Relationship, Barbados 1972–2001

Variable	Coefficient	Standard Error	*t* Statistic	Prob.
C	–3.318021	0.433380	–7.656154	0.0000
Ln *X*	0.582036	0.033566	17.34000	0.0000
R^2	0.914810	Mean dependent variable		4.178177
$\bar{R}^2$	0.911257	*F* statistic		300.6756
RSS	0.780257	Prob(*F* statistic)		0.000000

TABLE 1.6
OLS Results: Log Price and Money Relationship, Barbados 1972–2001

Variable	Coefficient	Standard Error	*t* Statistic	Prob.
C	3.636081	0.102867	35.34745	0.0000
X	9.60E-07	1.42E-07	6.756889	0.0000
R^2	0.619852	Mean dependent variable		4.178177
$\bar{R}^2$	0.606275	*F* statistic		45.65555
RSS	3.481769	Prob(*F* statistic)		0.000000

d) If the model above is replaced by a double log linear model, OLS estimation leads to the results shown in Table 1.5. The slope or the marginal effect is computed as:

$$\hat{\beta}(\bar{Y}/\bar{X}) = 0.582036(74.02667/564738.5) = 0.0000763$$

That is, a Bds $1000 increase in the money supply leads to a 0.0000763 increase in the retail price index. In this model $\hat{\beta}$ is the elasticity, since

$$\hat{\beta} = \frac{dLogY}{dLogX} = \frac{dY}{dX}\frac{X}{Y}$$

The elasticity is thus 0.582. That is, a 1 percent increase in the money supply brings about a 0.582 percent increase in the retail price index. The difference between the two elasticities is due to two facts. First, the two functional forms are different. Second, on one hand, the elasticity from the linear model is variable. Following the tradition, this elasticity was computed at the means of variables. On the other hand, the elasticity from the double log model is constant; that is, it is the same at every point. This elasticity is more reliable than the previous one if the model is truly a constant elasticity function.

e) Note that we can use OLS in all the models since the models are linear in parameters. The results of the log-lin model are shown in Table 1.6. The slope is given by:

$$\hat{\beta}\bar{Y} = 0.00000096 \times 74.02667 = 0.000071$$

TABLE 1.7
OLS Results: Price and Log Money Relationship, Barbados 1972–2001

Variable	Coefficient	Standard Error	*t* Statistic	Prob.
C	–367.9331	13.42816	–27.40012	0.0000
Ln X	34.31558	1.040036	32.99460	0.0000
R^2	0.974925	Mean dependent variable		74.02667
$\bar{R}^2$	0.974029	F statistic		1088.644
RSS	749.0897	Prob(F statistic)		0.000000

TABLE 1.8
OLS Results: Price and Reciprocal Money Relationship, Barbados 1972–2001

Variable	Coefficient	Standard Error	*t* Statistic	Prob.
C	104.8149	3.477738	30.13881	0.0000
$1/X$	–8016692	659909.8	–12.14816	0.0000
R^2	0.840527	Mean dependent variable		74.02667
$\bar{R}^2$	0.834831	F statistic		147.5779
RSS	4764.077	Prob(p value)		0.00000

That is, a Bds $1000 increase in the money supply brings about a 0.000071 increase in the retail price index. The elasticity is

$$\hat{\beta}\bar{X} = 0.000000960 \times 564738.5 = 0.542$$

That is, a 1 percent increase in the money supply brings about a 0.54 percent increase in the retail price index.

The results of the lin-log model are in Table 1.7. The slope is given by:

$$\hat{\beta}\left(1/\bar{X}\right) = 34.61558/564738.5 = 0.000061$$

That is, a Bds $1000 increase in the money supply leads to a 0.000061 increase in the retail price index. The elasticity is

$$\hat{\beta}\left(1/\bar{Y}\right) = 34.61558/74.02667 = 0.468$$

That is, a 1 percent increase in the money supply gives rise to a 0.47 percent increase in the retail price index.

The basic results of the estimation using the reciprocal model are presented in Table 1.8. The slope is given by:

$$-\hat{\beta}(1/\bar{X}^2) = 8016692/(564738.5)^2 = 0.0000251$$

TABLE 1.9
OLS Results: Log Money and Trend Relationship, Barbados 1972–2001

Variable	Coefficient	Standard Error	t Statistic	Prob.
C	11.26987	0.050165	224.6542	0.0000
T	0.103832	0.002826	36.74499	0.0000
R^2	0.979684	Mean dependent variable		12.87926
RSS	0.502489	F statistic		1350.195
		Prob(F statistic)		0.000000

That is, a Bds \$1000 increase in the money supply gives rise to a 0.0000251 increase in the retail price index. The elasticity is

$$-\hat{\beta}(1/\bar{X}\bar{Y}) = 8016692/41805710.58 = 0.191761$$

That is, a 1 percent increase in the money supply brings about a 0.192 percent increase in the retail price index. As can be seen, the slope and the elasticity derived from the reciprocal model here are different from their analogues in other models.

f) To obtain the instantaneous growth rate of money supply, we run the following regression:

$$Ln\,X = c + \beta\,T + u$$

where T represents the trend (here it goes from 1 to 30) and X is the money supply. OLS estimation gives the results shown in Table 1.9. The instantaneous growth rate is $0.104 \times 100\% = 10.4\%$. That is, over the period 1972–2001, the money supply grew at a rate of 10.4% per year. The compound growth rate is obtained from antilog(0.103831) – 1 = 0.109413. Thus, the compound rate is 0.109413*100% = 10.9%. Precisely, the money supply in Barbados grew at a compound rate of 10.9% per year during the period 1972–2001.

The absolute rate is obtained by running the following regression:

$$X = c + \beta\,T + u$$

According to the results in Table 1.10 the absolute increase in the money supply is Bds \$49,071,760.00. That is, over the period 1972–2001, the money supply in Barbados underwent on average an increase of Bds \$49,071,760.00 per year.

Answer 1.16

a) Supposing that all the CLM assumptions are fulfilled, the results indicate that income has a positive impact on saving. Indeed, a one dollar increase in income brings about a \$0.085 increase in saving. With no income (income

TABLE 1.10
OLS Results: Money and Trend Relationship, Barbados 1972–2001

Variable	Coefficient	Standard Error	*t* Statistic	Prob.
C	–195873.8	61259.70	–3.197433	0.0034
T	49071.76	3450.680	14.22089	0.0000
R^2	0.878385	Mean dependent variable		564732.1
$\bar{R}^2$	0.874041	F statistic		202.2338
RSS	7.49E+11	Prob(F statistic)		0.000000

at the zero level), the average dissaving is of the order of $648,123.60. The fit of the model is good, as 91 percent of the variation in saving is explained by income.

b) The consumption function is specified as follows:

$$C_t = \gamma + \delta Y_t + e_t \qquad \text{(A1.16.1)}$$

where t = 1,2,3,..., T is the time index, C stands for consumption, Y is income, γ is the autonomous consumption, δ is the marginal propensity to consume and e is the error term. We know that income = consumption + saving; that is,

$$\begin{aligned} Y_t &= C_t + S_t = \hat{C}_t + \hat{e}_t + \hat{S}_t + \hat{u}_t \\ &= \hat{C}_t + \hat{S}_t \end{aligned} \qquad \text{(A1.16.2)}$$

where $\hat{e}_t$ is the residual from the consumption regression (A1.16.1) and $\hat{u}_t$ is that from the saving regression (Q1.16.1). Note that $\hat{e}_t = -\hat{u}_t$ (see proof in Answer 2.20.a). Thus, the estimated consumption function is

$$\begin{aligned} \hat{C}_t &= \hat{\gamma} + \hat{\delta} Y_t = Y_t - \hat{S}_t \\ &= Y_t - (\hat{\alpha} + \hat{\beta} Y_t) = -\hat{\alpha} + (1 - \hat{\beta}) Y_t \end{aligned} \qquad \text{(A1.16.3)}$$

where the estimate of autonomous consumption is equal to the negative of the estimate of autonomous saving ($\hat{\gamma} = -\hat{\alpha}$) and the estimate of marginal propensity to consume is equal to one minus the estimate of marginal propensity to save ($\hat{\delta} = 1 - \hat{\beta}$).

Applying Equation (A1.16.3) to the results presented in the question section leads to:

$$\begin{aligned} \hat{C}_t &= Y_t - \hat{S}_t = Y_t - (-648.1236 + 0.084665 Y_t) \\ &= 648.1236 + 0.9153335 Y_t \end{aligned}$$

c) We want to show that $RSS_c = RSS_s$ where RSS stands for the residual sum of squares and the subscripts c and s refer to consumption function and saving function, respectively. We know that:

$$RSS_s = \sum (S_t - \hat{\alpha} - \hat{\beta} Y_t)^2 \tag{A1.16.4}$$

$$RSS_C = \sum (C_t - \hat{\gamma} - \hat{\delta} Y_t)^2 \tag{A1.16.5}$$

and

$$Y_t = C_t + S_t \tag{A1.16.6}$$

Equation (A1.16.6) in Equation (A1.16.5) gives:

$$\begin{aligned} RSS_C &= \sum (Y_t - S_t - \hat{\gamma} - \hat{\delta} Y_t)^2 \\ &= \sum (-S_t - \hat{\gamma} + (1 - \hat{\delta}) Y_t)^2 \\ &= \sum (-S_t + \hat{\alpha} + \hat{\beta} Y_t)^2 \qquad \text{(A1.16.7)} \\ &= \sum (S_t - \hat{\alpha} - \hat{\beta} Y_t)^2 \\ &= RSS_S \end{aligned}$$

d) We are asked to show in the first instance that:

$$Std_{\hat{\beta}} = Std_{\hat{\delta}}$$

We know that:

$$Std_{\hat{\beta}} = \hat{\sigma}_u \sqrt{\frac{1}{\sum (Y_t - \bar{Y})^2}} \tag{A1.16.8}$$

and

$$Std_{\hat{\delta}} = \hat{\sigma}_e \sqrt{\frac{1}{\sum (Y_t - \bar{Y})^2}} \tag{A1.16.9}$$

But

$$\hat{\sigma}_u = \hat{\sigma}_e = \sqrt{\frac{\text{RSS}}{n-2}} \quad \text{since} \quad \text{RSS} = \text{RSS}_c = \text{RSS}_s$$

Thus,

$$Std_{\hat{\beta}} = Std_{\hat{\delta}} \qquad \text{QED}$$

Similarly, we can show that the standard errors of the autonomous parts are the same.

e) The two R^2s are not strictly comparable since the dependent variables are different. If they were comparable, the regression with the higher variability of the explained variable would have a higher R^2 than the other one. Why?

Answer 1.17

a) For γ_2, the null and alternative hypotheses are, respectively, $H_0 : \gamma_2 = 0$ and $H_1 : \gamma_2 > 0$. The distribution of interest is the t distribution with the following critical value: $t_{(26-6),0.05} = 1.725$. The t calculated is

$$t = \frac{0.158-0}{\sqrt{0.026738}} = \frac{0.158}{0.1635} = 0.966$$

Since $0.966 < 1.725$, we do not reject H_0.

For γ_3, $H_0 : \gamma_3 = 0$ and $H_1 : \gamma_3 > 0$. The distribution of interest and critical value are as above. The t calculated is

$$t = \frac{1.097}{\sqrt{0.350372}} = \frac{1.097}{0.5919} = 1.853$$

Since $1.853 > 1.725$, we reject H_0.

For γ_4, $H_0 : \gamma_4 = 0$ and $H_1 : \gamma_4 < 0$. The distribution of interest is the same as above. The critical value is -1.725. The t calculated is

$$t = \frac{-0.152}{\sqrt{0.008131}} = \frac{-0.152}{0.0902} = -1.685$$

Since $-1.685 > -1.725$, we do not reject H_0.

For γ_5, $H_0 : \gamma_5 = 0$ and $H_1 : \gamma_5 < 0$. The distribution of interest and critical value are as above. The t calculated is

$$t = \frac{-0.685}{\sqrt{0.048476}} = \frac{-0.685}{0.2202} = -3.111$$

Since –3.111 < –1.725, we reject H_0.

For γ_6, $H_0 : \gamma_6 = 0$ and $H_1 : \gamma_6 < 0$. The distribution of interest and critical value are as above. The t calculated is

$$t = \frac{-1.007}{\sqrt{0.012637}} = \frac{-1.007}{0.1124} = -8.959$$

Since –8.959 < –1.725, we reject H_0.

b) The null and alternative hypotheses are, respectively, $H_0 : \gamma_6 = -1$ and $H_1 : \gamma_6 \neq -1$. The distribution of interest is the t with the following critical value: $t_{(20,0.025)} = -2.086$. The t calculated is

$$t = \frac{-1.007+1}{0.1124} = -0.0623$$

Since –0.0623 > –2.086, we do not reject H_0; that is, $\gamma_6 = -1$.

c) The null and alternative hypotheses are, respectively: $H_0 : \gamma_5 = \gamma_6$ and $H_1 : \gamma_5 \neq \gamma_6$ or $H_0 : \gamma_5 - \gamma_6 = 0$ and $H_1 : \gamma_5 - \gamma_6 \neq 0$. The distribution of interest is the t distribution with the critical value 2.086. The calculated t is

$$t = \frac{\left(\hat{\gamma}_5 - \hat{\gamma}_6\right) - 0}{\sqrt{\text{var}(\hat{\gamma}_5) + \text{var}(\hat{\gamma}_6) - 2\,\text{cov}\left(\hat{\gamma}_5 \hat{\gamma}_6\right)}}$$

$$t = \frac{-0.685 - (-1.007)}{\sqrt{0.048476 + 0.012637 - 2(0.011609)}} = \frac{0.322}{\sqrt{0.037895}} = \frac{0.322}{0.194666} = 1.654$$

Since 1.654 < 2.086, we do not reject H_0.

d) The unrestricted residual sum of squares is URSS = 0.100101 + 0.050142 = 0.150243. The distribution of interest, among others, is the F with the following critical value $F_{14}^{6} = 2.85$. The F calculated is

$$F = \frac{(\text{RRSS} - \text{URSS})/\#\text{constraints}}{\text{URSS}/(n-2k)}$$

$$F = \frac{(0.181067 - 0.150243)/6}{0.150243/(26-12)}$$

$$F = \frac{0.030824/6}{0.150243/14} = \frac{0.005137}{0.010732} = 0.479$$

Since $0.479 < 2.85$, we do not reject H_0; that is, the structural stability of regressions is not rejected.

e) This model attempts to explain the behaviour of international reserves in Barbados. The model indicates that a change in international reserves is positively related to an income change and negatively related to a money multiplier change as well as a domestic credit change. The model acknowledges structural stability with respect to the parameters of interest. Finally, the monetary approach to the balance of payments in Barbados is validated since $\gamma_6 = -1$.

1.4 SUPPLEMENTARY EXERCISES

Question 1.18 Suppose that the estimation of the function of expenditures on durables of a typical household in country Z gives rise to:

$$\hat{Y}_t = 44.610 + 0.0519X_{2t} - 0.347X_{3t}$$

where Y = expenditure on durables (in \$); $\hat{Y}$ = fitted values of Y; X_2 = household income (in \$); X_3 = price index; and $t = 1,2,3,\ldots, 15$. Important statistics are in the note.

a) Perform any standard test for judging the statistical significance of the explanatory variables and interpret the results. Use $\alpha = 0.05$ throughout.
b) Suppose that we are only interested in the hypothesis of the lack of impact of price on expenditures. Use a statistical test different from that utilized in (a) to test this null hypothesis.
c) Compute R^2. Is the latter significantly different from zero?
d) Which variable has the bigger impact on expenditures on durables (in absolute value)? (Make sure you justify your answer). (Adapted from UWI, EC36C, term test 1996.)

Note:

$$\text{RSS} = 1128.156 \quad Y'Y = 191460 \quad \bar{Y} = 112.3333 \quad \bar{X}_2 = 2058$$

$$\bar{X}_3 = 112.6667 \text{ and } Var\left(\hat{\beta}\right) = \begin{pmatrix} 2152.079 & -0.774167 & -4.904508 \\ & 0.000363 & 0.000247 \\ & & 0.039027 \end{pmatrix}$$

Moreover, RSS from the regression of Y_t on a constant and X_{2t} is equal to 1417.843.

Question 1.19 At the University of the West Indies, Barbados, Statistical Methods I is one of the prerequisites for Econometrics I. A regression of grades (in percent) obtained by thirty-eight students in Econometrics I in 1998 on grades (in percent)

TABLE 1.11
OLS Results: Econ98 on Stat97, UWI, Barbados, 38 Students

Variable	Coefficient	Standard Error	t Statistic	Prob.
C	2.613799	8.859956	0.295013	0.7697
Stat97	0.705869	0.144089	4.898853	0.0000
R^2	0.399988	Mean dependent variable		44.94737
RSS	5229.645	F statistic		23.99876
		Prob(F statistic)		0.000000

Note: Econ98, students' grades (%) in Econometrics I in 1998; Stat97, students' grades (%) in Statistical Methods I in 1997.

obtained in Statistical Methods I one year ago by the same cohort of students gives the results shown in Table 1.11.

a) Do the t ratio (which one?) and the F statistic convey the same message? Why or why not?
b) Fully interpret the results of the model.
c) Compute $\bar{R}^2$. Is the latter of any use here?
d) Is the model flawed? Justify your answer.

Question 1.20 Intuitively explain why the sample R^2 is a biased estimator of the population R^2. Likewise the adjusted R^2 is not better than the sample R^2 from the bias point of view (see also Wooldridge, 2000).

Question 1.21 The LR, W, and LM tests are the F test equivalent in large samples. Show why these tests follow a χ^2 distribution with the number of restrictions as the number of degrees of freedom, rather than an F distribution.

Question 1.22 Consider the following CLM:

$$Y_t = \alpha_0 + \alpha_1 X_t + \alpha_2 Z_t + e_t$$

where Y_t is the dependent variable, X_t and Z_t are the independent variables, t is the time index and e_t is a well behaved error term.

a) Test the assumption $\alpha_1 = -\alpha_2$ using two variants of the t test.
b) Test the above hypothesis using the F test.

Question 1.23 Consider Table 1.12 related to gross national income per capita (Gni_t) and gross domestic investment per capita (Gdi_t) for Gabon in the period 1973–1993.

a) Fit the following two regressions to the above data:

$$Gni_t = c + bGdi_t + u_t$$

TABLE 1.12
Per Capita Gross National Income and Per Capita Gross Investment for Gabon, 1973–1993

Year	Gni	Gdi	Year	Gni	Gdi
1973	4180.00	1350.00	1984	6480.00	2330.00
1974	6820.00	3630.00	1985	6040.00	2510.00
1975	7130.00	4290.00	1986	4350.00	2070.00
1976	8900.00	5850.00	1987	3430.00	950.00
1977	7550.00	4360.00	1988	3830.00	1820.00
1978	5590.00	1580.00	1989	3950.00	1440.00
1979	5730.00	1860.00	1990	4190.00	1210.00
1980	6740.00	1820.00	1991	4160.00	1300.00
1981	7200.00	2620.00	1992	3820.00	980.00
1982	6420.00	2400.00	1993	3740.00	1020.00
1983	6470.00	2250.00			

Note: Gni, gross national income per capita for Gabon in 1987 dollars; Gdi, gross domestic investment per capita in 1987 dollars.

Source: World's Table 95, World Bank, Washington, D.C.

$$LGni_t = \gamma + \delta LGdi_t + e_t$$

where variables in the first regression are defined as in the note to Table 1.12 and in the second, they are defined in logarithm forms; u_t and e_t represent the error terms.

b) Supposing that the assumptions of the classical linear model are fulfilled, compute and interpret the elasticities from the two models. Which elasticity do you prefer?

Question 1.24 Consider the following terms of trade for China for the period 1973–1993 (see Table 1.13). Test the hypothesis of deterioration of terms of trade.

TABLE 1.13
China Terms of Trade, 1973–1993

Year	TOT	Year	TOT
1973	121.3	1984	113.8
1974	116.3	1985	109.3
1975	108.1	1986	96.8
1976	111.3	1987	100.0
1977	117.8	1988	98.8
1978	108.1	1989	101.7
1979	108.0	1990	105.6
1980	115.4	1991	104.7
1981	119.5	1992	101.2
1982	121.4	1993	101.1
1983	111.4		

Note: TOT, terms of trade index.

Source: World Table 95, World Bank, Washington, D.C.

CHAPTER 2

Relaxation of Assumptions of the Classical Linear Model

2.1 INTRODUCTION

As seen above, there are key assumptions for a model to qualify as a classical linear regression model.

1. The model is linear in parameters. More precisely, the dependent variable is a linear function of a specific set of independent variables plus a disturbance term. Violation of this assumption, known as specification error, can take the form of wrong regressors (omission of relevant independent variables or inclusion of irrelevant variables); nonlinearity (the relation is nonlinear) and changing or varying parameters (the parameters vary instead of being constant: see Lucas critique). These different violations generally bring about specification bias and/or inefficiency of estimators.
2. On average, there are no errors in the model. Basically, positive and negative errors cancel out. The violation of this assumption brings about a biased constant term.
3. Error variance is constant; that is, error variance does not change with observations. This property is known as homoscedasticity. The violation of this property is known as heteroscedasticity. The latter is more prevalent in cross section data than in time series data. Inefficiency of OLS estimators and forecasts, wider confidence intervals and invalidation of test statistics are the consequences of heteroscedasticity.
4. Errors at different points in time or space are uncorrelated. This is known as absence of autocorrelation. The violation of the assumption brings about autocorrelation. As for heteroscedasticity, inefficiency of OLS estimators and invalidation of test statistics such as the t or F are the major consequences of autocorrelation. In many instances, assumptions (3) and (4) are combined and the non-fulfilment of at least one of them gives rise to errors that are nonspherical.
5. The independent variables are fixed in repeated samples. This implies a lack of correlation between the explanatory variables and the error term. This is desirable, as one wants to disentangle the respective impacts of the independent variables and the error on the dependent variable. The violation of this assumption can take the form of error in variables, autoregression

(lagged dependent variable) and endogeneity of variables, such as in simultaneous equations models. The violation of the assumption brings about bias and/or inconsistency of OLS estimators.

6. The number of observations is greater than the number of independent variables and an exact relationship does not exist between or among explanatory variables. The latter condition states that the rank of the matrix of independent variables is maximum. This condition is known as absence of multicollinearity. The violation of the assumption gives rise to multicollinearity. When the latter is perfect (exact), it is not possible to obtain all estimates. When it is imperfect, estimates are not precise.

These different issues can be recast in the problem of diagnostic checking and specification which can be discussed in the context of modelling strategy. In that connection, there are two tendencies: bottom-up and top-down (general-to-specific) strategies. The exercises in this chapter reflect different aspects of the points alluded to above.

2.2 QUESTIONS

2.2.1 Theoretical Exercises

Question 2.1 Write a concise note on each of the following using the following format: nature of the problem, causes, detection, consequences, and solutions:

a) Heteroscedasticity;
b) Autocorrelation;
c) Multicollinearity.

Question 2.2 Although the DW test statistic is the most popular test for autocorrelation, it has several limitations. Provide these limitations and suggest corresponding alternatives. (UWI, EC36C, final examination December 1996)

Question 2.3 Write short notes on the following tests:

a) Ramsey's RESET test for omitted variables;
b) Breusch–Godfrey LM test for autocorrelation;
c) Bera–McAleer test. (UWI, EC36C, final examination December 1996)

Question 2.4 Consider the following regression $Y = X\beta + u$ where Y is an $\mathbf{n} \times \mathbf{1}$ vector of observations on the dependent variables, X is an $n \times k$ matrix of explanatory variables including the column vector of ones, β is a $\mathbf{k} \times \mathbf{1}$ vector of parameters and u is an $\mathbf{n} \times \mathbf{1}$ vector of disturbances.

a) Provide four factors that affect the accuracy of the estimate of β, $\hat{\beta}$.
b) Provide and explain three possible causes for wrong signs associated occasionally with some components of $\hat{\beta}$.

c) Consider the existence of a competing model $Y = Z\gamma + e$ where variables and parameters are defined similarly as above and $Z \neq X$. Explain whether the J test proposed by Davidson and MacKinnon can be applied here to discriminate between the two models. If yes, explain its implementation and provide its limitations. (Adapted from UWI, EC36C, final examination December 2000.)

Question 2.5 Write careful notes on the following:

a) White's test;
b) Jarque–Bera test for normality.

Question 2.6 From the regression $Y = X\beta + u$ where Y is an $\mathbf{n} \times \mathbf{1}$ vector of observations on the dependent variable, X is an $n \times k$ matrix of explanatory variables including the column vector of ones, β is a $\mathbf{k} \times \mathbf{1}$ vector of parameters, u is an $\mathbf{n} \times \mathbf{1}$ vector of disturbances and $E(uu') = \sigma^2\Omega$ with $\Omega \neq I$ as a symmetric positive definite matrix:

a) Derive the GLS estimator of β.
b) Prove that the above estimator is unbiased. (UWI, EC36C, final examination December 1997)

Question 2.7 Consider the following classical linear regression model:

$$Y_t = \beta_1 + \beta_2 X_t + \beta_3 Z_t + \varepsilon_t \quad \text{(Q2.7.1)}$$

where $t = 1,2,\ldots, n$, $Z_t = bX_t$ and ε_t = a well-behaved error term.

a) Which problem does the above regression give rise to? What is (are) the consequence(s) of the problem?
b) Propose solutions to the problem. In each case state the properties of the resulting estimator(s).

Question 2.8 A true regression equation is given by:

$$Y_t = \beta_0 + \beta_1 Z_t + \beta_2 Z_t^2 + u_t \quad \text{(Q2.8.1)}$$

where Z_t is autocorrelated and u_t is a well-behaved error term. Suppose that instead of Equation (Q2.8.1), we estimate the following equation:

$$Y_t = \alpha_0 + \alpha_1 Z_t + \upsilon_t \quad \text{(Q2.8.2)}$$

a) Is υ_t a well-behaved error term?
b) Derive the small sample properties of the OLS estimator of α_1.
c) Is the above estimator consistent?

Question 2.9 A researcher interested in knowing the determining factors of wages regressed the latter variable on the level of education. Suspecting that the experience level also matters in wages determination, he decided to test whether experience level is an omitted variable in his model. To conduct the test he simply regressed the residuals from the above regression on the experience level. The test indicated that the coefficient of experience level was not significantly different from zero. The researcher thus rejected his suspicion and concluded that the experience level is irrelevant for wages. Comment on the validity of the results obtained by the researcher. (Adapted from SUNY Albany, PhD comprehensive examinations fall 1987.)

Question 2.10 Consider the following marginal cost model:

$$C_t = \beta_0 + \beta_1 Q_t + \beta_2 Q_t^2 + u_t \tag{Q2.10.1}$$

where C_t is marginal cost, Q_t is output and u_t is a well-behaved error term.

a) An investigator points out that one cannot estimate the model, because of perfect multicollinearity between Q_t and Q_t^2. Do you agree with this statement? Why or why not?
b) Suppose Q_t^2 is autocorrelated and we omit it from the basic regression. Do you think that the DW test statistic will reveal autocorrelation? If yes, can we say that the DW statistic is testing for first-order autocorrelation?

Question 2.11 Consider the five functional forms:

$$Y_t = \alpha_0 + \alpha_1 X_t + u_t \tag{Q2.11.1}$$

$$Y_t = \beta_0 + \beta_1 \log(X_t) + u_t \tag{Q2.11.2}$$

$$Y_t = \gamma_0 + \gamma_1 \frac{1}{X_t} + u_t \tag{Q2.11.3}$$

$$\log(Y_t) = \delta_0 + \delta_1 X_t + u_t \tag{Q2.11.4}$$

$$\log(Y_t) = a + b \log(X_t) + u_t \tag{Q2.11.5}$$

Conduct a thorough discussion on model choice.

Question 2.12 Consider the following model:

$$\mathbf{Y} = X\beta + \mathbf{U}$$

where **Y** is a vector of observations on the dependent variable, X is a matrix of explanatory variables including the column vector of ones, β is a vector of parameters and **U** is a vector of errors.

a) The use of OLS residuals gives rise to some difficulties in testing for heteroscedasticity or autocorrelation. Do you agree with this statement? Why or why not?
b) Cite one alternative if (a) is true.

Question 2.13 Consider the following model:

$$Y_t = \alpha + \beta X_t + u_t \qquad \text{(Q2.13.1)}$$

where Y_t is the dependent variable, X_t is the explanatory variable, t stands for time, and u_t is the error term. Suppose that X_t and u_t are not independent.

a) Provide three possible reasons for the dependence between X_t and u_t.
b) What are the consequences of the problem raised in (a)?
c) Suppose you have decided to solve the problem of the dependence between the two variables using an instrumental variable (IV), Z_t. Show that the estimator β^{IV} is consistent. (Adapted from UWI, EC36C, final examination December 2003.)

Question 2.14 Write careful notes on the following:

a) Omitted variables;
b) Irrelevant variables;
c) Proxy variables;
d) Dominant variables. (UWI, EC36C, final examination December 2003)

Question 2.15 In Hendry's methodology the following criteria are often used for the choice of a parsimonious model: data-admissible, theory-consistent, predictive-validity, data-coherency and encompassing. Explain the concepts.

Question 2.16 Consider the following consumption function:

$$C_t = \beta_0 + \beta_1(Y_t - T_t) + \beta_2 C_{t-1} + u_t \qquad \text{(Q2.16.1)}$$

where C_t stands for consumption expenditure, Y_t is income, T_t stands for taxes, C_{t-1} is one period lagged consumption and u_t is the error term. The same model may be rewritten as follows:

$$C_t = \alpha_0 + \alpha_1 Y_t + \alpha_2 T_t + \alpha_3 C_{t-1} + u_t \qquad \text{(Q2.16.2)}$$

where u_t is well behaved.

a) Is there any relationship between the R^2s in the two models? Explain carefully.
b) It is well known that consumption depends on disposable income. That is, Equation (Q2.16.1) is preferred to Equation (Q2.16.2). Under what conditions is $\beta_1 = \alpha_1$?
c) Are the two models nested? Why or why not? (Adapted from Kennedy, 1992 and Greene, 2003.)

2.2.2 Empirical Exercises

Question 2.17 The estimation of a labour demand for Barbados over the period 1970–1996 yields:

$$\hat{l}_t = -0.304 - 0.143 wr_t + 0.734\, gdp_t + 0.0003 nis_t$$

$$R^2 = 0.917 \; DW = 0.742 \quad \text{RSS} = 0.0225 \quad F = 84.715$$

$$Var(\hat{\beta}) = \begin{pmatrix} 0.2565 & -0.0072 & -0.0452 & 0.0084 \\ & 0.0046 & 0.0010 & 0.0002 \\ & & 0.0081 & -0.0017 \\ & & & 0.0005 \end{pmatrix}$$

where
l_t = natural logarithm of total employment;
$\hat{l}_t$ = fitted values of natural logarithm of total employment;
wr_t = natural logarithm of real wage index;
gdp_t = natural logarithm of real gross domestic product;
nis_t = natural logarithm of index of contributions of employers to national insurance;
t = time index;
RSS = residual sum of squares.

a) Evaluate the statistical significance of the results, supposing that all assumptions of CLM are fulfilled. Use α = 5% throughout.
b) Test for the first-order autocorrelation using the DW statistic. Does a significant DW necessarily mean presence of autocorrelation? (Be as explicit as possible.)
c) In light of your finding about autocorrelation in (b), reevaluate your answers given in (a).
d) A regression of l_t on the original regressors, $\hat{l}_t^2$ and a constant term yields the following statistics: R^2 = 0.950687 and RSS = 0.013347.

    i) Conduct a relevant test for omitted variables noting that the coefficient of $\hat{l}_t^2$ has a t statistic of 3.876.

ii) What is (are) the consequence(s) of omitted variables in a model? (UWI, EC36C, final examination December 2002)

Question 2.18 The estimation of a Cobb–Douglas production function for twenty firms of a given industry yields:

$$\hat{q}_i = -16.907 + 0.332 k_i + 2.777\, l_i$$

$$R^2 = 0.915 \;\; DW = 2.032 \; \text{RSS} = 0.461$$

$$Var(\hat{\beta}) = \begin{pmatrix} 4.939971 & & \\ 0.216639 & 0.031875 & \\ -0.857446 & -0.057229 & 0.166070 \end{pmatrix}$$

where

$\hat{q}_i$ = fitted value of natural logarithm of output (output expressed in 1000 tons);
k_i = natural logarithm of capital (capital expressed in machine hours);
l_i = natural logarithm of labour (labour is in hours);
RSS = residual sum of squares;
i = firm index.

a) Evaluate the statistical significance of the results, supposing that all assumptions of the classical linear model are fulfilled. Use $\alpha = 5\%$ throughout.
b) Test for autocorrelation using the DW statistic.
c) A regression of $\hat{u}_i^2$ (square of residuals) on the original regressors (see the basic regression), the squares of regressors and the pairwise cross-product of regressors, yields:

$$R^2 = 0.296041 \quad F = 1.77507 \; (p = 0.368382)$$

i) With this information, which test can you implement to deal with which problem?
ii) Implement the test and interpret the results.
iii) What is (are) the consequence(s) of the problem alluded to above on the estimators?

d) Which type of returns to scale is the industry characterized by? Back up your answer by a test. (Adapted from UWI, EC36C, final examination December 2002.)

Question 2.19 At the University of the West Indies, Cave Hill campus, the course Introductory Statistics is a prerequisite for Statistical Methods I. To some extent, the students' grades in Statistical Methods I are determined by their corresponding grades in Introductory Statistics. Using the information in Table 2.1 on eleven students:

a) Speculate on the meaning(s) of the constant term in the model:

TABLE 2.1
UWI Student Results

Statistical Methods I Grades (%) Y_i	Introductory Statistics Grades (%) X_i
89	74
56	74
60	57
56	51
40	41
60	71
20	55
81	81
76	76
73	68
54	65

Source: Department of Economics, UWI, Cave Hill campus.

$$Y_i = \alpha + \beta X_i + u_i$$

where variables are defined as in Table 2.1 and i stands for individual.

b) Using the data in Table 2.1 fit the regression line to $Y_i = \alpha + \beta X_i + u_i$.
c) Test for heteroscedasticity using the following information:

$$\hat{u}_i^2 = -15.94389 + 64.27750X_i - 0.554093X_i^2 \quad R^2 = 0.13082$$

Make sure to indicate the name of the test you use.

d) Test for omitted variables using the following information: a regression of Y on the intercept,

$$X_i, \hat{Y}_i^2 \text{ and } \hat{Y}_i^3$$

yields $R^2 = 0.544265$. Make sure to indicate the test that you use.

e) Test for the individual coefficients. Find r^2 and interpret it. How valid are these results given the outcomes in (c) and (d)?

Question 2.20 Using information provided in Question 1.16, do the following:

a) Show that the saving function and the derived consumption function have the same DW statistic.
b) Suppose that the DW statistic is equal to 0.91, infer whether there is autocorrelation in the models. If yes, suggest methods for correction.
c) Explain whether the following statement is true. An LM test statistic for autocorrelation (the Breusch–Godfrey LM) can be constructed by multiplying the size of the sample with r^2 of the saving or consumption function.

Question 2.21 Using information provided in Question 1.14, check whether all the assumptions of the CLM are fulfilled.

2.3 ANSWERS

Answer 2.1

(a) Heteroscedasticity: Consider the following model

$$Y_i = \alpha + \beta X_i + u_i$$

where u_i is the disturbance term and Y_i and X_i are variables of interest. Heteroscedasticity refers to the situation in which the variance of the disturbance term u_i is no longer constant from observation to observation. That is,

$$\mathrm{E}\left(u_i^2\right) = \sigma_i^2 \quad i = 1, 2, \ldots, n.$$

Among the reasons for such a situation, we can cite:

i) Error learning process – as time passes people's errors of behaviour decrease ($\hat{\sigma}_i^2$ decreases over time), as over time they develop the ability to correct their mistakes.
ii) Income changes – changes in income positively affect the scope of opportunities for individuals. As a consequence, $\hat{\sigma}_i^2$ is most likely positively correlated with income.
iii) Progress in data collection – as time passes, with improvement in technology, data collection becomes better and better. That is, errors in data decrease ($\hat{\sigma}_i^2$ decreases over time). (See Gujarati, 1995, 357–358.)

Heteroscedasticity is more likely to occur in cross section data than in time series data. This is due to the high likelihood of data heterogeneity in cross section data. This, however, does not mean heteroscedasticity does not occur in time series data. In fact, it often occurs in time series in the form of error clustering. This form of heteroscedasticity is known as autoregressive conditional heteroscedasticity (ARCH).

To detect heteroscedasticity, one can combine the nature of the problem, graphical methods and test statistics. The nature of the problem can help reveal heteroscedasticity. For example, cross section data are more likely to be heteroscedastic than time series data. Graphical methods encompass the plot of squared residuals against the fitted values of the dependent variable (or suspected explanatory variable). A changing pattern of squared residuals can easily be revealed by these methods. Test statistics are a more formal way of detecting heteroscedasticity. Among the most important tests, we can cite White's test, Ramsey's RESET test, the Breusch–Pagan test, the Goldfeld–Quandt test and the Gleyser test. Some of these tests require knowledge of the form of heteroscedasticity and others do not.

The consequences of heteroscedasticity are multiple. The estimators are still unbiased, but they are no longer efficient. Indeed, the estimates of their variances are biased. Tests of significance and confidence intervals consequently become invalid. Forecasts are unbiased but inefficient. Moreover, in the context of the limited dependent variable model, the estimators are biased and inconsistent. Summing up, under heteroscedasticity, the estimators are no longer BLUE.

There are basically two types of solution to heteroscedasticity. The first type of solution is related to the assumption about $\hat{\sigma}_i^2$. In this connection, $\hat{\sigma}_i^2$ may be known or unknown. In any case some types of generalized least squares (GLS), feasible GLS or weighted least squares (WLS) or maximum likelihood methods are appropriate to solve the problem. Recent advances include the White's heteroscedasticity-consistent variances and covariances matrix, which gives rise to robust standard errors under heteroscedasticity. The second type of solution concerns the possibility of transforming data into logs (if feasible). Indeed, in many instances, the logarithm transformation decreases the extent of heteroscedasticity.

b) Autocorrelation: Autocorrelation is the correlation or the dependence between units of series of observations ordered in time (as in time series data) or space (as in cross section data). In the classical linear regression model, autocorrelation, also known as serial correlation, concerns the disturbance u_i, that is, $E(u_i u_j) \neq 0$ for $i \neq j$. In other words, the disturbance relating to an observation is influenced by the disturbance relating to any other observation.

Autocorrelation can be positive or negative. A positive autocorrelation means that bigger (smaller) errors are followed by bigger (smaller) errors. Since economic variables seem to move together (due mainly to economic growth, cyclical patterns), positive autocorrelation is the most common form of autocorrelation. Moreover, autocorrelation is more prevalent in time series data than in cross section data.

There are several reasons autocorrelation occurs, some of which are as follows (see Gujarati, 1995, 402–405):

i) Inertia – sluggishness of economic time series implies that successive observations influence one another;
ii) Omitted variables – if omitted variables are indeed important u_i will be autocorrelated since the error term incorporates the influence of the excluded variables;
iii) Incorrect functional form – along the same line of reasoning as above;
iv) The cobweb phenomenon;
v) Manipulation of data – data averaging or interpolation, for example, may create patterns in the series that most likely did not exist.

These different causes are important to the extent that they need to be taken into account for autocorrelation correction.

The nature of the problem, visual inspection and test statistics can help detect the presence of autocorrelation. The nature of the problem is the first step in detection of autocorrelation. In that connection, use of time series data, omitted autocorrelated variables, missing dynamics and incorrect functional form are, among others, the first culprit of autocorrelation. Visual inspection of graphs, such as the plot of residuals against time or against previous residuals, for example, may reveal patterns indicative of autocorrelation. Formal test statistics are the ultimate way of detecting the presence of autocorrelation in errors. Among the most important tests are the DW test, the Durbin's h test and the Breusch–Godfrey LM test.

In the presence of autocorrelation, the β estimators are still unbiased but are no longer BLUE. Indeed, the β estimators are no longer efficient since their variances are larger (so are their confidence levels). The t ratios and confidence intervals are invalid since the variances of the β estimators are biased. The variance of the residuals, $\hat{\sigma}_i^2$, is likely to underestimate σ^2, hence the R^2 statistic is likely to be overestimated. Moreover, in the presence of lagged dependent variables, estimators are no longer consistent. Note that the forecasts are, in the presence of autocorrelation, unbiased but inefficient.

The solution depends on the nature of the autocorrelation. For pure autocorrelation, some variable differencing procedure or Cochrane–Orcutt iterative procedure or Hildreth–Lu search procedure are, among others, of interest. Advances have been made in the form of Newey–West HAC robust standard errors, which solve the problem of nonspherical errors assuming the sample is large. For other scenarios of autocorrelation, the nature of the autocorrelation dictates the course of action. For example, if autocorrelation is due to an omitted variable then if the latter is available one should introduce it in the model.

c) Multicollinearity: Multicollinearity refers to a situation of exact or approximately exact relationships among two or several explanatory variables (perfect multicollinearity and imperfect multicollinearity, respectively). The case of imperfect multicollinearity is more prevalent than that of perfect multicollinearity. In fact, multicollinearity is really a "question of degree and not of kind" (Gujarati, 1995, 335).

Since multicollinearity is a sample problem, there is no unique method of detecting or measuring its strength. There are, however, some rules of thumb (formal or informal): high R^2 but few significant t ratios; high pairwise correlation among regressors (a necessary but not sufficient condition); low partial correlations combined with high R^2; and wrong signs of estimators. There are some tests to detect multicollinearity (e.g., the Farrar–Glauber set of tests).

In both cases of multicollinearity, estimators are still BLUE. Nevertheless, concerning perfect multicollinearity, coefficients or estimates are impossible to obtain. Regarding imperfect multicollinearity, in practice, there is a loss of precision (variances are larger and confidence intervals are wider). Recall, multicollinearity is a sample problem.

As for the detection of multicollinearity, there is no unique method to solve the problem. Some methods include:

i) Enlarging the data set or obtaining another sample (this is, if feasible, the ideal solution, as multicollinearity is a sample problem);
ii) Using extraneous or prior information (issue: interpretation of results);
iii) Combining cross section and time series data (issue: interpretation of results);
iv) Omitting a highly collinear variable (issue: specification bias);
v) Transforming data, e.g., first difference (issue: autocorrelation);
vi) Using ridge regression (issue: difficulty of interpretation of estimates);
vii) Using principal components (issue: interpretation of estimates).

Answer 2.2

Limitations

i) The DW statistic tests only for first-order autocorrelation [*AR(1)* process].
ii) The test is inconclusive if the computed value lies between d_L (lower limit) and d_U (upper limit) or between $4 - d_U$ and $4 - d_L$.
iii) The test cannot be applied in models with lagged dependent variables.
iv) A significant DW statistic does not necessarily mean that there is autocorrelation. It can be indicative of omitted variables, functional misspecification or misspecified dynamics.
v) It can be an indication of autocorrelation other than *AR(1)*.

Alternatives

i) One can use the Breusch–Godfrey LM test instead (see Answer 2.3 for details about the test). Indeed, the latter tests for any type of autocorrelation [e.g., *AR(p), MA(q), ARMA(p q)*].
ii) One can use the Breusch–Godfrey LM test.
iii) One can use the Durbin's h test.
iv) To check whether there is an omitted variable, one can combine the DW test with the Ramsey's RESET test for omitted variables. To discriminate between autocorrelation and dynamic misspecification one can first test the restrictions in a dynamic model using a Wald test before commenting on autocorrelation.
v) One can use the Breusch–Godfrey LM test instead.

Answer 2.3

a) Ramsey's RESET test for omitted variables. As the name indicates, this is a test for omitted variables. Consider the following regression:

$$Y_i = \alpha + \beta X_i + u_i \tag{A2.3.1}$$

To construct the Ramsey's RESET test, first, estimate Equation (A2.3.1) and obtain powers of $\hat{Y}$: e.g., $\hat{Y}^2, \hat{Y}^3$. Second, regress

$$Y_i = \gamma_1 + \gamma_2 X_i + \delta_1 \hat{Y}_i^2 + \delta_2 \hat{Y}_i^3 + u_i \tag{A2.3.2}$$

Note that more powers of $\hat{Y}_i$ may be added to Equation (A2.3.2). In any case, third, construct an F test statistic:

$$F = \frac{\left(R^2\text{new} - R^2\text{old}\right) / \text{number of new regressors}}{\left(1 - R^2\text{new}\right) / \left(n - \text{number of parameters}\right)}$$

where "R^2 new" is R^2 derived from Equation (A2.3.2) and "R^2 old" is R^2 derived from Equation (A2.3.1), to test the null of the lack of omitted variables, $H_0 : \delta_1 = \delta_2 = 0$. The hypothesis is rejected if $F > F_{table}$; otherwise, it is not rejected.

b) Breusch–Godfrey LM test for autocorrelation. This is a more general test of autocorrelation than the DW test, as it can test for any type of autocorrelation. It proceeds as follows. Estimate Equation (A2.3.1) by OLS to get $\hat{u}_i$. Then using the latter run the following regression:

$$\hat{u}_i = \delta_1 + \delta_2 X_i + \sum_{j=1}^{p} \hat{u}_{i-j}\rho_j + \eta_i \tag{A2.3.3}$$

and test whether $\rho_1 = \rho_2 = \ldots \rho_p = 0$ using the following LM test statistic: $(n-p)R^2 \sim \chi^2_p$. H_0 is rejected if $LM = (n-p)R^2 > \chi^2_p$. Note that as the LM test statistic is not really distributed as a chi-square in small samples, for the latter use the F version.

c) Bera–McAleer test. (Answer adapted from Maddala, 1992, 222.) This is a specification test. It involves choosing between the log-linear and the linear forms, e.g.,

$$H_0 : \ln Z_t = \beta_0 + \beta_1 X_t + e_{0t} \qquad e_{0t} \sim IN\left(0, \sigma_0^2\right) \tag{A2.3.4}$$

$$H_1 : \; Z_t = \beta_0 + \beta_1 X_t + e_{1t} \qquad e_{1t} \sim IN\left(0, \sigma_1^2\right) \tag{A2.3.5}$$

Obtain the following predicted value from H_0 and H_1 and run the following.

$$\exp\left(\ln \hat{Z}_t\right) = \beta_0 + \beta_1 X_t + u_{1t} \tag{A2.3.6}$$

$$\ln \tilde{Z}_t = \beta_0 + \beta_1 X_t + u_{0t} \tag{A2.3.7}$$

Using the residuals from Equations (A2.3.6) and (A2.3.7), run the following artificial regressions:

$$\log Z_t = \beta_0 + \beta_1 X_t + \theta_0 \hat{u}_{1t} + \varepsilon_{0t} \tag{A2.3.8}$$

and

$$Z_t = \beta_0 + \beta_1 X_t + \theta_1 \hat{u}_{0t} + \varepsilon_{1t} \tag{A2.3.9}$$

The tests for H_0 and H_1 are based on θ_0 and θ_1 in the artificial regressions. Indeed, using the usual t test, if $\theta_0 = 0$, choose the log-linear model. If $\theta_1 = 0$, choose the linear model. It might be the case that both hypotheses are not rejected or rejected at the same time.

Answer 2.4

a) Answers are based largely on Koop (2000, 59–61).

i) Accuracy of estimation is affected by the sample size. A regression with a smaller number of data points is less reliable than a regression with larger data points. Note that the degrees of freedom should also matter here. Indeed, for example, when the number of observations is equal to the number of parameters, the fit is perfect. However, this is an "invalid" regression.

ii) Quality of information content. The information content matters in terms of accuracy of estimation. Indeed, a large data set with little information content is poor compared to a small data set with much information.

iii) Accuracy of estimation is improved by having smaller errors. Indeed, in the presence of smaller errors, the fit of the regression is improved since the RSS (or the variance of errors) is small; that is, the accuracy of the estimation is improved.

iv) Accuracy of estimation is improved by the presence of a larger variability of values of explanatory variable(s). Larger variance of explanatory variables (X) improves accuracy of estimation. This is the essence of regression. A regression with no important variation in explanatory variables is not really a regression.

b) There are no clear-cut causes for the existence of wrong signs (or wrong sizes) of the parameter estimates. Among others, there are:

i) Multicollinearity. In quite a number of situations a wrong sign is an indicator of the presence of serious but imperfect multicollinearity.

ii) Incorrect interpretations. A wrong sign (or wrong size) may simply be the result of treating an implicit form of the model as the explicit form of the model. Similarly to Rao and Miller (1971, 44–45), we illustrate this point by explaining the following income determination for Barbados from 1977–2001. Consider the following regression results:

$$\hat{Y}_t = \underset{(52.957)}{102.754} + \underset{(0.1953)}{0.8485} I_t + \underset{(0.042)}{0.886} Y_{t-1} \tag{A2.4.1}$$
$$\bar{R}^2 = 0.96$$

where Y_t = income captured by gross domestic product; I_t stands for investment and numbers in parentheses are standard errors. The reading of the investment multiplier from Equation (A2.4.1) reveals that the size of the multiplier is too small if the coefficient of I_t is taken as a long-run multiplier. Dropping Y_{t-1} leads to:

$$\hat{Y}_t = \underset{(406.838)}{155.617} + \underset{(0.536)}{5.388} I_t \qquad \text{(A2.4.2)}$$

$$\bar{R}^2 = 0.82$$

As can be seen the coefficient of investment has increased drastically. It seems to conform with the size of a long-run investment multiplier. This is not, however, a correct interpretation. Indeed, there are two problems here. First, if Y_{t-1} belongs to the true specification, Equation (A2.4.2) creates an omitted variable bias. Second, in Equation (A2.4.1) the coefficient of I_t is not a long-run multiplier but rather an impact multiplier. In fact, from Equation (A2.4.1), the long-run multiplier is

$$\frac{0.8485}{1-0.886} = 7.4.$$

The latter really conforms to the notion of long-run multiplier.

iii) Variables not appropriately defined. There are situations where a wrong sign of a coefficient is simply due to a variable that is not appropriately defined. Consider the following real demand for money equation:

$$Log(m_t) = \beta_0 + \beta_1 Log(Y_t / P_t) + \beta_2 Log(P_t / P_{t-1}) + \beta_3 r_t + u_t \qquad \text{(A2.4.3)}$$

where Log stands for logarithm; Y_t is nominal income; P_t is price level; m_t is real demand for money, defined as the ratio of nominal demand for money and price level; r_t is nominal interest rate; t is a time index and u_t is the error term.

Equation (A2.4.3) states that real demand for money depends on real income, inflation and interest rate. The equation can be rewritten as follows:

$$Log(m_t) = \beta_0 + \beta_1 Log(Y_t / P_t) + \beta_2 Log(P_t) - \beta_2 Log(P_{t-1}) + \beta_3 r_t + u_t \qquad \text{(A2.4.4)}$$

We know that real demand for money depends on real income and not nominal income. Suppose instead of using real income in the above we use nominal income, that is, Equation (A2.4.4) becomes:

$$Log(m_t) = \alpha_0 + \alpha_1 Log(Y_t) + \alpha_2 Log(P_t) - \alpha_2 Log(P_{t-1}) + \alpha_3 r_t + u_t \qquad \text{(A2.4.5)}$$

With respect to the correct specification the coefficient of Log(P_t) is not α_2 but rather $\beta_2 - \beta_1$ as in Equation (A2.4.6) derived from Equation (A2.4.4):

$$Log(m_t) = \beta_0 + \beta_1 Log(Y_t) + (\beta_2 - \beta_1) Log(P_t) - \beta_2 Log(P_{t-1}) + \beta_3 r_t + u_t \quad \text{(A2.4.6)}$$

c) The J test can be applied since the two models are non-nested (the explanatory variables in one model are not a subset of the explanatory variables in the other; at the limit, there is not a single common explanatory variable) and the J test is one of the appropriate tests to deal with such a situation.
The models of interest are:

$$H_0 : Y = X\beta + u \quad \text{(A2.4.7)}$$

$$H_1 : Y = Z\gamma + e \quad \text{(A2.4.8)}$$

A test of H_0 against H_1 is conducted as follows. Estimate Equation (A2.4.8) by OLS to obtain $\hat{\gamma}$ and $\hat{Y}_1$ (fit of Y). Then estimate the following regression:

$$Y = X\beta + a\hat{Y}_1 + \nu \quad \text{(A2.4.9)}$$

and test the null hypothesis $a = 0$. If the hypothesis is rejected, H_0 is not rejected by H_1; otherwise, it is rejected.
A test of H_1 against H_0 is conducted as follows. From Equation (A2.4.7) obtain $\hat{Y}_0 = X\hat{\beta}$ and run

$$Y = Z\gamma + b\hat{Y}_0 + \varepsilon \quad \text{(A2.4.10)}$$

If the hypothesis $b = 0$ is rejected, the H_1 model is not rejected by the H_0 model; otherwise, it is rejected.
The problem is that conflict may arise, as both models can be rejected or not rejected at the same time.

Answer 2.5

a) The White's test is an LM test for heteroscedasticity suggested by White. Note, however, that the White's test becomes a test of misspecification if the model is not correctly specified. There are two versions. The first version consists of the following steps. In the first instance, the basic regression, for example,

$$Y_t = \beta_0 + \beta_1 X_{1t} + \beta_2 X_{2t} + \beta_3 X_{3t} + u_t \quad \text{(A2.5.1)}$$

is run and the residuals $\hat{u}_t$ are retrieved. In the second step, a regression of the squared residuals on the original regressors, including the constant term, squares of regressors and cross products, is run:

$$\hat{u}_t^2 = \gamma_0 + \gamma_1 X_{1t} + \gamma_2 X_{2t} + \gamma_3 X_{3t} + \delta_1 X_{1t}^2 + \delta_2 X_{2t}^2 + \delta_3 X_{3t}^2 + \delta_4 X_{1t} X_{2t} + \delta_5 X_{2t} X_{3t} + \delta_6 X_{1t} X_{3t} + e_t \quad \text{(A2.5.2)}$$

In the third step, R^2 from this auxiliary regression is retrieved to help build an LM statistic:

$$LM = nR^2 \sim \chi^2_{df}$$

with n as the number of regressors and df the number of degrees of freedom (number of regressors except the constant term in the auxiliary regression). The LM tests the null hypothesis that the coefficients of all the regressors (except the constant term) are zero. If χ^2_{df} is less than the critical value, one does not reject the hypothesis of homoscedasticity; otherwise one rejects homoscedasticity in favour of heteroscedasticity. The second version of the White's test ignores the cross products in the auxiliary regression. Otherwise, other details are the same. As usual it is worth recalling that the LM test is a large sample test. In small samples its corresponding F version should be used.

b) The Jarque–Bera test is a test for normality of residuals. As such, it is an important test, as normality is required for the validity of many tests used in econometrics. The test is based on skewness and kurtosis and is given by:

$$JB = n\left[(m_3 / S^3)^2 + ((m_4 - 3) / S^4)^2\right] \sim \chi^2_2$$

where m_3 and m_4 are the third and fourth moment about the means of residuals, respectively, S is the standard error and n is the size of the sample. The null hypothesis (the disturbances are normally distributed) is rejected if

$$\chi^2_{calc} > \chi^2_{table}$$

Note that this is an asymptotic test. That is, it most likely does not have a good approximation for small samples.

Answer 2.6

Recall $Y = X\beta + u$ with $E(uu') = \sigma^2\Omega$.

a) Transform $Y = X\beta + u$ into $TY = TX\beta + Tu$ where the T matrix has the property: $T'T = \Omega^{-1}$. Indeed, such a T exists, as Ω is symmetric and positive definite.

GLS consists in minimizing $\hat{u}'T'T\hat{u}$; that is, minimize

$$\left(TY - TX\breve{\beta}\right)'\left(TY - TX\breve{\beta}\right)$$

$$\left(TY - TX\breve{\beta}\right)'\left(TY - TX\breve{\beta}\right) = Y'T'TY - \breve{\beta}'X'T'TY - Y'T'TX\breve{\beta} + \breve{\beta}'X'T'TX\breve{\beta}$$

First-order condition:

$$\frac{\partial \hat{u}'T'T\hat{u}}{\partial \breve{\beta}} = -2X'T'TY + 2'X'T'TX\breve{\beta} = 0$$

$$\breve{\beta} = \left(X'T'TX\right)^{-1} X'T'TY = \left(X'\Omega^{-1}X\right)^{-1} X'\Omega^{-1}Y$$

b) $E\left(\breve{\beta}\right) = \beta?$

$$\breve{\beta} = \left(X'\Omega^{-1}X\right)^{-1} X'\Omega^{-1}Y$$

$$\breve{\beta} = \left(X'\Omega^{-1}X\right)^{-1} X'\Omega^{-1}\left(X\beta + u\right) \qquad \text{using } Y = X\beta + u,$$

$$\breve{\beta} = \left(X'\Omega^{-1}X\right)^{-1} X'\Omega^{-1}X\beta + \left(X'\Omega^{-1}X\right)^{-1} X'\Omega^{-1}u$$

$$\breve{\beta} = \beta + \left(X'\Omega^{-1}X\right)^{-1} X'\Omega^{-1}u \qquad \text{since } \left(X'\Omega^{-1}X\right)^{-1} X'\Omega^{-1}X = I_{kxk}$$

$$E(\breve{\beta}) = \beta + \left(X'\Omega^{-1}X\right)^{-1} X'\Omega^{-1}\, E\left(u\right) \qquad \text{assuming that } X \text{ is fixed}$$

$$E\left(\breve{\beta}\right) = \beta \qquad \text{assuming that } E(u) = 0.$$

Answer 2.7

a) We have the problem of exact multicollinearity. This can be seen if Z_t is replaced by its value in Equation (A2.7.1):

$$Y_t = \beta_1 + \beta_2 X_t + \beta_3 b X_t + \varepsilon_t \qquad \text{(A2.7.1)}$$

As a consequence, it is not possible to get all estimates. However, with some transformations (linear combinations or others), there is the possibility of obtaining some estimates.

b) Among the solutions, there are:

i) Dropping Z_t. This gives rise to the following regression:

$$Y_t = \beta_1 + \beta_2 X_t + \varepsilon_t$$

If Z_t belongs to the true specification then an omitted variable bias has been created.

ii) Using first differences. This leads to the following equation:

$$Y_t - Y_{t-1} = \beta_2 \left(X_t - X_{t-1} \right) + \beta_3 \left(Z_t - Z_{t-1} \right) + \varepsilon_t - \varepsilon_{t-1} \qquad \text{(A2.7.2)}$$

If Equation (A2.7.2) were applied in the context of imperfect multicollinearity, the extent of multicollinearity could have been decreased. However, in the case of perfect (exact) multicollinearity, Equation (A2.7.2) does not solve the problem of exact multicollinearity at all. Indeed, the equation can be rewritten as:

$$Y_t - Y_{t-1} = \beta_2 \left(X_t - X_{t-1} \right) + \beta_3 \left(b\, X_t - b X_{t-1} \right) + \varepsilon_t - \varepsilon_{t-1} \qquad \text{(A2.7.3)}$$

or

$$Y_t - Y_{t-1} = \beta_2 \left(X_t - X_{t-1} \right) + \beta_3 b \left(X_t - X_{t-1} \right) + \varepsilon_t - \varepsilon_{t-1} \qquad \text{(A2.7.4)}$$

As can be seen, Equation (A2.7.4) expresses exact multicollinearity. As a consequence, the estimates of the parameters cannot be obtained from Equation (A2.7.3). Moreover, the errors are now autocorrelated.

iii) Using ratios. This gives rise to the following equation:

$$\frac{Y_t}{Z_t} = \beta_1 \frac{1}{Z_t} + \beta_2 \frac{X_t}{Z_t} + \beta_3 + \frac{\varepsilon_t}{Z_t} \qquad \text{(A2.7.5)}$$

As opposed to the case of imperfect multicollinearity, Equation (A2.7.5) in the case of perfect multicollinearity does not solve the problem at all. Indeed, expanding Equation (A2.7.5) leads to:

$$\frac{Y_t}{Z_t} = \beta_1 \frac{1}{Z_t} + \beta_2 \frac{X_t}{bX_t} + \beta_3 + \frac{\varepsilon_t}{Z_t} \qquad \text{(A2.7.6)}$$

or

$$\frac{Y_t}{Z_t} = \beta_1 \frac{1}{Z_t} + \beta_2 \frac{1}{b} + \beta_3 + \frac{\varepsilon_t}{Z_t} \qquad \text{(A2.7.7)}$$

In Equation (A2.7.7) the vector $1/b$ and the vector of ones are collinear. Thus, one cannot obtain the estimates of the parameters. Moreover, the new errors are now heteroscedastic (if one assumes the old errors are well behaved). Note that if Equation (A2.7.7) is written as:

$$\frac{Y_t}{Z_t}=\beta_1\frac{1}{Z_t}+\beta_4+\frac{\varepsilon_t}{Z_t} \tag{A2.7.8}$$

where $\beta_4 = b^{-1}\beta_2 + \beta_3$, then Equation (A2.7.8) leads to a problem of identification. That is, one cannot obtain the estimates of all the parameters of the model.

iv) Exploiting extraneous information. In this scenario, we rewrite the basic equation as follows:

$$Y_t-\hat{\beta}_3 Z_t=\beta_1+\beta_2 X_t+\varepsilon_t$$

where optimal $\hat{\beta}_3$ has been obtained outside the model (e.g., from a cross section study). The properties of the estimators will be dependent on the quality of the extraneous information.

v) Increasing the sample size. This is potentially an adequate solution since by increasing the sample size there is a possibility that the exact multicollinearity may disappear or become less severe.

vi) Using ridge regression estimation and/or principal components. Ridge regression estimation consists in adding a constant to the matrix of moments of the explanatory variables before obtaining the estimates. By so doing the variances are reduced but at the same time bias is created. Because the interpretation of results is not often clear-cut, we do not recommend it. The principal components in the present situation will also lead to the problem of interpretability of results. Summing up, perhaps the best solution is to enlarge the sample.

Answer 2.8

a) No; since

$$v_t=\beta_2 Z_t^2+u_t \tag{A2.8.1}$$

v_t will be autocorrelated.

b) We know that, from Equation (Q2.8.2):

$$\hat{\alpha}_1=\frac{\sum\left(Y_t-\bar{Y}\right)\left(Z_t-\bar{Z}\right)}{\sum\left(Z_t-\bar{Z}\right)^2}=\frac{\sum Y_t\left(Z_t-\bar{Z}\right)}{\sum\left(Z_t-\bar{Z}\right)^2}$$

Replace Y_t by its value in Equation (Q2.8.1) in the above expression:

$$\hat{\alpha}_1 = \frac{\sum(\beta_0 + \beta_1 Z_t + \beta_2 Z_t^2 + u_t)(Z_t - \bar{Z})}{\sum(Z_t - \bar{Z})^2}$$

$$= \beta_0 \frac{\sum(Z_t - \bar{Z})}{\sum(Z_t - \bar{Z})^2} + \beta_1 \frac{\sum(Z_t - \bar{Z})^2}{\sum(Z_t - \bar{Z})^2}$$

$$+ \beta_2 \frac{\sum(Z_t^2 - \overline{Z^2})(Z_t - \bar{Z})}{\sum(Z_t - \bar{Z})^2} + \frac{\sum u_t(Z_t - \bar{Z})}{\sum(Z_t - \bar{Z})^2}$$

since

$$\sum Z_t(Z_t - \bar{Z}) = \sum(Z_t - \bar{Z})^2,$$

$$\sum Z_t^2(Z_t - \bar{Z}) = \sum(Z_t^2 - \overline{Z^2})(Z_t - \bar{Z})$$

Using the fact that:

$$\sum(Z_t - \bar{Z}) = 0$$

The above estimator can be written as:

$$\hat{\alpha}_1 = \beta_1 + \beta_2 \frac{\sum(Z_t^2 - \overline{Z^2})(Z_t - \bar{Z})}{\sum(Z_t - \bar{Z})^2} + \frac{\sum u_t(Z_t - \bar{Z})}{\sum(Z_t - \bar{Z})^2}$$

The second term on the right-hand side is $\beta_2 b$ where b is the coefficient of the regression of

$$Z_t^2 = c + b\ Z_t + v_t$$

Thus,

$$E(\hat{\alpha}_1) = \beta_1 + \beta_2 b$$

since

$$E\left(\frac{\sum u_t(Z_t - \bar{Z})}{\sum(Z_t - \bar{Z})^2}\right) = 0$$

That is, $\hat{\alpha}_1$ is a biased estimator of β_1 unless $b = 0$ and/or $\beta_2 = 0$.

The second sample property is minimum variance. The variance of $\hat{\alpha}_1$ is compared to that of $\hat{\beta}_1$ in order to see whether it is smaller. Using the definition of variance and the value of $\hat{\alpha}_1$ such as above, we can write:

$$\begin{aligned} Var(\hat{\alpha}_1) &= E(\hat{\alpha}_1 - E(\hat{\alpha}_1))^2 \\ &= E\left[\frac{\sum u_t(Z_t - \bar{Z})}{\sum (Z_t - \bar{Z})^2}\right]^2 \\ &= \frac{\sum (Z_t - \bar{Z})^2}{\left[\sum (Z_t - \bar{Z})^2\right]^2}\sigma^2 \\ &= \frac{\sigma^2}{\sum (Z_t - \bar{Z})^2} \end{aligned}$$

To derive these results, we assumed Z_t is fixed. Similarly we can derive the variance of $\hat{\beta}_1$ (this is left as an exercise). It is

$$Var\left(\hat{\beta}_1\right) = \frac{\sigma^2}{\sum \left(Z_t - \bar{Z}\right)^2\left(1 - r^2_{Z^2Z}\right)}$$

where $r^2_{Z^2Z}$ is the square of the coefficient of correlation between Z_t^2 and Z_t.

As implication:

$$Var\left(\hat{\alpha}_1\right) \leq Var\left(\hat{\beta}_1\right)$$

since $0 \leq r^2_{z^2z} \leq 1$. That is, $\hat{\alpha}_1$ is minimum variance. However, since it is biased, it is not efficient.

c) We have to evaluate $\text{plim}\left(\hat{\alpha}_1\right)$ to answer the question of consistency. Using the above expression of $\hat{\alpha}_1$, we write:

$$\text{plim}\ \hat{\alpha}_1 = \text{plim}\ \beta_1 + \underset{n\to\infty}{\text{plim}}\,\beta_2 \frac{\sum\left(Z_t^2 - \overline{Z^2}\right)\left(Z_t - \bar{Z}\right)/n}{\sum\left(Z_t - \bar{Z}\right)^2/n} + \underset{n\to\infty}{\text{plim}} \frac{\sum u_t\left(Z_t - \bar{Z}\right)/n}{\sum\left(Z_t - \bar{Z}\right)^2/n}$$

$$\text{plim}\,\hat{\alpha}_1 = \beta_1 + \beta_2 \frac{\underset{n\to\infty}{\text{plim}} \sum\left(Z_t^2 - \overline{Z^2}\right)\left(Z_t - \bar{Z}\right)/n}{\underset{n\to\infty}{\text{plim}} \sum\left(Z_t - \bar{Z}\right)^2/n} + \frac{\underset{n\to\infty}{\text{plim}} \sum u_t\left(Z_t - \bar{Z}\right)/n}{\underset{n\to\infty}{\text{plim}} \sum\left(Z_t - \bar{Z}\right)^2/n}$$

We know that as n goes to infinity,

$$\underset{n\to\infty}{\text{plim}} \sum\left(Z_t^2 - \overline{Z^2}\right)\left(Z_t - \bar{Z}\right)\Big/ n = Cov(Z_t^2\ Z_t)$$

and

$$\underset{n\to\infty}{\text{plim}} \sum\left(Z_t - \bar{Z}\right)^2 \Big/ n = Var(Z_t)$$

thus

$$\text{plim}\ \hat{\alpha}_1 = \beta_1 + \beta_2 \frac{\text{cov}\left(Z_t^2 Z_t\right)}{\text{var}\left(Z_t\right)}$$

$\hat{\alpha}_1$ is not a consistent estimator of β_1 unless $\beta_2 = 0$ or $\text{cov}\left(Z_t^2 Z_t\right) = 0$.

Answer 2.9

The researcher's methodology is flawed and his results are dubious. Indeed, the coefficient of experience level from the regression of residuals on the experience level is inconsistent unless the parameter associated with the experience level is zero. In addition, as pointed out by Maddala (1992, 477), there are two problems. First, the standard errors are incorrect. Second, the distribution of the coefficient estimate is complex. The correct procedure is to regress the residuals on both the education and the experience level, and test whether the coefficient of the experience level is zero.

Answer 2.10

a) We disagree with the statement. Indeed, unless $\mathbf{Q_t}$ is a constant vector, $\mathbf{Q_t}$ and Q_t^2 are not linearly related. Recall, multicollinearity is concerned with *linear* relationships between or among variables.
b) The DW statistic will indicate the presence of autocorrelation. Although, the DW statistic is designed to test for AR(1) errors, in this particular case, it is testing for misspecification.

Answer 2.11

Model choice is related to model selection. The latter is concerned with choosing the model that best fits a given set of data. As Maddala (1992, 490–491) points out, the area of model selection consists of:

- Choosing between or among some models specified before any analysis;
- Simplifying complex models using the data (data-based simplification);
- Constructing a post-data model.

In this exercise we are concerned with the first and last points. Theil's $\bar{R}^2$ rule, which states that the best model is the one that maximizes $\bar{R}^2$ (or minimizes $\hat{\sigma}^2$), is one of the criteria for model choice. Another criterion is the sum of squares of studentized residuals (SSSR). This criterion stipulates that the best model is the one with the smallest SSSR. The two criteria are valid since their expected value is less for the true model than for the alternative models. To rephrase it, Theil's $\bar{R}^2$ is particularly interesting because it performs relatively well in terms of selecting regressors or choosing the correct model (although the presence of irrelevant variables decreases its ability to do so), as well as in terms of cross-validation.

Care should, however, be exercised, as in the case at hand the dependent variables are not the same. In that connection, there are two sets of comparable equations or models. One set consists of models (Q2.11.1), (Q2.11.2) and (Q2.11.3) and the other comprises (Q2.11.4) and (Q2.11.5). Thus, models (Q2.11.1), (Q2.11.2) and (Q2.11.3) are gauged together and the one with the highest $\bar{R}^2$ is selected as the best in its set. Similarly, we do the same with the second set. Finally, the two best models are put together for comparison. Since the dependent variables are not the same, one can use the Bera–McAleer test (developed in Answer 2.3.c) to discriminate between them. Alternatively, the best model with Y_t as dependent variable is transformed by multiplying Y_t by the inverse of its geometric mean. In other words, a new RSS is obtained by multiplying the old one with the inverse of the geometric mean of the dependent variable, Y_t. The new RSS is compared with the RSS from the model with logarithm Y as dependent variable. The best model is the one with the smaller RSS (higher $\bar{R}^2$ here). In fact, the latter method can be used at the outset for all models; that is, the ones with Y_t as dependent are transformed by generating new residuals which are the old ones times the inverse of the geometric mean of the dependent variables. All the residuals are compared. The one with the smallest RSS is chosen as the best model.

Note that the choice of the best model does not stop there. Other factors must be taken into account, such as sign (and size) of the coefficients.

Answer 2.12

a) Yes, we do agree with the statement. Precisely, the main difficulty is that OLS residuals will be heteroscedastic and autocorrelated even when the true errors are not. To understand that, let us derive the relationship between residuals and errors (disturbances). We know that:

$$\begin{aligned}\hat{U} &= Y - \hat{Y} = Y - X\hat{\beta} \\ &= Y - X\left(X'X\right)^{-1}X'Y \\ &= \left[I - X(X'X)^{-1}X'\right]Y \\ &= \left[\mathrm{I} - X(X'X)^{-1}X'\right](X\beta + U) \\ &= MU\end{aligned}$$

where $M = [I - X(X'X)^{-1}X']$ is a symmetric idempotent matrix. Multiplying $\hat{U}$ by $\hat{U}'$ and taking the expected value yields:

$$E(\hat{U}\hat{U}') = E(MUU'M) = E(UMU') = \sigma^2 M$$

Even if we assume that $E(UU') = \sigma^2 I$, most likely $M \neq I$ in the above; thus, in general, $\hat{U}$ will display varying variances and non-zero covariances.

b) In that case, one tests for heteroscedasticity and autocorrelation using tests based on recursive residuals, among others.

Answer 2.13

a) The three possible reasons are the following: errors in variables, autoregression (presence of lagged dependent variable) and endogeneity.

   i) Errors in explanatory variables. The errors can be in the dependent variables as well as in the explanatory variables. While the effects of errors in the dependent variables are benign, those in the explanatory variables are serious.

   ii) Autoregression or the presence of lagged dependent variables. The presence of lagged dependent variables among the explanatory variables is generally another source of the dependence between disturbances and explanatory variables.

   iii) Endogeneity. The case of the endogeneity in the explanatory variables often occurs in the context of simultaneous equations models. Recall an endogenous variable is a variable determined within the system.

b) Consequences

   i) Errors in explanatory variables. Consider the following model:

$$Y_t = \alpha + \beta X_t^{\bullet} + u_t \quad \text{(A2.13.1)}$$

where $X_t^{\bullet}$ is measured with errors (e_t is well-behaved).

$$X_t^{\bullet} = X_t + e_t \quad \text{(A2.13.2)}$$

That is,

$$Y_t = \alpha + \beta X_t + \beta e_t + u_t$$

or

$$Y_t = \alpha + \beta X_t + v_t \quad \text{(A2.13.3)}$$

As can be seen,

$$E(X_t v_t) \neq 0$$

Now,

$$\hat{\beta} = \frac{\sum (X_t - \bar{X})(Y_t - \bar{Y})}{\sum (X_t - \bar{X})^2} = \frac{\sum (X_t - \bar{X})Y_t}{\sum (X_t - \bar{X})^2}$$
$$= \frac{\sum x_t Y_t}{\sum x_t^2} \tag{A2.13.4}$$

where $x_t = X_t - \bar{X}$.

Replacing Y_t by its value in Equation (A2.13.4) gives:

$$\hat{\beta} = \frac{\sum x_t(\alpha + \beta X_t + v_t)}{\sum x_t^2}$$
$$= \beta + \frac{\sum x_t v_t}{\sum x_t^2}$$

The expected value of the estimator is

$$E(\hat{\beta}) = \beta + E\left[\frac{\sum x_t v_t}{\sum x_t^2}\right] \tag{A2.13.5}$$

The quantity in the numerator and that in the denominator are dependent. We know that with two random variables, for example, Y and Z, $E[Y/Z] \neq E(Y)/E(Z)$ in general. The expected value in brackets can only be computed by simulations. Monte Carlo simulations done by a number of authors indicate that the ratio is different from zero, that is, $\hat{\beta}$ is a biased estimator of β.

Let us analyse the consistency of $\hat{\beta}$. Using the above $\hat{\beta}$, we evaluate its probability limit:

$$\text{plim } \hat{\beta} = \text{plim } \beta + \frac{\underset{n\to\infty}{\text{plim}}(\sum x_t v_t)/n}{\underset{n\to\infty}{\text{plim}} \sum x_t^2/n}$$

Since

$$\underset{n\to\infty}{\text{plim}}(\sum x_t\, v_t)/n = Cov(X_t\, v_t) \neq 0$$

and

$$\underset{n\to\infty}{\text{plim}}(\sum x_t^2 / n) = \text{var}(X_t)$$

then

$$\text{plim } \hat{\beta} = \beta + \frac{Cov(X_t\ v_t)}{Var(X_t)} \tag{A2.13.6}$$

$\hat{\beta}$ is clearly inconsistent. Thus, the consequences are that $\hat{\beta}$ is biased and inconsistent.

ii) Autoregression. Consider the following model:

$$Y_t = \alpha + \beta Y_{t-1} + u_t \tag{A2.13.7}$$

Suppose also that $u_t \sim$ AR(1); that is,

$$u_t = \rho\, u_{t-1} + e_t \tag{A2.13.8}$$

with $|\rho| < 1$ and $e_t \sim N\left(0, \sigma^2\right)$. From the above, the OLS estimator of β is (see also Koutsoyiannis, 1977, 307–308):

$$\begin{aligned}\hat{\beta} &= \frac{\sum y_t y_{t-1}}{\sum y_{t-1}^2} = \frac{\sum Y_t y_{t-1}}{\sum y_{t-1}^2} = \frac{\sum(\alpha + \beta Y_{t-1} + u_t)\, y_{t-1}}{\sum y_{t-1}^2} \\ &= \beta + \frac{\sum u_t\, y_{t-1}}{\sum y_{t-1}^2} \\ &= \beta + \frac{\sum(\rho\, u_{t-1} + e_t)\, y_{t-1}}{\sum y_{t-1}^2} \\ &= \beta + \frac{\rho \sum u_{t-1}\, y_{t-1}}{\sum y_{t-1}^2} + \frac{\sum e_t\, y_{t-1}}{\sum y_{t-1}^2}\end{aligned} \tag{A2.13.9}$$

where lower case variables are deviations from the means. Thus,

$$
\begin{aligned}
E(\hat{\beta}) &= \beta + E\left[\frac{\rho\sum u_{t-1}\, y_{t-1}}{\sum y_{t-1}^2}\right] + E\left[\frac{\sum e_t\, y_{t-1}}{\sum y_{t-1}^2}\right] \\
&= \beta + E\left[\frac{\rho\sum u_{t-1}\, y_{t-1}}{\sum y_{t-1}^2}\right]
\end{aligned}
\tag{A2.13.10}
$$

We cannot evaluate analytically the expected value of the second term on the right-hand side since numerator and denominator are dependent (see above under measurement error). Monte Carlo simulations done by other authors indicate that the estimator is biased.

Let us check the consistency of the estimator. To proceed, let us examine further one of the components of Equation (A2.13.9):

$$
\frac{\sum u_{t-1}\, y_{t-1}}{\sum y_{t-1}^2} = \frac{\sum (y_{t-1} - \beta y_{t-2})\, y_{t-1}}{\sum y_{t-1}^2} = 1 - \beta\frac{\sum y_{t-2} y_{t-1}}{\sum y_{t-1}^2}
\tag{A2.13.11}
$$

using the fact that (in deviation with respect to the means), $u_{t-1} = y_{t-1} - \beta y_{t-2}$. Combining Equations (A2.13.9) and (A2.13.11) leads to:

$$
\begin{aligned}
\operatorname*{plim}\hat{\beta} &= \beta + \operatorname*{plim}_{n\to\infty}\frac{\rho\sum u_{t-1}\, y_{t-1}/n}{\sum y_{t-1}^2/n} + \operatorname*{plim}_{n\to\infty}\frac{\sum e_t\, y_{t-1}/n}{\sum y_{t-1}^2/n} \\
&= \beta + \rho - \rho\beta \operatorname*{plim}_{n\to\infty}\frac{\sum y_{t-2}\, y_{t-1}/n}{\sum y_{t-1}^2/n} + \operatorname*{plim}_{n\to\infty}\frac{\sum e_t\, y_{t-1}/n}{\sum y_{t-1}^2/n} \qquad \text{(A.13.12)} \\
&= \beta + \rho - \rho\beta \operatorname*{plim}_{n\to\infty}\hat{\beta}
\end{aligned}
$$

$$
\operatorname{plim}\hat{\beta} = \frac{\beta+\rho}{1+\beta\rho} = \beta + \frac{\rho(1-\beta^2)}{1+\beta\rho}
$$

Note that we use the following to derive Equation (A2.13.12):

$$
\frac{\sum y_{t-2}\, y_{t-1}}{\sum y_{t-1}^2} \approx \hat{\beta}
$$

in large samples, and

$$\operatorname*{plim}_{n\to\infty} \frac{\sum e_t\, y_{t-1}}{\sum y_{t-1}^2} = 0$$

since e_t is uncorrelated with y_{t-1}.

Thus, $\hat{\beta}$ is inconsistent with the asymptotic bias being $\rho(1 - \beta^2)/(1 + \beta\rho)$.

Conclusion: $\hat{\beta}$ is biased and inconsistent.

iii) Endogeneity. Consider the following regression:

$$Y_t = \alpha + \beta X_t + u_t \tag{A2.13.13}$$

If X_t is endogenous (or stochastic) then, in general, $E(X_t u_t) \neq 0$. Thus, similarly to the two previous cases, $\hat{\beta}$ is biased and inconsistent.

c) We know that:

$$\beta^{IV} = \frac{\sum(Z_t - \bar{Z})(Y_t - \bar{Y})}{\sum(Z_t - \bar{Z})(X_t - \bar{X})} = \frac{\sum(Z_t - \bar{Z})Y_t}{\sum(Z_t - \bar{Z})(X_t - \bar{X})} \tag{A2.13.14}$$

Replace Y_t by its value in Equation (A2.13.14):

$$\begin{aligned}\beta^{IV} &= \frac{\sum(Z_t - \bar{Z})(\alpha + \beta X_t + u_t)}{\sum(Z_t - \bar{Z})(X_t - \bar{X})} \\ &= \beta + \frac{\sum z_t\, u_t}{\sum z_t\, x_t}\end{aligned} \tag{A2.13.15}$$

where $z_t = Z_t - \bar{Z}$ and $x_t = X_t - \bar{X}$. Use Equation (A2.13.15) to evaluate plim $\hat{\beta}$:

$$\text{plim}\,\hat{\beta} = \text{plim}\,\beta + \frac{\operatorname*{plim}_{n\to\infty}(\sum z_t u_t)/n}{\operatorname*{plim}_{n\to\infty}(\sum z_t x_t)/n}$$

$$\text{plim}\,\hat{\beta} = \beta$$

since $\operatorname*{plim}_{n\to\infty} \sum z_t u_t / n = 0$ by assumption. Thus, the estimator is consistent.

Answer 2.14

a) Omitted or left-out variables are variables that were not used in a regression while theory suggests they belong to the true specification. This situation happens for at least two reasons. First, the researcher may be unaware of the relevant theory. Second, data may not be available. Moreover, a wrong search for a parsimonious model may also create this problem. As far as detection is concerned, the Ramsey's RESET type of test is appropriate. Alternatively, adding a trend to the omitted variable regression may help detect the existence of omitted variables (though not always). The consequences are as follows.

   - Coefficient estimates are biased and inconsistent if the omitted variables and included variables are correlated; if not, then only the estimate of the intercept is biased.
   - The variance of residuals is incorrectly estimated (biased upward).
   - Variances are biased upward.
   - The usual confidence interval and hypothesis testing procedures about the statistical significance of the parameter estimators are no longer valid. This results in invalidation of hypothesis testing and confidence intervals.

   If the omitted variable is available, then one should integrate it in the regression. If it is not available, then one should contemplate the use of trend, at least in the context of time series.

b) Irrelevant variables. As opposed to omitted variables, an irrelevant variable is a variable that does not belong to the model according to theory but is used in the regression. Theoretically the value of its coefficient in the regression must be zero. Care should be taken to detect irrelevant variables, because a non-significant coefficient does not necessarily mean that the corresponding variable is irrelevant as the lack of significance can be due to other reasons (e.g., multicollinearity and the presence of a dominant variable). Any test of significance can help detect redundant variables. The consequences are the following.

   - The estimators are unbiased and consistent.
   - The variance of the residual is estimated correctly.
   - The variances and covariances of estimators become larger because of the presence of irrelevant variables. Nevertheless, since the estimates of the variances of regression coefficients are unbiased the tests of hypothesis are still valid.

   Summing up, irrelevant variables bring about inefficiency of estimators, loss of degrees of freedom and (possible) multicollinearity. As a solution, if economic theory clearly establishes that a variable is irrelevant or redundant, then it must not enter the true specification.

c) Proxy variable. A proxy variable is a close substitute variable; that is, a variable that replaces another which theoretically belongs to a model but for which data are not available or cannot be measured. For example, rainfall is often a proxy for weather. The use of proxy variables biases the estimators. The bias is, however, less pronounced if the proxy variable is highly correlated with other included variables. The only test for detecting a proxy variable is the theory itself; that is, knowledge about true specification can help establish whether a variable is a proxy variable. Since a proxy variable introduces a bias in the estimate the question is whether one should get rid of the proxy. The answer depends on the extent of the bias. Practically, there is no harm if the bias is negligible. Note, however, that the proxy variable may also be capturing the effects of omitted variables. In that case, the bias may be substantial.

d) Dominant variable. A dominant variable is one that is part of the true specification but which explains almost all the variations in the dependent variable. In other words, it dominates all other included variables. This is often the case if the dependent variable is explained by the independent variable in fixed proportions. For example, raw material in some production functions is in some instances a dominant variable. Two major facts may signal the presence of a dominant variable: larger proportion of the variation in the dependent variable explained by the culprit variable and wrong signs (or/and wrong sizes) of the coefficients of other included variables. The presence of a dominant variable has "empirical consequences" rather than "theoretical consequences". The solution is generally to remove the dominant variable. This is a rare case where econometricians will have to learn to live with the bias.

Answer 2.15

a) Data-admissible. Predictions derived from the model that are not logically possible are excluded. For example, if the dependent variable is bound between 0 and 1, then a prediction of 2 is not admissible.
b) Theory-consistent. Economic theory must play a big role in modelling. The model must be in tune with economic theory. For example, if theory predicts that the long-run multiplier must be greater than one, than the results should conform to that prediction.
c) Predictive validity. The ex-post and ex-ante forecasts must be reasonable (parameter constancy).
d) Data coherency. Residuals must be white noise, otherwise the model has not exploited all patterns.
e) Encompassing. The model should be superior to its rivals.

(Adapted from Kennedy, 1992, 83.)

Answer 2.16

a) $R_2^2 \geq R_1^2$ where the subscript 2 means Equation (Q2.16.2) and subscript 1 stands for Equation (Q2.16.1). The inequality is justified to the extent that Equation (Q2.16.1) is a restricted form of Equation (Q2.16.2). As is well known, a restricted model has higher RSS than the unrestricted model. That is, the R^2 for the restricted model will be lower than that for the unrestricted model. Note that the two R^2 will be equal if the condition in (b) is fulfilled.
b) $\beta_1 = \alpha_1$ if $-\beta_1 = \alpha_2$. In this particular case the two regressions are equivalent, as in Equation (Q2.16.1) the coefficient of Y is the opposite of that of T_t and in Equation (Q2.16.2) the coefficient of Y_t is also the opposite of that of T_t.

c) Two models are nested if using some restrictions one can recover the set of explanatory variables of one model from the other model. The two models here are nested since Equation (Q2.16.2) can be written as Equation (Q2.16.1) if $-\beta_1 = \alpha_2$.

Answer 2.17

Let us write the model as:

$$l_t = \beta_0 + \beta_1 wr_t + \beta_2 gdp_t + \beta_3 nis_t + u_t$$

a) We examine individual coefficients and overall effects.

i) Individual coefficient tests.
Constant term: the null and alternative hypotheses are, respectively:

$$H_0 : \beta_0 = 0 \text{ and } H_1 : \beta_0 \neq 0$$

The distribution of interest is the t distribution with the following critical value:

$$t_{27\text{-}4,0.025} = 2.069$$

The calculated t is

$$t = \frac{\hat{\beta}_0 - \beta_0}{S_{\hat{\beta}_0}} = -\frac{-0.304}{\sqrt{0.2565}} = \frac{-0.304}{0.5065} = -0.600$$

Since $|-0.601| < |2.069|$, we do not reject H_0.

$$wr\text{:} \quad H_0 : \beta_1 = 0 \quad \text{and } H_1 : \beta_1 < 0$$

$$t = -\frac{-0.143}{\sqrt{0.0046}} = \frac{-0.143}{0.0678233} = -2.108$$

$$t_{23,0.05} = 1.714$$

Since $|-2.108| > |-1.714|$, we reject H_0.

$$gdp\text{:} \quad H_0 : \beta_2 = 0 \quad \text{and} \quad H_1 : \beta_2 > 0$$

$$t = \frac{0.734}{\sqrt{0.0081}} = \frac{0.734}{0.09} = 8.156$$

Since $8.156 > 1.714$, we reject H_0.

$$nis: \quad H_0 : \beta_3 = 0 \quad \text{and} \quad H_1 : \beta_3 < 0$$

$$t = \frac{0.0003}{\sqrt{0.0005}} = \frac{0.0003}{0.0223607} = 0.013$$

Since $0.013 > -1.714$, we do not reject H_0.

ii) Overall effects

$$H_0 : \beta_1 = \beta_2 = \beta_3 = 0 \text{ and } H_1\text{: at least one of the } \beta \neq 0$$

The statistic of interest is

$$F = \frac{R^2/(k-1)}{(1-R^2)/(n-k)} = \frac{0.917/3}{(1-0.917)/23} = \frac{0.305667}{0.0036087} = 84.703$$

Since $84.703 > F_{23}^{3} = 3.03$, we reject H_0.

iii) Conclusion. Summing up, the regression results indicate that all variables taken together do explain the level of employment in Barbados. In fact, precisely 91.7 percent of the variation of the level of employment is explained by the regression. Individually, real wages impact negatively on the level of employment; a 1 percent increase in real wages gives rise to a 0.143 percent decrease in the level of employment; GDP positively affects the level of employment; a 1 percent increase in real GDP brings about a 0.734 percent increase in the level of employment.

b) The lower limit of the DW test is equal to 1.162. As the DW value (0.742) is less than the lower limit of the distribution we conclude that there is a positive autocorrelation. A significant DW, however, does not necessarily mean the presence of autocorrelation (pure autocorrelation). Indeed, it can be indicative of omitted variables, misspecified functional form or misspecified dynamics.

c) As there is a positive autocorrelation, the results in (a) need to be reevaluated. Indeed, the existence of autocorrelation (pure autocorrelation) implies that the estimates are no longer efficient, and the variances are biased. That is, the test statistics used to interpret individual variables are no longer valid. To use these test statistics, there is a need to correct for autocorrelation (e.g., using the Cochrane–Orcutt iterative procedure). Note, however, since autocorrelation may be due to another cause, it is wise to pursue the matter; that is, to search for other sources of autocorrelation [see (d)]. If it turns out that it is due to an omitted variable, then the solution is to include the omitted variable if available.

d) i) Test for omitted variables. The appropriate test for omitted variables is, in this situation, the Ramsey's RESET test for omitted variables. Three approaches can be used here based on the fundamental regression:

$$\ell_t = \alpha_0 + \alpha_1 wr_t + \alpha_2 gdp_t + \alpha_3 nis_t + \alpha_4 \hat{\ell}_t^2 + v_t$$

where $\hat{\ell}_t^2$ is the square of the fitted value of $\hat{\ell}_t$. Higher powers of $\hat{\ell}_t$ are desirable. In any case, in the first instance, the t statistic can be used to test the hypothesis:

$$H_0 : \alpha_4 = 0 \text{ against } H_1 : \alpha_4 \neq 0$$

The t statistic of interest is

$$t = \frac{\hat{\alpha}_4}{Std_{\hat{\alpha}_4}} = 3.876$$

Since $3.876 > t_{22,0.025} = 2.074$, we reject H_0; that is, there are omitted variables.

The second method consists in using the F test (restricted versus unrestricted regression):

$$F = \frac{(\text{RRSS} - \text{URSS})/\#\text{of new regressors}}{\text{URSS}/\#\text{of df}}$$

$$= \frac{(0.0225 - 0.013347)/1}{0.013347/22} = \frac{0.009153}{0.000607} = 15.079$$

where RRSS stands for the restricted residual sum of squares (from the original regression without $\hat{\ell}_t^2$) and URSS is the unrestricted residual sum of squares (from the regression with $\hat{\ell}_t^2$). Since $15.079 > F_{22}^1 = 4.30$, the null $H_0 : \alpha_4 = 0$ is rejected.

The third method is a variant of the second where the R^2s are used instead of the RSSs. Thus, the F statistic is:

$$F = \frac{(R_U^2 - R_R^2)/\#\text{of new regressors}}{(1 - R_U^2/df}$$

$$= \frac{(0.950687 - 0.917)/1}{(1 - 0.950687)/22} = 15.029$$

where the subscripts U and R stand for unrestricted and restricted regressions, respectively. Since $15.029 > F_{22}^1 = 4.30$, we reject $H_0 : \alpha_4 = 0$. Thus, we conclude that there is (are) omitted variable(s). Note that the last two tests are fundamentally the same and also in this particular context (testing just for one extra variable) $F = t_{\hat{\alpha}_4}^2$.

ii) Consequences. Let Z_t be the omitted variable.
- If Z_t is correlated with included variables, then all the estimators are biased and inconsistent.
- If Z_t is uncorrelated with included variables, the parameter estimators are unbiased with the exception of the intercept.

- Variance of the error is incorrectly estimated.
- Var-Cov ($\hat{\beta}$) is generally biased upward.
- The usual confidence interval and hypothesis testing procedures about the statistical significance of the parameter estimators are no longer valid.

Answer 2.18

a) Let the original regression be given by:

$$q_t = \beta_0 + \beta_1 k_t + \beta_2 l_t + u_t$$

i) Individual significance. We test for individual coefficient significance following the procedure laid out in the previous exercises.

$$k_t\text{:} \quad H_0 : \beta_1 = 0 \text{ and } H_1 : \beta_1 > 0 \quad \alpha = 5\%$$

The t distribution is of interest here with a critical value of $t_{17,0.05} = 1.740$. The t calculated is

$$t_{\hat{\beta}_1} = \frac{0.332}{\sqrt{0.031875}} = \frac{0.332}{0.178536} = 1.860$$

Since $1.860 > 1.740$, we reject H_0 at the 5 percent level of significance.

$$l_t\text{:} \quad H_0 : \beta_2 = 0 \text{ and } H_1 : \beta_2 > 0$$

$$t_{\hat{\beta}_2} = \frac{2.777}{\sqrt{0.166070}} = \frac{2.777}{0.407517} = 6.814$$

Since $6.814 > 1.740$, we reject H_0.

ii) Overall significance.

$$H_0 : \beta_1 = \beta_2 = 0 \quad \text{and} \quad H_1 \text{ at least one of the } \beta \neq 0.$$

Since

$$F = \frac{R^2/(k-1)}{(1-R^2)/(n-k)} = \frac{0.915/2}{(1-0.915)/(20-3)} = 91.5 > F_{17}^2 = 3.59$$

we reject H_0.

Summing up, the results reveal that capital and labour are important in explaining output. Indeed, a 1 percent increase in capital yields a 0.332 percent increase in output. A 1 percent increase in labour brings about a 2.777 percent increase in output. All the inputs taken together affect output. Precisely, 91.5 percent of the variation in output is explained by the regression.

b) From the Durbin–Watson distribution table we know that the lower and upper limits of the DW statistic are, respectively, $d_L = 1.10$ and $d_U = 1.54$. Since $d_U < 2.032 < 4 - d_U$, we conclude there is no autocorrelation. Remember that a significant DW does not necessarily mean the presence of autocorrelation. It can be indicative of omitted variables, functional misspecification or misspecified dynamics.

c) i) White's test (in the F form) to test for heteroscedasticity.

ii) $F = 1.77507$ with p value $= 0.368382$. Since the p value is $> \alpha$, we do not reject H_0; that is, there is no heteroscedasticity.

iii) In the presence of heteroscedasticity, the estimators remain unbiased and consistent but are now inefficient and so are the forecasts. Since the variances are now biased, the usual tests of significance as well as the confidence intervals are no longer valid.

d) The null hypothesis is that there are constant returns to scale. The alternative hypothesis is there are increasing returns to scale. An F form of the Wald test has a value of 53.2394 (check it) with an associated p value of 0.000001. Clearly the null hypothesis is rejected. Alternatively, a t test can also be of interest. Its value is 7.299 (check it). This t ratio and the above F ratio are linked (find their link). In any case, we can assert that the industry is characterized by increasing returns to scale.

Answer 2.19

a) There are basically two interpretations. The first is that since there is no grade zero (or nearly so) in the data sample, the constant term is meaningless. However, you should be reminded that inference concerns population (where the value zero among grades can be the case). The second case is a mathematical interpretation. It is the grade obtained by a student who does not fulfil the prerequisite. It is thus the grade obtained by a student who got zero in Introductory Statistics. We favour the latter interpretation.

b) The slope is

$$\hat{\beta} = \frac{\sum x_i y_i}{\sum x_i^2} = \frac{\sum X_i Y_i - n\bar{X}\bar{Y}}{\sum X_i^2 - n\bar{X}^2} = 1.127184$$

and the constant term is

$$\hat{\alpha} = \bar{Y} - \hat{\beta}\bar{X} = 60.45455 - 1.127184(64.81818) = -12.60744$$

Thus, the fitted line is

$$\hat{Y}_i = -12.60744 + 1.127184 X_i$$

c) White's test. The White's test has two forms: the pure LM form and the F form. Here we use the F form, because the sample is small. The F is computed as:

$$F = \frac{R^2/2}{\left(1-R^2\right)/8} = \frac{0.13082/2}{(1-0.13082)/8} = \frac{0.06541}{0.1086475} = 0.602$$

Since $0.602 < F_8^2 = 4.46$, we accept H_0; that is, there is no heteroscedasticity.

d) Ramsey's RESET test. The null hypothesis is H_0: no omitted variables and the alternative is H_1: omitted variables. An F variant of the test is

$$F = \frac{\left(R_{\text{new}}^2 - R_{\text{old}}^2\right)/\#\text{of new regressors}}{\left(1-R_{\text{new}}^2\right)/df}$$

with:

$$R_{\text{old}}^2 = \hat{\beta}^2 \frac{\sum x_i^2}{\sum y_i^2} = \hat{\beta}\frac{\sum x_i y_i}{\sum y_i^2} = \frac{\left(\sum x_i y_i\right)^2}{\sum x_i^2 \sum y_i^2} = 0.511768$$

where variables are in deviation with respect to the means. Thus,

$$F = \frac{\left(0.544265-0.511768\right)/2}{\left(1-0.544265\right)/7} = \frac{0.0162485}{0.065105} = 0.250.$$

Since $F < 4.74$, we do not reject the null that there are no omitted variables.

e) Individual coefficient. Table 2.2 contains the results of the regression obtained using Eviews 4. As can be seen, the t statistic of the constant term is –0.521. The null hypothesis cannot be rejected. It means here that a student who does not fulfil the prerequisite has zero in Statistical Methods I. The t statistic of the slope is 3.071, which is significant at the 5 percent level. It means that a 1 percent increase in the Introductory Statistics grade brings about a 1.13 percent increase in the Statistical Method I grade. The r^2 is 0.51. With a p value of 0.013 for its associate F statistic, we can assert that r^2 or precisely its parametric equivalent is significantly different from zero. We conclude that 51 percent in the variation of Statistical Method I grades is explained by the regression (Introductory Statistics grades). Given the outcomes in (c), (d) and (e) we can assert the results obtained so far are valid.

TABLE 2.2
OLS Results: UWI Statistics, 11 students

Variable	Coefficient	Standard Error	t Statistic	Prob.
C	–12.60744	24.17529	–0.521501	0.6146
X	1.127184	0.366986	3.071462	0.0133
R^2	0.511768	Mean dependent variable		60.45455
Adjusted R^2	0.457521	S.D. dependent variable		19.42351
SE of regression	14.30604	Akaike information criterion		8.322206
RSS	1841.964	Schwarz criterion		8.394551
Log likelihood	–43.77213	F statistic		9.433878
Durbin-Watson	1.961937	Prob(F statistic)		0.013322

Note: X stands for student's grade in Introductory Statistics, in percent. Dependent variable is student's grade in Statistical Methods I, in percent.

Answer 2.20

a) Let us write the saving function with S_t as saving and Y_t as income, as follows:

$$S_t = \alpha + \beta Y_t + u_t \tag{A2.20.1}$$

and the consumption function with C_t as consumption, as follows:

$$C_t = \gamma + \delta Y_t + e_t \tag{A2.20.2}$$

From Equation (A2.20.1), the DW statistic can be computed as follows:

$$d_S = \frac{\sum (\hat{u}_t - \hat{u}_{t-1})^2}{\sum \hat{u}_t^2}$$

and from Equation (A2.20.2) the corresponding statistic is:

$$d_C = \frac{\sum (\hat{e}_t - \hat{e}_{t-1})^2}{\sum \hat{e}_t^2}$$

The question then is whether $d_s = d_c$. To proceed, it suffices to show first whether $\hat{u}_t = \hat{e}_t$ or $\hat{u}_t = -\hat{e}_t$. From Equation (A2.20.2) and exploiting the relationship $Y_t = C_t + S_t$, it can be seen that

$$\begin{aligned}\hat{e}_t &= C_t - \hat{\gamma} - \hat{\delta} Y_t \\ &= Y_t - S_t - \hat{\gamma} - \hat{\delta} Y_t \\ &= -S_t - \hat{\gamma} + (1 - \hat{\delta}) Y_t \\ &= -S_t + \hat{\alpha} + \hat{\beta} Y_t \qquad \text{since} \quad \hat{\gamma} = -\hat{\alpha} \quad \text{and} \quad (1 - \hat{\delta}) = \hat{\beta} \\ &= -(S_t - \hat{\alpha} - \hat{\beta} Y_t) \\ &= -\hat{u}_t\end{aligned}$$

$\hat{e}_t = -\hat{u}_t$ implies that

$$\sum (\hat{e}_t - \hat{e}_{t-1})^2 = \sum (-\hat{u}_t - (-\hat{u}_{t-1}))^2 = \sum (\hat{u}_t - \hat{u}_{t-1})^2$$

and

$$\sum \hat{e}_t^2 = \sum \hat{u}_t^2 \qquad \text{(A2.20.3)}$$

hence,

$$\frac{\sum (\hat{u}_t - \hat{u}_{t-1})^2}{\sum \hat{u}_t^2} = \frac{\sum (\hat{e}_t - \hat{e}_{t-1})^2}{\sum \hat{e}_t^2} \qquad \text{QED}$$

b) Yes, there is a positive autocorrelation, as $0.911 < d_L = 1.363$. First differences, the Cochrane–Orcutt iterative procedure, the Hildreth and Lu search procedure and Newey–West robust standard errors are a few alternatives to clean up autocorrelation.
c) No, the statement is false. The correct procedure is laid out in Answer (2.3.b).

Answer 2.21

This regression does not fulfil the assumptions of classical linear models. Indeed, three assumptions are violated. First, the absence of autocorrelation is violated. Indeed, there is a positive autocorrelation because the DW statistic has a value of 1, which is less than the lower limit ($d_L = 1.302$) of the Durbin–Watson distribution table. This result is also confirmed by the LM test in its F version with a value of 6.065 and an associated p value of 0.022.

Second, the hypothesis of homoscedasticity is also violated. Indeed, the White's test statistic in its F version has a value of 8.160634 and an associated p value of 0.002097. That is, there is presence of heteroscedasticity.

TABLE 2.3
Consumer Price Index: New OLS Results for Jamaica, 1972–1997

White Heteroscedasticity-Consistent Standard Errors and Covariance				
Variable	Coefficient	Standard Error	*t* Statistic	Prob.
C	2.217563	0.615647	3.602005	0.0015
IM	0.819308	0.095278	8.599094	0.0000
CPI2	0.001938	0.000969	2.000207	0.0574
R-squared	0.992686	Mean dependent variable		27.60000
Adjusted R-squared	0.992050	S.D. dependent variable		40.45678
S.E. of regression	3.607286	Akaike information criterion		5.511955
RSS	299.2877	Schwarz criterion		5.657120
Log likelihood	–68.65542	*F* statistic		1560.786
DW statistic	1.419572	Prob(*F* statistic)		0.000000

Note: CPI2: squared fitted value of CPI from the regression of CPI on a constant and import price index.

Third, there are omitted variables in the regression. Indeed, a regression of the residual from the basic regression on the constant, import price index and square of fitted consumer price index indicates that the coefficient of the latter is significant, with a t statistic of 2.973.

Tentatively, we deal with the problem of omitted variables by using the square of the fitted values of CPI. The results are shown in Table 2.3. The autocorrelation has disappeared as the LM test in its F form ($F = 0.197$ with p value $= 0.66$) indicates. That is, autocorrelation was most likely due to omitted variables. We use the White HCC standard errors to deal with the problem of heteroscedasticity although the sample is not large. Notice that the coefficient of import price index has not drastically changed. Recall, in the original regression it has a value of 1. Now, however, the constant term is significant.

2.4 SUPPLEMENTARY EXERCISES

Question 2.22 Write a comprehensive essay on the ARCH model including its derivatives.

Question 2.23 Explain the issues(s) that Sargan's common factor deals with. (See also Mizon, 1995.)

Question 2.24 Using information provided in Question 1.23 (see supplementary exercises to Chapter 1), check whether all the assumptions of the classical linear model are fulfilled.

CHAPTER 3

Dummy Variables and Limited Dependent Variables

3.1 INTRODUCTION

Applied econometrics requires the use of data, which are numerical by nature, that is, they capture quantitative phenomena. There are, however, instances in which data proxy qualitative phenomena, such as gender (male/female), race (white/non-white), sectors of industry (manufacturing/non-manufacturing), purchase of a house, decision to get married, seasonal effects, to name a few.

Qualitative phenomena presented in dichotomous form (characteristic/non-characteristic, e.g., male/female) are often quantified by a zero-one variable, called a dummy variable. A dummy variable takes a value of one if the attribute or the characteristic is present and zero otherwise. For example, in the case of gender, the value of one can be attributed to male and zero to female. The category with the value of zero is called the control or reference or base group. A dummy variable can also capture purely quantitative phenomena in certain circumstances. For example, it is well known that income values derived from surveys are often of poor quality, as the majority of respondents are reluctant to reveal their incomes. One way to "attenuate" the poor quality of data is to choose a cut off point and build a dummy variable with, for example, value one for individuals above the threshold and value zero for those below the threshold. The classification of countries into developed and developing countries is another example of such a dummy variable (for example, one for developed countries and zero for developing countries).

A dummy variable can be a regressor. For instance, the salary of teachers depends on their years of experience, their tenure position and their gender. Here, gender captured by a dummy variable is a regressor or explanatory variable.

An explanatory dummy variable can be used in a time series context, among others, as an indicator of the extent to which one time period is different from another (e.g., structural stability). In a cross section framework, a dummy variable regressor can capture differences between groups (Hardy, 1993, 5). In a panel data context, it can be an indicator of unit specificity or time specificity, such as in fixed effects models (see Chapter 9).

Naturally, a dummy variable can also be a regressand or an endogenous variable. In a model of a decision to buy a car, own a house or attend a particular university, the endogenous variable is a dummy variable. Models with dummy dependent variables are also known as discrete choice or qualitative response models. Models with binary choice include linear probability models, logit and probit models.

There are instances where the qualitative variable takes on more than two choices. These choices can be of several natures. For example, race can be decomposed into several categories: e.g., 3 for Asian, 2 for white, 1 for black and 0 for others. The categories in this case represent neither rank nor count. Another example concerns the opinion that individuals have on a candidate: 0 if the candidate is disliked, 1 if he or she does not generate a special interest, 2 if the candidate is liked and 3 if he or she is highly regarded. Here, the numbers characterize some ordering, although the difference between one and zero is not necessarily the same as the difference between three and two. Note that although most often multiple choices in the context of explanatory variables are transformed into binary choices for ease in interpretation, in a context of endogenous variables they are left as they are.

In some circumstances, the dependent variables take other forms in which, for example, they have both discrete and continuous characteristics. In the valuation of non-marketed goods, such as beaches, some people are willing to pay to access the amenity and others are not. In such a case the dependent variable will have two components: a set of zero values coupled with other values. The dependent variable in this scenario is called a limited dependent variable. The Tobit model is one example of a limited dependent variable model.

The exercises in this chapter focus more on dummy explanatory variables than on dummy endogenous variables.

3.2 QUESTIONS

3.2.1 Theoretical Exercises

Question 3.1 The zero-one values attributed to dummy variables are meaningless per se. Comment on this statement (UWI, EC36C, tutorial 2003).

Question 3.2 Explain the concept of the dummy variable trap.

Question 3.3 Use a model to show that the use of zero-one values to capture dummy variables gives rise to a straightforward interpretation of model results.

Question 3.4 Consider the following simple regression model:

$$Y_i = \beta_0 + \beta_1 D_{1i} + e_i \tag{Q3.4.1}$$

where Y_i is some quantitative variable (e.g., salary of teachers),

$$D_{1i} = \begin{cases} 1 \text{ if male} \\ 0 \text{ if female} \end{cases}$$

and e_i, the error term, is well behaved.

a) Show that $\hat{\beta}_0 = \bar{Y}_0$ and $\hat{\beta}_1 = \bar{Y}_1 - \bar{Y}_0$ where $\bar{Y}_0$ is the mean value of those Y observations associated with the zero values in D_{1i} and similarly $\bar{Y}_1$ refers to the mean of Y observations associated with $D_{1i} = 1$.
b) Derive $\text{var}(\hat{\beta})$ with $\hat{\beta} = (\hat{\beta}_0, \hat{\beta}_1)$.
c) Derive r^2. (UWI, EC36C, tutorial 2003)

Question 3.5 Consider the following seasonal models:

$$Y_t = \beta_0 + \beta_1 D_1 + \beta_2 D_2 + \beta_3 D_3 + u_t \quad \text{(Q3.5.1)}$$

$$Y_t = \gamma_0 + \gamma_2 D_2 + \gamma_3 D_3 + \gamma_4 D_4 + u_t \quad \text{(Q3.5.2)}$$

$$Y_t = \delta_0 + \delta_1 D_1 + \delta_3 D_3 + \delta_4 D_4 + u_t \quad \text{(Q3.5.3)}$$

$$Y_t = \alpha_0 + \alpha_1 D_1 + \alpha_2 D_2 + \alpha_4 D_4 + u_t \quad \text{(Q3.5.4)}$$

$$Y_t = a_1 D_1 + a_2 D_2 + a_3 D_3 + a_4 D_4 + u_t \quad \text{(Q3.5.5)}$$

where the D variables are seasonal dummies; that is,

$$D_1 = \begin{cases} 1 \text{ for first quarter} \\ 0 \text{ otherwise} \end{cases}$$

$$D_2 = \begin{cases} 1 \text{ for second quarter} \\ 0 \text{ otherwise} \end{cases}$$

$$D_3 = \begin{cases} 1 \text{ for third quarter} \\ 0 \text{ otherwise} \end{cases}$$

$$D_4 = \begin{cases} 1 \text{ for fourth quarter} \\ 0 \text{ otherwise} \end{cases}$$

Show that the four models are equivalent.

Question 3.6 Consider the following regression model:

$$Y_t = \beta_0 + \beta_1 X_t + \beta_2 D_t + \beta_3 (D_t X_t) + u_t \quad \text{(Q3.6.1)}$$

where $t = 1, 2, 3, \ldots, T$ is the time index; $T = T_1 + T_2$; Y_t and X_t are quantitative variables; D_t is a dummy variable with 1 for each of the first T_1 observations and 0 for each of the T_2 last observations; and u_t is the error term.

a) Provide an econometric issue that may be modelled as shown in Equation (Q3.6.1).
b) Explain what you learn by testing, individually or jointly, the significance of β_2 and β_3.
c) Is the methodology devised in (b) more advantageous than other similar methodology(ies) to deal with the issue in (a)?
d) What is (are) the assumption(s) for the validity of the test in (b)?

Question 3.7 Consider the following model:

$$Y_i = \beta_1 + \beta_2 X_i + \beta_3 D_i + u_i \qquad \text{(Q3.7.1)}$$

where Y_i and X_i are quantitative variables and D_i is a dummy variable such that:

$$D_i = \begin{cases} 1 \text{ characteristic present} \\ 0 \text{ otherwise} \end{cases}$$

a) Can we say that, holding X_i constant, the mean value of Y_i increases (decreases) by β_3 if D_i is increased by one unit? Why or why not?
b) If no, formulate the correct question.
c) Answer Question (b).

Question 3.8 Consider the following model:

$$Y_t = \beta_0 + \beta_1 D_t + \beta_2 X_t + \beta_3 Z_t + u_t \qquad \text{(Q3.8.1)}$$

where Y_t, X_t and Z_t are quantitative variables and D_t is a dummy variable with a value 1 for each of the first n_1 observations and a value 0 for each of the last n_2 observations.

a) Implement a full White's test for heteroscedasticity.
b) Suppose (a) reveals heteroscedasticity. Suppose also the errors are autocorrelated. Reevaluate what the White's test is testing.
c) If (b) is true suggest a solution to the two problems.

Question 3.9 Suppose that in a given country annual individual health care expenditure depends on income, race and level of education (primary, secondary and tertiary).

a) Write a model using the above variables with the particularity that the level of education only affects income and race acts only on the intercept.
b) Devise a test for the hypothesis that the level of education does not affect health expenditure.

c) Rewrite the above model with race affecting the intercept and the level of education impacting on both intercept and income.
d) Devise a test for the null hypothesis that race and level of education do not matter in explaining the level of health expenditure.

Question 3.10 Consider the following model:

$$LnY_i = \beta_1 + \beta_2 X_i + \gamma D_i + u_i \qquad \text{(Q3.10.1)}$$

where Y_i and X_i are quantitative variables, D_i is a dummy variable with value 1 if the characteristic is present and 0 otherwise, LnY_i is the logarithm of Y_i and u_i is the error term.

a) Can you interpret γ as the percent change in mean value of Y_i due to the dummy holding other factors constant? Why or why not?
b) If not, discuss the correct interpretation (including any properties of the estimator).

Question 3.11 Consider the following house ownership model:

$$Y_i = \alpha + \beta X_i + u_i \qquad \text{(Q3.11.1)}$$

where $i = 1, 2, \ldots, n$ is the family index, X_i is family income, Y_i is a dummy variable with value 1 if the family owns a house and 0 otherwise, and u is the error term.

a) Justify why Equation (Q3.11.1) is a linear probability model.
b) Identify three problems in estimating Equation (Q3.11.1).
c) Provide the solutions to the problems alluded to above.

Question 3.12 In the context of dummy dependent variables consider the following derivatives:

$$\frac{\partial}{\partial X_{il}}(X_i'\beta) = \beta_l \qquad \text{(Q3.12.1)}$$

$$\frac{\partial}{\partial X_{il}}\Phi(X_i'\beta) = \phi(X_i'\beta)\beta_l \qquad \text{(Q3.12.2)}$$

$$\frac{\partial}{\partial X_{il}}L(X_i'\beta) = \frac{\exp(X_i'\beta)}{[1+\exp(X_i'\beta)]^2}\beta_l \qquad \text{(Q3.12.3)}$$

where i stands for individual; $\mathbf{X}_{i1}$ is a vector (variable) of the matrix of quantitative explanatory variables, X_i; Φ stands for cumulative standard normal distribution; ϕ is the standard normal density; and L is a likelihood function.

a) These three derivatives come from three different models. Write down their corresponding models.
b) Explain the derivatives. (Read Maddala, 1983, 22–24.)

Question 3.13 Assume that the probability that a student is successful in an econometrics final examination is given by:

$$e^{\gamma+\delta X_i}\left(1+e^{\gamma+\delta X_i}\right)^{-1} \qquad \text{(Q3.13.1)}$$

where X_i is a dummy variable taking the value 1 for a local student and 0 for a foreign student. Suppose we have 100 students, of whom 20 are successful local students, 35 successful foreign students and 20 unsuccessful local students.

a) Model (Q3.13.1) is a logit model. Explain.
b) Provide the MLE of the probability that a student is successful in an econometrics final examination under the null hypothesis $\delta = 0$.
b) What are the MLE of γ and δ? (Partially adapted from Kennedy, 1992, 347.)

3.2.2 Empirical Exercises

Question 3.14 Consider the data shown in Table 3.1 on cruise ship passenger arrivals in Barbados for the period 1977–2002.

a) Fit a linear trend model to the data in Table 3.1 and interpret the results.
b) Fit the following regression to the data in Table 3.1 and explain the results:

TABLE 3.1
Cruise Ship Passenger Arrivals: Barbados, 1977–2002

Year	Arrivals	Year	Arrivals
1977	103,077	1990	362,611
1978	125,988	1991	372,140
1979	110,073	1992	399,702
1980	156,461	1993	428,611
1981	135,782	1994	459,502
1982	110,753	1995	484,670
1983	102,519	1996	509,975
1984	99,166	1997	517,888
1985	112,222	1998	506,610
1986	145,335	1999	432,854
1987	224,778	2000	533,278
1988	290,993	2001	527,597
1989	337,110	2002	523,253

Source: Central Bank of Barbados, *Economic and Financial Statistics*, November 2003.

TABLE 3.2
Crimes in the Turks and Caicos Islands, 1997:01–2000:12

Period	No. of Crimes	Period	No. of Crimes	Period	No. of Crimes
1997:01	80	1998:05	113	1999:09	124
1997:02	89	1998:06	88	1999:10	86
1997:03	104	1998:07	87	1999:11	112
1997:04	107	1998:08	63	1999:12	83
1997:05	87	1998:09	97	2000:01	90
1997:06	72	1998:10	106	2000:02	92
1997:07	63	1998:11	118	2000:03	129
1997:08	73	1998:12	129	2000:04	75
1997:09	91	1999:01	146	2000:05	106
1997:10	135	1999:02	81	2000:06	107
1997:11	85	1999:03	93	2000:07	119
1997:12	118	1999:04	134	2000:08	140
1998:01	151	1999:05	77	2000:09	125
1998:02	115	1999:06	88	2000:10	87
1998:03	94	1999:07	82	2000:11	99
1998:04	103	1999:08	96	2000:12	89

Source: Turks and Caicos Islands, *Yearbook of Statistics 2000.*

$$Y_t = \beta_0 + \beta_1 D_t + \gamma Tr + u_t \qquad \text{(Q3.14.1)}$$

where Y_t stands for cruise ship passenger arrivals, Tr captures trend, $t = 1, 2, \ldots, T$ represents time, D_t is a dummy variable for structural change with value of 1 for each year of the period before 1987 and value of 0 for each year from 1987 onwards, and u_t is the error term.

c) Suppose now D_t is redefined as 1 for each year in the period 1977–1986 and –1 for each year of the period 1987–2002. Reestimate Equation (Q3.14.1) and interpret the results.
d) Suppose now D_t is redefined as 2 for each year in the period 1977–1986 and 0 for each year of the period 1987–2002. Reestimate (Q3.14.1) and interpret the results.
e) Test for a full structural stability (intercept and slope).

Question 3.15 Consider the data in Table 3.2 on monthly crimes committed in the Turks and Caicos Islands.

a) Using a dummy variable approach, test for deterministic seasonality in "crime" in the Turks and Caicos Islands.
b) Check whether there is (are) any outlier(s).
c) Compute the instantaneous and compound crime growth rate in the period of interest.

TABLE 3.3
Variable Definitions for Forest Conversion Model

Name	Description
Droad	Distance to the nearest road in metres
Driver	Distance to the nearest river in metres
Drail	Distance to the nearest railway in metres
Dcity	Distance to the nearest city in metres
Toporg	Organic in top soil in percent
Subrock	Rock in subsoil in percent
Lownut	Low nutrient retention in percent
Lowpotas	Low ability to supply potassium in percent
Pir	Hig-P fixation due to iron in percent
Modacid	Moderate soil acidity in percent
Highali	High aluminum saturation in percent
Wetness	Excessive wetness in percent
Growb	Length of growing period in days
Sqi	Soil quality index

Question 3.16 Mamingi et al. (1996) attempted to explain the phenomenon "deforestation" in Cameroon and Zaire. They used a probit model with, as a dependent variable, a dummy variable with value 1 for non-forest land cover and 0 for forest. One of the models of interest is:

$$Conv_i = c + \beta_1 droad_i + \beta_2 driver_i + \beta_3 drail_i + \beta_1 dcity_i + \beta_1 sqi_i + u_i \qquad (Q3.16.1)$$

where i represents a pixel (sample point on a 5-km lattice); *conv* is the dummy variable for conversion, with 1 as non-forest land cover and 0 as forest; and other variables are defined as in Table 3.3. Note that the soil quality index, *sqi*, consists of agroclimatic characteristics such as the quality of soil (loam in top soil, organic in topsoil, rock in subsoil, sand in subsoil, loam in subsoil, low nutrient retention, iron, moderate soil acidity, high aluminum saturation), as well as excessive wetness.

The results of estimation of the above model for Cameroon are presented in Table 3.4.

a) In Table 3.4, what do "Coeff." and "dF/dX" represent?
b) Interpret the results of the model.

Question 3.17 Lewis and Mamingi (2003, 30–56) used the contingent valuation method to estimate the total economic value of Harrison's Cave of Barbados, a top tourist attraction. The total economic value of this non-marketed good is derived from two components: use value (entrance fees) and non-use value. To derive the use value of the amenity, the authors considered the following model:

$$WTP_i = c + \sum_j \alpha_j X_{ij} + u_i \qquad (Q3.17.1)$$

TABLE 3.4
Forest Conversion: Probit Estimation Results for Cameroon

No. of Observations	= 7138
χ^2_{13}	= 1573.78
Prob > χ^2	= 0.0000
Pseudo R^2	= 0.1938
Log Likelihood	= 3274.1425

Variables	Coefficient	Standard Error	z	dF/dX	Standard Error	z
Droad	–8.97e-06	1.11e-06	–8.092	–2.44e-06	2.76e-07	–8.846
Driver	–8.43e-06	1.08e-06	–7.777	–2.29e-06	2.85e-07	–8.042
Drail	–3.38e-06	4.09e-07	–8.255	–9.19e-07	1.05e-07	–8.736
Dcity	–3.31e-06	3.98e-07	–8.338	–9.01e-07	1.03e-07	–8.790
Toporg	–0.00613	0.0031248	–1.962			
Subrock	0.0051674	0.0026937	1.918			
Lownut	–0.0047851	0.0009374	–5.105			
Lowpotas	–0.00341	0.00154231	–2.210			
Pir	0.005227	0.020199	2.600			
Modacid	0.0088045	0.0012617	6.978			
Highali	0.0091483	0.0011772	7.771			
Wetness	–0.0090912	0.0018757	–4.847			
Growb	–0.00574	0.0008411	–6.824	–0.0015605	.0002082	–7.494
Sqi				0.2718622	0.0238033	11.421
C	2.097208	0.3351416	6.258			

Note: Variables are defined as in Table 3.3.

Source: Mamingi, Chomitz, Gray and Lambin (1996).

TABLE 3.5
Variables for the Valuation of Harrison's Cave, Barbados

Variables	Meanings
WTP	Willingness to pay an additional entrance fee in Bds$
Income	Yearly household income in Bds$
Expenditure	Expenditures in Bds$ incurred for the trip to Barbados
Impression	Impression of Harrison's Cave with respect to other attractions: 1 if most impressive; 0 otherwise
Visit cave	Individual visited Harrison's Cave: 1 if yes; 0 otherwise
Interest	Interest in caves: 1 if interested in caves; 0 otherwise
Education	Level of education reached: 1 if tertiary or above; 0 otherwise
Sex	Gender of the respondent: 1 if female and 0 otherwise
Type visitor	1: if long-stay visitor; 0 otherwise (e.g., cruise ship passenger)

Source: Lewis and Mamingi (2003).

where WTP_i is the willingness to pay an additional entrance fee to Harrison's Cave, X_{ij} is a set of variables defined as shown in Table 3.5, $i = 1, 2, \ldots, n$ is the respondent

TABLE 3.6
Tobit Estimates for Willingness to Pay an Additional Entrance Fee to Harrison's Cave

Variables	Tobit Estimates	Slopes
Constant	–18.858	–0.468
	(–2.000)	
Expenditure	0.0007	0.0002
	(1.361)	
Income	6.7×10^{-5}	1.7×10^{-6}
	(0.777)	
Interest	6.749	0.168
	(1.467)	
Type visitor	8.225	0.204
	(2.094)	
Visit cave	–8.262	–0.205
	(–1.772)	
Sex	–3.829	–0.095
	(–0.949)	
Education	12.110	0.301
	(2.454)	
Sample size	72	
Positive bids	34	
MWTP (Bds$)	6.10	

Note: Variables are defined as in Table 3.5. Slopes: marginal effects; MWTP: average WTP computed from the bid curve. Values in parentheses are Z statistics. Equation (Q3.17.1) is of interest.

Source: Lewis and Mamingi (2003).

index, j is the variable index, and u is a well-behaved error term. Data were obtained through a survey.

Tobit estimation results of Equation (Q3.17.1) are presented in Table 3.6.

a) Why is the Tobit estimation method used here instead of OLS?
b) Why is R^2 not presented in Table 3.6?
c) Using a 10 percent level of significance, interpret the results of the model. (UWI, EC36D, tutorial 2003)

3.3 ANSWERS

Answer 3.1

Yes, the zero-one values attributed to dummy variables are meaningless per se. They can be replaced by another set of values such as two-three. The zero-one dichotomy simply captures attribute/no-attribute status, which any other dichotomy can do. Note, however, the zero-one division is chosen to characterize dummy variables because in regression it lends itself to a straightforward interpretation of results.

Answer 3.2

Consider the following model:

$$Y_i = \beta_0 + \beta_1 D_{1i} + e_i$$

where i is an index for individual (i = 1, 2, …, n), be it individual per se or time; Y_i is a quantitative variable; D_{1i} is a dummy variable (0-1 variable) and e_i is the error term. To be more precise, let

$$D_{1i} = \begin{cases} 1 \text{ if male} \\ 0 \text{ if female} \end{cases}$$

In such a situation we can well contemplate the possibility of a second dummy variable,

$$D_{2i} = \begin{cases} 1 \text{ if female} \\ 0 \text{ if male} \end{cases}$$

A regression with a constant term and two dummies:

$$Y_i = \alpha_0 + \alpha_1 D_{1i} + \alpha_2 D_{2i} + e_i$$

is problematic to the extent that it is not estimable. Indeed, there is perfect multicollinearity between explanatory variables. Precisely, the vector of ones attached to the constant term and the two dummies are linearly dependent. This is a case of perfect multicollinearity and it is impossible to estimate the coefficients of the model. This is the essence of the dummy variable trap: too many dummies with a constant term do not allow the estimation of the model. As a remedy, in the presence of a constant term, one only introduces (s – 1) dummy variables, where s stands for the number of groups. In our case, there are two groups, thus we must only introduce one dummy variable. The constant term captures the reference group. Of course, the use of all the dummies without the constant term does not lead to a dummy variable trap.

Answer 3.3

Consider the following model:

$$Y_i = \beta_0 + \beta_1 D_{1i} + e_i \qquad \text{(A3.3.1)}$$

where

Y_i = the salary of teachers,

$$D_{1i} = \begin{cases} 1 \text{ if male} \\ 0 \text{ if female} \end{cases}$$

e_i = the usual error term.

Suppose that the error fulfils all the assumptions of a classical linear model, then:

$$E(Y_i / D_{1i} = 0) = \beta_0 \tag{A.3.3.2}$$

and

$$E(Y_i / D_{1i} = 1) = \beta_0 + \beta_1 \tag{A.3.3.3}$$

Here β_0 is the intercept for females, which represents the average salary for females; $\beta_0 + \beta_1$ is the intercept for males, which captures the average salary for males; and β_1 is the intercept differential, which indicates whether females are discriminated against ($\beta_1 > 0$) or not ($\beta_1 < 0$). To the best of our knowledge this straightforward interpretation would not be available with another pair of values (e.g., 3-4) for dummy variables.

Answer 3.4

a) Rewrite Equation (Q3.4.1):

$$Y_i = \beta_0 + \beta_1 D_{1i} + e_i \tag{A3.4.1}$$

The residual sum of squares (RSS) from Equation (A3.4.1) is given by:

$$\text{RSS} = \sum \hat{e}_i^2 = \sum \left(Y_i - \hat{\beta}_0 - \hat{\beta}_1 D_{1i}\right)^2$$

The first-order condition for the minimization of RSS leads to the following:

$$\begin{gathered}\frac{\partial \text{RSS}}{\partial \hat{\beta}_0} = -2\sum \left(Y_i - \hat{\beta}_0 - \hat{\beta}_1 D_{1i}\right) = 0 \\ \sum Y_i = n\hat{\beta}_0 + \hat{\beta}_1 \sum D_{1i}\end{gathered} \tag{A3.4.2}$$

$$\begin{gathered}\frac{\partial \text{RSS}}{\partial \hat{\beta}_1} = -2\sum \left(Y_i - \hat{\beta}_0 - \hat{\beta}_1 D_{1i}\right) D_{1i} = 0 \\ \sum Y_i D_{1i} = \hat{\beta}_0 \sum D_{1i} + \hat{\beta}_1 \sum D_{1i}^2\end{gathered} \tag{A3.4.3}$$

Equations (A3.4.2) and (A3.4.3) are normal equations. By Cramer's rule, we have:

$$\hat{\beta}_0 = \frac{\begin{vmatrix} \sum Y_i & \sum D_{1i} \\ \sum Y_i D_{1i} & \sum D_{1i}^2 \end{vmatrix}}{\begin{vmatrix} n & \sum D_{1i} \\ \sum D_{1i} & \sum D_{1i}^2 \end{vmatrix}} = \frac{\sum Y_i \sum D_{1i}^2 - \sum D_{1i} \sum Y_i D_{1i}}{n\sum D_{1i}^2 - \left(\sum D_{1i}\right)^2}$$

$$= \frac{n_1 \sum Y_i - n_1 \sum Y_1}{nn_1 - n_1^2} = \frac{n_1\left(\sum Y_i - \sum Y_1\right)}{nn_1 - n_1^2}$$

$$= \frac{\sum Y_i - \sum Y_1}{n - n_1} = \frac{\sum Y_0}{n_0} = \bar{Y}_0 \qquad \text{QED} \qquad \text{(A3.4.4)}$$

where n is the overall size of the sample ($n = n_1 + n_0$), n_1 is the size of the elements that have value 1 in D_{1i}, n_0 is the size of the elements that have value 0 in D_{1i}, Y_1 is Y_i corresponding to elements with value 1 in D_{1i}, and Y_0 is Y_i corresponding to elements with value 0 in D_{1i}. Similarly, the estimator $\hat{\beta}_1$ is given by (see also Mukherjee et al., 1998, 300–301):

$$\hat{\beta}_1 = \frac{\begin{vmatrix} n & \sum Y_i \\ \sum D_{1i} & \sum Y_i D_{1i} \end{vmatrix}}{\begin{vmatrix} n & \sum D_{1i} \\ \sum D_{1i} & \sum D_{1i}^2 \end{vmatrix}} = \frac{n\sum Y_i D_{1i} - \sum Y_i \sum D_{1i}}{n\sum D_{1i}^2 - \left(\sum D_{1i}\right)^2}$$

$$= \frac{n\sum Y_1 - n_1 \sum Y_i}{nn_1 - n_1^2} = \frac{(n_1 + n_0)\sum Y_1 - n_1 \sum (Y_1 + Y_0)}{n_1(n - n_1)}$$

$$= \frac{n_1 \sum Y_1 + n_0 \sum Y_1 - n_1 \sum Y_1 - n_1 \sum Y_0}{n_1 n_0}$$

$$= \bar{Y}_1 - \bar{Y}_0 \qquad \text{QED} \qquad \text{(A3.4.5)}$$

Alternative Method

Rewrite the model as:

$$Y = X\beta + e \qquad \text{(A3.4.6)}$$

with $X = [\delta\ D_{1i}]$, $\beta = [\beta_0\ \beta_1]'$ and $\delta = (1\ 1\ 1\ \ldots\ 1)'$. The RSS is:

$$\begin{aligned}\text{RSS} &= \left(Y - X\hat{\beta}\right)'\left(Y - X\hat{\beta}\right)\\ &= Y'Y - \hat{\beta}'X'Y - YX\hat{\beta} + \hat{\beta}'X'X\hat{\beta}\\ &= Y'Y - 2\hat{\beta}'X'Y + \hat{\beta}'X'X\hat{\beta}\end{aligned}$$

The first-order condition leads to:

$$\frac{\partial \text{RSS}}{\partial \hat{\beta}} = -2X'Y + 2\left(X'X\right)\hat{\beta} = 0$$

Thus:

$$\hat{\beta} = \left(X'X\right)^{-1} X'Y$$

Without loss of generality we can write:

$$X' = \begin{pmatrix} 1 & 1 & 1 & \cdots & 1 & 1 & \cdots & \cdots & \cdots & \cdots & 1 \\ 1 & 1 & 1 & \cdots & 1 & 0 & \cdots & \cdots & \cdots & \cdots & 0 \end{pmatrix}$$

Thus:

$$\left(X'X\right)^{-1} = \begin{pmatrix} n & n_1 \\ n_1 & n_1 \end{pmatrix}^{-1} = \frac{\begin{pmatrix} n_1 & -n_1 \\ -n_1 & n \end{pmatrix}}{nn_1 - n_1^2} \tag{A3.4.7}$$

and

$$X'Y = \begin{pmatrix} \sum Y_i \\ \sum Y_1 \end{pmatrix} \tag{A3.4.8}$$

Equations (A3.4.7) and (A3.4.8) give the following:

$$\begin{aligned}\left(X'X\right)^{-1} X'Y &= \frac{\begin{pmatrix} n_1 & -n_1 \\ -n_1 & n \end{pmatrix}}{nn_1 - n_1^2}\begin{pmatrix} \sum Y_i \\ \sum Y_1 \end{pmatrix}\\ &= \begin{pmatrix} \dfrac{n_1 \sum Y_i - n_1 \sum Y_1}{nn_1 - n_1^2} \\ \dfrac{-n_1 \sum Y_i + n \sum Y_1}{nn_1 - n_1^2} \end{pmatrix}\end{aligned}$$

Thus:

$$\hat{\beta}_0 = \frac{n_1\sum Y_i - n_1\sum Y_1}{nn_1 - n_1^2} = \frac{\sum Y_i - \sum Y_1}{n - n_1} = \frac{\sum Y_0}{n_0} = \bar{Y}_0$$

$$\hat{\beta}_1 = \frac{-n_1\sum Y_i + n\sum Y_1}{nn_1 - n_1^2} = \frac{-n_1\sum (Y_0 + Y_1) + n\sum Y_1}{nn_1 - n_1^2}$$

$$= \frac{-n_1\sum Y_0 - n_1\sum Y_1 + n_1\sum Y_1 + n_0\sum Y_1}{nn_1 - n_1^2}$$

$$= \frac{n_0\sum Y_1 - n_1\sum Y_0}{n_1 n_0} = \bar{Y}_1 - \bar{Y}_0 \quad \text{QED} \tag{A3.4.9}$$

b) As is well known:

$$\text{var}(\hat{\beta}) = \text{E}\left[\left(\hat{\beta} - \text{E}(\hat{\beta})\right)\left(\hat{\beta} - \text{E}(\hat{\beta})\right)'\right]$$

Recall:

$$\hat{\beta} = (X'X)^{-1} X'Y$$

Using the value of Y in the above leads to:

$$\hat{\beta} = (X'X)^{-1} X'(X\beta + u)$$

$$\hat{\beta} = \beta + (X'X)^{-1} X'u \tag{A3.4.10}$$

The expected value of the above is:

$$\text{E}(\hat{\beta}) = \beta$$

Thus:

$$\text{var}(\hat{\beta}) = \text{E}\left[(\hat{\beta} - \beta)(\hat{\beta} - \beta)'\right]$$

Equation (A3.4.10) in the above variance-covariance matrix gives rise to:

$$\text{var}(\hat{\beta}) = \text{E}\left[\left(X'X\right)^{-1} X'uu'X\left(X'X\right)^{-1}\right]$$

$$= \sigma^2\left(X'X\right)^{-1}$$

Using Equation (A3.4.7) leads to:

$$\text{var}(\hat{\beta}) = \sigma^2 \begin{pmatrix} n & n_1 \\ n_1 & n_1 \end{pmatrix}^{-1} \quad \text{(A3.4.11)}$$

c) In a simple regression of the type shown in Equation (A3.4.1) with a constant and one explanatory variable, X, it is well known that the coefficient of determination is given by:

$$r^2 = \frac{\text{ESS}}{\text{TSS}} = \frac{\hat{\beta}_1^2 \sum (X_i - \bar{X})^2}{\sum (Y_i - \bar{Y})^2} \quad \text{(A3.4.12)}$$

Here, however, the explanatory variable is D_{1i}. The latter in Equation (A3.4.12) leads to:

$$r^2 = \frac{\hat{\beta}_1^2 \sum \left(D_{1i} - \bar{D}_1\right)^2}{\sum \left(Y_i - \bar{Y}\right)^2} = \frac{\left(\bar{Y}_1 - \bar{Y}_0\right)^2 \sum \left(D_{1i} - \bar{D}_1\right)^2}{\sum \left(Y_i - \bar{Y}\right)^2} \quad \text{since} \quad \hat{\beta}_1 = \bar{Y}_1 - \bar{Y}_0$$

$$= \frac{\left(\bar{Y}_1 - \bar{Y}_0\right)^2 \sum \left(D_{1i}^2 - 2D_{1i}\bar{D}_1 + \bar{D}_1^2\right)}{\sum \left(Y_i - \bar{Y}\right)^2}$$

since $\sum D_{1i} = n_1$ and $\bar{D}_1 = \dfrac{n_1}{n}$

$$r^2 = \frac{\left(\bar{Y}_1 - \bar{Y}_0\right)^2 \left(n_1 - n\left(\frac{n_1}{n}\right)^2\right)}{\sum \left(Y_i - \bar{Y}\right)^2}$$

Since $n_1 - n\left(\frac{n_1}{n}\right)^2 = n_1\left(1-\frac{n_1}{n}\right) = n_1\left(\frac{n-n_1}{n}\right) = \frac{n_1 n_0}{n}$

$$r^2 = \frac{n_1 n_0}{n} \frac{\left(\bar{Y}_1 - \bar{Y}_0\right)^2}{\sum\left(Y_i - \bar{Y}\right)^2} \tag{A3.4.13}$$

Answer 3.5

The five models are equivalent since the following holds:

$$a_1 = \alpha_0 + \alpha_1 = \delta_0 + \delta_1 = \gamma_0 = \beta_0 + \beta_1$$

$$a_2 = \alpha_0 + \alpha_2 = \delta_0 = \gamma_0 + \gamma_2 = \beta_0 + \beta_2$$

$$a_3 = \alpha_0 = \delta_0 + \delta_3 = \gamma_0 + \gamma_3 = \beta_0 + \beta_3$$

$$a_4 = \alpha_0 + \alpha_4 = \delta_0 + \delta_4 = \gamma_0 + \gamma_4 = \beta_0$$

Answer 3.6

a) The model attempts to address the issue of structural change (or structural stability).

b) By testing jointly the significance of parameters we can make a statement about the overall regression stability. The null hypothesis of interest in Equation (Q3.6.1) is $H_0 : \beta_2 = \beta_3 = 0$. The alternative is that at least one of the two values for β is different from zero. The test of interest is the Chow F test:

$$F = \frac{(\text{RRSS} - \text{URSS})/q}{\text{URSS}/(T-k)} \tag{A3.6.1}$$

where RRSS stands for the restricted residual sum of squares from the regression modelled in Equation (Q3.6.1) without the dummy and URSS is the unrestricted residual sum of squares from Equation (Q3.6.1), k is the number of parameters in Equation (Q3.6.1) and q is the number of restrictions. It is well known that the F distribution is characterized by two sets of degrees of freedom: the numerator, which is the number of restrictions (here 2), and the denominator, captured by the difference between the number of observations and the number of parameters (T – 4 here). If F calculated is greater than F of table, we reject the null hypothesis; otherwise, we do not reject it. In the case of rejection of the null hypothesis, testing of individual parameters informs us about the origin of regression instability.

c) This methodology is advantageous compared to the Chow methodology per se, which consists in dividing Equation (Q3.6.1) into two regressions: Equation (Q3.6.1) related to the first period (T_1) and Equation (Q3.6.1) related to the second period (T_2), and testing for structural stability using the above Chow test. The advantage of the dummy variable method is that in the case where the null hypothesis is rejected, it enables us to tell whether only the intercepts are different, only the slopes are different or both intercepts and slopes are different. In many instances, the *t* test statistic is of great help.

d) The key assumption, as for the Chow methodology, is that the variance must remain constant in the two scenarios (restricted and unrestricted regressions).

Answer 3.7

a) The question does not make sense. Indeed, D_i being a dummy variable, it cannot be increased by one unit.
b) The correct question should read as follows: "Can we say that, holding X_i constant, the mean value of Y_i increases (decreases) by β_3 for the group that has the characteristic compared to that which does not?"
c) Yes, holding X_i constant, the mean value of Y_i is higher (lower) by β_3 for the entity that has the characteristic compared to one that does not. An alternative way of answering the question is, holding X_i constant, the mean value of the entity that does have the characteristic is $\beta_1 + \beta_3$.

Answer 3.8

a) In the first step, we run the original regression to obtain $\hat{u}_t^2$. In the second step, we run the following auxiliary regression:

$$\hat{u}_t^2 = \beta_0 + \beta_1 D_1 + \beta_2 X_t + \beta_3 Z_t + \beta_4 X_t^2 + \beta_2 Z_t^2$$
$$+ \beta_6 D_1 X_t + \beta_7 D_1 Z_t + \beta_8 X_t Z_t + v_t$$

It is worth noting that $D_1^2 = D_1$. In the third step, we form $nR^2 \sim \chi_p^2$, where p is the number of regressors in the above regression; for example, here p = 8. If $nR^2 > \chi_p^2$, we reject the H_0; that is, there is heteroscedasticity; otherwise, there is none.

b) The White's test is about misspecification in this situation.
c) We can use the Newey–West heteroscedasticity-autocorrelation covariance matrix to obtain robust standard errors, at least in large samples.

Answer 3.9

a) The model can be written as follows:

$$HE_i = \alpha + \alpha_1 R_i + \alpha_2 Y_i + \beta_2 (Y_i D_{2i}) + \beta_3 (Y_i D_{3i}) + u_i \qquad \text{(A3.9.1)}$$

where *HE* stands for individual health care expenditure; *R* is a dummy variable for race, with value 1 for white and 0 for others; *Y* stands for income; D_2 is a dummy variable, with value 1 for secondary education level and 0 for others; D_3 is a dummy variable, with value 1 for tertiary education level and 0 for others; $i = 1, 2, \ldots, n$ stands for individuals; and *u* is the error term.

b) An F test (restricted versus unrestricted) can be implemented to test the null hypothesis, $\beta_2 = \beta_3 = 0$. Note that Equation (A3.9.1.) is the unrestricted regression with URSS as the unrestricted residual sum of squares. Subsequently, Equation (A3.9.1) without the terms (Y_iD_{2i}) and (Y_iD_{3i}) is the restricted regression with RRSS as the restricted residual sum of squares. The F test statistic is thus:

$$F = \frac{\left(\text{RRSS} - \text{URSS}\right)/q}{\text{URSS}/df} \qquad \text{(A3.9.2)}$$

where URSS and RRSS are defined as above, q is the number of constraints or restrictions, df is the degrees of freedom of the unrestricted regression (number of observations minus number of parameters). If $F > F_{df}^{q}$ we reject the null hypothesis; otherwise we do not reject it. Note here $q = 2$.

c) The model is now:

$$HE_i = \alpha + \alpha_1 R_i + \alpha_2 Y_i + \gamma_2 D_{2i} + \gamma_3 D_{3i} + \beta_2 (Y_i D_{2i}) + \beta_3 (Y_i D_{3i}) + u_i \quad \text{(A3.9.3)}$$

where variables are defined as above.

d) Testing proceeds as in (b), except that the null hypothesis is:

$$\alpha_1 = \gamma_2 = \gamma_3 = \beta_2 = \beta_3 = 0.$$

Answer 3.10 (Answer adapted from Van Garderen and Shah, 2002.)

a) The interpretation given above is only correct for a continuous variable. In Equation (Q3.10.1), D_i is a dummy variable, that is, it is a discrete variable. In this context γ represents the discontinuous impact of the presence of the characteristic captured by the dummy variable (see Halvorsen and Palmquist, 1980, 474).

b) In the case of a discrete variable, such as a dummy variable, the percentage change is $H = 100(Y_1 - Y_0)/Y_0$, which is different from 100γ. Note that Y_1 represents values of Y for $D_i = 1$ and similarly, Y_0 is values of Y for $D_i = 0$. To be more explicit, it is known that

$$\begin{aligned}(Y_1 - Y_0)/Y_0 &= (Y_1/Y_0) - 1\\ &= \exp\{\beta_1 + \beta_2 X_i + \gamma.1 + u_i\}/\exp\{\beta_1 + \beta_2 X_i + \gamma.0 + u_i\} - 1\\ &= \exp\{\gamma\} - 1.\end{aligned}$$

The percentage H derived by Halvorsen and Palmquist (1980) is given by:

$$H = 100\,(\exp\{\gamma\} - 1). \qquad \text{(A3.10.1)}$$

Note that the parameter γ in Equation (A3.10.1) needs to be estimated. Kennedy (1981) showed that a good approximation of the above percentage is:

$$\hat{H} = 100\,(\exp\{\hat{\gamma} - (1/2)V(\hat{\gamma})\} - 1) \qquad \text{(A3.10.2)}$$

instead of Halvorsen and Palmquist's (1980) estimator:

$$\hat{H} = 100\,(\exp\{\hat{\gamma}\} - 1) \qquad \text{(A3.10.3)}$$

where $V(\hat{\gamma})$ is the OLS estimate of the variance of $\hat{\gamma}$. Van Garderen and Shah (2002) pointed out that Equation (A3.10.2), while improving on Halvorsen and Palmquist's (1980) estimator [Equation (A3.10.3)], is still biased. According to Van Garderen and Shah (2002), the exact minimum variance unbiased estimator of the percentage change in Y due to the dummy variable change from 0 to 1 is given by:

$$\hat{H} = 100\{\exp(\hat{\gamma})\ {}_0F_1(r; -\frac{1}{2} rV(\hat{\gamma})) - 1\} \qquad \text{(A3.10.4)}$$

where $r = (n - k)/2$, n is the sample size, k is the number of regressors and ${}_0F_1$ is the hypergeometric function. For example,

$$\left({}_0F_1(r;z) = \sum_{s=0}^{\infty} \frac{z^s}{s!(r)_s} \right) \quad \text{with} \quad (r)_s = r(r+1)\cdots(r+s-1).$$

The exact minimum variance unbiased estimator of the variance is given by:

$$V(\hat{H}) = 100^2 \exp(2\hat{\gamma})\{[{}_0F_1(r; -\frac{1}{2} rV(\hat{\gamma}))]^2 - {}_0F_1(r; -2rV(\hat{\gamma}))\} \qquad \text{(A3.10.5)}$$

A good approximation to Equation (A3.10.5) is:

$$V(\hat{H}) = 100^2 \exp\{2\hat{\gamma}\}[\exp\{-V(\hat{\gamma})\} - \exp\{-2V(\hat{\gamma})\}] \qquad \text{(A3.10.6)}$$

Monte Carlo simulations in Van Garderen and Shah (2002) indicate that in empirical work the Kennedy estimator [see Equation (A3.10.2)] and the variance, such as Equation (A3.10.6), can be used because their biases are negligible.

Answer 3.11

a) The model is called a probability linear model because $E(Y_i/X_i)$ can be given a probability interpretation to the extent that $P(Y_i = 1/X_i) = E(Y_i/X_i)$. To explain better, let P_i be the probability that an event i occurs ($Y_i = 1$) and $(1 - P_i)$ the probability that the event does not occur ($Y_i = 0$), thus:

$$E(Y_i) = P_i(1) + (1 - P_i)(0) = P_i$$

or

$$E(Y_i / X_i) = \alpha + \beta X_i = P_i$$

b) The three problems are the following: non-normality of disturbances, heteroscedastic disturbances and lack of guarantee that $0 \leq E(Y_i/X_i) \leq 1$.

The lack of normality results from the fact that Y_i can only have two values, either one or zero. Hence, the disturbances are also binary; that is, they follow a binomial distribution. Naturally, if the objective of the exercise is simply estimation, then the above has no bearing on the outcome of estimation. Moreover, in large samples, the central limit theory can be advocated to justify OLS since the estimators will be normally distributed.

The disturbances are heteroscedastic since the variance depends on the conditional expectation of Y_i which is a function of X_i:

$$\text{var}(u_i) = P_i(1 - P_i) = E(Y_i / X_i)(1 - E(Y_i / X_i))$$

The third problem is a major problem. Indeed, there is "no guarantee" that the estimated values of Y_i, $\hat{Y}_i$, will be confined within the interval 0–1.

c) As said above, lack of normality is irrelevant if the objective of the exercise is simply to obtain the estimates. If hypothesis testing or obtaining confidence intervals is of interest, then enlarging the sample size (if small) helps get around the problem of lack of normality of disturbances to the extent that the central limit theory can be used to justify the transition of binomial disturbances into normal disturbances.

The issue of heteroscedastic disturbances can be resolved by using the weighted least squares estimation method. There are two types of solutions for the lack of fulfilment of $0 \leq E(Y_i/X_i) \leq 1$. The first solution consists simply of transforming the negative values of Y_i into zero and the values of Y_i above one into one. The second set of solutions consists of using appropriate models which guarantee that $0 \leq E(Y_i/X_i) \leq 1$. Two such models are the logit model and the probit model.

Answer 3.12

a) The first derivative comes from the linear probability model; for example,

$$Y_i = X_i\beta + u_i \qquad \text{(A3.12.1)}$$

where $Y_i = 1$ if the characteristic is present and $Y_i = 0$ if not.

The second derivative comes from the following type of model:

$$Y_i^* = X_i\beta + u_i \tag{A3.12.2}$$

where Y^* is a latent variable which follows the law:

$$Y = 1 \text{ if } Y^* > 0$$

$$Y = 0 \text{ otherwise}$$

If u_i follows a normal distribution, then the derivative (Q3.12.2) is from Equation (A3.12.2).

The third derivative also comes from Equation (A3.12.2) but with u_i following a logistic distribution.

b) The derivative (Q3.12.1) represents the marginal effect of a variable X_{i1} on the predicted value of Y_i (probability of belonging to a given group). The derivative is constant. Its major drawback is that it is incapable of capturing the nonlinear relations between Y_i and X_i so common in probability models.

The derivatives (Q3.12.2) and (Q3.12.3) also represent the marginal effects of a variable X_{i1} on the predicted value of Y_i. These derivatives, however, vary with the values of X_{i1}. To restrict variability they are computed at the means or some relevant values. Note that with respect to (Q3.12.1) the parameters are not marginal effects here.

Answer 3.13

a) Equation (Q3.13.1) represents a logit model. This is so since in the model below u_i follows a logistic distribution:

$$Y_i = \gamma + \delta X_i + u_i \tag{A3.13.1}$$

where

$$Y_i = \begin{cases} 1 & \text{if } \; Y_i^* > 0 \\ 0 & \text{otherwise} \end{cases}$$

Y^* is a latent variable and X is the explanatory variable. Put differently, if u_i follows a logistic distribution in Equation (A3.13.1) then P_i, the probability of success, is given by

$$P_i = \frac{\exp\{\gamma + \delta X_i\}}{1 + \exp\{\gamma + \delta X_i\}} \quad \text{(see details below).}$$

b) Model (A3.13.1) is of interest here with $Y_i = 1$ if a student is successful and 0 if not, X_i is a dummy variable that represents nationality: 1 if a local student and 0 if a foreign student. As is well known, the likelihood function of Equation (A3.13.1) is given by:

$$\begin{aligned} L &= \prod_{Y_i=1} P_i \prod_{Y_i=0} (1-P_i) \\ &= \prod_{Y_i=1} \left[1-F(-\gamma-\delta X_i)\right] \prod_{Y_i=0} F(-\gamma-\delta X_i) \end{aligned} \tag{A3.13.2}$$

where F is the cumulative distribution function of u, and P_i is the probability of success.

If the cumulative distribution function of u is the logistic distribution, then:

$$F(-\gamma-\delta X_i) = \frac{\exp(-\gamma-\delta X_i)}{1+\exp(-\gamma-\delta X_i)} = \frac{1}{1+\exp(\gamma+\delta X_i)}$$

and

$$1-F(-\gamma-\delta X_i) = \frac{\exp(\gamma+\delta X_i)}{1+\exp(\gamma+\delta X_i)}$$

Thus, the likelihood can be written as:

$$\begin{aligned} L &= \prod_{i=1}^{n} \left(\frac{1}{1+\exp(\gamma+\delta X_i)}\right)^{1-Y_i} \left(\frac{\exp(\gamma+\delta X_i)}{1+\exp(\gamma+\delta X_i)}\right)^{Y_i} \\ &= \frac{\exp\left(\gamma \sum Y_i + \delta \sum X_i Y_i\right)}{\prod_{i=1}^{n} \left[1+\exp(\gamma+\delta X_i)\right]} \end{aligned} \tag{A3.13.3}$$

Since $\delta = 0$, Equation (A3.13.3) becomes:

$$L = \frac{\exp\left(\gamma \sum Y_i\right)}{\prod_{i=1}^{n} \left[1+\exp(\gamma)\right]} \tag{A3.13.4}$$

The log likelihood of Equation (A3.13.4) is:

$$\log L = \gamma \sum_{i=1}^{n} Y_i - \sum_{i=1}^{n} \ln\left[1+\exp(\gamma)\right] \tag{A3.13.5}$$

Maximization of Equation (A3.13.5) with respect to γ gives:

$$\frac{\partial LogL}{\partial \gamma} = \sum_{i=1}^{n} Y_i - \sum_{i=1}^{n} \frac{\exp(\gamma)}{1+\exp(\gamma)} = 0 \tag{A3.13.6}$$

This gives:

$$\sum_{i=1}^{n} Y_i = \sum_{i=1}^{n} \frac{\exp(\hat{\gamma})}{1+\exp(\hat{\gamma})} \tag{A3.13.7}$$

Let us define the predicted probability as:

$$\hat{P}_i = \frac{\exp(\hat{\gamma})}{1+\exp(\hat{\gamma})} \tag{A3.13.8}$$

Thus, Equations (A3.13.7) and (A3.13.6) point out that predicted frequency is equal to actual frequency, that is,

$$\sum_{i=1}^{n} Y_i / n = n_1 / n \tag{A3.13.9}$$

where n_1 is the size of $Y_i = 1$. Hence,

$$\hat{P}_i = \frac{55}{100}$$

is the probability that a student will be successful in the econometrics final examination.

c) Computation of MLE of γ and δ. Using the framework laid out above, the likelihood is:

$$L = \left[e^{\gamma}/\left(1+e^{\gamma}\right)\right]^{20} \left(1+e^{\gamma}\right)^{-25} \left[e^{\gamma+\delta}/\left(1+e^{\gamma+\delta}\right)\right]^{20} \left(1+e^{\gamma+\delta}\right)^{-35} \tag{A3.13.10}$$

The log likelihood is:

$$\log L = 20\left[\gamma - \ln\left(1+\exp\gamma\right)\right] - 25\ln\left(1+\exp\left(\gamma\right)\right)$$
$$+20\left[\left(\gamma+\delta\right) - \ln\left(1+\exp(\gamma+\delta)\right)\right] - 35\ln\left(1+\exp\left(\gamma+\delta\right)\right)$$

or

$$LogL = 40\gamma + 20\delta - 20\ln\left(1+\exp\left(\gamma\right)\right) - 25\ln\left(1+\exp\left(\gamma\right)\right)$$
$$-20\ln\left(1+\exp\left(\gamma+\delta\right)\right) - 35\ln\left(1+\exp\left(\gamma+\delta\right)\right)$$
$$= 40\gamma + 20\delta - 45\ln\left(1+\exp\left(\gamma\right)\right) - 55\ln\left(1+\exp\left(\gamma+\delta\right)\right)$$

Maximization of Log L gives:

$$\frac{\partial LogL}{d\gamma} = 40 - 45\frac{\exp\left(\gamma\right)}{1+\exp\left(\gamma\right)} - 55\frac{\exp\left(\gamma+\delta\right)}{1+\exp\left(\gamma+\delta\right)} = 0 \qquad \text{(A3.13.11)}$$

$$\frac{\partial LogL}{d\delta} = 20 - 55\frac{\exp\left(\gamma+\delta\right)}{1+\exp\left(\gamma+\delta\right)} = 0 \qquad \text{(A3.13.12)}$$

From Equation (A3.13.12), it can be deduced that:

$$\frac{\exp\left(\hat{\gamma}+\hat{\delta}\right)}{1+\exp\left(\hat{\gamma}+\hat{\delta}\right)} = \frac{20}{55} \qquad \text{(A3.13.13)}$$

Equation (A3.13.13) into Equation (A3.13.11) gives:

$$40 - 45\frac{\exp\left(\hat{\gamma}\right)}{1+\exp\left(\hat{\gamma}\right)} - 20 = 0$$

$$\frac{\exp\left(\hat{\gamma}\right)}{1+\exp\left(\hat{\gamma}\right)} = \frac{20}{45} = \frac{4}{9}$$

That is:

$$\exp(\hat{\gamma}) = \frac{4}{9}\left(1 + \exp(\hat{\gamma})\right)$$

or

$$\frac{5}{9}\exp(\hat{\gamma}) = \frac{4}{9}$$

That is:

$$\hat{\gamma} = \ln\left(\frac{4}{5}\right) \tag{A3.13.14}$$

Let us expand Equation (A3.13.13):

$$55\exp\left(\hat{\gamma} + \hat{\delta}\right) = 20\left(1 + \exp\left(\hat{\gamma} + \hat{\delta}\right)\right)$$

or

$$35\exp\left(\hat{\gamma} + \hat{\delta}\right) = 20$$

That is:

$$35\exp(\hat{\gamma})\exp\left(\hat{\delta}\right) = 20 \tag{A3.13.15}$$

Use Equation (A3.13.14) in Equation (A3.13.15):

$$35\,\frac{4}{5}\exp\left(\hat{\delta}\right) = 20$$

$$\exp\left(\hat{\delta}\right) = \frac{20}{28} = \frac{5}{7}$$

$$\hat{\delta} = \ln\left(\frac{5}{7}\right) \tag{A3.13.16}$$

Thus, the MLEs of γ and δ are

$$\hat{\gamma} = \ln\left(\frac{4}{5}\right) \text{ and } \hat{\delta} = \ln\left(\frac{5}{7}\right), \text{ respectively.}$$

TABLE 3.7
Cruise Ship Passenger Arrivals Regression Results:
Barbados 1977–2002, the Trend Model

Variable	Coefficient	Standard Error	t Statistic	Prob.
C	25509.85	34796.16	0.733123	0.4706
Tr	21224.19	1928.454	11.00581	0.0000
R^2	0.898176	Mean dependent variable		312036.5
Adjusted R^2	0.893934	SD dependent variable		171288.6
SE of regression	55784.98	Akaike information criterion		24.77020
RSS	7.47E+10	Schwarz criterion		24.86698
Log likelihood	–320.0126	F statistic		211.7014
DW statistic	0.427232	Prob(F statistic)		0.000000

Note: Dependent variable is cruise ship passenger arrivals; *Tr* stands for trend. Regression is corrected for autocorrelation with the Newey–West HAC.

TABLE 3.8
Cruise Ship Passenger Arrivals Regression Results:
Barbados 1977–2002, the Dummy Variable D_1 Case

Variable	Coefficient	Standard Error	t Statistic	Prob.
C	165155.9	58776.88	2.809879	0.0099
T	14422.56	2787.605	5.173818	0.0000
D_1	–124342.4	46649.62	–2.665453	0.0138
R^2	0.935649	Mean dependent variable		312036.5
Adjusted R^2	0.930054	SD dependent variable		171288.6
SE of regression	45301.34	Akaike information criterion		24.38823
RSS	4.72E+10	Schwarz criterion		24.53339
Log likelihood	–314.0470	F statistic		167.2083
DW statistic	0.653686	Prob(F statistic)		0.000000

Note: Dependent variable is cruise ship passenger arrivals. Regression is corrected for autocorrelation using the Newey–West HAC. D_1 is a dummy variable: 1 for each year in the period 1977–1986 and 0 for each year of the period 1987–2002.

Answer 3.14

a) The OLS results for the linear trend model are presented in Table 3.7. The results indicate that over the period 1977–2002 on average the number of cruise ship passenger arrivals increased at the absolute rate of 21,224 arrivals per year. Note that the trend explains about 90 percent of the variation in cruise ship passenger arrivals.
b) The dummy-trend regression produces the results presented in Table 3.8. As can be seen, cruise ship passenger arrivals have increased over time. Over the period 1977–2002, on average, the number of cruise ship passenger

TABLE 3.9
Cruise Ship Passenger Arrivals Regression Results: Barbados 1977–2002, the Dummy Variable D_2 Case

Variable	Coefficient	Standard Error	t Statistic	Prob.
C	102984.7	40057.12	2.570947	0.0171
Tr	14422.56	2787.605	5.173818	0.0000
D_2	–62171.19	23324.81	–2.665453	0.0138
R^2	0.935649	Mean dependent variable		312036.5
Adjusted R^2	0.930054	SD dependent variable		171288.6
SE of regression	45301.34	Akaike information criterion		24.38823
RSS	4.72E+10	Schwarz criterion		24.53339
Log likelihood	–314.0470	F statistic		167.2083
DW statistic	0.653686	Prob(F statistic)		0.000000

Note: Dependent variable: cruise ship passenger arrivals; D_2 is a dummy variable with 1 for the period 1977–1986 and –1 for 1987–2002. Regression corrected for autocorrelation using the Newey–West HAC.

arrivals increased at the absolute rate of 14,423 per year, holding other factors constant. That is, there was an upward trend. However, there was a difference in average arrivals between the first period (1977–1986) and the second period (1987–2002). Indeed, while the yearly average of cruise ship passenger arrivals is 165,156 + 14,423 arrivals in the second period, in the first period it is 124,342 arrivals less than in the second period. Put differently, holding the trend constant, the yearly average number of arrivals is 40,814 and 165,156 in the first and second periods, respectively.

c) Table 3.9 gives the results of the model above but with a different dummy variable configuration. To repeat here, D_2 takes on value 1 for the observations 1977–1986 and –1 for the observations 1987–2002. Table 3.9 conveys the same message as Table 3.8. Indeed, as for the latter table, holding the trend constant, the annual average of cruise ship passenger arrivals in the first period is 102,985 – 62,171 = 40,814 arrivals; in the second period, it is 102,985 – 62,171*(–1) = 165,156 arrivals. Holding other factors constant, on average the absolute rate of increase of cruise ship passenger arrivals is 14,423 arrivals per year.

d) Table 3.10 shows the results of the trend-dummy model but with a dummy defined as follows: D_3 takes on value 2 for the observations 1977–1986 and 0 for the observations 1987–2002. As for the previous cases, controlling for the trend the yearly mean of arrivals is 165,155.9 – 2* 62,171.19 = 40,814 arrivals in the first period and 165,156 arrivals in the second period. As can be seen the three cases combined indicate that the value assigned to the dichotomous variable does not matter at all. However, in our view, preference is given to the 0-1 dummy since it gives rise to a straightforward interpretation of results.

e) We test the structural stability using a dummy-variable approach with the following regression:

TABLE 3.10
Cruise Ship Passenger Arrivals Regression Results: Barbados 1977–2002, the Dummy Variable D_3 Case

Variable	Coefficient	Standard Error	t Statistic	Prob.
C	165155.9	58776.88	2.809879	0.0099
Tr	14422.56	2787.605	5.173818	0.0000
D_3	–62171.19	23324.81	–2.665453	0.0138
R^2	0.935649	Mean dependent variable		312036.5
Adjusted R^2	0.930054	SD dependent variable		171288.6
SE of regression	45301.34	Akaike information criterion		24.38823
RSS	4.72E+10	Schwarz criterion		24.53339
Log likelihood	–314.0470	F statistic		167.2083
DW statistic	0.653686	Prob(F statistic)		0.000000

Note: Dependent variable: cruise ship passenger arrivals; D_3 is a dummy variable with 2 for the period 1977–1986 and 0 for 1987–2002. Regression corrected for autocorrelation using the Newey–West HAC.

$$Y_t = \beta_0 + \beta_1 D_1 + \gamma Tr + \beta_2 (D_1 Tr) + u_i \qquad \text{(A3.14.1)}$$

where Y is cruise ship passenger arrivals, $(D_1 Tr)$ is the interaction term and other variables are defined as above. The lack of change of structure is tested using the null hypothesis $H_0 : \beta_1 = \beta_2 = 0$.

The regression (A3.14.1) gives rise to the results shown in Table 3.11. Neither autocorrelation nor heteroscedasticity is present, as the relevant statistics in the table indicate. The F test for $H_0 : \beta_1 = \beta_2 = 0$ with a value of 19.85 and an associated p value of 0.0000 clearly indicates the reject of the null hypothesis; that is, there exists a structural change in the cruise ship passenger arrivals pattern. The question of whether this structural change originates from the intercept alone or the slope or both is answered by looking at the individual t statistics of interest. The latter reveals that only the slope is changing. Note also that this regression dominates the previous ones using the basic statistics for comparison ($\bar{R}^2$, Akaike information criterion, Schwarz information criterion).

Answer 3.15

a) Deterministic seasonality can be analysed through the behaviour of the dummy variables D_1 through D_{11} in Table 3.12. The latter table reveals that none of the dummy coefficients is significant at the 5 or 10 percent levels of significance. This means that deterministic seasonality is not present in the crime pattern in the Turks and Caicos Islands. The more formal F test (restricted versus unrestricted) with a value of 0.422 confirms the above finding with a p value of 0.9358. The regression is, however, problematic, since the adjusted R^2 is negative. That is, there is a need to revisit the specification. That is exactly what is implicitly done in the next item.

TABLE 3.11
Structural Change, Cruise Ship Passenger Arrivals Regression Results: Barbados 1977–2002

Variable	Coefficient	Standard Error	*t* Statistic	Prob.
C	101571.6	35975.28	2.823373	0.0099
D_1	17146.97	43117.80	0.397677	0.6947
T	17859.55	1886.913	9.464953	0.0000
$D_1{*}T$	–17601.55	4270.103	–4.122043	0.0004
R^2	0.963691	Mean dependent variable		312036.5
Adjusted R^2	0.958740	SD dependent variable		171288.6
SE of regression	34792.96	Akaike information criterion		23.89286
RSS	2.66E+10	Schwarz criterion		24.08641
Log likelihood	–306.6071	*F* statistic		194.6393
DW statistic	1.341916	Prob(*F* statistic)		0.000000
Breusch–Godfrey Serial Correlation LM Test (2 lags)				
F statistic	1.057259	Probability		0.366037
Observed*R^2	2.486035	Probability		0.288512
White Heteroscedasticity Test				
F statistic	0.716601	Probability		0.618406
Observed*R^2	3.950222	Probability		0.556605
Wald Test				
Null Hypothesis	$\beta_1 = 0 \quad \beta_2 = 0$			
F statistic	19.84842	Probability		0.000012
Chi-square	39.6984	Probability		0.000000

b) Table 3.13 presents the results without seasonal dummies. As can be seen, D_{outlier}, a dummy variable with value 1 in 1998:01 and 0 elsewhere, is an outlier. Indeed, its associated coefficient is significant. Moreover, the model with the results presented in this table is superior to the previous one. Indeed, for example, the adjusted R^2 is now positive, and the R^2 is significant, as the associated p value of the F test statistic indicates ($p <$ nominal level of significance).

c) Table 3.14 provides us with the results for computing growth rate of crime in the Turks and Caicos Islands. As can be seen, holding the outlier effect constant, the crime grew at the instantaneous rate of 100*0.0034, which is 0.34 percent per year. This translates into a compound rate of 100*(exp(0.0034)-1); that is, the crime has been increasing at a compound rate of 0.341 percent per year. Coincidentally, both rates are the same.

Answer 3.16

a) Coeff. stands for the parameter estimates of the model. They are not, however, the marginal effects. The latter are given by $\partial F / \partial X_j = \phi(X_i \beta)\beta_j$ where X_j stands for any variable, X_i is the matrix of explanatory variables, β is a vector of parameters, F is the cumulative standard normal distribution and ϕ is the standard normal density.

TABLE 3.12
Crime Regression Results:
The Turks and Caicos Islands, Seasonality Effects

Variable	Coefficient	Standard Error	*t* Statistic	Prob.
C	95.41341	12.98889	7.345770	0.0000
D_1	3.384311	16.79003	0.201567	0.8415
D_2	–7.387803	15.59888	–0.473611	0.6388
D_3	3.050978	15.56513	0.196014	0.8458
D_4	2.489758	15.53488	0.160269	0.8736
D_5	–6.821462	15.50813	–0.439864	0.6628
D_6	–14.13268	15.48491	–0.912674	0.3678
D_7	–15.44390	15.46524	–0.998620	0.3250
D_8	–10.50512	15.44913	–0.679981	0.5011
D_9	5.433659	15.43658	0.351999	0.7270
D_{10}	–0.627561	15.42762	–0.040678	0.9678
D_{11}	–0.938780	15.42223	–0.060872	0.9518
$D_{outlier}$	48.15642	25.25171	1.907056	0.0650
T	0.311220	0.235269	1.322825	0.1947

R^2	0.261646	Mean dependent variable	100.5833
Adjusted R^2	–0.020666	SD dependent variable	21.58588
SE of regression	21.80779	Akaike information criterion	9.240905
RSS	16169.72	Schwarz criterion	9.786672
Log likelihood	–207.7817	*F* statistic	0.926796
DW statistic	1.818454	Prob(*F* statistic)	0.536983

Note: Dependent variable: total crimes; the Ds are seasonal dummies; e.g., D_1 is 1 for January and 0 elsewhere; D_2 is 1 for February and 0 elsewhere; etc.; $D_{outlier}$ is a dummy with a value of 1 for 1998:01 and 0 elsewhere. T is trend.

TABLE 3.13
Crime Regression Results:
The Turks and Caicos Islands, 1997:01–2000:12

Variable	Coefficient	Standard Error	*t* Statistic	Prob.
C	91.60459	6.019712	15.21744	0.0000
$D_{outlier}$	55.24185	20.57367	2.685075	0.0101
T	0.319505	0.212111	1.506311	0.1390

R^2	0.160848	Mean dependent variable	100.5833
Adjusted R^2	0.123553	SD dependent variable	21.58588
SE of regression	20.20844	Akaike information criterion	8.910539
RSS	18377.14	Schwarz criterion	9.027489
Log likelihood	–210.8529	*F* statistic	4.312797
DW statistic	1.776337	Prob(*F* statistic)	0.019338

TABLE 3.14
Log Crime Regression Results:
The Turks and Caicos Islands 1997:01–2000:12

Variable	Coefficient	Standard Error	*t* Statistic	Prob.
C	4.496644	0.060154	74.75243	0.0000
T	0.003356	0.002120	1.583405	0.1203
D_{outlier}	0.477006	0.205589	2.320196	0.0249
R^2	0.136359	Mean dependent variable		4.588807
Adjusted R^2	0.097975	SD dependent variable		0.212623
SE of regression	0.201939	Akaike information criterion		–0.301241
RSS	1.835071	Schwarz criterion		–0.184291
Log likelihood	10.22978	F statistic		3.552480
DW statistic	1.736608	Prob(F statistic)		0.036940

b) We interpret the model (Q3.16.1) results using the marginal effects. The overall estimate of the model is significant at the $p = 0.00001$ level. Non-forest land cover declines in probability with increasing distance to roads, rivers, railways and cities. Indeed, at sample means, an increase of 1 km in distance to the road decreases the non-forest probability by 0.24 percentage points, *ceteris paribus*. Similarly, an increase of 1 km in distance to the river decreases the non-forest probability by 0.23 percentage points, *ceteris paribus*. An increase of 1 km in distance to the railways decreases the non-forest probability by 0.092 percentage points, *ceteris paribus*. An increase of 1 km in distance to the city decreases the non-forest probability by 0.09 percentage points. Soil quality index, constructed by summing the observed soil characteristics weighted by their estimated coefficients, is positively related to non-forest land cover. On average, high quality soil boosts the probability of non-forest land cover by 27 percent. This means that good soils can result in forest conversion even at considerable distances from transport corridors. (See Mamingi et al., 1996 for details.)

Answer 3.17

a) Tobit estimation is of interest here to avoid estimate bias due to zero bids. Indeed, in this case OLS estimators are biased since the error term does not have a zero mean as a result of truncation due to the use of positive values of the dependent variable only.
b) It is not presented because it is not a valid goodness of fit measure in the case at hand. Some alternatives have been proposed in the literature (see Veall and Zimmermann, 1994). It is our view that consensus has not yet emerged.
c) An examination of Table 3.6 indicates that all variables with the exception of income have impact on the willingness to pay (WTP) an additional entrance fee to Harrison's Cave at the 10 percent level of significance. Expenditure impact is counterintuitive. However, it is possible that it is a proxy for income where data quality was dubious. A Bds \$1,000 increase in expenditure leads to Bds \$0.20 increase in WTP an extra entrance fee

to Harrison's Cave. For those who are interested in caves, the average WTP an extra entrance fee is Bds \$0.17 higher than those who are not interested, holding everything else constant. The mean WTP an extra entrance fee is Bds \$0.20 higher for long-stay visitors than cruise ship visitors, *ceteris paribus*. The average WTP an extra entrance fee for those who visited Harrison's Cave is Bds \$0.20 lower than that of those who did not visit the cave, everything else being equal. The higher the level of education, the higher is the WTP an extra entrance fee to the cave. Indeed, the mean WTP an extra entrance fee of those with tertiary or graduate level education is Bds \$0.30 higher than those with at most a secondary level education, *ceteris paribus*. The constant term that captures the overall average effect of omitted variables indicates that the latter depresses WTP by Bds \$0.47. (Answer taken from Lewis and Mamingi, 2003, 43.)

3.3 SUPPLEMENTARY EXERCISES

Question 3.18 Using a dummy variable approach, provide an example of a piecewise linear regression model.

Question 3.19 Compare and contrast censored regressions and truncated regressions.

Question 3.20 It has been argued by Ai and Norton (2003) that an interaction term does not fully capture the interaction effect in a nonlinear model, such as a probit model. Comment.

Question 3.21 Should we use a Tobit model each time we have zero observations in our sample? Why or why not? (See Maddala, 1992, 345.)

Part Two

Simultaneous Equations Models

Part Two deals with simultaneous equations models, and consists of one chapter. Chapter 4 is concerned with exercises dealing with some issues related to simultaneous equations models.

Chapter 4

Simultaneous Equations Models

4.1 INTRODUCTION

One of the key assumptions of the classical linear model is that the explanatory variable(s) and the disturbances must be independent. This condition is automatically fulfilled if the explanatory variables are exogenous in the sense they are fixed or determined outside the model. In reality, however, there are at least two situations that result in a non-zero correlation between the explanatory variable(s) and the disturbances: measurement errors in explanatory variables and endogeneity due to simultaneity. The issue of measurement errors has been alluded to above. This chapter concentrates on endogeneity of explanatory variables in the context of simultaneous equations models (SEM), that is, on the situation where some explanatory variables are jointly determined with the dependent variables, most likely through an equilibrium mechanism.

To fix ideas, consider the following demand equation:

$$q_{dt} = \alpha + \beta P_t + u_t \tag{4.1.1}$$

where q_{dt} is the quantity demanded of, for example, sugar cane; P_t is the price of sugar cane; t is time and u_t is disturbances. In general, q_{dt} and P_t are determined simultaneously; that is, P_t is an endogenous variable just like q_{dt}. In other words, there is a missing equation that should be brought in. In this situation it is the supply equation:

$$q_{st} = \gamma + \delta P_t + \tau R_t + e_t \tag{4.1.2}$$

where q_{st} is the quantity supplied of sugar cane; P_t is the price of sugar cane; R_t stands for rainfall and e_t represents disturbances. In general, what we observe is equilibrium quantity and price, hence the need to add the equilibrium condition:

$$q_{dt} = q_{st} = q_t \tag{4.1.3}$$

Equations (4.1.1), (4.1.2) and (4.1.3) represent a system of simultaneous equations. The system is known as the structural form to the extent that its equations are a direct econometric translation or representation of the structure of an economy or the behaviour of an economic agent. The particularity here is that all explanatory variables are not necessarily exogenous or predetermined. Note that because of the equilibrium condition, the three-equation model can be reduced into a two-equation model. We can derive from the above a system of equations that expresses endogenous variables as a function of exogenous or predetermined variables only. This new system is called the reduced form:

$$\begin{aligned} P_t &= \pi_{11} + \pi_{12}R_t + v_{1t} \\ q_t &= \pi_{21} + \pi_{22}R_t + v_{2t} \end{aligned} \tag{4.1.4}$$

In Equation (4.1.4) the vs are the new errors and the different πs are a mixture of structural parameters; for example,

$$\pi_{11} = \frac{-\alpha + \gamma}{\beta - \delta}$$

At this juncture, the question of interest is whether one can retrieve the structural parameters from the reduced form parameters. This is the question of identification; in other words, the question of whether one can obtain "meaningful" structural parameter estimates from reduced form parameters. For identification to hold, a certain number of restrictions need to be imposed. The most popular one is the so-called zero restrictions, which means that some variables do not enter other equations. An equation can be just-identified (exactly identified), overidentified or underidentified (unidentified or not identified). In the latter case, it is impossible to recover the structural parameters from the reduced form parameters. Just-identification exists whenever numerical values of the structural parameters can be obtained uniquely. Overidentification exists if more than one value exists for some reduced form parameters. If the equation is identified, the next question is which method of estimation to apply to obtain the structural parameters. There are two sets of methods: single-equation methods and system methods. The single-equation methods include the following: ordinary least squares (OLS), indirect least squares (ILS), instrumental variables (IV), two-stage least squares (TSLS or 2SLS) and limited information maximum likelihood (LIML). The system methods include three-stage least squares (3SLS) and full information maximum likelihood (FIML). Two remarks are important. OLS is problematic, because it gives rise to biased and inconsistent estimators. Other methods produce consistent estimators. In the particular case of overidentification, an appropriate method of estimation such as the 2SLS will force the multiple estimates of a structural parameter to become unique.

The exercises below touch on some aspects of what has been discussed. Theoretical exercises will be emphasized here. The proliferation of powerful computers (and software) forces us to change focus.

4.2 QUESTIONS

4.2.1 Theoretical Exercises

Question 4.1 In the context of simultaneous equations models, carefully define the concepts of endogeneity, exogeneity and predetermined variable.

Question 4.2 What are the main issues involved with simultaneous equations models?

Question 4.3 In some situations, OLS can be validly applied in a simultaneous equations model. Discuss.

Question 4.4 Consider the following model:

$$Y_t = \beta_0 + \beta_1 Z_t + u_{1t} \tag{Q4.4.1}$$

$$X_t = \gamma_0 + \gamma_1 Y_t + \gamma_2 S_t + u_{2t} \tag{Q4.4.2}$$

where

$$u = (u_{1t}\ u_{2t})' \text{ and } \Sigma = \mathrm{E}\left(uu'\right) = \begin{pmatrix} \sigma_{11} & \sigma_{12} \\ \sigma_{21} & \sigma_{22} \end{pmatrix}$$

a) Is this system fully recursive? Why or why not?
b) Suggest an estimation method.

Question 4.5 Suppose the following system of equations:

$$y_1 = \alpha_0 + \alpha_2 y_2 + \alpha_4 x_1 + \alpha_5 x_2 + \alpha_6 x_3 + u_1$$

$$y_2 = \beta_0 + \beta_1 y_1 + \beta_4 x_1 + \beta_5 x_2 + \beta_6 x_3 + u_2$$

$$y_3 = \gamma_0 + \gamma_1 y_1 + \gamma_2 y_2 + \gamma_4 x_1 + \gamma_5 x_2 + \gamma_6 x_3 + u_3$$

where the *y*s are endogenous variables and the *x*s are predetermined variables. Assume that errors across equations are uncorrelated and individual errors are well behaved.

a) Study the identifiability of the third equation.
b) Whatever your answer to (a), carefully explain why OLS yields consistent estimators of the related structural parameters.

Question 4.6 Not all sets of equations are simultaneous. Provide an example and suggest a method of estimation.

Question 4.7 Show that in the case of a just-identified equation, the ILS and 2SLS estimates are identical.

Question 4.8 Show that when $n = k$ (number of observations equals number of predetermined variables), the 2SLS estimator reduces to the OLS estimator. What is the implication?

Question 4.9 In the context of the simultaneous equations model:

a) Explain the concept of "observational equivalence in structures or theories".
b) Compare and contrast "single-equation methods" with "system methods".

Question 4.10 Consider the following market model for sugar cane:

$$q_d = \alpha + \beta P + e_1 \tag{Q4.10.1}$$

$$q_s = \gamma + \delta P + \eta R + e_2 \tag{Q4.10.2}$$

$$q_d = q_s = q \tag{Q4.10.3}$$

where
q_d = quantity demanded
q_s = quantity supplied
P = price
R = rainfall
e = disturbances

Assume that R is predetermined or exogenous, $E(e) = 0$ with $e = (e_1, e_2)$ and $E(e_i e_j) = \sigma_{ij} I$ (the errors in the different equations are contemporaneously correlated but are independent over time).

a) Obtain the reduced form of the above system.
b) What is meant by the identification problem in simultaneous equations models? (Use this exercise to explain the concept.)
c) Using order and rank conditions, determine whether the demand function is identified.
d) Using order and rank conditions, determine whether the supply function is identified.
e) The equilibrium condition is always identified. Prove that it holds here.
f) Which method would you use to estimate the parameters of the identified equation(s)? Why?
g) Show that $\text{Cov}(Pe_1) \neq 0$. (State clearly any assumption you use.)
h) Show that the OLS estimator of β is inconsistent.
i) Suppose that we modify the demand function by adding an exogenous variable called income (Y). What happens to the identification problem? (Adapted from UWI, EC36C final examination December 2001.)

Question 4.11 Consider the following demand-and-supply model for money:

Demand for money: $$M_t^d = \beta_0 + \beta_1 Y_{1t} + \beta_2 R_t + \beta_3 P_t + u_{1t} \tag{Q4.11.1}$$

Supply of money: $$M_t^s = \gamma_0 + \gamma_1 Y_{1t} + \gamma_4 T_t + u_{2t} \tag{Q4.11.2}$$

where M_t^d is demand for money, M_t^s is money supply, Y_t is income, R_t is interest rate, P_t is price, T is trend and the u_ts are errors. Money and income are endogenous. The parameters of missing variables in a given equation have the value zero (e.g., $\beta_4 = 0$ for the variable T in the first equation).

a) Something is apparently missing in this model. What is it? Explain.
b) After taking care of the issue in (a), study the identifiability of both equations.
c) For the interest rate variable provide the following quantities:
    i) total effect on money;
    ii) direct effect on money;
    iii) indirect effect on money;
d) Study the identifiability of the system using the following restrictions:

$$\beta_2 + \beta_3 = 0, \beta_4 = 0, \ \gamma_4 = 0.$$

Question 4.12 Consider the following model:

$$\beta_{11}Y_{1t} + \beta_{12}Y_{2t} + \gamma_{11}X_{1t} + \gamma_{12}X_{2t} = u_{1t}$$

$$\beta_{21}Y_{1t} + \beta_{22}Y_{2t} + \gamma_{21}X_{1t} + \gamma_{22}X_{2t} = u_{2t}$$

where the *Y*s are endogenous variables and the *X*s exogenous variables.

Study the identifiability of each equation using the following restrictions:

a) $\beta_{11} = 1; \ \ \gamma_{11} + \gamma_{12} = 1; \ \ \beta_{22} = 1, \beta_{21} + \gamma_{21} = 1$
b) $\beta_{11} = 1; \ \ \gamma_{11} = -\gamma_{12}; \ \ \beta_{22} = 1; \ \ \gamma_{22} = 0$

Question 4.13 Consider the following model:

$$y_1 + \beta_{11}x_1 + \beta_{12}x_2 = u_1$$

$$\alpha_{21}y_1 + y_2 + \beta_{21}x_1 + \beta_{22}x_2 = u_2$$

where the *y*s are endogenous variables and the *x*s are exogenous variables.

a) With no further restrictions, study the identifiability of each equation.
b) Suppose that the variance-covariance of errors is:

$$E(uu') = \Sigma = \begin{pmatrix} \sigma_{11} & 0 \\ 0 & \sigma_{22} \end{pmatrix} \text{ where } u = \begin{pmatrix} u_1 \\ u_2 \end{pmatrix}$$

Study the identifiability of each equation. Comment on the results.

c) Redo (b) with

$$\Sigma = \begin{pmatrix} \sigma_{11} & \sigma_{12} \\ \sigma_{21} & \sigma_{22} \end{pmatrix}$$

Question 4.14 Consider the following model:

$$y_t = \gamma x_t + u_t$$

$$x_t = \delta y_t + v_t$$

where t stands for time, y_t and x_t are the variables of interest defined as deviations from their respective means, u_t and v_t are independent, normally distributed random variables each with mean zero, and with

$$Var(u_t) = \sigma_u^2, Var(v_t) = \sigma_v^2 \quad \text{and} \quad \text{cov}(u_t\, v_t) = 0$$

a) Obtain the reduced form equations.
b) Find plim $\hat{\gamma}$ where $\hat{\gamma}$ is the OLS estimator of γ.
c) Indicate and explain intuitively the conditions for consistency of $\hat{\gamma}$.
d) Suppose the second equation is replaced by:

$$x_t = \delta\, s_t + v_t$$

where s_t is an exogeneous variable. Compute plim $\hat{\gamma}$ assuming cov($u_t v_t$) = 0. (Adapted from Maddala, 1977, Exercise 11.3.)

4.2.2 Empirical Exercises

Question 4.15 Consider the following two-equation model capturing the labour market in Barbados for the period 1970–1996:

$$lblabor_t = \alpha_1 + \alpha_2 Lbwager_t + \alpha_3 Lbgdp_t + \alpha_4 Lbniscor_t + u_{1t}$$

$$lblabor_t = \beta_1 + \beta_2 Lbwager_t + \beta_3 T + \beta_4 Lbnisee_t + u_{2t}$$

where variables are logarithms of variables, defined as in Table 4.1, with the exception of the trend *T*. Use a 10 percent level of significance throughout.

The first equation of the system represents labour demand and the second, labour supply; *lblabor* and *Lbwager* are the endogenous variables of the model.

a) In this system the left-hand-side variables are the same. Why is this so?
b) Is the system complete? Why or why not?
c) What are the expected signs of the parameters of the model?

TABLE 4.1
Some Labour Statistics for Barbados, 1970–1996

Year	Blabor	Bwage	Bwager	Bgdp	Bniscor	Bnisee
1970	83.600	30.6	1.159091	627.600	85.71	100.00
1971	83.300	35.3	1.188552	629.500	100.00	100.00
1972	83.400	39.4	1.238994	637.600	100.00	100.00
1973	84.600	43.1	1.158602	654.640	100.00	100.00
1974	86.400	48.3	0.936047	640.000	100.00	100.00
1975	88.500	53.1	0.853698	627.800	100.00	100.00
1976	87.600	58.2	0.892638	655.300	100.00	100.00
1977	88.200	70.0	0.990099	679.400	101.43	100.00
1978	88.800	77.5	1.001292	712.500	101.43	100.00
1979	95.000	83.2	0.919337	768.600	100.00	100.00
1980	100.300	100.0	0.967118	802.300	100.00	100.00
1981	101.900	110.5	0.931703	786.800	141.14	158.30
1982	96.600	123.0	0.940367	748.000	185.71	216.70
1983	95.700	130.1	0.944808	751.800	228.57	266.70
1984	93.100	142.0	0.985427	778.500	228.57	266.70
1985	92.100	148.9	0.992667	786.900	217.86	250.00
1986	96.100	155.2	1.024422	827.000	217.86	250.00
1987	105.200	157.8	1.006378	848.200	257.14	325.00
1988	108.300	169.4	1.031669	877.500	257.14	325.00
1989	111.700	174.0	0.996564	909.100	257.14	325.00
1990	113.300	182.8	1.016120	879.100	257.14	325.00
1991	107.100	184.4	0.964435	844.800	275.00	370.80
1992	101.700	181.1	0.892998	796.200	339.29	416.70
1993	100.400	184.0	0.897212	802.900	307.14	341.70
1994	105.600	181.0	0.881637	834.700	253.57	266.70
1995	110.100	181.0	0.871030	858.900	253.57	266.70
1996	114.400	181.0	0.850964	903.600	253.57	266.70

Note: Blabor = Barbados labour employment in thousands; Bwage: Barbados wage index; Bwager: Barbados real wage index (bwage/consumer price index); Bgdp: Barbados gross domestic product at constant prices (Bds$ millions); Bniscor: index of contributions of employers to the national insurance scheme; Bnisee: index of contributions of employees to the national insurance scheme.

Sources: Downes, A.S. and McLean, W. (1988). The estimation of missing values of employment in Barbados, Research Paper 13, Centre of Statistics of Trinidad and Tobago, 115–35; Central Bank of Barbados, *Annual Statistical Digest*, 1998.

d) Study the identification of the model.
e) Obtain the OLS estimates of the parameters. Fully comment on the results.
f) Obtain the ILS estimates of the parameters.
g) Obtain the 2SLS estimates of the parameters. Fully comment on the results (e.g., compare these results with those obtained with OLS).
h) What are the total effect, the direct effect and the indirect effect of GDP on labour?

Question 4.16 Consider the following model for joint determination of unemployment rate, price inflation and wage inflation:

$$\pi_t = \beta_0 + \beta_1 wi_t + \beta_2 AD_t + \beta_3 T + u_{1t} \quad \text{(Q4.16.1)}$$

$$UN_t = \alpha_0 + \alpha_1 \pi_t + \alpha_2 \text{Prod}_t + u_{2t} \quad \text{(Q4.16.2)}$$

$$wi_t = \gamma_0 + \gamma_2 UN_t + \gamma_3 \pi_t + u_{3t} \quad \text{(Q4.16.3)}$$

where
UN_t = unemployment rate;
π_t = inflation rate;
wi_t = wage inflation (rate of change of wages);
$Prod_t$ = productivity defined as GDP/total employment;
AD_t = rate of change of aggregate demand (GDP growth);
T = time trend.

a) Tentatively explain the presence of the variable T in the inflation equation.
b) Study the identifiability of each equation and of the system.
c) What are the additional restrictions to make the system (i) triangular; (ii) fully recursive.

Suppose we have the data shown in Table 4.2 for Barbados.

d) Estimate the model by all appropriate methods. Comment on the results. Use a 10 percent level of significance throughout.
e) Test for the endogeneity of inflation rate in the unemployment rate equation.

4.3 ANSWERS

Answer 4.1

One of the main characteristics of simultaneous equations models is the classification of variables into endogenous variables and exogenous variables. This classification is based largely on economic theory.

To explain the difference between the two types of variables, consider the following macromodel:

Consumption: $$C_t = \beta_0 + \beta_1 Y_t + \beta_2 C_{t-1} + \beta_3 Y_{t-1} + u_t \quad \text{(A4.1.1)}$$

Investment: $$I_t = \gamma_0 + \gamma_1 r_t + \gamma_2 Y_t + v_t \quad \text{(A4.1.2)}$$

Demand: $$Y_t = C_t + I_t + G_t \quad \text{(A4.1.3)}$$

TABLE 4.2
Data for Simultaneous Determination of Price Inflation, Wage Inflation and Unemployment Rate: The Case of Barbados, 1975–1996

Obs	π (%)	*wi* (%)	UN (%)	AD (%)	PROD
1975	18.6833	9.4745	22.40000	−1.9247	7.093785
1976	4.7104	9.1708	16.20000	4.2872	7.480594
1977	8.0986	18.4610	17.00000	3.6117	7.702948
1978	9.0541	10.1783	12.20000	4.7570	8.023649
1979	15.6363	7.0969	13.40000	7.5791	8.090526
1980	13.3255	18.3923	12.90000	4.2912	7.999003
1981	13.7152	9.9845	10.80000	−1.9509	7.721295
1982	9.7913	10.7169	13.70000	−5.0571	7.743271
1983	5.1408	5.6119	15.20000	0.5067	7.855799
1984	4.5430	8.7524	17.20000	3.4899	8.361976
1985	4.0128	4.7448	18.70000	1.0732	8.543974
1986	0.9950	4.1440	18.40000	4.9704	8.605619
1987	3.4385	1.6614	18.00000	2.5312	8.062738
1988	4.6114	7.0934	17.90000	3.3960	8.102493
1989	6.1412	2.6793	17.70000	3.5378	8.138765
1990	2.9903	4.9337	17.60000	−3.3556	7.759047
1991	6.0919	0.8715	17.20000	−3.9799	7.887955
1992	5.8900	−1.8058	23.00000	−5.9250	7.828909
1993	1.1277	1.5985	24.30000	0.8380	7.997012
1994	0.0975	−1.6537	21.70000	3.8842	7.904356
1995	1.2104	0.0000	19.60000	2.8580	7.801090
1996	2.3307	0.0000	15.80000	5.0734	7.898601

Note: *wi*: wage inflation computed as 100*[Log(wage) – Log(wage(–1))]; π: price inflation computed as 100*[Log(CPI) – Log(CPI(–1))]; UN: unemployment rate in percent; AD: GDP growth as 100*[Log(GDP – Log(GDP(–1))]; PROD: productivity as the ratio of real GDP to labour employment.

Sources: Downes, A.S. and McLean, W. (1988). The estimation of missing values of employment in Barbados, Research Paper 13, Centre of Statistics of Trinidad and Tobago, 115–35; Central Bank of Barbados, *Annual Statistical Digest*, 1998.

where C_t is consumption expenditure, Y_t is income, I_t is investment, r_t is interest rate, G_t is government expenditure, and u_t and v_t are disturbances. The model explains consumption behaviour and investment behaviour along with the equilibrium condition (identity).

Endogenous variables are those variables that are determined within the system. In the context of simultaneous equations models, all endogenous variables are jointly determined. In other words, a shock to one disturbance term of the system affects all the endogenous variables. For example, in the system above a shock to u_t affects C_t, which in turn affects Y_t and which in turn affects I_t. Thus, C_t, I_t and Y_t are endogenous variables.

Aside from endogenous variables, there are variables known as exogenous variables. The latter are determined outside the system. Precisely, in causal terms, exogenous variables impact on endogenous variables without being affected by the latter. Put differently, a shock to an exogenous variable affects the paths of all endogenous variables without being affected by the latter (feedback). They can serve as policy variables in the context of SEM. In our system, G_t, r_t and the constant term are exogenous variables. Exogeneity is related to "predeterminedness". In a large sense, predetermined variables, in the context of simultaneous equations, include exogenous and lagged endogenous variables. As the name indicates, lagged endogenous variables are past values of endogenous variables. These are predetermined variables to the extent they are endogenous variables that are determined at the current period. In other words, in a strict sense predetermined variables are independent of current and future errors. In our system, Y_{t-1} and C_{t-1} are such variables. In the same vein, (strictly) exogenous variables are independent of past, current and future errors.

Three remarks are in order here. First, it is worth noting that for a lagged endogenous variable to claim the status of a predetermined variable it must be uncorrelated with the current and future errors. This condition is fulfilled as long as the errors are not autocorrelated. Second, "predeterminedness" of a lagged endogenous variable is in doubt if the related endogenous variable is strongly autocorrelated (indicated by Maddala, 1977). Third, the notion of endogenous variable is very relative. That is, a variable that is endogenous in a given environment can become exogenous in another environment.

Answer 4.2

a) The main issues involved in simultaneous equations models are:

   i) The classification of variables into endogenous and exogenous or predetermined variables as well as the establishment of the direction of causality relationships;
   ii) The problem of identification, that is, the issue of whether several theories are consistent with the same data; and
   iii) The problem of estimation.

b) Exogeneity such as defined above has been questioned by some econometricians. The "time series analysts" emphasize the concept of exogeneity with respect to some parameters. In any case, the reaction to endogeneity/exogeneity overemphasized in simultaneous equations models has given rise to a new approach to econometric modelling, called the VAR approach. In the VAR approach, the question of classifying variables into endogenous and exogenous does not arise, at least in the reduced form VAR. Indeed, all variables are endogenous and in each equation an endogenous variable is expressed in terms of its own past, the past of other variables as well as a serially uncorrelated error term. Note, however, that recently other forms of VAR have come into existence that acknowledge the distinction between endogenous variables and exogenous variables. Recursive VAR and structural VAR (see Chapter 6) are such forms. The literature has gone full circle.

Answer 4.3

This is the case of a fully recursive model. The latter has the following characteristics: (i) the matrix of endogenous variables is (lower) triangular; and (ii) the variance-covariance matrix of errors is diagonal, emphasizing the lack of correlation across equation errors.

To explain better, consider the following model:

$$Y_t = \alpha_0 + \alpha_1 Z_t + \alpha_2 V_t + u_{1t}$$

$$X_t = \beta_0 + \beta_1 Y_t + \beta_2 Z_t + \beta_3 V_t + u_{2t}$$

where $E(u_{1t}) = 0$, $E(u_{2t}) = 0$, $E(u_{1t}u_{2t}) = 0$, $\mathrm{E}(u_1 u_1') = \sigma_1^2 \mathrm{I}$, $\mathrm{E}(u_2 u_2') = \sigma_2^2 \mathrm{I}$.

As can be seen, the first equation can be consistently estimated by OLS, because there are no endogenous variables on the right-hand side and the error term is well behaved. Although Y_t is correlated with u_{1t}, the lack of correlation between the two error terms implies that Y_t is uncorrelated with u_{2t}. Hence, OLS can validly be applied to the second equation.

Answer 4.4

a) No. Although the matrix of endogenous variables is lower triangular, the variance-covariance of errors is not diagonal.
b) A feasible GLS can be applied to the whole system (see Lahiri and Schmidt, 1978).

Answer 4.5

a) The order condition indicates that the third equation is underidentified. Indeed, the number of excluded variables in the equation is less than the number of endogenous variables in the system minus one; that is, $0 < 2$. The rank condition involves building a matrix of endogenous and predetermined variables, striking out the row of interest (equation of interest) and constructing a submatrix with zero entries in the row alluded to above. If the rank of the submatrix is equal to the number of equations of the system minus one, then the equation is identified; otherwise, it is underidentified. Let us apply the above rule to the following A matrix. The latter is a matrix of structural parameters of dimension $g^*(g + k)$, with g being the number of endogenous variables and k the number of predetermined variables; that is,

$$A = \begin{pmatrix} 1 & -\alpha_2 & 0 & -\alpha_0 & -\alpha_4 & -\alpha_5 & -\alpha_6 \\ -\beta_1 & 1 & 0 & -\beta_0 & -\beta_4 & -\beta_5 & -\beta_6 \\ -\gamma_1 & -\gamma_2 & 1 & -\gamma_0 & -\gamma_4 & -\gamma_5 & -\gamma_6 \end{pmatrix}$$

The submatrix does not exist since there are no zero entries in the third equation. That is, the rank of the submatrix is zero. Since it is less than the number of equations in the model (number of endogenous variables in the system) minus one, which is 2, the third equation is underidentified. Summing up, order and rank conditions indicate that the third equation is unidentified.

b) OLS can, however, be validly applied to this equation since the system is block recursive. To recall, a system of equations is said to be block recursive if it can be divided into blocks such that while within each block equations are simultaneous, across blocks equations are recursive (see Pindyck and Rubinfeld, 1981, 323). Indeed, a quick look at the model reveals that y_1 and y_2 are each independent of the equation error term, u_3. OLS estimates from this equation will be consistent assuming u_3 is well behaved.

Answer 4.6

Seemingly unrelated regressions (SUR) are a case in point. SUR represents a set of equations that, on the surface, are uncorrelated but which in reality are related through the cross equation errors. SUR has often been used in the context of systems of demand equations. An example is Stone's expenditure system (see Greene, 2003, 362):

$$\log q_i = \beta_i + \beta_i \log\left(\frac{Y}{P}\right) + \sum_{j=1}^{r} \gamma_{ij} \log\left(\frac{P_j}{P}\right) + u_i$$

where *i* represents commodity, *j* represents another commodity, *Y* is income, *P* is price index, and *q* is quantity demanded. We can rewrite the equation as follows:

$$Z_1 = X_1\,\delta_1 + u_1$$

$$Z_2 = X_2\,\delta_2 + u_2$$

$$\vdots$$

$$Z_r = X_r\,\delta_r + u_r$$

where $Z_i = \log q_i$ and X_i is a matrix of explanatory variables. Equivalently:

$$\begin{bmatrix} Z_1 \\ Z_2 \\ \vdots \\ Z_r \end{bmatrix} = \begin{bmatrix} X_1 & & & \\ & X_2 & & \\ & & \ddots & \\ & & & X_r \end{bmatrix} \begin{bmatrix} \delta_1 \\ \delta_2 \\ \vdots \\ \delta_r \end{bmatrix} + \begin{bmatrix} u_1 \\ u_2 \\ \vdots \\ u_r \end{bmatrix}$$

where $E(u_i u_i') = \sigma_{ii}I$ and $E(u_i u_j') = \sigma_{ij}I$, $i = 1, 2, \ldots, r$, $j = 1, 2, \ldots, r$.

The variance-covariance of errors is indeed

$$\Sigma = \begin{bmatrix} \sigma_{11} & \sigma_{12} & \cdots & \sigma_{1r} \\ \sigma_{21} & \sigma_{22} & \cdots & \sigma_{2r} \\ \vdots & & & \\ \sigma_{r1} & \sigma_{r2} & \cdots & \sigma_{rr} \end{bmatrix} \otimes \mathrm{I}$$

where ⊗ is a Kronecker product.

Because of the cross-correlation of errors, GLS is the appropriate method of obtaining parameter estimates. Note that if $X_1 = X_2 = \ldots X_r$ or errors are uncorrelated across equations, then OLS = SUR.

Answer 4.7

Answers can be found in many econometrics textbooks (for example, Johnston, 1984, 439–443). Let us illustrate the equality between ILS and 2SLS by way of a Keynesian consumption function (see Johnston, 1984):

$$C_t = a + bY_t + e_t$$
$$Y_t = C_t + I_t \tag{A4.7.1}$$

where C_t stands for consumption, Y_t is disposable income, I_t is investment and e_t stands for disturbances.

a) Derivation of ILS estimator
   The corresponding reduced form system to Equation (A4.7.1) is:

$$C_t = \frac{a}{1-b} + \frac{b}{1-b} I_t + v_t$$

$$Y_t = \frac{a}{1-b} + \frac{1}{1-b} I_t + v_t$$

   where $v_t = e_t/(1 - b)$. Rewriting the reduced form as:

$$C_t = \pi_{11} + \pi_{12} I_t + v_t$$

$$Y_t = \pi_{21} + \pi_{22} I_t + v_t$$

   leads to:

$$b_{ILS} = \frac{\pi_{12}}{\pi_{22}} = \frac{\sum ci}{\sum i^2} \bigg/ \frac{\sum yi}{\sum i^2} = \frac{\sum ci}{\sum yi} \tag{A4.7.2}$$

where variables are deviations to the respective means, for example, $c = C - \bar{C}$.

b) Derivation of 2SLS estimator
Regress Y_t on all predetermined variables of the system. Using the deviation form and taking into account that I_t is the only predetermined variable of the system leads to the following:

$$y_t = \gamma i_t + v_t \qquad \text{(A4.7.3)}$$

The estimator of γ is:

$$\hat{\gamma} = \frac{\sum yi}{\sum i^2} \qquad \text{(A4.7.4)}$$

Using the above estimator, the fitted value of $\hat{y}_t$ is:

$$\hat{y}_t = \hat{\gamma} i_t = \left(\frac{\sum yi}{\sum i^2} \right) i_t \qquad \text{(A4.7.5)}$$

Using the deviation form and using $\hat{y}$ from Equation (A4.7.5) for y_t in the first equation of (A4.7.1) give rise to:

$$c_t = b\hat{y}_t + u_t \qquad \text{(A4.7.6)}$$

The 2SLS estimator is the OLS estimator from Equation (A4.7.6):

$$b_{2SLS} = \frac{\sum c\,\hat{y}}{\sum \hat{y}^2} = \frac{\hat{\gamma}\sum c\,i}{\hat{\gamma}^2 \sum i^2} = \frac{\sum yi}{\sum i^2} \frac{\left(\sum i^2\right)^2}{\left(\sum yi\right)^2} \frac{\sum ci}{\sum i^2} = \frac{\sum ci}{\sum yi} \qquad \text{(A4.7.7)}$$

Equations (A4.7.2) and (A4.7.7) reveal that $b_{\text{ILS}} = b_{\text{2SLS}}$.

Answer 4.8

Consider the following equation (see Johnston, 1984, 479–480):

$$y = Y_1\alpha + X_1\beta + u$$

as part of a simultaneous equations model. Suppose also that the equation is overidentified. Moreover, y and Y_1 are endogenous variables. Let X be the matrix of predetermined variables in the system.

We know that Y_1 is correlated with u. In the 2SLS method we replace it by its fitted value, $\hat{Y}_1$, obtained as:

$$\hat{Y}_1 = X\left(X'X\right)^{-1} X'Y_1$$

Now since $n = k$, X is square, and in the absence of multicollinearity:

$$\hat{Y}_1 = XX^{-1}(X')^{-1}X'Y_1 = Y_1$$

In other words, the 2SLS estimator is equal to the OLS estimator. This implies that the 2SLS estimator is inconsistent.

Answer 4.9

a) Observational equivalence
The issue of "observational equivalence in structures" is at the core of the problem of identification in simultaneous equations models. The identification problem in this context is a mathematical problem related to whether or not the reduced form parameters give rise to meaningful structural form parameters (see Kennedy, 1992, 153). In that connection, an equation can be just-identified, overidentified and underidentified. In the latter case, it is not possible to obtain structural parameters from the reduced form parameters. The main reason for this state of affairs is the existence of several indistinguishable theories that are consistent with the same data (see Greene, 2003, 384); in other words, the theories or structures are "observationally equivalent".

b) Single-equation methods and system methods
Both sets of methods attempt to obtain structural parameter estimates of the SEM. In this connection, the single-equation method estimates "one equation at once", that is, it does not take into account constraints embedded in the other equations. OLS, ILS, 2SLS and LIML fall in this category. On the contrary, the system method estimates, when feasible, all the parameters of the model simultaneously "(at once)", that is, it uses all the restrictions of the model to derive estimates of the parameters. 3SLS and FIML fall in this category.

The two approaches yield desirable properties; they are all consistent with the exception of OLS. In the absence of specification errors, the system methods yield estimators that are asymptotically more efficient than those obtained under the single-equation methods. This, however, only holds if there are correlations among errors in different equations and/or cross equation restrictions.

Of great importance is the comparison between 3SLS estimators and 2SLS estimators. The 3SLS estimators are equivalent to 2SLS estimators: (a) if each equation of the system is just-identified; and (b) if there are no contemporaneous correlations between errors in different equations.

Note that the small sample performances of estimators from the two approaches (single-equation methods and system methods) are not clear cut, although 2SLS estimators seem to have an edge over all other estimators in terms of small bias.

Answer 4.10

a) Rewrite the system as:

$$q = \alpha + \beta P + e_1 \tag{A4.10.1}$$

$$q = \gamma + \delta P + \eta R + e_2 \tag{A4.10.2}$$

The reduced form is obtained by expressing each endogenous variable as a function of all predetermined variables of the system. The two equations combined give rise to:

$$\gamma + \delta P + \eta R + e_2$$

That is:

$$P = \frac{-\alpha + \gamma}{\beta - \delta} + \frac{\eta R}{\beta - \delta} + \frac{e_2 - e_1}{\beta - \delta}$$

$$q = \frac{-\alpha\delta + \beta\gamma}{\beta - \delta} + \frac{\beta\eta R}{\beta - \delta} + \frac{\beta e_2 - \delta e_1}{\beta - \delta}$$

or

$$P = \pi_{11} + \pi_{12} R + v_1$$

$$q = \pi_{21} + \pi_{22} R + v_2$$

b) The identification problem in the context of a simultaneous equations model deals with the issue of whether meaningful estimates of the structural parameters can be obtained from the reduced form parameters. Precisely, here it is a question of whether the πs enable us to obtain the structural parameters (α, β, γ, δ and η). In that connection, an equation (or the structural parameters of an equation) can be just (exactly) identified (unique values of the structural parameters can be derived); overidentified (more than such values are derived) or underidentified (structural parameters cannot be derived from the reduced form parameters).

c) The order condition consists in finding out whether the number of variables excluded in the equation of interest exceeds or is equal to or less than the number of equations (endogenous variables in the system) minus one.

Applying the rule to the demand equation gives 1 = 2 – 1. That is, the demand equation is just-identified. The rank condition involves building a matrix of endogenous and predetermined variables, striking out the row of interest and constructing a submatrix with zero entries in the row alluded to above. If the rank of the submatrix is equal to the number of equations minus one, then the equation is identified.

Let us apply the above rule to the following *A* matrix. The latter is a matrix of structural parameters of dimension $g*(g+k)$, with g being the number of endogenous variables and k the number of predetermined variables; that is:

$$A = \begin{pmatrix} 1 & -\beta & -\alpha & 0 \\ 1 & -\delta & -\gamma & -\eta \end{pmatrix}$$

The submatrix alluded to above is $(-\eta)$. Clearly the rank of this submatrix is 1 if we assume $\eta \neq 0$. Thus, since the rank is equal to 2 – 1, the demand equation is identified; precisely, just-identified, as the number of columns of the submatrix is equal to the rank. Summing up, both order and rank conditions indicate that the demand equation is just-identified.

d) Applying the same line of reasoning to the supply equation gives rise to the following:

Order condition: 0 < 2 – 1; that is, the supply equation is underidentified.

Rank condition:

$$\begin{pmatrix} 1 & -\beta & -\alpha & 0 \\ 1 & -\delta & -\gamma & -\eta \end{pmatrix}$$

The submatrix does not exist; that is, its rank is zero. Since the rank is less than 2 – 1 = 1, the supply equation is underidentified. Summing up, both order and rank conditions indicate that the supply equation is underidentified.

e) To show that the equilibrium condition is always identified, we use the original system of equations. Using the rank condition, we have:

$$\begin{pmatrix} 1 & 0 & -\beta & -\alpha & 0 \\ 0 & 1 & -\delta & -\gamma & -\eta \\ 1 & -1 & 0 & 0 & 0 \end{pmatrix}$$

The submatrix of interest is:

$$\begin{pmatrix} -\beta & -\alpha & 0 \\ -\delta & -\gamma & -\eta \end{pmatrix} = 2$$

Since 2 = 3 – 1, the equilibrium condition is identified.

f) The equation of interest is the demand equation since it is exactly identified. We can use indirect least squares. However, we can also use two stage least squares since in this case the latter is equivalent to the former. We use these methods because they are appropriate in these circumstances. Indeed, they allow us to obtain the structural parameters from the reduced form parameters and, more important, they yield consistent estimators.

g) By definition:

$$
\begin{aligned}
Cov(Pe_1) &= \mathrm{E}\left[\left(P-\mathrm{E}(P)\right)\left(e_1-\mathrm{E}(e_1)\right)\right] \\
&= \mathrm{E}\left[\left(P-\mathrm{E}(P)\right)e_1\right] \qquad \text{since } \mathrm{E}(e_1)=0
\end{aligned}
$$

From the reduced form equation of *P*, we know that:

$$
\mathrm{E}(P)=\frac{-\alpha+\gamma}{\beta-\delta}+\frac{\eta R}{\beta-\delta}
$$

Thus:

$$
P-\mathrm{E}(P)=\frac{e_2-e_1}{\beta-\delta} \tag{A4.10.3}
$$

That is:

$$
\begin{aligned}
Cov(Pe_1) &= \mathrm{E}\left[\left(P-\mathrm{E}(P)\right)e_1\right] \\
&= \mathrm{E}\left[\frac{e_2-e_1}{\beta-\delta}e_1\right] \\
&= \frac{1}{\beta-\delta}\left[\mathrm{E}(e_1e_2)-\mathrm{E}(e_1^2)\right] \\
&= \frac{1}{\beta-\delta}\left(\sigma_{12}-\sigma_1^2\right)
\end{aligned} \tag{A4.10.4}
$$

Assuming that $\sigma_{12} \neq \sigma_1^2$, then Cov($Pe_1$) $\neq 0$.

h) We know that:

$$
\begin{aligned}
\hat{\beta} &= \frac{\sum(q-\bar{q})(P-\bar{P})}{\sum(P-\bar{P})^2} \\
&= \frac{\sum q(P-\bar{P})}{\sum(P-\bar{P})^2}
\end{aligned} \tag{A4.10.5}
$$

Using the value of q from Equation (A4.10.1) in Equation (A4.10.5) gives the following:

$$\hat{\beta} = \frac{\sum(\alpha + \beta P + e_1)(P - \bar{P})}{\sum(P - \bar{P})^2}$$
$$= \frac{\alpha\sum(P - \bar{P}) + \beta\sum P(P - \bar{P}) + \sum e_1(P - \bar{P})}{\sum(P - \bar{P})^2} \tag{A4.10.6}$$

Since $\sum(P - \bar{P}) = 0$, and $\sum P(P - \bar{P}) = \sum(P - \bar{P})^2$, Equation (A4.10.6) leads to:

$$\hat{\beta} = \beta + \frac{\sum e_1(P - \bar{P})}{\sum(P - \bar{P})^2} \tag{A4.10.7}$$

We know that an estimator $\hat{\beta}$ is a consistent estimator of β if $\text{plim}\,\hat{\beta} = \beta$. Applying plim to Equation (A4.10.7) gives rise to:

$$\text{plim}\,\hat{\beta} = \text{plim}\,\beta + \frac{\underset{n\to\infty}{\text{plim}} \sum e_1(P - \bar{P})/n}{\underset{n\to\infty}{\text{plim}} \sum(P - \bar{P})^2/n}$$

As $n \to \infty$,

$$\underset{n\to\infty}{\text{plim}} \sum e_1(P - \bar{P})/n = Cov(Pe_1) = \frac{\sigma_{12} - \sigma_1^2}{\beta - \delta}$$

and

$$\underset{n\to\infty}{\text{plim}} \sum(P - \bar{P})^2/n = Var(P) = \frac{\sigma_1^2 + \sigma_2^2 - 2\sigma_{12}}{(\beta - \delta)^2}$$

Thus:

$$\underset{n\to\infty}{\text{plim}}\,\hat{\beta} = \beta + (\beta - \delta)\frac{\sigma_{12} - \sigma_1^2}{\sigma_1^2 + \sigma_2^2 - 2\sigma_{12}} \tag{A4.10.8}$$

Assuming that $\sigma_{12} \neq \sigma_1^2$ and $\beta \neq \delta$, $\hat{\beta}$ is inconsistent since $\text{plim}\,\hat{\beta} \neq \beta$.

i) Now both supply and demand are just-identified (check it).

Answer 4.11

a) If we assume that the market is in equilibrium, then the equilibrium condition is missing. Without that condition, the system is incomplete since there are three endogenous variables and two equations.

b) After adding the equilibrium condition ($M_t^s = M_t^d = M_t$), the system reads as follows:

$$\text{Demand for money:} \quad M_t = \beta_0 + \beta_1 Y_t + \beta_2 R_t + \beta_3 P_t + u_{1t} \tag{A4.11.1}$$

$$\text{Supply of money:} \quad M_t = \gamma_0 + \gamma_1 Y_t + \gamma_4 T + u_{2t} \tag{A4.11.2}$$

The matrix A for rank condition is given by:

$$A = \begin{pmatrix} 1 & -\beta_1 & -\beta_0 & -\beta_2 & -\beta_3 & 0 \\ 1 & -\gamma_1 & -\gamma_0 & 0 & 0 & -\gamma_4 \end{pmatrix}$$

As can be seen for the first equation the resulting submatrix is ($-\gamma_4$), with rank equal to one assuming that the parameter value is not zero. Since the rank is equal to the number of endogenous variables of the system minus one, the equation is identified (here just-identified since the number of columns is equal to the rank).

For the second equation, the resulting submatrix is ($-\beta_2$ – β_3). Unless $\beta_2 = \beta_3 = 0$, its rank is 1. Once more the equation is identified (here overidentified).

c) To answer the question we need to derive the reduced form:

$$\begin{aligned} Y_t &= \frac{\gamma_0 - \beta_0}{\beta_1 - \gamma_1} - \frac{\beta_2 R_t}{\beta_1 - \gamma_1} - \frac{\beta_3 P_t}{\beta_1 - \gamma_1} + \frac{\gamma_4 T}{\beta_1 - \gamma_1} + \frac{u_{2t} - u_{1t}}{\beta_1 - \gamma_1} \\ M_t &= \frac{\gamma_0 \beta_1 - \gamma_1 \beta_0}{\beta_1 - \gamma_1} - \frac{\beta_2 \gamma_1 R_t}{\beta_1 - \gamma_1} - \frac{\beta_3 \gamma_1 P_t}{\beta_1 - \gamma_1} + \frac{\beta_1 \gamma_4 T}{\beta_1 - \gamma_1} + \frac{\beta_1 u_{2t} - \gamma_1 u_{1t}}{\beta_1 - \gamma_1} \end{aligned} \tag{A4.11.3}$$

i) The total effect of interest rate on money can be read off the reduced form. It is:

$$-\frac{\beta_2 \gamma_1}{\beta_1 - \gamma_1}$$

ii) The direct effect can be read off the structural form. It is β_2.

iii) The indirect effect can be deduced from total and direct effects:

$$-\frac{\beta_2 \gamma_1}{\beta_1 - \gamma_1} - \beta_2 = -\frac{\beta_2 \beta_1}{\beta_1 - \gamma_1}$$

d) Restrictions are a key ingredient of structural parameter identification. Restrictions used so far are called zero restrictions. There are other types of restrictions, including linear and nonlinear restrictions.

In this part of the question we are interested in homogeneous linear restrictions of type $\delta_i + \delta_j = 0$. The rule for identification is as follows: the order condition remains the same except that the number of excluded variables now reads the number of restrictions. That is, an equation is just-identified, overidentified or underidentified if the number of restrictions is equal to, greater or less than the number of endogenous variables of the system minus one $(g - 1)$, respectively.

The rank condition involves the use of two types of matrices: (1) ϕ_i, the matrix of restrictions (in a given equation i) of dimension $(g + k) \times q$ where $g + k$ is the total number of variables in the system and q stands for restrictions, with one column per restriction; and (2) A, the matrix of structural parameters of dimension $g \times (g + k)$. The equation is identified if $r(A\phi_i) = g - 1$, where r stands for rank.

Let us examine the demand equation. It can be observed that we have in fact two restrictions: $\beta_2 + \beta_3 = 0$ as well as $\beta_4 = 0$. The order condition gives $2 > 2 - 1$. Thus, the demand-for-money equation is overidentified.

For the rank condition, the matrix ϕ_i is as follows:

$$\phi_1 = \begin{pmatrix} 0 & 0 \\ 0 & 0 \\ 0 & 0 \\ 1 & 0 \\ 1 & 0 \\ 0 & 1 \end{pmatrix}$$

where the first column represents the linear restrictions $\beta_2 + \beta_3 = 0$ and the second $\beta_4 = 0$. The A matrix has already been presented above. The multiplication of the A and ϕ_i matrices leads to:

$$A\phi_1 = \begin{pmatrix} 1 & -\beta_1 & -\beta_0 & -\beta_2 & -\beta_3 & 0 \\ 1 & -\gamma_1 & -\gamma_0 & 0 & 0 & -\gamma_4 \end{pmatrix} \begin{pmatrix} 0 & 0 \\ 0 & 0 \\ 0 & 0 \\ 1 & 0 \\ 1 & 0 \\ 0 & 1 \end{pmatrix}$$

$$= \begin{pmatrix} -\beta_2 - \beta_3 & 0 \\ 0 & -\gamma_4 \end{pmatrix}$$

$$= \begin{pmatrix} 0 & 0 \\ 0 & -\gamma_4 \end{pmatrix} \quad \text{since } -\beta_2 - \beta_3 = \beta_2 + \beta_3 = 0$$

$$= \begin{pmatrix} 0 & 0 \\ 0 & 0 \end{pmatrix} \quad \text{since } \gamma_4 = 0$$

The demand for money is underidentified. Since the rank condition is a sufficient condition, the final answer is that the demand for money is no longer identified.

Let us examine the supply-of-money equation. There are three restrictions in total: $\gamma_2 = 0$, $\gamma_3 = 0$ and $\gamma_4 = 0$. Note that the first two restrictions were already embedded in the equation. Since 3 > 2 – 1, the supply of money is overidentified by order condition. For the rank condition, the ϕ_i matrix is as follows:

$$\phi_2 = \begin{pmatrix} 0 & 0 & 0 \\ 0 & 0 & 0 \\ 0 & 0 & 0 \\ 1 & 0 & 0 \\ 0 & 1 & 0 \\ 0 & 0 & 1 \end{pmatrix}$$

where the first column deals with the restriction $\gamma_2 = 0$, the second with $\gamma_3 = 0$ and the last with $\gamma_4 = 0$. Multiplication of the A matrix with ϕ_2 gives:

$$A\phi_2 = \begin{pmatrix} 1 & -\beta_1 & -\beta_0 & -\beta_2 & -\beta_3 & 0 \\ 1 & -\gamma_1 & -\gamma_0 & 0 & 0 & -\gamma_4 \end{pmatrix} \begin{pmatrix} 0 & 0 & 0 \\ 0 & 0 & 0 \\ 0 & 0 & 0 \\ 1 & 0 & 0 \\ 0 & 1 & 0 \\ 0 & 0 & 1 \end{pmatrix}$$

$$= \begin{pmatrix} -\beta_2 & -\beta_3 & 0 \\ 0 & 0 & -\gamma_4 \end{pmatrix}$$

$$= \begin{pmatrix} -\beta_2 & -\beta_3 & 0 \\ 0 & 0 & 0 \end{pmatrix} \qquad \text{since } \gamma_4 = 0$$

Unless $\beta_2 = \beta_3 = 0$, the rank of the above submatrix is 1. Since 1 = 2 – 1, the supply equation is identified; precisely, it is overidentified (number of columns > rank). Note that, alternatively, in this particular case we could have placed all the restrictions in the A matrix:

$$A = \begin{pmatrix} 1 & -\beta_1 & -\beta_0 & -\beta_2 & -\beta_3 & 0 \\ 1 & -\gamma_1 & -\gamma_0 & 0 & 0 & 0 \end{pmatrix}$$

As above, the resulting submatrix is of rank 1; that is, the same conclusion will be reached.

Answer 4.12

a) The linear restrictions examined in Question 4.11 are all homogeneous to the extent that they correspond to zero restrictions in terms of specified coefficients or linear combinations of coefficients. In economic theory, however, quite a number of restrictions are nonhomogeneous; that is, they are not set equal to zero. For example, constant returns to scale in production function. There is a need to recourse to some normalization to give meanings to nonhomogeneous restrictions.

As can be seen, in the first equation (page 119), $\gamma_{11} + \gamma_{12} = 1$ is a nonhomogeneous restriction. However, using the normalization $\beta_{11} = 1$, that nonhomogeneous restriction can be transformed into an homogeneous one: $\beta_{11} - \gamma_{11} - \gamma_{12} = 0$. In the second equation, the restriction thus becomes $\beta_{22} - \beta_{21} - \gamma_{21} = 0$.

Using the rank condition, for the first equation, the matrix (vector) ϕ_i is:

$$\phi_1 = \begin{pmatrix} 1 \\ 0 \\ -1 \\ -1 \end{pmatrix}$$

and the matrix A is

$$A = \begin{pmatrix} \beta_{11} & \beta_{12} & \gamma_{11} & \gamma_{12} \\ \beta_{21} & \beta_{22} & \gamma_{21} & \gamma_{22} \end{pmatrix}$$

Thus:

$$\begin{aligned} A\phi_1 &= \begin{pmatrix} \beta_{11} & \beta_{12} & \gamma_{11} & \gamma_{12} \\ \beta_{21} & \beta_{22} & \gamma_{21} & \gamma_{22} \end{pmatrix} \begin{pmatrix} 1 \\ 0 \\ -1 \\ -1 \end{pmatrix} \\ &= \begin{pmatrix} \beta_{11} - \gamma_{11} - \gamma_{12} \\ \beta_{21} - \gamma_{21} - \gamma_{22} \end{pmatrix} \\ &= \begin{pmatrix} 0 \\ \beta_{21} - \gamma_{21} - \gamma_{22} \end{pmatrix} \qquad \text{since } \beta_{11} - \gamma_{11} - \gamma_{12} = 0 \end{aligned}$$

The rank is 1 if $\beta_{21} - \gamma_{21} - \gamma_{22} \neq 0$. Since the rank is equal to $g - 1$, that is $2 - 1$, the equation is identified (just-identified).

For the second equation the matrix $A\phi_2$ gives:

$$A\phi_2 = \begin{pmatrix} \beta_{11} & \beta_{12} & \gamma_{11} & \gamma_{12} \\ \beta_{21} & \beta_{22} & \gamma_{21} & \gamma_{22} \end{pmatrix} \begin{pmatrix} -1 \\ 1 \\ -1 \\ 0 \end{pmatrix}$$

$$= \begin{pmatrix} -\beta_{11} + \beta_{12} - \gamma_{11} \\ -\beta_{21} + \beta_{22} - \gamma_{21} \end{pmatrix}$$

$$= \begin{pmatrix} -\beta_{11} + \beta_{12} - \gamma_{11} \\ 0 \end{pmatrix}$$

Assuming that $-\beta_{11} + \beta_{12} - \gamma_{11} \neq 0$, $r(A\phi_2) = 1$. Thus, the equation is (just) identified.

b) We incorporate normalization information in the A matrix. Thus:

$$A = \begin{pmatrix} 1 & \beta_{12} & \gamma_{11} & \gamma_{12} \\ \beta_{21} & 1 & \gamma_{21} & \gamma_{22} \end{pmatrix}$$

Moreover, $\gamma_{11} = -\gamma_{12}$ can be rewritten as $\gamma_{11} + \gamma_{12} = 0$. Thus, in the first equation the ϕ_i matrix is:

$$\phi_1 = \begin{pmatrix} 0 \\ 0 \\ 1 \\ 1 \end{pmatrix}$$

and in the second equation it is:

$$\phi_2 = \begin{pmatrix} 0 \\ 0 \\ 0 \\ 1 \end{pmatrix}$$

For the first equation:

$$A\phi_1 = \begin{pmatrix} 1 & \beta_{12} & \gamma_{11} & \gamma_{12} \\ \beta_{21} & 1 & \gamma_{21} & \gamma_{22} \end{pmatrix} \begin{pmatrix} 0 \\ 0 \\ 1 \\ 1 \end{pmatrix}$$

$$= \begin{pmatrix} \gamma_{11} + \gamma_{12} \\ \gamma_{21} + \gamma_{22} \end{pmatrix}$$

$$= \begin{pmatrix} 0 \\ \gamma_{21} + \gamma_{22} \end{pmatrix}$$

$$= \begin{pmatrix} 0 \\ \gamma_{21} \end{pmatrix} \qquad \text{since } \gamma_{22} = 0.$$

The resulting rank is 1, assuming that $\gamma_{21} \neq 0$. Thus, the equation is just-identified.

For the second equation:

$$A\phi_2 = \begin{pmatrix} 1 & \beta_{12} & \gamma_{11} & \gamma_{12} \\ \beta_{21} & 1 & \gamma_{21} & \gamma_{22} \end{pmatrix} \begin{pmatrix} 0 \\ 0 \\ 0 \\ 1 \end{pmatrix}$$

$$= \begin{pmatrix} \gamma_{12} \\ \gamma_{22} \end{pmatrix} = \begin{pmatrix} \gamma_{12} \\ 0 \end{pmatrix}$$

The rank is 1 provided that $\gamma_{12} \neq 0$. Since the rank is equal to $g - 1$ $(2 - 1)$, the equation is identified (just-identified).

Answer 4.13

a) The A matrix is:

$$A = \begin{pmatrix} 1 & 0 & \beta_{11} & \beta_{12} \\ \alpha_{21} & 1 & \beta_{21} & \beta_{22} \end{pmatrix}$$

As can be seen, the first equation is just-identified. The second equation is not identified.

b) Following Johnston (1984, 463–466), we build an admissible transformation matrix, T, a $g \times g$ non-singular matrix. The latter is said to be admissible if its product with the matrix A satisfies all *a priori* restrictions on A. Thus:

$$T = \begin{bmatrix} \delta_{11} & \delta_{12} \\ \delta_{21} & \delta_{22} \end{bmatrix} = \begin{bmatrix} 1 & 0 \\ \delta_{21} & 1 \end{bmatrix}$$

Now with this transformation the new error term is Tu_t; that is:

$$V = \mathrm{E}\left(Tu_t \left(Tu_t \right)' \right)$$

$$= \mathrm{E}\left(Tu_t u_t' T' \right)$$

$$= T \Sigma T'$$

Since

$$\Sigma = \begin{bmatrix} \sigma_{11} & 0 \\ 0 & \sigma_{22} \end{bmatrix}$$

V must "obey the restriction that the covariance between the two transformed errors is zero" (p. 464); that is:

$$\delta_1 \Sigma \delta_2' = 0 \text{ with } \delta_1 = (1\ 0) \text{ and } \delta_2 = (\delta_{21}\ 1)$$

or, precisely,

$$\begin{pmatrix} 1 & 0 \end{pmatrix} \begin{bmatrix} \sigma_{11} & 0 \\ 0 & \sigma_{22} \end{bmatrix} \begin{bmatrix} \delta_{21} \\ 1 \end{bmatrix} = 0$$

This leads to:

$$\delta_{21}\sigma_{11} = 0 \Rightarrow \delta_{21} = 0$$

Thus, the only admissible transformation matrix is:

$$T = \begin{pmatrix} 1 & 0 \\ 0 & 1 \end{pmatrix}$$

That is, the first equation is just-identified and so is the second equation. Thus, the zero covariance of errors has aided to identify the equations. In fact, with a diagonal matrix of errors, the system is fully recursive.

c) With respect to (a) no further information is added, that is, no restrictions are added. Thus, Σ cannot aid in identifying parameters. As seen in (a) the first equation is just-identified and the second is underidentified. This system is, however, peculiar. It is triangular. A feasible GLS on the system is the appropriate method of estimation (see Lahiri and Schmidt, 1978).

Answer 4.14

a) The reduced form is as follows:

$$y_t = \frac{\gamma v_t}{1-\gamma\delta} + \frac{u_t}{1-\gamma\delta}$$

$$x_t = \frac{v_t}{1-\gamma\delta} + \frac{\delta u_t}{1-\gamma\delta}$$

The variables of interest depend only on the random shocks.

b) Let us compute $\operatorname{plim}\hat{\gamma}$ as:

$$\underset{n\to\infty}{\operatorname{plim}}\hat{\gamma} = \underset{n\to\infty}{\operatorname{plim}}\frac{\sum x_t y_t}{\sum x_t^2} = \underset{n\to\infty}{\operatorname{plim}}\frac{\sum x_t(\gamma x_t + u_t)}{\sum x_t^2}$$

$$= \gamma + \underset{n\to\infty}{\operatorname{plim}}\frac{\sum x_t u_t / n}{\sum x_t^2 / n}$$

But:

$$\underset{n\to\infty}{\operatorname{plim}}\sum x_t u_t / n = Cov(x_t u_t) = E(x_t u_t) = \frac{\delta\sigma_u^2 + \sigma_{uv}}{1-\gamma\delta}$$

and

$$\underset{n\to\infty}{\operatorname{plim}}\sum x_t^2 / n = Var(x_t) = E(x_t^2) = \frac{(\delta^2\sigma_u^2 + \sigma_v^2 + 2\delta\sigma_{uv})}{(1-\gamma\delta)^2}$$

Using $\sigma_{uv} = 0$,

$$\underset{n\to\infty}{\operatorname{plim}}\hat{\gamma} = \gamma + (1-\gamma\delta)\frac{\delta\sigma_u^2}{(\delta^2\sigma_u^2 + \sigma_v^2)}$$

c) The estimator is consistent if either one of the following is true:

i) $\gamma\delta = 1 \;\Rightarrow\; \delta = \frac{1}{\gamma}$ with $\gamma \neq 0$
ii) $\delta = 0$
iii) $\sigma_u^2 = 0$

Condition (i) states that one regression is simply the reverse of the other. This happens when $R^2 = 1$. This means one regression contains full information about the other. In this particular case the right-hand-side endogeneity is irrelevant.

Condition (ii) means that the system is recursive. Indeed, the matrix of endogenous variables is (upper) triangular and the matrix of errors is diagonal. Thus, OLS is consistent.

Condition (iii) means that there are no errors in the first equation. That is, the first equation is purely deterministic. The reasoning is as follows. The variance of the errors is zero, meaning that the error term is not a random variable but rather a constant vector. If we add that the mean of errors is zero, then the constant vector is a zero vector.

d) As in (b):

$$\underset{n\to\infty}{\text{plim}}\,\hat{\gamma} = \gamma + \underset{n\to\infty}{\text{plim}} \frac{\sum x_t u_t / n}{\sum x_t^2 / n}$$

But

$$\begin{aligned}\underset{n\to\infty}{\text{plim}} \sum x_t u_t / n &= Cov(X_t u_t) \\ &= \text{E}\left[\left(\delta s_t + v_t\right) u_t\right] \\ &= \delta\,\text{E}\left(s_t u_t\right) + \text{E}\left(u_t v_t\right) \\ &= 0\end{aligned}$$

Since z_t is exogenous and $\text{Cov}(u_t v_t) = 0$

$$\underset{n\to\infty}{\text{plim}} \sum x_t^2 / n = Var\left(X_t\right) = \delta^2\sigma_s^2 + \sigma_v^2$$

Thus:

$$\begin{aligned}\text{plim}\,\hat{\gamma} &= \gamma + \frac{0}{\delta^2\sigma_s^2 + \sigma} \\ &= \gamma\end{aligned}$$

Now the estimator $\hat{\gamma}$ is consistent.

Answer 4.15

a) They are the same, because we assume that the market is in equilibrium; that is, demand for labour is equal to labour supply.
b) Yes, the system is complete, because the number of equations is equal to the number of endogenous variables.
c) Concerning the demand-for-labour equation, the expected signs are the following:

$\alpha_1 \neq 0$ since we do not have any prior expectation for the constant term here;
$\alpha_2 < 0$ since, everything being equal, higher real wage decreases labour demand due to increases in labor costs;
$\alpha_3 > 0$ since, everything being equal, an increase in GDP boosts labour demand;
$\alpha_4 < 0$ since, everything being equal, an increase in employer's contributions to the national insurance scheme depresses labour demand, as the cost has increased.

Concerning the supply of labour equation, the expected signs are the following:

$\beta_1 \neq 0$ since we do not have any prior expectation for the constant term here;
$\beta_2 > 0$ since, *ceteris paribus*, higher real wage increases labour supply;
$\beta_3 \neq 0$ since we do not have any prior expectation for the trend, which captures here the effect of omitted variables;
$\beta_4 < 0$ since, everything being equal, an increase in employee's contributions to the national insurance scheme depresses labour supply, as these contributions represent a cost for the employee.

d) Let us use both order and rank conditions.
Order condition
Demand equation As can be seen, the number of excluded variables in the equation, which is 2, exceeds the number of endogenous variables in the system minus 1, which is 2 – 1. This means that the demand for labour is overidentified.
Supply equation As above, the number of excluded variables in the equation (2) exceeds the number of endogenous variables in the system minus one, that is, 2 – 1. Hence, the supply equation is overidentified.
Rank condition The A matrix is:

$$A = \begin{pmatrix} 1 & -\alpha_2 & -\alpha_1 & -\alpha_3 & -\alpha_4 & 0 & 0 \\ 1 & -\beta_2 & -\beta_1 & 0 & 0 & -\beta_3 & -\beta_4 \end{pmatrix}$$

The identification of the demand for labour proceeds as follows. Strike out the first row, which represents the demand for labour, and build the submatrix associated with the zero entries in the first row. This results in the submatrix $(-\beta_3 \quad -\beta_4)$. Find out the rank of the submatrix. With no further assumptions, the rank is one. If the rank is equal to the number of equations minus one, then the equation is identified. This is the case here; that is, the labour demand equation is identified. Since the number of columns in the submatrix is greater than the rank of the submatrix, the equation is overidentified.

Following the same procedure as above, we establish that the submatrix of interest for the supply equation is $(-\alpha_3 \quad -\alpha_4)$. With no further assumptions, the rank of this submatrix is one. That is, it is equal to the number of equations minus one. This means that the equation is identified. But since the number of columns is greater than the rank, the equation is overidentified.

Summing up, both order and rank conditions indicate the equations of the system are each overidentified. That is, the system is identified.

e) OLS Estimation Results: Table 4.3 and Table 4.4 present the OLS results for the estimation of labour demand and labour supply, respectively. Computations were done by Eviews 4 and TSP 4.4. As far as labour demand is concerned, the upper part of Table 4.3 indicates that all coefficients have the correct signs. Moreover, real wage and real GDP significantly impact

TABLE 4.3
OLS Results for Demand for Labour Equation, Barbados 1970–1996

Variable	Coefficient	Standard Error	*t* Statistic	Prob.
C	–0.304274	0.506496	–0.600742	0.5539
Lbwager	–0.143113	0.067479	–2.120850	0.0449
Lbgdp	0.734320	0.090125	8.147772	0.0000
Lbniscor	0.000265	0.023422	0.011306	0.9911
R^2	0.917011	Mean dependent variable		4.571220
Adjusted R^2	0.906187	SD dependent variable		0.102027
SE of regression	0.031250	LM test for heteroscedasticity		0.909339
RSS	0.022461	*p* value		0.340000
Log likelihood	57.42820	*F* statistic		84.71545
DW statistic	0.741638	Prob(*F* statistic)		0.000000
Hildreth–Lu Grid Technique for Autocorrelation Correction				
C	–0.499821	0.627964	–.795940	0.4260
Lbwager	–0.190780	0.081960	–2.32771	0.0200
Lbgdp	0.758977	0.103355	7.34337	0.0000
Lbniscor	0.005712	0.028712	.198955	0.8420
ρ (autocorrelation coefficient)	0.600000	DW statistic		1.5280

Note: *C*: constant term; Lbwager: logarithm of Barbados real wage index; Lbgdp: logarithm of Barbados gross domestic product; Lbniscor: logarithm of index of contributions of employers to the national insurance scheme.

on labour demand at the 10 percent level of significance, as the associated *p* values of the *t* ratios show. The LM test for heteroscedasticity through its *p* value indicates the presence of homoscedasticity. In addition, the size of the DW statistic shows there is autocorrelation. The lower part of the table contains the results with autocorrelation correction (Hildreth–Lu grid technique). The basic results do not change: real wage and real GDP impact significantly on labour demand.

Regarding labour supply, the upper part of Table 4.4 indicates that only trend (*T*) has a significant impact on labour supply at the 10 percent level of significance. The regression has, however, an autocorrelation problem (why?). The autocorrelation correction (see the lower part of Table 4.4) does not change the above message.

As pointed out in the theoretical discussion, OLS gives rise to biased and inconsistent estimators in the case of a genuine simultaneous equations model.

f) This is a trap. ILS is only applicable to equations that are just-identified.

g) The 2SLS (TSLS) estimates are obtained as follows. Regress each right-hand-side endogenous variable of the model on all predetermined variables of the model. Then replace each right-hand-side endogenous variable by its estimate in the equation used. Run a new regression to obtain the 2SLS estimates. The results with and without autocorrelation correction are given in Table 4.5 and Table 4.6.

TABLE 4.4
OLS Results for Supply of Labour Equation, Barbados 1970–1996

Variable	Coefficient	Standard Error	*t* Statistic	Prob.
C	4.478637	0.176516	25.37242	0.0000
Lbwager	0.050818	0.127422	0.398813	0.6937
T	0.012986	0.003286	3.951364	0.0006
Lbnisee	–0.016869	0.041282	–0.408636	0.6866
R^2	0.814187	Mean dependent variable		4.571220
Adjusted R^2	0.789950	SD dependent variable		0.102027
SE of regression	0.046760	LM test for heteroscedasticity		3.673380
RSS	0.050290	*p* value		0.055000
Log likelihood	46.54668	*F* statistic		33.59338
DW statistic	0.659190	Prob(*F* statistic)		0.000000
Hildreth–Lu Grid Technique for Autocorrelation Correction				
C	4.549150	0.214701	21.18830	0.0000
Lbwager	–0.036975	0.122705	–0.301333	0.7630
T	0.013872	0.004186	3.313530	0.0010
Lbnisee	–0.033710	0.041519	–0.708920	0.4780
ρ (autocorrelation coefficient)	0.700000	Durbin Watson		0.9812

Note: *C*: constant term; *T*: trend; Lbwager: logarithm of Barbados real wage index; Lbnisee: logarithm of index of contributions of employees to the national insurance scheme.

A look at the demand-for-labour results (see Table 4.5) indicates that all the estimates have the expected signs. The upper part of Table 4.5 reveals the presence of autocorrelation (see the size of the Durbin–Watson statistic). The lower part contains the correction of autocorrelation with robust standard errors. The variables real wage and GDP significantly impact on labour demand in Barbados at the 10 percent level of significance. Indeed, a 1 percent increase in real wage now depresses labour demand by 0.22 percent. A 1 percent increase in GDP increases demand for labour in the order of 0.72 percent.

As far as supply is concerned, Table 4.6 presents the 2SLS results with and without autocorrelation correction. We interpret the lower part of the table. Only the constant term and the trend are significant. Most likely there are significant omitted variables that need to be taken into account in the model. The reader is invited to check whether the omission of variables was the source of autocorrelation.

With respect to OLS, concerning demand for labour we notice that the key results are statistically the same (at least the results corrected for autocorrelation). This is not surprising, as the R^2 is very high. As far as supply of labour is concerned, both estimation techniques convey the same message. However, we note that while the 2SLS estimators are consistent, those of OLS are not.

TABLE 4.5
2SLS Results for Demand of Labour, Barbados 1970–1996

Variable	Coefficient	Standard Error	t Statistic	Prob.
C	–0.181248	0.534890	–0.338851	0.7378
Lbwager	–0.221058	0.103504	–2.135746	0.0436
Lbgdp	0.717490	0.094173	7.618837	0.0000
Lbniscor	–0.002298	0.024224	–0.094873	0.9252
R^2	0.912197	Mean dependent variable		4.571220
Adjusted R^2	0.900745	SD dependent variable		0.102027
SE of regression	0.032144	RSS		0.023764
F statistic	80.17387	DW statistic		0.701730
Prob(F statistic)	0.000000			
Newey–West HAC Standard Errors and Covariance				
C	–0.181248	0.523827	–0.346008	0.7325
Lbwager	–0.221058	0.110392	–2.002470	0.0572
Lbgdp	0.717490	0.089752	7.994140	0.0000
Lbniscor	–0.002298	0.026417	–0.086998	0.9314
R^2	0.912197	Mean dependent variable		4.571220
Adjusted R^2	0.900745	SD dependent variable		0.102027
SE of regression	0.032144	RSS		0.023764
F statistic	80.17387	DW statistic		0.701730
Prob(F statistic)	0.000000			

Note: C: constant term; Lbwager: logarithm of Barbados real wage index; Lbgdp: logarithm of Barbados gross domestic product at constant prices; Lbniscor: logarithm of index of contributions of employers to the national insurance scheme.

h) To compute the total effect, we need to derive the reduced form. The coefficient of the policy variable in that equation represents the total effect. The direct effect is read off the structural form results. The indirect effect is derived from the total and direct effects. The reduced form (not reported here) reveals that the total effect of GDP is 0.434205 percent. According to Table 4.5 the direct effect of GDP on labour is 0.717490 percent. Thus, the indirect effect is 0.434205 – 0.717490 = –0.283285 percent.

Answer 4.16

a) In the inflation equation, the variable T tentatively captures omitted variables.

b) Let us use the rank condition to study the identifiability of each equation and of the system. The matrix A is:

$$A = \begin{pmatrix} 1 & 0 & -\beta_1 & -\beta_2 & -\beta_3 & 0 & -\beta_0 \\ -\alpha_1 & 1 & 0 & 0 & 0 & -\alpha_2 & -\alpha_0 \\ -\gamma_3 & -\gamma_2 & 1 & 0 & 0 & 0 & -\gamma_0 \end{pmatrix}$$

TABLE 4.6
2SLS Results for Supply of Labour, Barbados 1970–1996

Variable	Coefficient	Standard Error	*t* Statistic	Prob.
C	5.026795	0.485274	10.35867	0.0000
Lbwager	0.974198	0.656702	1.483471	0.1515
T	0.028317	0.011818	2.396226	0.0251
Lbnisee	–0.159002	0.120624	–1.318166	0.2004
R^2	0.389938	Mean dependent variable		4.571220
Adjusted R^2	0.310365	SD dependent variable		0.102027
SE of regression	0.084728	RSS		0.165113
F statistic	10.94933	DW statistic		0.883301
Prob(*F* statistic)	0.000115			
Newey–West HAC Standard Errors and Covariance				
C	5.026795	0.409730	12.26855	0.0000
Lbwager	0.974198	0.805353	1.209652	0.2387
T	0.028317	0.013406	2.112350	0.0457
Lbnisee	–0.159002	0.110279	–1.441809	0.1628
R^2	0.389938	Mean dependent variable		4.571220
Adjusted R^2	0.310365	SD dependent variable		0.102027
SE of regression	0.084728	RSS		0.165113
F statistic	10.94933	DW statistic		0.883301
Prob(*F* statistic)	0.000115			

Note: *C*: constant term; *T*: trend; Lbwager: logarithm of Barbados real wage index; Lbnisee: logarithm of index of contributions of employees to the national insurance scheme.

The inflation submatrix is:

$$\begin{pmatrix} 1 & -\alpha_2 \\ -\gamma_2 & 0 \end{pmatrix}$$

Unless $\alpha_2 = 0$ and/or $\gamma_2 = 0$ the rank of the above submatrix is 2. It is equal to the number of endogenous variables of the system minus one. Thus, the equation is identified, precisely, just-identified.

The unemployment rate submatrix is:

$$\begin{pmatrix} -\beta_1 & -\beta_2 & -\beta_3 \\ 1 & 0 & 0 \end{pmatrix}$$

The rank is 2, unless $\beta_1 = \beta_2 = \beta_3 = 0$. Since $2 = 3 - 1$, the unemployment rate equation is identified; precisely, overidentified.

The wage equation submatrix is:

$$\begin{pmatrix} -\beta_2 & -\beta_3 & 0 \\ 0 & 0 & -\alpha_2 \end{pmatrix}$$

TABLE 4.7
2SLS Results for Inflation Equation, Unemployment Equation and Wage Equation, Barbados 1975–1996

Variable	Coefficient	Standard Error	t Statistic	Prob.
Inflation Equation				
C	98.0979	467.8234	0.209690	0.8347
wi	–6.005280	33.26935	–0.180505	0.8588
AD	0.151899	2.778390	0.054672	0.9570
T	–0.048554	0.236479	–0.205321	0.8396
R^2	–14.121881	Mean dependent variable		6.4380
RSS	8118.80	DW statistic		2.3007
Unemployment Equation				
C	55.66406	21.71748	2.563099	0.0190
π	–0.544935	0.219572	–2.481805	0.0226
$Prod$	–4.390103	2.630715	–1.668787	0.1116
R^2	0.223615	Mean dependent variable		17.31364
RSS	202.045	DW statistic		1.50559
Wage Inflation Equation				
C	27.1042	17.78608	1.523901	0.1440
UN	–0.014405	0.904921	–1.591855	0.1279
π	0.596611	0.431443	1.382828	0.1828
R^2	0.154604	Mean dependent variable		6.0048
RSS	566.3039	DW statistic		1.83034

Note: C: constant term; wi: wage growth; AD: aggregate demand; T: trend; π: inflation; $Prod$: productivity; UN: unemployment rate.

The rank is 2, unless $\beta_2 = \beta_3 = 0$ and/or $\alpha_2 = 0$. The equation is overidentified. Thus, the system is identified since each equation is identified.

c) i) To make the system triangular, the restriction is $\beta_1 = 0$.

ii) To make the system fully recursive, the following restrictions must hold:

$$\beta_1 = 0 \text{ and } \Sigma = \begin{pmatrix} \sigma_{11} & 0 & 0 \\ 0 & \sigma_{22} & 0 \\ 0 & 0 & \sigma_{33} \end{pmatrix}$$

d) We estimate each equation of the model by the 2SLS since each equation is identified. Results of the estimation are shown in Table 4.7. Concerning the inflation equation, no explanatory variable has a significant impact on price inflation. The lack of significance is not likely due to multicollinearity. Indeed, the negative R^2 points to the misspecification of the equation. Regarding the unemployment equation, inflation negatively affects unemployment at the 10 percent significance level. There is no evidence of

TABLE 4.8
3SLS Results for Inflation Equation, Unemployment Equation and Wage Equation, Barbados 1975–1996

Variable	Coefficient	Standard Error	*t* Statistic	Prob.
Inflation Equation				
C	20.9897	412.0763	0.050936	0.09596
wi	–0.486172	29.329520	–0.016596	0.9868
AD	–0.579375	2.368457	–0.244621	0.8076
T	–0.932519	20.8247	–0.044779	0.9644
R^2	0.398443	Mean dependent variable		6.437995
RSS	322.9706	DW statistic		1.236001
Unemployment Equation				
C	53.64542	19.83807	2.704166	0.0091
π	–0.533417	0.20.2950	–2.628315	0.0111
Prod	–4.145086	2.402885	–1.725046	0.0900
R^2	0.228998	Mean dependent variable		17.31364
RSS	200.6039	DW statistic		1.487374
Wage Inflation Equation				
C	30.11942	16.25041	1.853456	0.0691
UN	–1.595183	0.826552	–1.929925	0.0587
π	0.544243	0.397499	1.369170	0.1764
R^2	0.066176	Mean dependent variable		6.004845
RSS	625.5424	DW statistic		1.749313

Note: *C*: constant term; *AD*: aggregate demand; *T*: trend; π: inflation; *Prod*: productivity; *UN*: unemployment rate.

autocorrelation. The R^2 is rightly signed. Concerning the wage equation, there is no significant explanatory variable at the 10 percent level of significance.

We also calibrate the model with 3SLS. Results are shown in Table 4.8. Concerning (price) inflation, the R^2 is now good. However, all variables are still insignificant.

Regarding the unemployment equation, inflation and productivity negatively affect unemployment. In the wage inflation equation, unemployment negatively affects wage inflation.

In principle, under the assumption of correct model specification the 3SLS estimates are theoretically better (more efficient) than those under 2SLS when the errors in different equations are correlated and/or there are cross-equations restrictions. In the present case, model 1 (the inflation equation) is probably misspecified. It means that we have to rethink the model.

e) We use the Hausman specification test. The null hypothesis and the alternative hypothesis are, respectively:

H_0: Inflation rate and unemployment rate are independent;
H_1: Inflation rate and unemployment rate are dependent.

We build the m statistic (see Maddala, 1992):

$$m = \frac{\hat{q}^2}{Var(\hat{q})} \sim \chi_1^2$$

with $\hat{q} = \hat{\gamma}_1 - \hat{\gamma}_0$ and $Var(\hat{q}) = Var(\hat{\gamma}_1) - Var(\hat{\gamma}_0)$ where $\hat{\gamma}_1$ is the 2SLS estimate of π in the unemployment equation and $\hat{\gamma}_0$ is the OLS estimate of π in the unemployment equation. Note that $\hat{\gamma}_0$ is consistent and efficient under H_0 but inconsistent under H_1. By the same token, $\hat{\gamma}_1$ is consistent under both H_0 and H_1 but is inefficient under H_0. Computation of the statistic m gives the following:

$$m = \frac{(-0.544935 - 0.392935)^2}{(0.048212 - 0.023257)} = 35.247$$

Since $m > 2.705$ (critical value at the 10 percent level of significance), we reject the null hypothesis and conclude that inflation is endogenous in the unemployment equation.

4.4 SUPPLEMENTARY EXERCISES

Question 4.17 Write a comprehensive essay on the problem of identification in simultaneous equations models.

Question 4.18 One reviewer of this manuscript wrote the following: "Identification (over or exact) means that the structural form parameters can be determined *uniquely* from the reduced form parameters. In reality, the reduced form estimates are linked with the structural parameters by more than one relation. Theoretically, the same structural form values are derived from the reduced form, exactly or overidentified." Evaluate the statement.

Question 4.19 Explain the concept of "overidentification restrictions". How can they be tested?

Question 4.20 Suppose the following model:

$$y_1 + \beta_{11}x_1 + \beta_{12}x_2 = u_1$$

$$\alpha_{21}y_1 + y_2 + \beta_{21}x_1 + \beta_{22}x_2 = u_2$$

$$\alpha_{31}y_1 + \alpha_{32}y_2 + \alpha_{33}y_3 + \beta_{31}x_1 + \beta_{32}x_2 = u_3$$

$$\alpha_{41}y_1 + \alpha_{42}y_2 + \alpha_{43}y_3 + \alpha_{44}y_4 + \beta_{41}x_1 + \beta_{42}x_2 = u_4$$

where the *y*s are the endogenous variables, the *x*s are the exogenous variables and the *u*s are the usual error terms.

a) With no further restrictions, study the identifiability of each equation of the system.
b) Suppose that the variance-covariance of errors of the system is:

$$\Sigma = \begin{pmatrix} \sigma_{11} & 0 & 0 & 0 \\ & \sigma_{22} & 0 & 0 \\ & & \sigma_{33} & 0 \\ & & & \sigma_{44} \end{pmatrix}$$

Study the identifiability of each equation of the system. Comment on the results.

c) Redo (b) with:

$$\Sigma = \begin{pmatrix} \sigma_{11} & \sigma_{12} & 0 & 0 \\ & \sigma_{22} & 0 & 0 \\ & & \sigma_{33} & 0 \\ & & & \sigma_{44} \end{pmatrix}$$

Comment on the results.

Question 4.21 Using the data and model in Question 4.15, obtain the LIML and 3SLS estimates of the parameters. Compare and contrast these results with those presented in Answer 4.15.

Part Three

Dynamic Regression Models

Part Three focuses on dynamic regression models. It consists of three chapters, which tackle various aspects of dynamic regression models. Chapter 5 deals with exercises related to the more traditional (classical) aspect of dynamic regression models. Autoregressive distributed lag models fall in this category. Chapter 6 concerns the modern approach to dynamic regression models. Exercises dealing with cointegration, vector autoregression models, and error correction models constitute the core of the chapter. Chapter 7 focuses on data frequency in the context of time series. Issues of aggregation over time are reflected in the exercises.

CHAPTER 5

Dynamic Regression Models

5.1 INTRODUCTION

Part Three deals with dynamic regression models. Dynamic regressions are regressions that contain some lags to emphasize that the relationships between the dependent variable(s) and independent variable(s) are not instantaneous. Strictly speaking, it is the presence of the lagged dependent variable that gives the characteristic of "dynamic" to a static regression.

The reasons for the existence of lags in a model can be grouped into at least three broad categories: (1) non-instantaneous transmission of effects of policy changes into the dependent variables; (2) adaptive expectations and partial adjustments types of behaviour from the economic agents; (3) other institutional, psychological and technological motives.

The three chapters in Part Three are concerned with various aspects of dynamic regression models. This chapter focuses on dynamic regression models in the traditional (classical) sense. More precisely, the exercises deal with issues related to autoregressive models, distributed lag (DL) models and autoregressive distributed lag (ADL) models. They emphasize stationarity, invertibility, parameter meanings in ADL models, properties of estimators, similarities and differences between Koyck transformation, adaptive expectations and partial adjustment models.

5.2 QUESTIONS

5.2.1 Theoretical Exercises

Question 5.1 Write a careful note on "stationarity".

Question 5.2 Write a careful note on "invertibility".

Question 5.3 State the Wold's theorem or decomposition.

Question 5.4 Consider the following moving average process of order one [$MA(1)$]:

$$Y_t = \varepsilon_t + 1.2\varepsilon_{t-1}$$

where ε_t is a white noise process.

a) Prove that Y_t is stationary.
b) Show that Y_t is not invertible.
c) Find the corresponding invertible representation of the above process.

Question 5.5 Consider the following models:

$$X_t = \varepsilon_t + \alpha_1 \varepsilon_{t-1} + \alpha_2 \varepsilon_{t-2} \quad \text{(Q5.5.1)}$$

and

$$X_t = \beta_1 X_{t-1} + \beta_2 X_{t-2} + \varepsilon_t \quad \text{(Q5.5.2)}$$

where ε_t is white noise. Find the conditions for stationarity or invertibility wherever appropriate.

Question 5.6 Consider the following model:

$$Y_t = \alpha + \beta Y_{t-1} + e_t \quad \text{(Q5.6.1)}$$

with $e_t \sim IID\left(0, \sigma_e^2\right)$.

a) If $\alpha \neq 0$ and $|\beta| < 1$, which process does Y_t follow?
b) If $\alpha \neq 0$ and $|\beta| = 1$, which process does Y_t follow?
c) Show that the OLS estimator of β in (a) is biased but consistent.
d) Suppose now that $e_t = \rho e_{t-1} + \varepsilon_t$ where $|\rho| < 1$ and ε_t is a well-behaved process. Show that the OLS estimator of β in (a) is biased and inconsistent.

Question 5.7 In the context of distributed lag models, explain the following concepts:

a) impact multiplier;
b) intermediate multiplier;
c) long-run multiplier;
d) mean lag;
e) median lag. (See, for example, Johnson and Dinaro, 1997; Hendry, 1995.)

Question 5.8 The Koyck transformation, partial adjustment and adaptive expectations models are similar but conceptually different. Comment.

Question 5.9 Let a simple economy be characterized by the following set of equations (variables are expressed in logarithms):

$$y_t = y_{t-1} + \beta\left(p_t - E_{t-1} p_t\right) + u_t \quad \text{(Q5.9.1)}$$

$$m_t - p_t = y_t + v_t \quad \text{(Q5.9.2)}$$

$$m_t = m^* - \gamma y_{t-1} \quad \text{(Q5.9.3)}$$

where
y_t = real output;
p_t = price level;
$E_{t-1}p_t$ = expected price based on all information available at time $t - 1$;
m_t = money supply;
m^* = anticipated money supply;
u_t and v_t are error terms.

a) Explain what each equation represents.
b) Using the method of undetermined coefficients, solve the model for output and price. Does monetary policy (the choice of m^* and γ) affect the level of output? Give both an intuitive economic explanation and a mathematical explanation.
c) Now replace Equation (Q5.9.3) by the following equation:

$$m_t = m^* + \delta u_t \tag{Q5.9.4}$$

The coefficient δ is a policy parameter chosen by the Central Bank. Discuss what the above policy rule means intuitively and whether or not it is a reasonable assumption. Solve the model again and determine whether monetary policy (the choice of m^* and γ) can affect output. (SUNY Albany PhD Macroeconomics comprehensive examinations, 1988)

5.2.2 Empirical Exercises

Question 5.10 Consider the following rational lag model:

$$Y_t = \left(\left(0.4 + 2L\right) / \left(1 - 0.4L + 0.4L^2\right)\right) X_t + \hat{e}_t \tag{Q5.10.1}$$

where L is the lag operator, that is, $LX_t = X_{t-1}$, and $\hat{e}_t$ is the residual term.

a) Find and explain the short-run multiplier.
b) Find and explain the long-run multiplier.
c) Find and explain the mean lag.

Question 5.11 Consider the following distributed lag model:

$$Y_t = 2 + 0.40X_t + 0.35X_{t-1} + 0.25X_{t-2} + 0.20X_{t-3} + 0.10X_{t-4} + \hat{e}_t \tag{Q5.11.1}$$

where Y_t is the dependent variable, X_t and lagged X_t are the explanatory variables.

a) Which two major econometric problems are associated with this type of regression?
b) Compute the impact multiplier.
c) Compute the long-run multiplier.

d) Compute the mean lag.
e) Compute the median lag. Explain what it means.

Question 5.12 Consider the following *MA*(2) process:

$$Y_t = \left(1 + 3.8L + 1.36L^2\right)u_t \qquad \text{(Q5.12.1)}$$

$$\mathrm{E}\left(u_t u_s\right) = \begin{cases} 1 \text{ if t = s} \\ 0 \text{ otherwise} \end{cases}$$

where L is the lag operator and u_t is the error term.

a) Calculate the autocovariances and autocorrelations of the series.
b) Show that the above *MA*(2) is not invertible.
c) Find the corresponding invertible representation of the process.
d) Calculate the autocovariances and autocorrelations of the new process. Compare them with those obtained in (a). (Adapted from Hamilton, 1994 and UWI, EC36D term test 1998.)

Question 5.13 The following model:

$$Y_t = \beta_0 + \beta_1 Y_{t-1} + \beta_2 X_t + u_t$$

gives rise to the following OLS results using a time series data of 27 observations:

$$\hat{Y}_t = \underset{(0.4)}{2.1} + \underset{(0.29)}{0.97}\, Y_{t-1} + \underset{(1.2)}{3.2}\, X_t$$

$$DW = 0.37$$

where figures in parentheses are standard errors.

a) An econometrician points out that the DW statistic is too low. He concludes that there is positive autocorrelation. To reinforce his idea, he points out that the t statistics are too good. Carefully comment on his position.
b) If there is indeed autocorrelation, advise on an appropriate method of estimation.
c) In the absence of autocorrelation, is the estimator of β_1 biased?
d) An econometrician says that this is a Koyck scheme, another thinks it is an adaptive expectations model and yet another thinks it is a partial adjustment model. Evaluate their positions.

Question 5.14 In Barbados, exports and imports are highly correlated. According to many people this is an indication of a highly open country. An econometrician argues that imports (Y) depend on the expected or permanent level of exports and he formulates the following model:

TABLE 5.1
Exports and Imports in Barbados, 1972–2001

Year	Exports	Imports	Year	Exports	Imports
1972	252.000	329.000	1987	1,340.000	1,325.000
1973	298.000	398.000	1988	1,510.000	1,495.000
1974	386.000	472.000	1989	1,724.000	1,725.000
1975	469.000	515.000	1990	1,689.000	1,780.000
1976	406.000	566.000	1991	1,610.000	1,701.000
1977	493.000	607.000	1992	1,588.000	1,330.000
1978	646.000	760.000	1993	1,727.000	1,537.000
1979	882.000	1,027.000	1994	1,960.000	1,683.000
1980	1,214.000	1,247.000	1995	2,265.000	2,503.000
1981	1,138.000	1,315.000	1996	2,450.000	2,199.000
1982	1,270.000	1,323.000	1997	2,438.000	2,511.000
1983	1,490.000	1,466.000	1998	2,521.900	2,619.700
1984	1,656.000	1,547.000	1999	2,545.900	2,823.200
1985	1,633.000	1,448.000	2000	2,582.900	2,919.200
1986	1,496.000	1,435.000	2001	2,592.800	2,735.300

Note: Imports of goods and services: Y variable in the model; exports of goods and services: X variable in the model. Variables are in Bds$ millions.

Source: International Monetary Fund, Washington, D.C., *International Financial Statistics*, various issues.

$$Y_t = \alpha + \beta X_t^* + e_t \qquad \text{(Q5.14.1)}$$

where X_t^* is expected exports and e_t is the error term. The former variable is unknown and the econometrician assumes expectations are adaptive:

$$X_t^* - X_{t-1}^* = \gamma(X_t - X_{t-1}^*) \qquad \text{(Q5.14.2)}$$

where $0 < \gamma \leq 1$.

a) What are the major criticisms that a "rational expectations" follower will formulate against the "adaptive expectations" scheme such as in Equation (Q5.14.2)?
b) Obtain an estimable form of Equation (Q5.14.1).
c) Fit the model developed in (b) to the data in Table 5.1.
d) Fully interpret the results (including the properties of estimators).
e) Are the errors autocorrelated? Why or why not?
f) Whatever your answer to (e), the errors from the estimable form were expected to be autocorrelated. If your answer to (e) is no, explain why this is so. If not, proceed to question (g).
g) Test $\beta = 1$.

Suppose your estimable model is now:

$$Y_t = a + b_0 X_t + b_1 X_{t-1} + \delta Y_{t-1} + u_t \tag{Q5.14.3}$$

h) Estimate the new model and interpret the results.
i) What is the long-run impact of exports on imports?

5.3 ANSWERS

Answer 5.1

Stationarity is an important concept in econometrics for at least three reasons. First, most test statistics have been derived under the assumption of stationarity. In other words, the non-fulfilment of the stationarity assumption generally brings about non-standard distributions, which are not always tractable. Second, in some circumstances the lack of stationarity gives rise to nonsense results (e.g., nonsense or spurious regressions). Third, according to the Wold's theorem any stationary process can be decomposed into two parts: a deterministic part and a nondeterministic part (a moving average of infinite order). But what do econometricians or statisticians mean by stationary process?

A set of random variables ordered in time is known as a stochastic process. The latter can be stationary or not. A stochastic process can be strictly stationary or weakly stationary. A stochastic process $\{Y_t \; t \in T\}$ is said to be strictly stationary if the joint distribution of $Y_{t_1},\cdots,Y_{t_n}$ is the same as $Y_{t_{1+s}},\cdots,Y_{t_{n+s}}$. This is a rather strong condition. A weaker form concentrates on the first and second moments of the distribution. A stochastic process is characterized as weak or wide or covariance stationary if the mean and the variance of the process are constant and the covariance between, for example, Y_{t_1} and Y_{t_2} only depends on the distance $s = t_1 - t_2$.

Summing up, a stationary process is a process that is mean reverting; that is, a process that constantly returns to its mean after some deviations. A white noise series and an autoregressive process of order one are examples of stationary series.

How to detect stationarity? There are basically three ways of detecting stationarity in a series: graphical methods, use of a correlogram and test statistics. Graphical methods allude to the shape of the plot of the series against time. A stationary series is erratic (does not wander forever). Correlogram or autocorrelation functions (acf) is the graph of different autocorrelation coefficients against the different lags. A stationary series has the characteristic of having an acf that dies out fast as the number of lags increases. The test statistics are basically the tests for unit roots (non-stationarity versus stationarity). They are developed in Chapter 6. It is our view that a combination of the three methods will usually enable the researcher to be at ease with his or her conclusion about the stationarity/non-stationarity of a series.

Answer 5.2

The concept of invertibility is defined in the context of the moving average process (MA). Recall, a process Y_t follows a moving average if it can be written out as follows:

$$Y_t = \varepsilon_t + \beta_1\varepsilon_{t-1} + \beta_2\varepsilon_{t-2} + \beta_3\varepsilon_{t-3} + \cdots \quad \text{(A5.2.1)}$$

where ε_t is a white noise process (purely random process) and β represents any constants. Equation (A5.2.1) is an infinite-order moving average, $MA(\infty)$. Note that a constant (e.g., mean of the series) can be added to Equation (A5.2.1).

A moving average is said to be invertible if it can be represented as an autoregressive process of infinite order, $AR(\infty)$. To explain, consider the following $MA(q)$:

$$Y_t = \varepsilon_t + \beta_1\varepsilon_{t-1} + \beta_2\varepsilon_{t-2} + \cdots + \beta_q\varepsilon_{t-q} \quad \text{(A5.2.2)}$$

or

$$Y_t = B_q(L)\varepsilon_t$$

where $B_q(L) = 1 + \beta_1 L + \beta_2 L^2 + \cdots + \beta_q L^q$ and L is the backward shift operator, that is, $LY_t = Y_{t-1}$. We can rewrite $B_q(L)$ as:

$$\left(1 + \beta_1 L + \beta_2 L^2 + \cdots + \beta_q L^q\right) = \left(1 - \lambda_1 L\right)\left(1 - \lambda_2 L\right)\cdots\left(1 - \lambda_q L\right) \quad \text{(A5.2.3)}$$

where $\lambda_1, \lambda_2, \ldots, \lambda_q$ are the roots of the equation:

$$Z^q + \beta_1 Z^{q-1} + \cdots + \beta_q = 0 \quad \text{(A5.2.4)}$$

If $|\lambda_i| < 1$ for all i, then the process shown in Equation (A5.2.2) is said to be invertible, that is, Equation (A5.2.2) can be rewritten as:

$$\varepsilon_t = \left[B_q(L)\right]^{-1} Y_t \quad \text{(A5.2.5)}$$

or

$$\varepsilon_t = Y_t + \alpha_1 Y_{t-1} + \alpha_2 Y_{t-2} + \alpha_3 Y_{t-3} + \cdots \quad \text{(A5.2.6)}$$

that is:

$$Y_t = -\alpha_1 Y_{t-1} - \alpha_2 Y_{t-2} - \alpha_3 Y_{t-3} - \cdots + \varepsilon_t \quad \text{(A5.2.7)}$$

which is an infinite-order autoregressive process.

Summing up, if $|\lambda_i| < 1$, the roots of Equation (A5.2.2) are all outside the unit circle, and the equation is said to be invertible.

With the exception of $|\lambda_i| = 1$, $|\lambda_i| < 1$ corresponds to $|\lambda_i| > 1$, that is, to each invertible representation corresponds a noninvertible representation and vice versa.

The striking feature is that both processes (invertible and corresponding noninvertible representations) have identical moments.

Although invertible and noninvertible representations of data well characterize MA processes, preference is given to invertible representations for at least two reasons. First, to find the innovation ε at time t, there is a need to know current and past values of Y_t. On the contrary, for the corresponding ε in the noninvertible representation knowledge of future values of Y_t is required. Clearly since the past of Y_t is known it is advantageous to work with the invertible representation. Second, some methods for estimating parameters and generating forecasts require the use of the invertible representation for their validity (see Hamilton, 1994, 67).

Answer 5.3

Wold's theorem or Wold's decomposition states that any covariance stationary process (e.g., Y_t) can be decomposed into two parts: a deterministic part and a nondeterministic part (a moving average of infinite order):

$$Y_t = C + \sum_{i=0}^{\infty} \theta_i \varepsilon_{t-i}$$

where ε_t is a white noise process (nondeterministic part) and C is the deterministic part. The two parts are uncorrelated. Wold's decomposition implies that any AR process has an MA representation.

Answer 5.4

a) It suffices to show (i) the first and second moments are not dependent on time t; (ii) the covariance between Y_t and Y_{t-s} depends only on the distance between t and $t - s$.

$$\begin{aligned} E(Y_t) &= E\left[\varepsilon_t + 1.2\varepsilon_{t-1}\right] \\ &= E(\varepsilon_t) + 1.2E(\varepsilon_{t-1}) \\ &= 0 + 0 = 0 \qquad \text{since } \varepsilon_t \text{ is white noise.} \end{aligned}$$

$$\begin{aligned} \text{var}(Y_t) &= E\left(Y_t - E(Y_t)\right)^2 \\ &= E\left(Y_t^2\right) \qquad \text{since } E(Y_t) = 0 \\ &= E\left(\varepsilon_t + 1.2\varepsilon_{t-1}\right)^2 \\ &= E\left(\varepsilon_t^2 + 2.4\varepsilon_t\varepsilon_{t-1} + 1.44\varepsilon_{t-1}^2\right) \\ &= (1 + 1.44)\sigma_\varepsilon^2 \quad \text{since } E\left(\varepsilon_t^2\right) = E\left(\varepsilon_{t-1}^2\right) = \sigma_\varepsilon^2 \text{ and } \mathrm{E}\left(\varepsilon_t\varepsilon_{t-1}\right) = 0 \\ \text{var}(Y_t) &= 2.44\sigma_\varepsilon^2 \end{aligned}$$

$$
\begin{aligned}
Cov\left(Y_t Y_{t-1}\right) &= E\left(Y_t Y_{t-1}\right) - E\left(Y_t\right)E\left(Y_{t-1}\right) \\
&= E\left(Y_t Y_{t-1}\right) \qquad \text{since } E\left(Y_t\right) = 0 \\
&= E\left[\left(\varepsilon_t + 1.2\varepsilon_{t-1}\right)\left(\varepsilon_{t-1} + 1.2\varepsilon_{t-2}\right)\right] \\
&= E\left(\varepsilon_t\varepsilon_{t-1}\right) + 1.2E\left(\varepsilon_{t-1}^2\right) + 1.2E\left(\varepsilon_t\varepsilon_{t-2}\right) + 1.44E\left(\varepsilon_{t-1}\varepsilon_{t-2}\right) \\
&= 1.2\sigma_\varepsilon^2
\end{aligned}
$$

Since the first and second moments are constant and the covariance does not depend on t, Y_t is a second-order stationary process.

b) $Y_t = \varepsilon_t + 1.2\varepsilon_{t-1}$
Y_t is not invertible since $|1.2| > 1$.

c) The invertible representation is given by:

$$Y_t = \varepsilon_t^* + \frac{1}{1.2}\varepsilon_{t-1}^*$$

where ε_t^* is the new innovation (for details, see Answer 5.12).

Answer 5.5

In Equation (Q5.5.1) we are interested in invertibility. We can rewrite that equation as follows:

$$X_t = \left(1 + \alpha_1 L + \alpha_2 L^2\right)\varepsilon_t$$

The polynomial in L has two roots and we can write:

$$X_t = \left(1 - \pi_1 L\right)\left(1 - \pi_2 L\right)\varepsilon_t$$

where π_1 and π_2 are the roots of the equation

$$S^2 + \alpha_1 S + \alpha_2 = 0$$

The condition $|\pi_i| < 1$ gives rise to:

$$\left|\frac{-\alpha_1 \pm \sqrt{\alpha_1^2 - 4\alpha_2}}{2}\right| < 1$$

This means that α_1 and α_2 must satisfy:

$$\alpha_1 + \alpha_2 > -1$$

$$\alpha_2 - \alpha_1 > -1$$

$$|\alpha_2| < 1$$

The last condition comes from $\alpha_2 = \pi_1\pi_2$ and the first two are derived from:

$$\alpha_1^2 - 4\alpha_2 < (2+\alpha_1)^2 \quad \text{or} \quad \alpha_1^2 - 4\alpha_2 < (2-\alpha_1)^2$$

The condition of stationarity can be developed in the context of Equation (Q5.5.2). As for invertibility, the equation can be rewritten as follows:

$$(1-\beta_1 L - \beta_2 L^2)X_t = \varepsilon_t$$

where π_1 and π_2 are the roots of the equation:

$$S^2 - \beta_1 S - \beta_2 = 0$$

Put differently, $|\pi_i| < 1$ implies that:

$$\left|\frac{\beta_1 \pm \sqrt{\beta_1^2 + 4\beta_2}}{2}\right| < 1$$

This means that β_1 and β_2 must satisfy:

$$\beta_1 + \beta_2 < 1$$

$$\beta_2 - \beta_1 < 1$$

$$|\beta_2| < 1$$

(See Maddala and Kim, 1998, 12–15.)

Answer 5.6

a) This is an autoregressive process of order 1, *AR*(1).
b) This is a random walk with a drift.
c) Minimization of the residual sum of squares gives rise to:

$$\hat{\beta}_{OLS} = \frac{\sum_{t=2}^{T}\left(Y_t - \overline{Y}\right)\left(Y_{t-1} - \overline{Y_{-1}}\right)}{\sum_{t=2}^{T}\left(Y_{t-1} - \overline{Y_{-1}}\right)^2} = \frac{\sum_{t=2}^{T} Y_t\left(Y_{t-1} - \overline{Y_{-1}}\right)}{\sum_{t=2}^{T}\left(Y_{t-1} - \overline{Y_{-1}}\right)^2}$$

$$= \frac{\sum\left(\alpha + \beta Y_{t-1} + e_t\right)\left(Y_{t-1} - \overline{Y_{-1}}\right)}{\sum\left(Y_{t-1} - \overline{Y_{-1}}\right)^2} \qquad \text{(A5.6.1)}$$

$$= \frac{\alpha\sum\left(Y_{t-1} - \overline{Y_{-1}}\right)}{\sum\left(Y_{t-1} - \overline{Y_{-1}}\right)^2} + \frac{\beta\sum\left(Y_{t-1} - \overline{Y_{-1}}\right)^2}{\sum\left(Y_{t-1} - \overline{Y_{-1}}\right)^2} + \frac{\sum e_t\left(Y_{t-1} - \overline{Y_{-1}}\right)}{\sum\left(Y_{t-1} - \overline{Y_{-1}}\right)^2}$$

$$= \beta + \frac{\sum e_t\left(Y_{t-1} - \overline{Y_{-1}}\right)}{\sum\left(Y_{t-1} - \overline{Y_{-1}}\right)^2}$$

We know that many terms in the numerator of the second term on the right-hand side of Equation (A5.6.1) are correlated with those in the denominator. In other words, the numerator and denominator are a ratio of two random variables, for example, z_t and v_t. It is known that in such a case $E(z_t/v_t) \neq E(z_t)/E(v_t)$ in general. Monte Carlo simulations of

$$\mathrm{E}\left[\frac{\sum e_t\left(Y_{t-1} - \overline{Y_{-1}}\right)}{\sum\left(Y_{t-1} - \overline{Y_{-1}}\right)^2}\right] \qquad \text{(A5.6.2)}$$

done by some authors and not reported here, indicate that this expected value is different from zero. Hence,

$$\mathrm{E}\left(\hat{\beta}_{OLS}\right) = \beta + \mathrm{E}\left[\frac{\sum e_t\left(Y_{t-1} - \overline{Y_{-1}}\right)}{\sum (Y_{t-1} - \overline{Y_{-1}})^2}\right] \qquad \text{(A5.6.3)}$$

is different from β, that is, $\hat{\beta}$ is a biased estimator of β.

To prove the consistency of $\hat{\beta}$, we evaluate its probability limit. Using Equation (A5.6.1), we can write:

$$\operatorname*{plim}_{T\to\infty}\hat{\beta}_{OLS} = \operatorname*{plim}_{T\to\infty}\beta + \frac{\operatorname*{plim}_{T\to\infty}\sum e_t\left(Y_{t-1} - \overline{Y_{-1}}\right)/T}{\operatorname*{plim}_{T\to\infty}\sum\left(Y_{t-1} - \overline{Y_{-1}}\right)^2/T} \qquad \text{(A5.6.4)}$$

Since:

$$\underset{T\to\infty}{\text{plim}} \frac{\sum e_t\left(Y_{t-1}-\overline{Y_{-1}}\right)}{T}=0 \quad \text{as} \quad \mathrm{E}\left[e_t\left(Y_{t-1}-\overline{Y_{-1}}\right)\right]=0 \qquad \text{(A5.6.5)}$$

and

$$\underset{T\to\infty}{\text{plim}} \frac{\sum \left(Y_{t-1}-\overline{Y_{-1}}\right)}{T}=Var\left(Y_t\right) \qquad \text{(A5.6.6)}$$

thus

$$\text{plim}\,\hat{\beta}_{OLS}=\beta$$

That is, $\hat{\beta}_{OLS}$ is a consistent estimator of β.

d) i) To show that $\hat{\beta}$ is a biased estimator of β, we use Equation (A5.6.3), which is still valid. Now since Y_{t-1} is correlated with e_t through $e_t = \rho e_{t-1} + \varepsilon_t$, $\hat{\beta}$ is biased (using the argument as in part [c]).

ii) Inconsistency of $\hat{\beta}$. That is, $\text{plim}\,\hat{\beta} \neq \beta$. This has been shown in Answer 2.13.b.

Answer 5.7

Consider the following distributed lag model:

$$Y_t=\alpha+\sum_{i=0}^{p}\beta_i X_{t-i}+e_t$$

where e_t is a white noise process and

$$\sum_{i=0}^{p}\beta_i<\infty$$

a) Impact multiplier (short-run multiplier): The impact multiplier captured by β_0 in the above is the contemporaneous change in the mean value of Y_t due to a unit change in X_t in the same time period; that is:

$$\frac{\partial Y_t}{\partial X_t}=\beta_0$$

b) Interim multiplier(s): The interim, or intermediate, multiplier is the average response of Y_t due to a unit change in X_t in any of the previous periods:

$$\beta_i=\partial Y_t \big/ \partial X_{t-i}$$

This is the impact multiplier of order i. Impact multipliers (in plural) represent the partial sums of the β_i. For example, if the change in X_t is maintained at the same level thereafter, then $(\beta_0 + \beta_1)$ gives the change in mean value of Y_t in the next period.

c) Long-run or total distributed lag multiplier: The long-run multiplier is the total sum of impacts:

$$\beta = \sum_{i=0}^{p} \beta_i$$

This supposes that the economy is at a steady state. In other words, it indicates the extent to which, after the whole period, the mean value of Y_t (dependent variable) has increased as a result of a permanent increase in X_t (explanatory variable).

d) Mean lag: This is a "lag weighted average time". That is, the average period of time it takes for an effect of an explanatory variable to be transmitted into the dependent variable. For example, having a mean lag of 3 years means that it takes 3 years for the effect of X_t to be transmitted to Y_t.

e) Median lag: The median lag is similar to the mean lag. It stands for the number of periods of time it takes for 50 percent of the total effect of X_t to be achieved.

Answer 5.8

To do justice to the topic, we explain briefly what each model stands for. Consider the following infinite distributed lag model:

$$Y_t = \alpha + \sum_{i=0}^{\infty} \beta_i X_{t-i} + e_t \qquad \text{(A5.8.1)}$$

The estimation of this structure is marred with econometric problems. The three most important ones are multicollinearity, autocorrelation of errors and insufficient degrees of freedom given the usual size of economic data. Several models have been suggested in the literature to restrict the above lag model to a few underlying parameters. Among others, there are the Koyck or geometric lag model, the Pascal lag distribution, the Jorgenson's rational lag distribution and the Gamma distribution. Of the long list of approximations, in our view the Koyck scheme has withstood time.

The Koyck model is derived as follows (see, for example, Maddala, 1977, 359–363; Johnston, 1984, 343–383). Suppose all the β_i are of the same sign and β_i is declining geometrically; that is, the distant past is less important than the near past:

$$\beta_i = \beta_0 \lambda^i \qquad \text{(A5.8.2)}$$

where $0 < \lambda < 1$ is the coefficient of decay and β_0 is the impact multiplier. Noting that β is the long-run multiplier, Equation (A5.8.2) can also be written as:

$$\beta_i = \beta(1-\lambda)\lambda^i \tag{A5.8.3}$$

where

$$\beta = \sum_{i=0}^{\infty} \beta_i$$

and $w_i = (1-\lambda)\lambda^i$ is the lag weight. Equation (A5.8.3) into (A5.8.1) gives rise to:

$$\begin{aligned} Y_t &= \alpha + \sum_{i=0}^{\infty} \beta w_i X_{t-i} + e_t \\ &= \alpha + \beta \sum_{i=0}^{\infty} w_i X_{t-i} + e_t \qquad \text{(A5.8.4)} \\ &= \alpha + \beta(1-\lambda) \sum_{i=0}^{\infty} \lambda^i X_{t-1} + e_t \end{aligned}$$

Using the lag operator L (i.e., $LY_t = Y_{t-1}$), Equation (A5.8.4) can be rewritten as:

$$Y_t = \alpha + \beta B(L) X_t + e_t \tag{A5.8.5}$$

where

$$B(L) = (1-\lambda)(1 + \lambda L + \lambda^2 L^2 + \lambda^3 L^3 + \cdots) = \frac{1-\lambda}{1-\lambda L}$$

Thus, Equation (A5.8.5) is:

$$Y_t = \alpha + \beta \frac{1-\lambda}{1-\lambda L} X_t + e_t$$

or

$$(1-\lambda L)Y_t = \alpha(1-\lambda L) + \beta(1-\lambda)X_t + (1-\lambda L)e_t$$

or

$$Y_t = \alpha(1-\lambda) + \lambda Y_{t-1} + \beta(1-\lambda)X_t + v_t \tag{A5.8.6}$$

where $\alpha(1 - \lambda L) = \alpha(1 - \lambda)$ and $v_t = e_t - \lambda e_{t-1}$.

Equation (A5.8.6) is the Koyck scheme or representation of Equation (A5.8.1). With respect to the latter it has the advantage of having only three parameters to estimate: λ, α, and β.

Equation (A5.8.6) has been derived rather mechanically, to the extent that it is devoid of any economic content. Economists or econometricians have succeeded in giving an economic content to the equation. Two such attempts are the so-called adaptive expectation models and the partial adjustment models.

Adaptive expectations models are models of the following type (see, for example, Maddala, 1992):

$$Y_t = \alpha + \beta X^*_{t+1} + e_t \qquad \text{(A5.8.7)}$$

where X^*_{t+1} is the expected value of X_t at time $t + 1$. For example, today's production depends on tomorrow's expected sales; demand for money depends on expected long-run interest rate.

Equation (A5.8.7) cannot be estimated as it stands. There is a need for a mechanism of expectations formation. An example of such a mechanism is the so-called adaptive expectations, which states:

$$X^*_{t+1} - X^*_t = (1-\lambda)(X_t - X^*_t) \qquad 0 \le \lambda \le 1 \qquad \text{(A5.8.8)}$$

Equation (A5.8.8) means expectations get revised each period using the latest information about the actual value of the variables. Using the lag operator L Equation (A5.8.8) can be rewritten as:

$$\begin{aligned} X^*_{t+1} &= X^*_t + (1-\lambda)X_t - (1-\lambda)X^*_t \\ X^*_{t+1} &= \lambda X^*_t + (1-\lambda)X_t \\ (1-\lambda L)X^*_{t+1} &= (1-\lambda)X_t \\ X^*_{t+1} &= \frac{(1-\lambda)}{(1-\lambda L)}X_t \end{aligned} \qquad \text{(A5.8.9)}$$

Equation (A5.8.9) into (A5.8.7) gives:

$$\begin{aligned} Y_t &= \alpha + \beta\frac{(1-\lambda)}{(1-\lambda L)}X_t + e_t \\ (1-\lambda L)Y_t &= \alpha(1-\lambda L) + \beta(1-\lambda)X_t + (1-\lambda L)e_t \\ Y_t &= \alpha(1-\lambda) + \lambda Y_{t-1} + \beta(1-\lambda)X_t + v_t \end{aligned} \qquad \text{(A5.8.10)}$$

The adaptive expectations model [Equation (A5.8.10)] is thus "identical" to the Koyck model [Equation (A5.8.6)].

The second rationalization of the Koyck scheme is the partial adjustment model. The latter posits a model of the following type:

$$Y_t^* = \alpha + \beta X_t + e_t \tag{A5.8.11}$$

That is, the explanatory variables are linked to some desired levels of endogenous variables. In general, there is a gap between the desired level and the actual level. There is thus a partial adjustment of actual level toward desired level. This can be written as follows:

$$Y_t - Y_{t-1} = (1-\lambda)(Y_t^* - Y_{t-1}) \tag{A5.8.12}$$

where $0 \leq \lambda \leq 1$. Rearranging the above gives:

$$\begin{aligned}(1-\lambda)Y_t^* &= Y_t - Y_{t-1} + (1-\lambda)Y_{t-1} \\ (1-\lambda)Y_t^* &= Y_t - \lambda Y_{t-1} \\ Y_t^* &= \frac{1}{(1-\lambda)}(Y_t - \lambda Y_{t-1})\end{aligned} \tag{A5.8.13}$$

Equation (A5.8.13) into Equation (A5.8.11) gives:

$$Y_t = \alpha(1-\lambda) + \lambda Y_{t-1} + \beta(1-\lambda)X_t + (1-\lambda)e_t \tag{A5.8.14}$$

Equation (5.8.14) is the partial adjustment model equivalent of the Koyck scheme. Except for the error term, they are both the same.

Putting the three models together, it can be said that they bear striking resemblance to each other. In fact, they are the same in the context used here. However, the autocorrelation structures are different for the partial adjustment model, which does not have autocorrelation, at least if we assume that the original error is well behaved. On the contrary, the errors for the Koyck and adaptive expectations models are generally autocorrelated. This has implications in terms of appropriate methods of estimation. Moreover, while the Koyck scheme is an ad hoc procedure, the two other models are grounded in economic theory. The adaptive expectations model is centered on uncertainty, and the partial adjustment model emphasizes the gap between the desired level and the actual level of a variable due to some costs (e.g., adjustment costs).

In conclusion, it is always imperative to ask oneself about the type of model that has generated the results with which one is working, as the results are subject to different interpretations with different models.

Answer 5.9

a) Equation (Q5.9.1) is a variant of the Lucas supply curve: real output depends on price surprises and past real output. Note that there is no strong theoretical justification for the presence of y_{t-1} except that it boosts the fit of the equation; otherwise, y_t will simply be a noise. Equation (Q5.9.2) represents money demand: real money depends on real output. Equation (Q5.9.3) represents the money supply rule: money supply equals a fixed target (m^*) plus a feedback from output disturbance that is influenced by the Central Bank.

b) Using undetermined coefficients, we can derive the following:

$$y_t = \pi_y y_{t-1} + \pi_m m^* + \pi_u u_t + \pi_v v_t \quad \text{(A5.9.1)}$$

$$p_t = \theta_y y_{t-1} + \theta_m m^* + \theta_u u_t + \theta_v v_t \quad \text{(A5.9.2)}$$

where the πs and θs are undetermined coefficients. Equations (A5.9.1) and (A5.9.2) in Equations (Q5.9.2), (Q5.9.3) and (Q5.9.1) give:

$$m^* - \gamma y_{t-1} = \pi_y y_{t-1} + \pi_m m^* + \pi_u u_t + \pi_v v_t + \theta_y y^*_{t-1} + \theta_m m^* + \theta_u u_t + \theta_v v_t + v_t \quad \text{(A5.9.3)}$$

$$\pi_y y_{t-1} + \pi_m m^* + \pi_u u_t + \pi_v v_t = y_{t-1} + \beta(\theta_u u_t + \theta_v v_t) + u_t \quad \text{(A5.9.4)}$$

From Equations (A5.9.3) and (A5.9.4) we have the following:

$$\begin{cases} \pi_m + \theta_m - 1 & = 0 \\ \pi_y + \theta_y + \gamma & = 0 \\ \pi_u + \theta_u & = 0 \\ \pi_v + \theta_v + 1 & = 0 \\ \pi_m & = 0 \\ \pi_y - 1 & = 0 \\ \pi_u - \beta\theta_u - 1 & = 0 \\ \pi_v - \beta\theta_v & = 0 \end{cases} \quad \text{(A5.9.5)}$$

Equation (A5.9.5) is a system of eight equations with eight unknowns. The solutions are the following:

$$\pi_m = 0, \quad \theta_m = 1, \quad \pi_y = 1, \quad \theta_y = -1 - \gamma,$$

$$\pi_u = \frac{1}{1+\beta}, \quad \theta_u = \frac{-1}{1+\beta}, \quad \pi_v = \frac{-\beta}{1+\beta}, \quad \theta_v = \frac{-1}{1+\beta}.$$

Thus:

$$\begin{cases} y_t = y_{t-1} + \dfrac{1}{1+\beta} u_t - \dfrac{\beta}{1+\beta} v_t \\ p_t = -(1+\gamma) y_{t-1} + m^* - \dfrac{1}{1+\beta} u_t - \dfrac{1}{1+\beta} v_t \end{cases} \tag{A5.9.6}$$

Equation (A5.9.6) indicates that monetary policy does not affect real output. Indeed, neither m^* nor γ enter the output equation: y_t is only affected by its own past and surprises (the Lucas supply curve: only unexpected price [inflation] affects output).

c) If the last equation is replaced by $m_t = m^* + \delta u_t$ then (check it):

$$y_t = y_{t-1} + \frac{\delta - 1}{1+\beta} u_t - \frac{\beta}{1+\beta} v_t$$

$$p_t = -y_{t-1} + m^* - \frac{\delta - 1}{1+\beta} u_t - \frac{1}{1+\beta} v_t$$

Yes, monetary policy affects output through the parameter δ. Indeed, δ enters the y_t equation as seen above. Intuitively, the Central Bank has superior information on the shock u_t. That is why it can use δ to influence y_t.

Answer 5.10

a) The first term of the division of $0.4 + 2L$ by $1 - 0.4L + 0.4L^2$ is 0.4. That is $0.4X_t$ is the first term on the right-hand side of Equation (Q5.10.1). The short-run multiplier is then 0.4. If X_t increases by one unit the contemporaneous increase in the mean value of Y_t is 0.4.

b) Equation (Q5.10.1) is a rational lag model. Let us rewrite it in general terms:

$$Y_t = \frac{B(L)}{C(L)} X_t + e_t \tag{A5.10.1}$$

The long-run multiplier or equilibrium multiplier is:

$$\beta = \sum \beta_i = \frac{B(1)}{C(1)} = D(1)$$

where $B(1)$ is simply $B(L)$ with $L = 1$, and similarly for $C(1)$. Reverting to (Q5.10.1), the long-run multiplier is:

$$\beta = \frac{0.4 + 2}{1 - 0.4 + 0.4} = 2.4$$

That is, if the values of X_t were permanently fixed at $\bar{X}$ (steady state), then a one unit shock to $\bar{X}$ will bring about a 2.4 unit change in Y_t. This is the total cumulative effect on Y_t due to a shock to $\bar{X}$.

c) Using Equation (A5.10.1), we know that the mean lag is:

$$\frac{D'(1)}{D(1)} = \frac{B'(1)}{B(1)} - \frac{C'(1)}{C(1)}$$

From Equation (Q5.10.1) we have:

$$B(L) = 0.4 + 2L \qquad B'(L) = 2 \qquad B'(1) = 2$$

$$C(L) = 1 - 0.4L + 0.4L^2 \qquad C'(L) = -0.4 + 0.8L \qquad C'(1) = 0.4$$

$$B(1) = 2.4 \qquad C(1) = 1$$

Thus:

$$\text{Mean lag } = \frac{2}{2.4} - \frac{0.4}{1} = 0.4$$

It means that it takes on average 0.4 unit of time for the effect of X_t to be transmitted to Y_t.

Answer 5.11

a) The two major problems in this type of regression are multicollinearity and autocorrelation of errors. Multicollinearity is often present if the X_t values are highly autocorrelated. Unfortunately, this is usually the case. This results in imprecision of estimates. Autocorrelation too is often present in this type of regression. This often arises when there are omitted lagged autocorrelated X_t. This type of autocorrelation leads to biased, inconsistent and inefficient estimators (why?).

b) The impact multiplier is 0.4.

c) The long-run multiplier is 0.40 + 0.35 + 0.25 + 0.20 + 0.10 = 1.30.

d) The mean lag is:

$$\frac{\sum i\beta_i}{\sum \beta_i} = \frac{0.35 + (2 \times 0.25) + (3 \times 0.20) + (4 \times 0.10)}{1.30} = 1.42.$$

e) We start by computing standardized coefficient w_i:

$$w_i = \frac{\beta_i}{\sum \beta_i}$$

Thus:

$$w_0 = \frac{\beta_0}{\beta} = \frac{0.4}{1.3} = 0.308 \qquad w_1 = \frac{0.35}{1.3} = 0.269$$

$$w_2 = \frac{0.25}{1.3} = 0.192 \qquad w_3 = \frac{0.20}{1.3} = 0.154 \qquad w_4 = \frac{0.10}{1.3} = 0.077$$

Period	0	1	2	3	4
w_i	$\frac{0.4}{1.3}$	$\frac{0.35}{1.3}$	$\frac{0.25}{1.3}$	$\frac{0.20}{1.3}$	$\frac{0.10}{1.3}$
Cumulative effect	$\frac{0.4}{1.3}$	$\frac{0.75}{1.3}$	$\frac{1}{1.3}$	$\frac{1.2}{1.3}$	1

$$\text{Median lag } = 0 + \frac{0.50-(0.40/1.3)}{(0.75/1.3)-(0.40/1.3)} = 0.71.$$

That is, it takes 0.71 periods for 50 percent of the total effect in Y_t due to a change in X_t to be achieved.

Answer 5.12

a) Let us compute first the autocovariances. Recall the autocovariance of order zero is the variance itself:

$$\gamma_0 = Cov(Y_t\, Y_t) = \mathrm{E}(Y_t - \mathrm{E}(Y_t))^2 \tag{A5.12.1}$$

Using Equation (Q5.12.1) in Equation (A5.12.1) gives:

$$\gamma_0 = \mathrm{E}(Y_t - \mathrm{E}(Y_t))^2 = \mathrm{E}(Y_t^2)$$

since:

$$\mathrm{E}(Y_t) = \mathrm{E}(u_t + 3.8u_{t-1} + 1.36u_{t-2}) = 0$$

Thus:

$$\gamma_0 = \mathrm{E}(u_t^2) + 3.8^2\mathrm{E}(u_{t-1}^2) + 1.36^2\mathrm{E}(u_{t-2}^2) \;\text{ since }\; Cov(u_t\; u_{t-s}) = 0$$

$$\begin{aligned}\gamma_0 &= (1 + 3.8^2 + 1.36^2)\sigma_u^2 \\ &= (1 + 14.44 + 1.8496) \\ &= 17.2896\end{aligned}$$

since

$$E(u_t^2) = E(u_{t-1}^2) = E(u_{t-2}^2) = \sigma_u^2 \quad \text{and} \quad \sigma_u^2 = 1$$

The autocovariance of order one, γ_1, is defined as:

$$\gamma_1 = Cov(Y_t\, Y_{t-1}) = E(Y_t\, Y_{t-1}) \tag{A5.12.2}$$

since $E(Y_t) = E(Y_{t-1}) = 0$ here. As above:

$$\begin{aligned}\gamma_1 &= E[(u_t + 3.8u_{t-1} + 1.36u_{t-2})\,(u_{t-1} + 3.8u_{t-2} + 1.36u_{t-3})]\\ &= 3.8\sigma_u^2 + (1.36 \times 3.8)\sigma_u^2\\ &= 8.968\end{aligned}$$

Similarly, autocovariance of order 2, γ_2, is:

$$\begin{aligned}\gamma_2 &= E[(u_t + 3.8u_{t-1} + 1.36u_{t-2})\,(u_{t-2} + 3.8u_{t-3} + 1.36u_{t-4})]\\ &= 1.36\end{aligned}$$

The autocorrelations are simply the ratios of covariances and variance. The autocorrelation of order 0 is:

$$\rho_0 = \frac{\gamma_0}{\gamma_0} = 1$$

The autocorrelation of order 1 is:

$$\rho_1 = \frac{\gamma_1}{\gamma_0} = \frac{8.968}{17.2896} = 0.519$$

The autocorrelation of order 2 is:

$$\rho_2 = \frac{\gamma_2}{\gamma_0} = \frac{1.36}{17.2896} = 0.079$$

Note that by definition of *MA*(2), autocovariances and autocorrelations of order higher than 2 are all zero (check it). The graph or the plot of autocorrelation coefficients against different lags is called the autocorrelation function (acf) or the correlogram.

b) The MA is not invertible if the $|Z| < 1$ or the $|\lambda| > 1$. To repeat, if the roots of

$$(1 + 3.8Z + 1.36Z^2) = 0 \tag{A5.12.3}$$

lie inside the unit circle, Equation (A5.12.3) cannot be written as an $AR(\infty)$. Solving for the roots in Equation (A5.12.3) gives the following:

$$Z_1, Z_2 = \frac{-3.8 \pm \sqrt{3.8^2 - 4(1.36)}}{2(1.36)}$$

$$= \frac{-3.8 \pm 3}{2.72}$$

$$Z_1 = -2.5 \text{ and } Z_2 = \frac{-0.8}{2.72}$$

Note that factorization of the $MA(2)$ process gives:

$$(1 + \theta_1 L + \theta_2 L^2) = (1 - \lambda_1 L)(1 - \lambda_2 L) \tag{A5.12.4}$$

with

$$\lambda_1 = \frac{1}{Z_1} \text{ and } \lambda_2 = \frac{1}{Z_2}$$

This means that $\lambda_1 = \dfrac{1}{-2.5} = -.4$ and $\lambda_2 = \dfrac{1}{-0.8/2.72} = \dfrac{-2.72}{0.8} = -3.4$

Since $|Z_2| < 1$ or $|\lambda_2| > 1$, the $MA(2)$ is not invertible.

c) Some theory is needed to answer the question (see Hamilton, 1994, 66–68). Note that the original $MA(2)$ can be expressed in terms of roots as follows:

$$Y_t = c + \prod_{i=1}^{q} (1 - \lambda_i L) u_t \tag{A5.12.5}$$

where $|\lambda_i| < 1$ for $i = 1, 2, 3, \cdots, l$

$|\lambda_i| > 1$ for $i = l + 1, \cdots, q$

$$E(u_t u_s) = \begin{cases} \sigma^2 \text{ for } t = s \\ 0 \text{ otherwise} \end{cases}$$

The corresponding invertible representation of Equation (A5.12.5) is:

$$Y_t = c + \left[\prod_{i=1}^{\ell} (1 - \lambda_i L) \prod_{i=l+1}^{q} (1 - \lambda_i^{-1} L) \right] u_t^* \qquad \text{(A5.12.6)}$$

with

$$E(u_t^* u_s^*) = \begin{cases} \sigma^2 \lambda_{l+1}^2 \cdots \lambda_q^2 \text{ for } t = s \\ 0 \text{ otherwise} \end{cases}$$

In our case there are only two λs. One gives rise to noninvertibility ($\lambda_2 = -3.4$). Thus, the error pattern is:

$$E(u_t^* u_s^*) = \begin{cases} \sigma^2(-3.4)^2 = 11.56 \text{ for } t = s \\ 0 \quad \text{otherwise} \end{cases}$$

The new *MA*(2) process is thus:

$$\begin{aligned} Y_t &= (1 + 0.4L)\left(1 + \frac{0.8}{2.72} L\right) u_t^* \\ &= \left(1 + 0.4L + \frac{0.8}{2.72} L + 0.4 \frac{0.8}{2.72} L^2\right) u_t^* \\ &= \left(1 + \frac{1.888}{2.72} L + \frac{0.32}{2.72} L^2\right) u_t^* \\ &= \left(1 + 0.69412\, L + 0.11765 L^2\right) u_t^* \end{aligned} \qquad \text{(A5.12.7)}$$

Equation (A5.12.7) is the invertible representation to Equation (Q5.12.1).

d) Autocovariances: As in part (a),

$$\begin{aligned} \gamma_0 &= E\left(u_t^* + 0.69412 u_{t-1}^* + 0.11765 u_{t-2}^*\right)^2 \\ &= \left(1 + 0.69412^2 + 0.11765^2\right) \sigma_{u^*}^2 \\ &= \left(1 + 0.69412^2 + 0.11765^2\right) 11.56 \\ &= (1 + 0.481636 + 0.013924) 11.56 \\ &= 1.495644022 \times 11.56 \\ &= 17.2896 \end{aligned}$$

$$\gamma_1 = E\left[\left(u_t^* + 0.694\,12u_{t-1}^* + 0.11765u_{t-2}^*\right)\left(u_{t-1}^* + 0.694\,12u_{t-2}^* + 0.11765\,u_{t-3}^*\right)\right]$$

$$= \left(0.69412 + \left(0.11765 \times 0.69412\right)\right)\sigma_{u^*}^2$$

$$= 0.775783218 \times 11.56$$

$$= 8.968$$

$$\gamma_2 = E\left[\left(u_t^* + 0.69412u_{t-1}^* + 0.11765u_{t-2}^*\right)\left(u_{t-2}^* + 0.69412u_{t-3}^* + 0.11765u_{t-4}^*\right)\right]$$

$$= 0.11765\,\sigma_{u^*}^2$$

$$= 0.11765 \times 11.56$$

$$= 1.36$$

Autocorrelations: As in part (a),

$$\rho_0 = \frac{\gamma_0}{\gamma_0} = 1\,,\ \rho_1 = \frac{\gamma_1}{\gamma_0} = \frac{8.968}{17.2896} = 0.519\,,\ \rho_2 = \frac{1.360}{17.2896} = 0.079$$

Autocovariances and autocorrelations obtained from the invertible *MA*(2) process are the same as those obtained from the corresponding noninvertible process.

Answer 5.13

a) To begin with, the DW is not the appropriate statistic to use in this situation because of the presence of a lagged dependent variable. A Durbin's *h* test or a Breusch-Godfrey LM test are appropriate tests in this case. Moreover, good *t* statistics do not necessarily mean the presence of autocorrelation. The bottom line is that without further information we cannot say whether there is autocorrelation.
b) If there is autocorrelation then OLS gives rise to biased and inconsistent estimators. An instrumental variable or ML procedure are viable solutions to the problem.
c) Yes, it is biased (see Answer 5.6.[c]).
d) All three models can find their account here. Without further information it is difficult to say which of these models fits the data. In any case, if there is autocorrelation, then most likely it is either a Koyck scheme or an adaptive expectations model. If there is no autocorrelation then most likely it is a partial adjustment model. Naturally, it might be the case that it is none of them.

TABLE 5.2
OLS Results: Import Model for Barbados, 1972–2001

Variable	Coefficient	Standard Error	*t* Statistic	Prob.
C	49.02822	67.53422	0.725976	0.4743
X_t	0.754811	0.147218	5.127172	0.0000
Y_{t-1}	0.243221	0.145592	1.670567	0.1068
R^2	0.959005	Mean dependent variable		1552.152
Adjusted R^2	0.955852	SD dependent variable		733.6011
SE of regression	154.1409	Akaike information criterion		13.01131
RSS	617744.5	Schwarz criterion		13.15275
Log likelihood	–185.6640	*F* statistic		304.1118
DW statistic	1.914670	Prob(*F* statistic)		0.000000
Breusch–Godfrey Serial Correlation LM Test (1 lag)				
F statistic	0.077179	Probability		0.783442
Obs*R-squared	0.089252	Probability		0.765130

Note: Y, imports; X, exports.

Answer 5.14

a) A "rational expectations" follower will raise the issue that an adaptive expectations model scheme will not allow us to get around the trap of eternal mistake maker. Moreover, expectations are only based on past information; thus, expectations are suboptimal in the sense they do not incorporate all available information.

b) The estimable form can be obtained in a manner similar to that shown in Answer 5.8 or textbooks (e.g., Gujarati, 1995, 597; Watson and Teelucksingh, 2002). It is:

$$Y_t = \alpha\gamma + \beta\gamma X_t + (1-\gamma)Y_{t-1} + e_t - (1-\gamma)e_{t-1} \qquad \text{(A5.14.1)}$$

c) Table 5.2 contains OLS estimation of Equation (A5.14.1).

d) The absence of autocorrelation, such as indicated by the *p* value of the Breusch-Godfrey LM test statistic, justifies the use of OLS in the estimation of Equation (A5.14.1). The impact multiplier is in the order of 0.75; that is, an increase in exports of Bds \$1.00 boosts imports by Bds \$0.75. The long-run parameter is 0.7548/(1 – 0.2432) = 0.997. That is, a Bds \$1.00 permanent increase in exports leads to an increase of imports by almost Bds \$1.00. The adjustment coefficient (expectational coefficient) of about 0.76 leans towards a strict pragmatism. The estimators are consistent and asymptotically normally distributed. Since we assume that the errors are normally distributed, these OLS estimators are also ML estimators. However, because of the presence of the lagged dependent variable, the estimators are biased in finite samples.

e) The question has been fully answered in (d).
f) Indeed, we were expecting autocorrelation of errors in this model (adaptive expectations model). One possible explanation of the gap is that the original error had a peculiar autocorrelation which helped cancel the autocorrelation in the final model. To explain, suppose that in Equation (Q5.14.1):

$$e_t = (1-\gamma)e_{t-1} + \varepsilon_t \tag{A5.14.2}$$

where ε_t is white noise. We know that in Equation (A5.14.1) the error is:

$$v_t = e_t - (1-\gamma)e_{t-1} \tag{A5.14.3}$$

Equation (A5.14.2) in Equation (A5.14.3) gives:

$$v_t = \varepsilon_t \tag{A5.14.4}$$

Hence, v_t is white noise.
g) Recall that the long-run parameter β is:

$$\beta = \frac{\beta\gamma}{\gamma} = \frac{b}{1-d}$$

The null hypothesis $\beta = 1$ means that

$$\frac{b}{1-d} = 1$$

The restriction is clearly nonlinear. However, it can be transformed into a linear one; for example $q = b + d - 1 = 0$. Testing the above null hypothesis gives the same result using either linear restrictions or nonlinear restrictions if the sample is large; otherwise, there is no guarantee that the results will be the same.

Exploiting Taylor's expansion, the standard deviation of β using the nonlinear restriction is given by:

$$\sigma_\beta = \sqrt{Var(\beta)} = \sqrt{\left(\frac{\partial\beta}{\partial b}\right)^2 \text{var}(b) + \left(\frac{\partial\beta}{\partial d}\right)^2 \text{var}(d) + 2\left(\frac{\partial\beta}{\partial b}\right)\left(\frac{\partial\beta}{\partial d}\right)\text{cov}(bd)}$$

The relevant Z test statistic to test the null hypothesis is:

$$Z = \frac{\hat{\beta} - \beta}{\sqrt{\text{var}(\hat{\beta})}}$$

where

$$\sqrt{\text{var}(\hat{\beta})}$$

is the estimate of

$$\sqrt{\text{var}(\beta)}$$

Using the regression information,

$$Z = \frac{0.997 - 1}{\sqrt{(1.7461 * 0.21673) + (1.7371 * 0.021197) + 2(1.3214 * 1.3180 * -0.020615)}}$$

$$= -0.0561$$

The absolute value of the statistic is smaller than the critical value (1.96) at the 5 percent level of significance. That is, we do not reject the null hypothesis $\beta = 1$.

The linear approach gives rise to var(q) = var(b) + var(d) + 2cov(bd). The appropriate t is

$$t = \frac{0.997 - 1}{\sqrt{0.021673 + 0.021197 + 2 * (-0.020615)}} = -0.0741$$

Since $-0.0741 > t_{26,\,0.025} = -2.056$, we do not reject the null hypothesis. That is, the long-run parameter is not statistically different from 1. Here the two approaches lead to the same conclusion although the statistic values are different.

h) Table 5.3 presents the results of estimation of the autoregressive distributed lag of the order one model, *ADL*(1,1). The LM test for autocorrelation indicates no evidence of autocorrelation. At the 5 percent level of significance only exports have a significant impact on imports. A Bds $1.00 dollar increase in exports increases imports by about Bds $0.87. The model fit is good. All variables taken together explain 96 percent of the variation in imports.

i) The long-run parameter is given by:

$$\beta = \frac{0.8664 - 0.1873}{1 - 0.3197} = 0.998.$$

That is, a Bds $1.00 increase in permanent level of export brings about a Bds $1.00 increase in imports. Note that here both scenarios [adaptive expectations and the *ADL*(1,1) model] bring about the same long-run parameter.

TABLE 5.3
Autoregressive Distributed Lag Model of Order One:
The Case of Imports in Barbados, 1972–2001

Variable	Coefficient	Standard Error	*t* Statistic	Prob.
C	36.45731	71.16942	0.512261	0.6130
Y_{t-1}	0.319684	0.190682	1.676536	0.1061
X_t	0.866394	0.231099	3.749022	0.0009
X_{t-1}	–0.187264	0.296536	–0.631506	0.5334
R^2	0.959649	Mean dependent variable		1552.152
Adjusted R^2	0.954807	SD dependent variable		733.6011
SE of regression	155.9545	Akaike information criterion		13.06445
RSS	608044.9	Schwarz criterion		13.25304
Log likelihood	–185.4345	F statistic		198.1862
DW statistic	2.145760	Prob(F statistic)		0.000000
Breusch–Godfrey Serial Correlation LM Test (1 lag)				
F statistic	1.671986	Probability		0.208302
	1.888736	Probability		0.169345

5.4 SUPPLEMENTARY EXERCISES

Question 5.15 Write an essay on the Almon distributed lag model.

Question 5.16 Some measures have been proposed in the literature to determine the lag length of a distributed lag model. Present two such measures. Fully point out their flaws if any.

Question 5.17 Lag weights present some problems of interpretation. Succinctly explain those problems. (See Judge et al., 1985, 405–408.)

Question 5.18 Consider the following model:

$$Y_t = \alpha + \beta_1 X_t + \beta_2 Y_{t-1} + u_t$$

a) If u_t is well behaved, provide the properties of OLS estimators.
b) If u_t follows an $AR(1)$ process, provide the properties of OLS estimators, IV estimators and ML estimators.
c) If u_t follows an $ARMA(0,1)$ process, provide the properties of OLS and ML estimators, respectively.

Question 5.19 In time series, compare and contrast ergodicity and stationarity. (See, for example, Ghosh, 1991, 529–530.)

Question 5.20 Exploiting the data in Question 1.15 and using the distributed lag framework, fit and interpret several variants of the relationships between money supply and price in Barbados.

Question 5.21 Using the data in Table 5.1, reestimate the model shown in Equation (A5.14.1) using the IV and Hatanaka two step methods.

CHAPTER 6

Unit Root, Vector Autoregressions, Cointegration and Error Correction Models

6.1 INTRODUCTION

This chapter deals with another aspect of dynamic regression models. It is concerned with a more modern approach to econometrics, which is essentially the (new) time series approach to econometrics, qualified in some quarters as "atheoretical" econometrics.

The recent econometrics revolution started with the vector autoregressions initiated by Sims (1980) and culminated with the cointegration approach to econometrics launched by Granger (1983) and Engle and Granger (1987) as well as its associated error correction models, which can be traced back to the work of Phillips (1954).

The exercises in this chapter deal with the different aspects of unit root, vector autoregression, cointegration and error (or equilibrium) correction models.

6.2 QUESTIONS

6.2.1 Theoretical Exercises

Question 6.1 Explain the concept of unit root.

Question 6.2

a) Mention some popular unit root tests.
b) Point out the issues involved in testing for unit root.

Question 6.3 Why is there a great deal of proliferation of unit root tests?

Question 6.4 Consider the following model:

$$Y_t = \alpha + Y_{t-1} + e_t \qquad \text{(Q6.4.1)}$$

where $e_t \sim iid\left(0, \sigma^2\right)$ and $\alpha \neq 0$.

a) Which type of process does Y_t follow?
b) Show that the model contains implicitly a deterministic trend.
c) Explain the constant term.

Question 6.5 Consider the following model:

$$Y_t = Y_{t-1} + e_t \qquad \text{(Q6.5.1)}$$

where $e_t \sim iid\left(0, \sigma^2\right)$.

a) Show that the model is nonstationary.
b) Show that the model is integrated of order one, $I(1)$.
c) What is the name of the process?

Question 6.6 Write a comprehensive essay on vector autoregressions (including error correction models). (UWI, EC36D, final examination May 2003)

Question 6.7 In the context of VAR models, explain the following concepts:

a) Granger causality;
b) Impulse response functions;
c) Variance decomposition.

Question 6.8 Consider the following VAR model:

$$\begin{aligned} Y_t &= \alpha_1 + \beta_{11}Y_{t-1} + \beta_{12}Y_{t-2} + \beta_{13}Y_{t-3} + \delta_{11}X_{t-1} + \delta_{12}X_{t-2} + \delta_{13}X_{t-3} + e_{1t} \\ X_t &= \alpha_2 + \beta_{21}Y_{t-1} + \beta_{22}Y_{t-2} + \beta_{23}Y_{t-3} + \delta_{21}X_{t-1} + \delta_{22}X_{t-2} + \delta_{23}X_{t-3} + e_{2t} \end{aligned} \qquad \text{(Q6.8.1)}$$

where e_{1t} and e_{2t} are two uncorrelated white noise error terms.

a) Why is it often useless to interpret individual coefficients in this type of model? Name a few alternatives that bypass the interpretation of individual coefficients in the VAR context.
b) Devise Granger causality tests for this model.
c) Suppose you have been told that Y_t and X_t are not individually covariance stationary. What course of action will you take? Explain.

Question 6.9 Consider the following model:

$$Y_t = \alpha + \beta X_t + u_t \qquad \text{(Q6.9.1)}$$

where $Y_t \sim I(1)$, $X_t \sim I(1)$ and u_t is the error term.

a) When can we say the above regression is spurious? What does it mean?

b) Under which conditions does cointegration between the variables hold? What does cointegration mean?
c) Suppose the Engle–Granger test for cointegration and the Johansen procedure for cointegration reveal the existence of cointegration between the two variables. However, the regression results given by the two approaches are different. Which approach is to be trusted and why?

Question 6.10 Consider the following data generation process based on the permanent-income hypothesis:

$$y_t = y_t^P + y_t^T \tag{Q6.10.1}$$

$$y_t^P = y_{t-1}^P + u_t \tag{Q6.10.2}$$

$$c_t = y_t^P \tag{Q6.10.3}$$

$$p_t = p_{t-1} + e_t \tag{Q6.10.4}$$

where y_t stands for income, c_t stands for consumption, p_t is price level, superscripts P and T stand for permanent and transitory, respectively, and u_t and e_t are well-behaved uncorrelated innovations.

a) Briefly explain the model above.

In each of the following models guess what the econometrician is trying to check. Explain whether it makes sense. Note that the error term is present in each model.

b) $c_t = \beta_1 + \beta_2 p_t$
c) $c_t = \gamma_1 + \gamma_2 t$
d) $\Delta c_t = \beta_3 + \beta_4 \Delta y_t$
e) $\Delta c_t = \delta_3 + \delta_4 y_{t-1}$
f) $c_t = a_1 + a_2 y_t$ (Adapted from Stock and Watson, 1988a.)

Question 6.11 Consider the following model:

$$Y_t = \alpha + \beta X_t + \gamma Z_t + \delta V_t + u_t \tag{Q6.11.1}$$

where $Y_t \sim I(1)$, $X_t \sim I(1)$, $Z_t \sim I(1)$, $V_t \sim I(1)$ and $u_t \sim I(0)$.

a) What problem does one have if the Engle–Granger test reveals the existence of more than one cointegrating relationship?

b) If more than one cointegrating relationship is revealed by the Johansen procedure (*trace* and *maximum eigenvalue* tests), what issue(s) does it entail?

Question 6.12 Write a concise note on the relationship between unit root, cointegration, error correction models and Granger causality using a bivariate framework. (UWI, EC36D, final examinations May 1998, 1999, 2000, 2001, 2002)

Question 6.13 Explain the concept of exogeneity in econometrics.

Question 6.14 Consider the following models:

$$y_t = \alpha + \beta_1 x_t + u_t \quad \text{(Q6.14.1)}$$

$$y_t = \alpha + \beta_1 x_t + \beta_2 x_{t-1} + u_t \quad \text{(Q6.14.2)}$$

$$y_t = \alpha + \beta_3 y_{t-1} + u_t \quad \text{(Q6.14.3)}$$

$$y_t = \alpha + \beta_2 x_{t-1} + u_t \quad \text{(Q6.14.4)}$$

$$y_t = \alpha + \beta_2 x_{t-1} + \beta_3 y_{t-1} + u_t \quad \text{(Q6.14.5)}$$

$$y_t = \alpha + \beta_1 x_t + \beta_3 y_{t-1} + u_t \quad \text{(Q6.14.6)}$$

$$\Delta y_t = \alpha + \beta_1 \Delta x_t + u_t \quad \text{(Q6.14.7)}$$

$$\Delta y_t = \alpha + \beta_1 \Delta x_t + (\beta_3 - 1)(y_{t-1} - \delta x_{t-1}) + u_t \quad \text{(Q6.14.8)}$$

where y_t and x_t are variables and u_t is the error term.

a) The eight models above may be thought of as coming from a common model. Provide the common model.
b) In each case, provide the name of the model and the constraint(s) used to derive the model from the common model. (Adapted from Ericsson, 1997 and others.)

Question 6.15 Let a model of interest be:

$$y_t = \alpha + \beta x_t + u_t \qquad t = 1, 2, 3, \cdots, n$$

where u_t is the error term, $y_t \sim I(1)$ and $x_t \sim I(1)$.

a) If $u_t \sim I(0)$, indicate whether $\hat{\beta}$ (the OLS estimator of β) is a long-run estimator of the parameter β and justify your answer.
b) Provide and explain the properties of $\hat{\beta}$.
c) Explain how to test for Granger causality between the two variables of interest. (UWI, EC36D, final examination May 2002)

Question 6.16 Suppose that $y_t \sim I(1)$ and $x_t \sim I(1)$. Consider the following regressions:

$$y_t = \alpha + \beta x_t + u_t \qquad t = 1,2,3,\cdots,n$$

and

$$x_t = \gamma + \delta y_t + e_t \qquad t = 1,2,3,\cdots,n$$

Which problem(s) do these regressions entail if a researcher is testing for cointegration between the two variables using the Engle–Granger procedure?

Question 6.17 Consider the following data generation process due to Engle and Granger (1987):

$$y_t + \beta x_t = e_{1t} \qquad e_{1t} = e_{1,t-1} + u_{1t} \qquad \text{(Q6.17.1)}$$

$$y_t + \alpha x_t = e_{2t} \qquad e_{2t} = \rho e_{2,t-1} + u_{2t} \qquad \text{(Q6.17.2)}$$

$$|\rho| < 1$$

where x_t and y_t are the variables of interest and the us are white noise series.

a) Equations (Q6.17.1) and (Q6.17.2) reveal that $e_{1t} \sim I(1)$ and $e_{2t} \sim I(0)$. An econometrician points out the possibility of having $y_t \sim I(2)$ and $x_t \sim I(2)$. Do you agree with the conjecture? Why or why not?
b) The two equations may well be considered as a system of two equations with two endogenous variables. Is the model internally consistent?
c) Derive the error correction models (ECMs) corresponding to the system of equations above.
d) What factors aided in identifying the parameters of interest? (Parts [b] and [d] are adapted from Maddala, 1992, 590–591.)

6.2.2 Empirical Exercises

Question 6.18 Consider the series shown in Table 6.1 on money supply for Jamaica (J$ millions) for the period 1970 to 1999. Conduct a full study on the unit root of the money supply.

TABLE 6.1
Money Supply: Jamaica 1970–1999

Year	1970	1971	1972	1973	1974	1975
Money	127	160	173	218	258	322
Year	1976	1977	1978	1979	1980	1981
Money	339	474	570	629	717	775
Year	1982	1983	1984	1985	1986	1987
Money	876	1066	1319	1520	2140	2252
Year	1988	1989	1990	1991	1992	1993
Money	3445	3153	4016	7818	13391	16903
Year	1994	1995	1996	1997	1998	1999
Money	21252	29320	35548	34470	36664	46795

Note: Money supply is in J$ millions.

Source: *International Financial Statistics,* International Monetary Fund, Washington, D.C., 2000.

Question 6.19 Mamingi (1999) tested for cointegration between log real per capita GDP of Barbados and log real per capita GDP of the Organization of Eastern Caribbean States (OECS) as a whole. The model used is as follows:

$$Lba_t = c + bLoecs_t + u_t \qquad \text{(Q6.19.1)}$$

where *Lba* stands for the logarithm of Barbados per capita real GDP, *Loecs* is the logarithm of the OECS per capita real GDP and u is the error term. The variables are individually $I(1)$.

The Engle–Granger procedure and the Johansen procedure are used to test for cointegration. Results of the testing are presented in Table 6.2.

a) What can be concluded from the results in terms of cointegration between the two variables of interest?
b) Standard errors were not presented in the Engle–Granger procedure. Is this an omission? Why or why not?
c) The Engle–Granger procedure and the Johansen procedure have given rise to similar estimates of parameters. Is this always the case?
d) Suppose the Johansen procedure indicates the existence of two cointegrating vectors. What does it mean?
e) Suppose the Johansen procedure indicates the existence of zero cointegrating vector. What does it mean?

Question 6.20 Consider the data shown in Table 6.3 on money supply and price for South Africa.

a) Conduct tests for the unit root for money supply and price.
b) Evaluate the monetarist position according to which money growth leads to inflation in the long run.

TABLE 6.2
Testing for Cointegration between Log Real per Capita GDP of Barbados and Log Real per Capita GDP of the OECS, 1978–1996

Engle–Granger Procedure		Johansen Procedure	
C	*Loecs*	*C*	*Loecs*
7.637	0.141	7.167 (0.127)	0.135 (0.016)
$R^2 = 0.317$	DW = 0.971	$LR(0) = 23.725$	CV = 19.96
$AEG(1) = -2.569$	CV = −3.27	$LR(1) = 3.099$	CV = 9.24
$t_{ec} = -2.921$	CV = −1.77		

Note: The model shown in Equation (Q6.19.1) is of interest. Lba_t and $Loecs_t$ are defined as above. AEG = augmented Engle–Granger test statistic with one lag. t_{ec} = t test statistic of the coefficient of the lagged error correction term in the Engle–Granger error correction model (ECM). $LR(0)$ and $LR(1)$ are likelihood ratio statistics that test for the presence of no cointegration and one cointegration relationship, respectively. CV = critical value of the corresponding test statistic. (…) = standard errors. The level of significance is 5 percent.

Source: Mamingi (1999).

TABLE 6.3
Money and Price for South Africa, 1970–1999

Year	Price (CPI)	Money	Year	Price (CPI)	Money
1970	5.4	2,259.000	1985	28.8	21,332.000
1971	5.8	2,446.000	1986	34.1	23,207.000
1972	6.1	2,808.000	1987	39.6	32,026.000
1973	6.7	3,382.000	1988	44.7	39,934.000
1974	7.5	4,011.000	1989	51.3	43,343.000
1975	8.5	4,286.000	1990	58.7	50,354.000
1976	9.5	4,437.000	1991	67.6	60,800.000
1977	10.5	4,648.000	1992	77.0	70,809.000
1978	11.6	5,133.000	1993	84.5	75,550.000
1979	13.1	6,198.000	1994	92.1	94,511.000
1980	15.0	8,398.000	1995	100.0	111,844.000
1981	17.2	11,273.000	1996	107.4	147,664.000
1982	19.7	13,124.000	1997	116.5	173,335.000
1983	22.2	16,586.000	1998	124.6	213,532.000
1984	24.8	23,413.000	1999	131.0	259,937.000

Note: Money supply is in millions of rands and price stands for consumer price index (CPI).

Source: *International Financial Statistics,* International Monetary Fund, Washington, D.C., 2000.

c) Formally test for causality between money growth and inflation.
d) Conduct impulse responses and variance decomposition analyses.

TABLE 6.4
Monetary Approach to the Balance of Payments of Barbados: ECM Results

Regressors	Coefficient	t statistic
Constant	0.045	1.914
ECM1	–0.002	–2.450
$\Delta P/P$	0.250	1.667
$\Delta Y/Y$	1.372	2.548
$\Delta i/i$	–0.207	–2.488
$\Delta m/m$	–0.444	–2.024
$\Delta D/(R + D)$	–1.006	–10.062
$R^2 = 0.874$	$F = 20.851$	$p = 0.000$
SE = 0.087	LM(5) = 0.423	$p = 0.824$
DW = 2.12	Chow = 0.894	$p = 0.542$

Note: Dependent variable is $\Delta R/(R + D)$, R = international reserves of monetary authorities; D = domestic credit; P = price level; Y = real income; i = interest rate; m = the money multiplier; *ECM1* = the lagged error correcting term; Δ = the first difference operator, SE = standard error of the regression; p = the p value of the corresponding statistic.

Source: Howard and Mamingi (2002).

Question 6.21 Using the data of Question 1.17, in the published version of the paper of interest, Howard and Mamingi (2002) found that the variables of interest are cointegrated. Moreover, fitting the ECM to the data produced the results shown in Table 6.4.

a) Is the above a valid ECM? Why or why not?
b) Carefully explain why the results obtained in Answer 1.17 are not too different from the ones obtained here?

Question 6.22 Consider the following wage model for Barbados for the period 1975–1996 (see Table 6.5):

$$wi_t = C + \beta UN_t + \gamma \pi_t + u_t \qquad \text{(Q6.22.1)}$$

where wi_t is wage growth in percent, UN_t is unemployment rate in percent and π_t is inflation in percent. Conduct a full study of cointegration among the three variables.

6.3 ANSWERS

Answer 6.1

A process is said to contain a unit root if it does not revert to its mean as time passes. Basically, it exhibits a systematic pattern in its movement. The latter is itself unpredictable. That is, a unit root process has a stochastic trend. A unit root thus belongs to the class of nonstationary processes.

TABLE 6.5
Wage Growth, Unemployment and Inflation in Barbados, 1975–1996

Year	*wi* (%)	*UN* (%)	π (%)	Year	*wi* (%)	*UN* (%)	π (%)
1975	9.474537	22.40000	18.68333	1986	4.143967	18.40000	0.995033
1976	9.170843	16.20000	4.710447	1987	1.661380	18.00000	3.438548
1977	18.46099	17.00000	8.098610	1988	7.093437	17.90000	4.611409
1978	10.17827	12.20000	9.054121	1989	2.679252	17.70000	6.141245
1979	7.096941	13.40000	15.63631	1990	4.933736	17.60000	2.990350
1980	18.39228	12.90000	13.32551	1991	0.871465	17.20000	6.091886
1981	9.984533	10.80000	13.71515	1992	−1.805795	23.00000	5.890027
1982	10.71688	13.70000	9.791295	1993	1.598476	24.30000	1.127739
1983	5.611903	15.20000	5.140797	1994	−1.653709	21.70000	0.097466
1984	8.752367	17.20000	4.543010	1995	0.000000	19.60000	1.210375
1985	4.744788	18.70000	4.012779	1996	0.000000	15.80000	2.330664

Note: *wi*: Log(wage)-Log(wage(−1)); *UN*: unemployment rate in %;

π: inflation: Log(cpi)-Log(cpi(−1)); *w* and π have been multiplied by 100.

Sources: Central Bank of Barbados, *Annual Statistical Digest*, 1998; Downes, A. and McLean, W. *The Estimation of Missing Values of Employment in Barbados*, Research Paper 13, Centre of Statistics of Trinidad and Tobago (1988, 115–116).

To explain better, consider the following model:

$$y_t = a + by_{t-1} + u_t \tag{A6.1.1}$$

where, for example, u_t is white noise. If $b = 1$, the process is $AR(1)$ with a unit root (the root of the $AR(1)$ process is equal to one). A unit root process is also said to be an integrated process. Precisely, in the above model with $b = 1$, the process is integrated of order one, $I(1)$; that is, it needs to be differenced once to become stationary. Summing up, a process that contains a unit root (e.g., log of money supply in Jamaica; see Figure 6.2) has the following characteristics. It does not revert to its mean (not mean reverting). Its variance is not time-independent and goes to infinity as time approaches infinity. Its empirical correlogram dies out very slowly compared to that of a stationary process (see, for example, Figures 6.4 and 6.5).

Examples of unit root processes include any type of ARIMA models, for example, the random walk process (see below). Most economic variables are unit root processes as they exhibit strong stochastic trends. Examples include consumption, income and prices.

Answer 6.2

a) Unit root tests are basically of two categories (for a good discussion, see Maddala and Kim, 1998, 45–154). One category of the tests uses nonstationarity (unit root) as the null hypothesis. Basically these are tests of unit autoregressive root. The most popular unit root tests fall in this category: the Dickey–Fuller (DF) test, the augmented Dickey–Fuller (ADF) test and the Phillips–Perron (PP) test. To this list we can add the Elliot–Rothenberg–Stock

(DF-GLS) test (a modification of the DF or ADF tests) and the Perron and Ng test (a modification of the PP test). Another category exploits the null hypothesis of stationarity. These can be considered as tests of the unit moving-average root. The most popular of these tests is the Kwiatkoswki–Phillips–Schmidt–Shin (KPSS) test.

b) The important issues involved in testing for unit root are the following. (i) Most unit root tests have low powers. In this connection, the popular tests such as the ADF, the PP and the KPSS tests do not perform well. The DF-GLS and the P-Ng are better, according to Maddala and Kim (1998). (ii) The question of which null hypothesis to use (nonstationarity or stationarity) is an important point. (iii) Since most unit root tests have low powers, there is the question of how to boost their powers. Hence, the issue of whether one should increase data frequency or the data span, or resort to panel data to increase the power of tests. (iv) Another issue of interest is the consequences of uncertainty about unit roots. (v) Finally, the appropriate level of significance to use to test for unit root is as important as the issues raised above, particularly when using the test of unit root as a pretest. (Adapted from Maddala and Kim, 1998, 98–146.)

Answer 6.3

There is a proliferation of unit root tests simply because up to now there does not exist a uniformly most powerful unit root test.

Answer 6.4

a) This is a random walk with a drift.
b) Using substitution, we have the following:

$$Y_t = \alpha + Y_{t-1} + e_t$$

$$Y_t = (\alpha + \alpha) + Y_{t-2} + e_{t-1} + e_t$$

$$Y_t = (\alpha + \alpha + \alpha) + Y_{t-3} + e_{t-2} + e_{t-1} + e_t$$

$$\vdots$$

$$Y_t = t\alpha + Y_0 + \sum_{i=0}^{t-1} e_{t-i}$$

where Y_0 is the initial value of Y_t. As can be seen, the parameter α is multiplied by the time trend t. Thus, there is a deterministic trend in Y_t.

c) The constant term is called drift. It gives the general pattern to the random walk. At each instant in time the random walk jumps by α. If $\alpha > 0$, there is an upward trend; if $\alpha < 0$, there is a downward trend.

Answer 6.5

a) Using substitution, we can rewrite the model as follows:

$$Y_t = Y_{t-1} + e_t$$

$$Y_t = Y_{t-2} + e_{t-1} + e_t$$

$$Y_t = Y_{t-3} + e_{t-2} + e_{t-1} + e_t$$

$$\vdots$$

$$Y_t = Y_0 + \sum_{i=0}^{t-1} e_{t-i}$$

where Y_0 is the initial value of Y. As can be seen:

$$E(Y_t) = E\left(Y_0 + \sum_{i=0}^{t-1} e_{t-i}\right) = Y_0 \quad \text{since} \quad E(e_{t-i}) = 0 \quad \text{and} \quad E(Y_0) = Y_0$$

$$Var(Y_t) = Var\left(Y_0 + \sum_{i=0}^{t-1} e_{t-i}\right) = \sum_{i=0}^{t-1} \text{var}(e_{t-i}) = t\sigma^2$$

since $Var\sum_{i=0}^{t-1} e_{t-i} = \sum_{i=0}^{t-1} Var(e_{t-i}), Var(e_{t-i}) = \sigma^2$ and $Var(Y_0) = 0$.

The covariance is:

$$Cov(Y_t, Y_{t+s}) = E\left[\sum_{i=0}^{t-1} e_{t-i} \sum_{i=0}^{t+s-1} e_{t+s-i}\right] = (t-s)\,\sigma^2$$

The results show that variance and covariance depend on time t. By definition this is the case of a series that is not covariance stationary.

b) The model is integrated of order one, since

$$Y_t - Y_{t-1} = \Delta Y_t = e_t \sim I(0)$$

that is,

$$\Delta Y_t \sim I(0) \rightarrow Y_t \sim I(1).$$

c) This is a random walk process.

Answer 6.6

Vector autoregression models result from the reaction to the main issue, in simultaneous equations models, of classifying variables into endogenous and exogenous. Often, economists disagree on which variables are endogenous and which are exogenous. Moreover, the simultaneous equations model approach emphasizes economic theory, which helps point out identifying restrictions. Again, economists may have different opinions on identifying restrictions according to their schools of thought affiliations. To bypass these problems, Sims (1980) developed the idea of vector autoregression (VAR) which is a generalization of single autoregressive models; that is, an n-equation model in which each variable is a function of its own past, the past of other remaining variables, as well as uncorrelated error terms. By doing so the issue of endogeneity versus exogeneity is put to rest, as each variable is now considered endogenous. This approach, which does not rely on economic theory, is qualified as "atheoretical" by some as it is really data-based ("let the data speak for themselves").

The VAR, as conceived by Sims, has several limitations. First, its detractors point out that VAR is linked to simultaneous equations models to the extent that it is simply an overfit of the reduced form of SEM. That is why the VAR as described above has been known as the reduced-form VAR. Put differently, the criticism here is that VAR uses an unnecessarily large number of lags. Second, the number of parameters to be estimated can be incredibly large, requiring a very long time series, which is usually not available in many instances. Third, VAR requires covariance stationarity of variables.

To answer some of the limitations, other types of VARs have been added: Bayesian VAR, recursive VAR, structural VAR and error correction models (ECMs). The Bayesian VAR introduced by Litterman (1979) uses some shrinking methods to reduce the number of parameters to estimate. The recursive VAR is similar to recursive models in the context of simultaneous equations models. Basically contemporaneous endogenous variables are added judiciously on the right-hand side of the equations in such a way that the matrix of endogenous variables is triangular and that of errors, diagonal. By doing so economic theory makes its entry timidly into the VAR methodology. It is worth noting that few VAR models conform to the recursive model reality. Acknowledging fully the importance of economic theory, the structural VAR somehow goes back to the simultaneous equations framework. In other words, using economic theory, the structural VAR builds up structure at the image of SEM. As pointed out by Stock and Watson (2001, 103), identifying assumptions that allow correlation to be interpreted as causality is required in structural VARs. As far as covariance stationarity is concerned, VAR in levels is valid if variables are stationary. If they are not, VAR in differences is the appropriate model if variables are not cointegrated; if they are cointegrated, an error correction model is the appropriate model. The error correction models are known as restricted VARs because they incorporate the restrictions in the VAR, which are in the form of lagged error correcting terms. Error correction models go back to the work of Phillip (1954), popularized by Sargan (1964), and are recently associated with Engle and Granger (1987) as well as Johansen (1988). Put differently, there are two types of ECMs: the Sargan–Hendry type of ECM and the Engle–Granger–Johansen type of ECM. The Sargan–Hendry ECM type includes some contemporaneous variables (levels or differences) on the right-hand side of the equation. The Engle–Granger–Johansen type is really the VAR type proposed by Sims, to the extent that the right-hand side contains only lagged variables and a lagged error correcting term.

In terms of the four major goals of macroeconomics (data description, macroeconomic forecasts, inference and macroeconomic policy), it seems that VARs have a good record in addressing data description and forecasting. As far as the two other goals (structural inference and policy analysis) are concerned, the results are dubious as the solution to the identification problem (causality versus correlation) requires economic theory or institution knowledge. (For details, see Stock and Watson, 2001, 102.)

Answer 6.7

a) Granger causality: Causality is a difficult and subtle concept to deal with, because it contains a variety of controversial meanings or interpretations. In economics two major attempts have been made to deal with the concept: the "Cowles Commission approach" (the simultaneous equations model approach) and the "time series approach" (Mamingi, 1984).

The Cowles Commission explains or establishes causality in the context of simultaneous equations models. For the Commission, causality has to deal with the possibility of classifying causal relations into a hierarchy of sets, levels I, II, III, etc., in the context of simultaneous equations models and under the realm of economic theory. Precisely, variables in the lower-number sets are said to cause variables in higher-number sets if the former influence the latter without the reverse being true (see Ando et al., 1963, 2). That is, causality is an "asymmetrical relation" between or among some variables (Ando et al., 1963, 3).

The proponents of the time series approach use a statistical criterion to formalize the concept of causality. One such prominent representative is Granger. Granger (1969) starts from the premise that the future cannot cause the present or the past, in order to formalize his concept of causality, which in reality is linked to prediction or forecasting. Indeed, for him a variable X_t causes another variable Y_t if the past of the former helps better predict Y_t than the past of Y_t alone; that is, X_t contains information that helps better predict Y_t than the past of Y_t alone. With two variables (X_t and Y_t), one may have the following causal relationship: X_t causes Y_t ($X_t \rightarrow Y_t$), Y_t causes X_t ($Y_t \rightarrow X_t$), or bidirectional causality.

Granger causality testing in the time series framework can be conducted using either a VAR or an ECM framework depending on the behaviour of variables in terms of stationarity. In any case, to conduct the test for Granger causality, one exploits restrictions on variables. An F (restricted versus unrestricted) or a Wald-type test is often of interest. Granger causality testing results may be affected by the lag structure, the ordering of variables (if more than two variables are involved), and omitted variables.

b) Impulse response function: Impulse response functions trace the effects of a shock to an innovation of an endogenous variable on the variables in the VAR. Consider the following VAR model:

$$y_{1t} = \alpha_1 + \alpha_{11} y_{1,t-1} + \alpha_{12} y_{2,t-1} + e_{1t}$$

$$y_{2t} = \alpha_2 + \alpha_{21} y_{1,t-1} + \alpha_{22} y_{2,t-1} + e_{2t}$$

written more compactly as:

$$Y_t = \mu + \theta Y_{t-1} + e_t$$

where

$$Y_t = (y_{1t}\ y_{2t})',\ \theta = \begin{pmatrix} \alpha_{11} & \alpha_{12} \\ \alpha_{21} & \alpha_{22} \end{pmatrix} \quad \text{and} \quad e_t = (e_{1t}\ e_{2t})'$$

represents the innovations. A shock in e_{1t} gives rise to an "immediate and one-for-one effect" on y_{1t} but has no effect on y_{2t}. However, in period t + 1 and thereafter it affects both $y_{1,t+s}$ and $y_{2,t+s}$ with s ≥ 1: In other words the shock leads to a chain reaction in the system. The objective of the impulse response function is to capture these chain reactions. Concretely, this is done by inverting the system; that is by transforming the VAR into a vector moving average (VMA). The above system can be rewritten in VMA as follows:

$$\begin{bmatrix} y_{1t} \\ y_{2t} \end{bmatrix} = \begin{bmatrix} \bar{y}_1 \\ \bar{y}_2 \end{bmatrix} + \sum_{i=0}^{\infty} \begin{bmatrix} \delta_{11}(i) & \delta_{12}(i) \\ \delta_{21}(i) & \delta_{22}(i) \end{bmatrix} \begin{bmatrix} e_{1,t-i} \\ e_{2,t-i} \end{bmatrix}$$

The matrix

$$\delta_s = \frac{\partial Y_{t+s}}{\partial e_s}$$

represents the impulse response and the plot of these different responses against s, the horizon, is called the impulse response function (IRF). The impulse responses are linked to dynamic multipliers.

There are two major issues associated with the IRF. First, the errors in different equations must be uncorrelated. If that is not the case, then responses of endogenous variables to an innovation shock are confound responses. That is, a response can be attributed to several shocks. To solve this issue, one orthogonalizes the errors to make them uncorrelated. However, the orthogonality using the Chowleski decomposition leads to the second issue: that of the influence of ordering on the resulting IRF. Precisely, changing the order of variables may affect resulting IRFs. Recently Pesaran and Shin (1998), among others, have solved the two problems in

IRF by constructing an orthogonal set of innovations that are independent of the VAR ordering.

c) Variance decomposition: This is another alternative for depicting the dynamics of the system. The variance decomposition provides information concerning the relative importance of each innovation towards explaining the behaviour of endogenous variables. In that connection, at the extreme, one may have an endogenous variable that evolves completely independently of an innovation at all horizons. This means that the variable is exogenous. On the other hand, an innovation shock can explain all the forecast error variance of an endogenous variable at all forecast horizons; that is, the latter variable is endogenous. The two problems advocated in the context of IRF are also issues here. As above, Pesaran and Shin (1998) have given them the same response.

Summing up, Granger causality, IRFs and variance decomposition can be useful tools to examine the relationships among economic variables in the context of VAR methodology.

Answer 6.8

a) It is often useless to interpret individual coefficients in the VAR type model because they are often plagued by multicollinearity. Insignificant coefficients and/or wrong signs are often the result. To solve these problems, the VAR proponents have focused on the interpretation of sets of coefficients. Granger causality, IRFs and variance decomposition fit that concern.

b) Assuming the sample is small, we recommend an F test to test for Granger causality. The F test in this context is based on restricted and unrestricted models. For example, suppose we want to test that X_t does not cause Y_t. This translates into the following:

$$H_0 : \delta_{11} = \delta_{12} = \delta_{13} = 0$$

Taking this restriction into account leads to the restricted model. Thus:

$$F = \frac{(\text{RRSS} - \text{URSS}) / \#\text{ of restrictions}}{\text{URSS}/(n-k)}$$

where RRSS stands for the restricted residual sum of squares from the restricted model and URSS is the corresponding residual sum of squares in the unrestricted regression, n is the sample size and k is the number of parameters.

If $F_{\text{calculated}} > F$ then the null hypothesis is rejected; otherwise, it is not rejected. In large samples, we may use the Wald test.

c) Basically, at least two courses of action can be taken.

i) If $Y_t \sim I(1)$, $X_t \sim I(1)$ and $e_t \sim I(1)$, then a VAR in first differences is advisable as a model.

ii) If $Y_t \sim I(1)$, $X_t \sim I(1)$ and $e_t \sim I(0)$, then an error correction model is suitable as a model.

Answer 6.9

a) It is spurious if $u_t \sim I(1)$. It means the apparent relationship between variables is false. Indeed, it is simply the trends in the variables that make the two variables correlated (see Granger and Newbold, 1974; Phillips, 1986).
b) Cointegration between the two variables holds if their linear combination, u_t, is integrated of order zero; that is, it is stationary. Cointegration means a long-run equilibrium between nonstationary variables. Note that cointegration is basically a statistical concept. As economists, however, we are interested in cointegration relationships that have economic meanings.
c) In general, the Johansen procedure is more reliable than the Engle–Granger approach. In particular, the estimators from the Engle–Granger procedure, although superconsistent, are biased in small samples. The bias can be substantial. Moreover, because of nonstationarity, the usual conventional asymptotic theory cannot be used. Hence, the t statistics are of limited use.

Answer 6.10

Answers are adapted from Stock and Watson (1988a) and Banerjee et al. (1993, 190–191).

a) This is a model to explain permanent income hypothesis according to Milton Friedman. Equation (Q6.10.1) states that income consists of two components: a permanent component (y_t^P) and a transitory component (y_t^T). Equation (Q6.10.2) indicates that the permanent income follows a random walk process. Equation (Q6.10.3) indicates a one to one correspondence between consumption and permanent income. Equation (Q6.10.4) points to the fact that price level is a random walk process.
b) The econometrician is most likely trying to check money illusion. The inference from this regression is not valid since the error from the regression will be $I(1)$; that is, the regression is spurious. Note that this is the case because the two variables do not have a common trend.
c) The econometrician is trying to see whether consumption has a deterministic trend. It turns out to be a bad idea, because consumption has a stochastic trend and not a deterministic trend. The regression is also spurious.
d) The econometrician is trying to compute the marginal propensity to consume. The regression seems plausible; however, there is a downward bias for the marginal propensity to consume. The reason is that income is measured with error (transitory part).
e) The econometrician is trying to test the permanent income hypothesis itself. The approach is not appropriate, as the regression is unbalanced (variables are of different orders of integration). The inferences on the coefficients are misleading (coefficients are biased).
f) The econometrician is trying to test whether consumption and income are cointegrated. Cointegration exists because there is a common trend. This

is a valid regression. Note that although the estimators are superconsistent, they are biased in small samples. Moreover, the t results are not reliable because of autocorrelation.

Answer 6.11

a) The problem does not exist to the extent that the Engle–Granger test can only reveal one cointegrated relationship if cointegration exists.
b) The issue is the identification of cointegrated relationships. Basically, some restrictions need to be made to derive meaningful cointegrated relationships.

Answer 6.12

Consider the following model

$$y_t = \alpha + \beta x_t + u_t$$

where y_t and x_t are the variables of interest and u_t is the error term. The validity of the above equation requires, among others, knowing first the properties of individual variables; that is, whether y_t and x_t are individually stationary or nonstationary. To study nonstationarity we use the unit root tests, such as the ADF or the PP test. Suppose that $y_t \sim I(1)$ and $x_t \sim I(1)$, then the above equation is only valid if u_t is stationary. In that case, the variables are said to be cointegrated. That is, they have a long-run equilibrium. To test for cointegration, residual tests or nonresidual tests can be used. The most popular residual test for cointegration is the augmented Engle–Granger test, which is the equivalent of the ADF test in the cointegration context. The most popular nonresidual test is the LR Johansen test, which can be either a trace test or a maximum eigenvalue test.

By the Granger representation theorem, if two variables are cointegrated, there exists a valid error correction model; that is, a restricted VAR with the lagged error correcting term as the restriction term. In the bivariate case, we have, for example:

$$\Delta y_t = \beta_1 u_{t-1} + \sum_{i=1}^{p} \gamma_i \Delta y_{t-i} + \sum_{i=1}^{p} \delta_i \Delta x_{t-i} + e_t$$

$$\Delta x_t = \beta_2 u_{t-1} + \sum_{i=1}^{p} a_i \Delta y_{t-i} + \sum_{i=1}^{p} b_i \Delta x_{t-i} + v_t$$

A constant term and other deterministic terms may be added to the model. An ECM is valid in this context if $\beta < 0$. Note that the theorem says that at least one β_j or both are negative. In the above models, u_{t-1} is the lagged error correcting term whose role is to correct for the previous disequilibrium.

By the Granger representation theorem, it is also known that if two variables are cointegrated then there exists Granger causality in at least one direction.

Answer 6.13

Exogeneity, like causality, is a subtle concept. The proponents of the Cowles Commission and those of the more modern econometrics (mainly time series proponents) define the concept differently.

The proponents of the Cowles Commission (the simultaneous equations approach) basically link exogeneity with something *external*. Precisely, a variable is exogenous if it is determined outside the system. This is relative, to the extent that what is external in one system may be determined within the system in another context. In a given system, different schools of thought do not necessarily agree on which variables are exogeneous. In any event, the Cowles Commission sharpens the concept of exogeneity by breaking it down into "predeterminedness" and strict exogeneity. A variable is predetermined in a given equation if it is independent of the current or contemporaneous and future errors. Lagged endogenous variables are examples. A variable is strictly exogenous in a given equation if it is independent of the past, current or contemporaneous and future errors. Weather-like variables are typical exogenous variables.

The time series proponents question the definition of exogeneity given by the Cowles Commission. They are interested in the question, "exogeneity for what?" To borrow from Engle, Hendry and Richard (1983), consider the model:

$$y_t = bx_t + e_t \qquad \text{(A6.13.1)}$$

where b is an unknown parameter, y_t and x_t are the variables of interest and e_t is an error term. Suppose that we rewrite the model as follows:

$$y_t = dx_t + u_t \qquad \text{(A6.13.2)}$$

where $d = b + 1$ is an unknown parameter and $u_t = e_t - x_t$ is the new error term. As pointed out by the authors if $E(e_t/x_t) = 0$ then $E(u_t/x_t) \neq 0$. That is, exogeneity is dependent on the parameter of interest. Hence the question, "exogeneity for what?" They defined three concepts of exogeneity, each related to one of the major purposes of econometrics (inferences about parameters of interest, forecasting and testing for stability).

Weak exogeneity: A variable x_t is weakly exogenous for estimating a given parameter if the conditional distribution of the endogenous variable given x_t contains all the information for the parameter of interest and the marginal distribution of x_t does not add any information for estimating the parameter.

Strong exogeneity: A variable x_t is strongly exogenous for estimating a given parameter if it is weakly exogenous and it is not Granger caused by any endogenous variable of the system.

Super-exogeneity: A variable x_t is super-exogenous for estimating a given parameter if the conditional distribution of the parameters of the conditional distribution remain invariant to changes in the marginal distribution of x_t. This notion is linked to the Lucas critique.

Answer 6.14

a) The eight models come from the following autoregressive distributed lag model of order one, *ADL*(1,1):

$$y_t = \alpha + \beta_1 x_t + \beta_2 x_{t-1} + \beta_3 y_{t-1} + u_t \quad \text{(A6.14.1)}$$

where u_t is *iid*$(0, \sigma^2)$.

b) Equation (Q6.14.1) is a static model, as there are no dynamics. The constraint of interest is $\beta_2 = \beta_3 = 0$ in Equation (A6.14.1).

Equation (Q6.14.2) is a distributed lag model. The constraint used in Equation (A6.14.1) is $\beta_3 = 0$.

Equation (Q6.14.3) is an autoregressive model, as the right-hand side only contains the lagged dependent variable. The constraint is thus $\beta_1 = \beta_2 = 0$.

Equation (Q6.14.4) is a leading indicator model, as only the past of the explanatory variable explains the dependent variable. The constraint of interest is $\beta_1 = \beta_3 = 0$.

Equation (Q6.14.5) represents a reduced-form model. The constraint is $\beta_1 = 0$.

Equation (Q6.14.6) is the partial adjustment model. The constraint is $\beta_2 = 0$.

Equation (Q6.14.7) is the growth rate model. The constraints are $\beta_2 = -\beta_1$ and $\beta_3 = 1$.

Equation (Q6.14.8) is an error correction model arrived at by making $\delta = -(\beta_1 + \beta_2)/(\beta_3 - 1)$ and $\beta_3 \neq 1$. (Answer adapted in part from Ericsson, 1997.)

Answer 6.15

a) Yes, it is a long-run estimate because the variables of interest are cointegrated.

b) $\hat{\beta}$ is superconsistent; that is, it goes to its true value at a faster rate (T) than the regular OLS estimator $\left(\sqrt{T}\right)$ (see Stock, 1987a). However, this estimator is most often biased in small samples (see Banerjee et al., 1986, 1993). Moreover, $\hat{\beta}$ is most often affected by autocorrelation in errors and endogeneity of variables. Autocorrelation will result in inefficiency and invalidation of test statistics. Last, because variables are integrated of the order of at least one, the t statistic has a nonstandard distribution (see Banerjee et al., 1993, 162–168).

c) An error correction model will be implemented.

Answer 6.16

The major problem that a researcher may encounter is that one regression may reveal cointegration and another one no cointegration, as in general $\hat{\delta} \neq 1/\hat{\beta}$ unless $R^2 = 1$. That is, there is the issue of normalization of variables.

Answer 6.17

a) No. We can argue in two ways. First, we know that $I(2) + I(2) = I(2)$ or $I(1)$ in particular cases. Since $I(2) + I(2)$ cannot give $I(0)$ and we know that $e_{2t} \sim I(0)$, then y_t is not $I(2)$ and so is not x_t. Second we can, as done by many authors, derive the full expression for both variables of interest. Using Equations (Q6.17.1) and (Q6.17.2) gives the following:

$$y_t = \frac{\alpha}{\alpha - \beta} e_{1t} - \frac{\beta}{\alpha - \beta} e_{2t} \quad \text{(A6.17.1)}$$

$$x_t = -\frac{1}{\alpha - \beta} e_{1t} - \frac{1}{\alpha - \beta} e_{2t} \quad \text{(A6.17.2)}$$

Since $e_{1t} \sim I(1)$ and $e_{2t} \sim I(0)$ and $I(1) - I(0) = I(1)$, thus $y_t \sim I(1)$ and $x_t \sim I(1)$.

b) The model is internally consistent as long as $\alpha \neq \beta$ (why?). (See Maddala, 1992, 590.)

c) From the reduced forms of Equations (A6.17.1) and (A6.17.2) we obtain:

$$\Delta y_t = \frac{1}{\alpha - \beta}(\alpha \Delta e_{1t} - \beta \Delta e_{2t}) \quad \text{(A6.17.3)}$$

$$\Delta x_t = \frac{1}{\alpha - \beta}(-\Delta e_{1t} + \Delta e_{2t}) \quad \text{(A6.17.4)}$$

Exploiting the values of e_{1t} and e_{2t} as in Equations (Q6.17.1) and (Q6.17.2) and using Equations (A6.17.3) and (A6.17.4), we arrive at (check it):

$$\Delta y_t = \beta \gamma u_{2,t-1} + \eta_{1t} \quad \text{(A6.17.5)}$$

$$\Delta x_t = -\gamma u_{2,t-1} + \eta_{2t} \quad \text{(A6.17.6)}$$

where

$$\gamma = \frac{\rho - 1}{\alpha - \beta}$$

and η_{1t} and η_{2t} are combinations of u_{1t} and u_{2t}. Equations (A6.17.5) and (A6.17.6) are the ECMs corresponding to the data generation process (DGP).

d) The fact that the two errors were integrated at different levels help identify the structural parameters (see Maddala, 1992, 591).

Answer 6.18

Unit root analysis is conducted at three levels: graphical inspection, correlogram inspection and unit root test examinations. Figure 6.1 contains the graph of raw data (original series) on money supply in Jamaica. The figure indicates that money supply in Jamaica

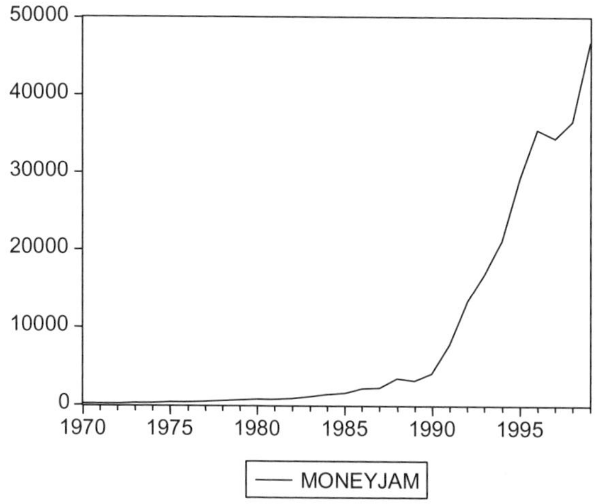

FIGURE 6.1
Money supply in Jamaica 1970–1999 (millions of Jamaican dollars)

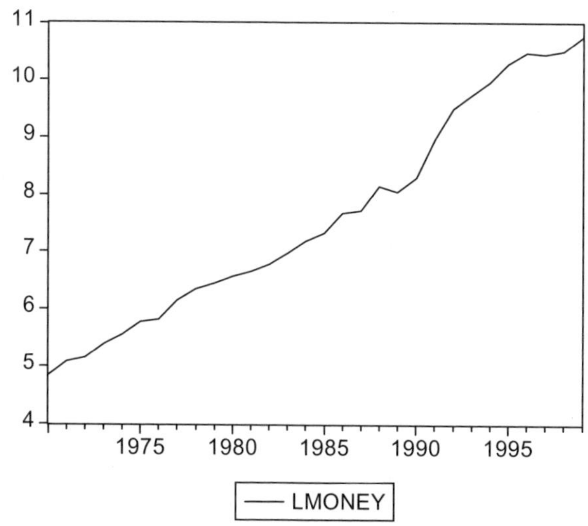

FIGURE 6.2
Log of money supply in Jamaica 1970–1999

is trending up, most likely exponentially. Given this shape, it is advisable to transform the series into a logarithm form. The graph of the level series for the logarithm of money supply is presented in Figure 6.2. It can be seen clearly that the series contains a stochastic trend, with possibly a linear deterministic trend.

At this stage, it is interesting to examine the type of shape we get if we use the first difference of the series. Figure 6.3 contains the result of the exercise. We can see the series is now stationary, as it seems to revert to its mean each time it wanders.

Now let us see what the second instrument of analysis reveals, that is, the examination of the correlogram or autocorrelation function (acf). Note that we are

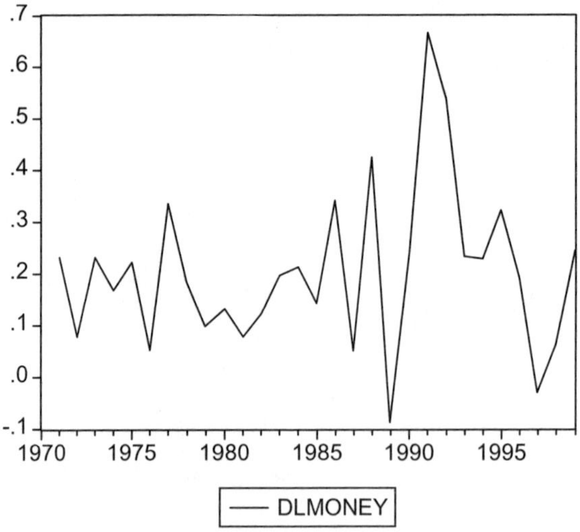

FIGURE 6.3
Money growth in Jamaica 1970–1999

Autocorrelation	Partial Correlation		AC	PAC	Q-Stat	Prob
. |****** |	. |****** |	1	0.817	0.817	22.081	0.000
. |***** |	.*| . |	2	0.645	-0.066	36.342	0.000
. |**** |	.*| . |	3	0.484	-0.069	44.686	0.000
. |*** |	. | . |	4	0.347	-0.036	49.135	0.000
. |**. |	. | . |	5	0.260	0.052	51.727	0.000
. |**. |	. | . |	6	0.200	0.015	53.327	0.000
. |* . |	. | . |	7	0.153	-0.014	54.298	0.000
. |* . |	. | . |	8	0.125	0.022	54.980	0.000
. |* . |	. | . |	9	0.107	0.012	55.500	0.000
. |* . |	. | . |	10	0.087	-0.013	55.863	0.000
. |* . |	. | . |	11	0.068	-0.010	56.096	0.000
. | . |	. | . |	12	0.053	0.005	56.246	0.000

FIGURE 6.4
Correlogram of log of money supply in Jamaica 1970–1999
Note: the dotted line represents the 5 percent two standard deviation bounds.

only concerned with the acf (why?). Figure 6.4 contains the acf and the partial autocorrelation function (pacf) of the log of money supply. As can be seen, the acf dies out slowly. This is one of the characteristics of a nonstationary series. Care should be taken, however, since the correlogram of a near-unit root process dies out slowly too. That is why it is often useful to combine the three instruments to have a clear picture of stationarity/nonstationarity.

Autocorrelation	Partial Correlation		AC	PAC	Q-Stat	Prob
. |* . |	. |* . |	1	0.109	0.109	0.3827	0.536
. | . |	. | . |	2	-0.010	-0.022	0.3859	0.825
. | . |	. | . |	3	0.005	0.009	0.3868	0.943
. |* . |	. |* . |	4	0.131	0.131	1.0071	0.909
. | . |	. | . |	5	-0.009	-0.039	1.0102	0.962
. | . |	. | . |	6	0.040	0.051	1.0732	0.983
. | . |	. | . |	7	-0.010	-0.022	1.0774	0.993
. | . |	. | . |	8	0.034	0.022	1.1261	0.997
. | . |	. | . |	9	0.051	0.053	1.2441	0.999
. | . |	. | . |	10	-0.014	-0.039	1.2528	1.000
. |* . |	. |* . |	11	0.080	0.099	1.5734	1.000
. | . |	. | . |	12	-0.015	-0.050	1.5857	1.000

FIGURE 6.5
Correlogram of money growth in Jamaica 1970–1999

TABLE 6.6
Tests for Unit Root (Stationarity) for Log of Money Supply in Jamaica, 1970–1999

	ADF Test	KPSS Test
Level	0.487 [0, 0.9832]	0.697
First difference	–4.604 [0, 0.0010]	0.171
Critical values	–3.679, –2.968, –2.623	0.739, 0.463, 0.347

Note: The ADF test is the augmented Dickey–Fuller test result. In brackets, the first figure is the optimal lag and the second figure is the p value. The KPSS is the Kwiatkowski–Phillips–Schmidt–Shin test statistic. Critical values are critical values of the corresponding test at the 1 percent, 5 percent, and 10 percent level of significance, respectively.

Figure 6.5 indicates that money growth is stationary, as all autocorrelations are within two standard deviations. The series becomes white noise in fact. Summing up, the second instrument reveals that the log of money supply is nonstationary to the extent that it is integrated of order one (the level is nonstationary and the first difference is stationary).

The last instrument to be used is the formal testing for unit roots. Two tests are of interest here: the ADF test and the KPSS test. Recall, the ADF uses unit root as the null hypothesis. On the contrary, the KPSS uses stationarity as the null hypothesis. According to the ADF test results (Table 6.6), the log of money supply is integrated of order one. Indeed, the p value of the level is greater than the level of significance (5 percent), implying the non-rejection of the null hypothesis. The p value of the first difference (money growth) is, on the contrary, smaller than the level of significance, leading to the rejection of the null hypothesis.

According to the KPSS test results (see Table 6.6), the log of money supply is integrated of order one too. Indeed, the value of the test for the level is greater than the 5 percent value, leading to the rejection of the null hypothesis (stationarity). Note here it is smaller than the 1 percent value (this clearly is at odds with respect to what the graph reveals). The value of the statistic of the first difference is unquestionably smaller than any critical value exhibited in the table, leading to the non-rejection of the null hypothesis.

In conclusion, the three means for detecting stationarity/nonstationarity convey the same message: the log of money supply in Jamaica during the period of investigation is nonstationary; precisely, integrated of order one.

Answer 6.19

a) An examination of the results reveals the following. The AEG test indicates the absence of cointegration, as the statistic is, in absolute value, less than the critical value. However, the *t* ratio statistic of the error correcting term reveals cointegration. For the trace statistic from the Johansen procedure, the critical value is less than the value of the statistic for no cointegration and the reverse for one cointegration, implying there is one cointegrated vector. Overall, there is cointegration between the two variables.
b) No, it is not an omission. The standard errors are not presented because they are not reliable, for several reasons. Among others, the regressions are plagued by autocorrelation rending variances (and standard errors) biased and *t* invalid. Moreover, the variables are nonstationary; that is, standard distribution does not apply.
c) No; from time to time the two methods give conflicting results. In that case, one leans toward the Johansen procedure results, because the Johansen procedure does not suffer from the major flaws of the Engle–Granger procedure alluded to elsewhere.
d) Theoretically, this should not be the case, as the maximum number of cointegrating relationships one may have is $n - 1$, with n being the number of variables. In any case, the existence of n cointegrating vectors means that the original variables are already stationary, at least if the prior is that variables are individually $I(1)$.
e) It means that variables are individually integrated of order one without having a long-run relationship. Their short-run relationships are obtained using their first differences.

Answer 6.20

a) Unit root (stationarity) tests. Let us adopt the following definitions. Money growth is captured by $Gmsa = (m_t - m_{t-1})/m_{t-1}$, where m_t is money supply. Inflation is defined as $Gpsa = (p_t - p_{t-1})/p_{t-1}$, where p_t is price (consumer price index). Table 6.7 shows that money growth is stationary by the two tests. As far as inflation is concerned, the results of the two tests diverge. Indeed, while the KPSS test clearly indicates a strong stationarity, the ADF test underlines that inflation is integrated of order one. Since we have some

TABLE 6.7
Testing for Unit Root (Stationary) in Money Growth and Inflation in South Africa, 1970–1999

	Gpsa	*Gmsa*	Critical Value
ADF: level	–1.363 (0)	–4.464 (1)	–3.69, –2.97, –2.63
KPSS: level	0.196	0.181	0.739, 0.463, 0.347
ADF: first difference	–4.689 (1)		

Note: Variables are defined in the text. The numbers in parentheses for the ADF test results are the optimal lag.

TABLE 6.8
ARMA Structure of Inflation

Variable	Coefficient	Standard Error	*t* Statistic	Prob.
C	0.116682	0.014432	8.084766	0.0000
AR(1)	0.569512	0.185600	3.068495	0.0051
MA(1)	0.685271	0.121983	5.617771	0.0000
R^2	0.696182	Mean dependent variable		0.118271
SE of regression	0.019506	Akaike information criterion		–4.935247
RSS	0.009512	Schwarz criterion		–4.792511
Log likelihood	72.09346	*F* statistic		28.64305
DW statistic	2.228340	Prob(*F* statistic)		0.000000

problem deciding on the type of process that inflation follows, we recourse to another method. We fit the inflation model to try to see whether it is stationary or not.

Table 6.8 indicates that inflation is an *ARMA*(1,1) process. The root for stationarity is far from the unit circle. Note that the ADF test in the presence of a large MA component loses a great deal of its power (has the tendency to accept the null hypothesis more than it should do). Thus, we conclude inflation is stationary.

b) We have found that both variables are stationary. Thus, there is no point in checking for cointegration. However, to see how this theory fares, we still run cointegration tests following the Johansen procedure to illustrate some of the problems that we may encounter while testing for cointegration.

Using an ECM with one lag, according to the results of Table 6.9, if we follow the Akaike information criterion then the optimal model (the one with the smallest value of the criterion) is the one with a quadratic trend. The results indicate a cointegration rank of 2. This means that individual variables are stationary. If we choose the Schwarz information criterion, then the optimal model is the one with neither intercept nor trend. It indicates the existence of one cointegrated relationship. This is contradictory, as variables were found to be stationary.

A search indicates that the optimal number of lags is 2. That is, we rerun the Johansen test with an optimal lag of 2. Results of the exercise are

TABLE 6.9
Cointegration Test (Johansen Procedure) with One Lag: Inflation and Money Growth in South Africa, 1970–1999

Data Trend	None	None	Linear	Linear	Quadratic
Rank	No intercept No trend	Intercept No trend	Intercept No trend	Intercept Trend	Intercept Trend
Trace	1	1	2	1	2
Max-eig	1	1	2	0	2
Akaike Information Criterion					
0	–5.742896	–5.742896	–5.595623	–5.595623	–5.637089
1	–5.938831	–5.977901	–5.903858	–5.925967	–6.022303*
2	–5.649449	–5.804345	–5.804345	–5.971554	–5.971554
Schwarz Information Criterion					
0	–5.550920	–5.550920	–5.307660	–5.307660	–5.253137
1	–5.554879*	–5.545955	–5.423919	–5.398034	–5.446375
2	–5.073522	–5.132430	–5.132430	–5.203650	–5.203650

Note: Lag interval of 1; Rank: number of cointegrating relationships; (*): smallest value; Trace: Trace test; Max-eig: maximum eigenvalue test.

TABLE 6.10
Cointegration Test (Johansen) with Two Lags: Inflation and Money Growth in South Africa, 1970–1999

Data Trend	None	None	Linear	Linear	Quadratic
Rank	No intercept No trend	Intercept No trend	Intercept No trend	Intercept Trend	Intercept Trend
Trace	0	0	0	0	0
Max-Eig	0	0	0	0	0
Akaike Information Criterion					
0	–6.248450*	–6.248450*	–6.110491	–6.110491	–6.104361
1	–6.130476	–6.120675	–6.059602	–6.092861	–6.133041
2	–5.844278	–5.767361	–5.767361	–5.860246	–5.860246
Schwarz Information Criterion					
0	–5.861344*	–5.861344*	–5.626607	–5.626607	–5.523701
1	–5.549816	–5.491627	–5.382165	–5.367036	–5.358828
2	–5.070065	–4.896371	–4.896371	–4.892479	–4.892479

Note: Lag interval of 2; Rank: number of cointegrating relationships; (*): smallest value; Trace: Trace test; Max-eig: maximum eigenvalue test.

TABLE 6.11
Vector Autoregression Estimates: Inflation and Money Growth in South Africa, 1973–1999

	GPSA	GMSA
GPSA(–1)	1.016634	0.733681
	[4.90665]	[0.61319]
GPSA(–2)	–0.306877	–0.530757
	[–1.47063]	[–0.44046]
GMSA(–1)	0.016002	0.166404
	[0.44163]	[0.79527]
GMSA(–2)	0.016863	–0.308380
	[0.48288]	[–1.52916]
C	0.029078	0.188392
	[1.56534]	[1.75618]
R^2	0.649948	0.112227
SE equation	0.020618	0.119061
F statistic	10.21195	0.695276
Log likelihood	69.25692	21.91271
Akaike information criterion	–4.759772	–1.252793
Schwarz criterion	–4.519802	–1.012824
Determinant residual covariance		5.52E-06
Log Likelihood (df adjusted)		86.82921
Akaike information criteria		–5.691053
Schwarz criterion		–5.211113

Note: *t* Statistics are in brackets.

presented in Table 6.10. The table indicates that with two lags, the cointegration rank is zero for both tests. This means that both variables are nonstationary. This clearly contradicts our unit root analysis and also at the same time raises the question whether we should use the unit root tests as pretests for cointegration. If yes, we should be wary about the level of significance to use.

In any case the analysis of cointegration is dismissed given the unit root results and we conclude that there is no long-run relationship between money growth and inflation in South Africa. Put differently, no long-run causality exists in either sense between money growth and inflation. Monetarist views are not supported by these data.

c) Granger causality. We use a VAR in level to test for causality, as variables were found to be stationary. Note here the level variables are money growth and inflation. The VAR results are presented in Table 6.11. The results point to the lack of relationship between the two variables at the 5 percent or 10 percent level of significance.

TABLE 6.12
Pairwise Granger Causality Tests

Lags: 2

Null Hypothesis:	No. of Observations	F Statistic	Prob.
GPSA does not Granger cause GMSA	27	0.19059	0.82782
GMSA does not Granger cause GPSA		0.24858	0.78207

The results of a formal Granger causality are presented in Table 6.12. They clearly demonstrate the lack of causality between money growth and inflation in South Africa in the period of investigation. Indeed, the p value is greater than any standard level of significance. These results are robust across different lag structures (check it for yourself).

d) We derive the impulse response functions (Figure 6.6) as well as the variance decomposition (Figure 6.7) from the VAR in Table 6.11 using Pesaran–Shin decomposition. The impulse response functions indicate that a one standard deviation (SD) shock to inflation innovation increases inflation by 2 percent in the first two years before decreasing and completely leveling off from year seven and onwards; the same shock depresses money growth by about 4 percent in the first year before undergoing slight increase and leveling off at year four. One SD shock to money growth innovation leads to a slight decrease in inflation in the order of 0.5 percent, which levels off from year 3 and onwards. On the contrary, the shock has a bigger impact on money growth itself. It increases by more than 10 percent in the first year but quickly decreases before leveling off by year 6. The impulse response results seem to reinforce the story about the lack of causality between money growth and inflation in South Africa, at least in the period of investigation.

Figure 6.7 presents variance decomposition results. It indicates that inflation is largely explained by shocks to its own innovation. That is, a one SD shock to innovation in money growth has no explanatory power in the variance of inflation. This also reinforces the lack of causality from money growth to inflation. A one SD shock to inflation innovation explains about 10 percent variance of money growth. If there is causality, it would run from inflation to money growth and not the other way round.

Answer 6.21

a) Yes, the ECM is valid. Indeed, the lagged error correcting term enters significantly (negatively) in the model, as the t statistic indicates.
b) The results are not too different, as the size of the error correcting term is very small. This is most likely the reflection of a lower degree of cointegration among variables. (See also Downes et al., 2004, 540–541 for the ECM.)

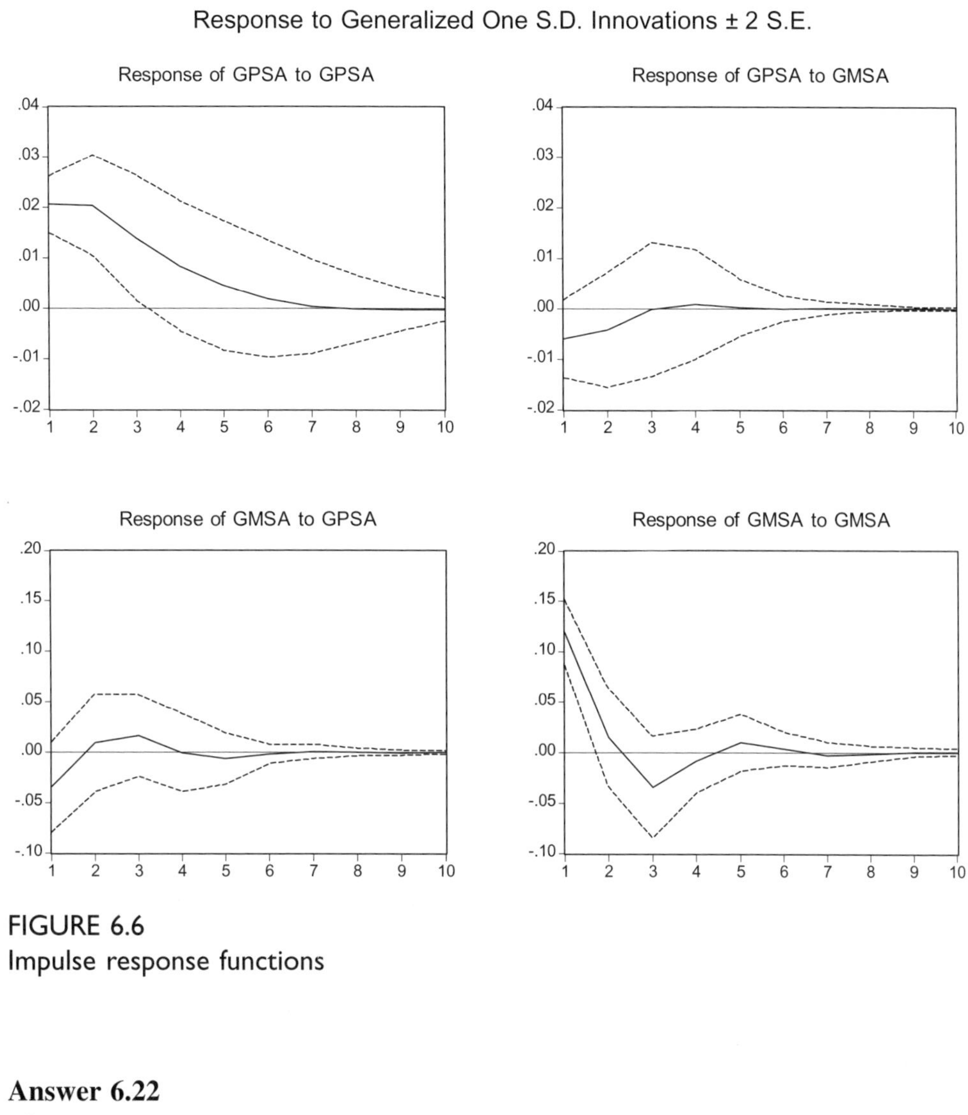

FIGURE 6.6
Impulse response functions

Answer 6.22

We leave the search for the degree of integration of each variable to the reader. As a warning, however, for some variables a combination of several methods is necessary to have a final say. In any event, we found that the variables are integrated of order one, although inflation is not a clear-cut story. We proceed to test for cointegration by using the residual and nonresidual tests for cointegration (the Engle–Granger and the Johansen LR tests).

Concerning the Engle–Granger procedure, we start by running the basic regression as in Equation (Q6.22.1). We augment the regression with a trend since two individual variables have a strong deterministic trend. We retrieve the residuals that we call $\hat{u}_t$. We then run the following regression:

$$\Delta \hat{u}_t = \alpha \hat{u}_{t-1} + e_t \tag{A6.22.1}$$

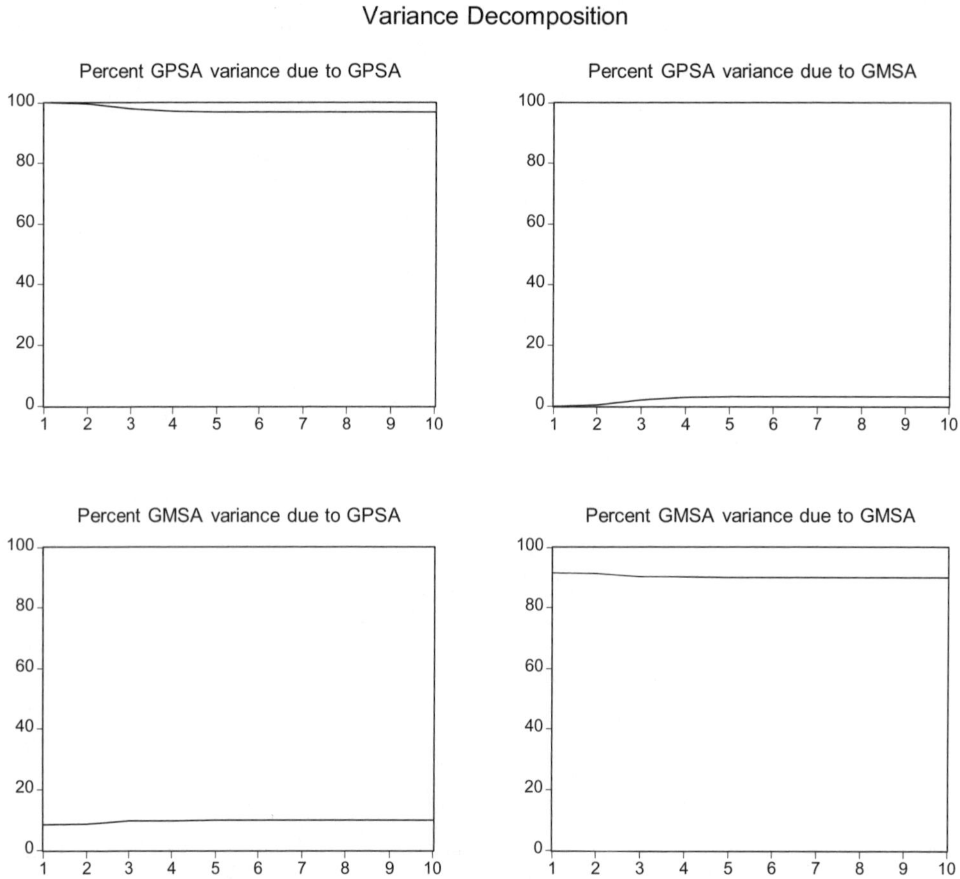

FIGURE 6.7
Variance decomposition

The t statistic of α is the Engle–Granger t test. The latter does not follow a t distribution. Critical values can be found in Engle and Granger (1987) as well as in Engle and Yoo (1987).

The Engle and Granger regression results are shown in the upper part of Table 6.13. As can be seen, R^2 is high. However, the DW statistic is also high; in fact, far higher than R^2. There is a presumption that the variables are cointegrated. The formal t test derived from Equation (A6.22.1) has a value of –7.523 (see Table 6.14). As it is greater in absolute value than the critical value, –4.1193, at the 5 percent level of significance, we reject the null hypothesis of non-cointegration.

Let us turn now to the Johansen procedure. Results not reported here indicate the existence of one cointegrated relationship in the presence of a deterministic trend. The cointegration regression results are presented in the lower part of Table 6.13. All the variables are statistically significant. A 1 percent increase in the permanent value of unemployment decreases wage growth by 0.19 percent. A 1 percent increase in permanent inflation increases wage growth by 0.17 percent. Note that the Engle–Granger procedure and the Johansen procedure in general give different results for the variables of interest. As said elsewhere, in this case we trust the Johansen procedure results.

TABLE 6.13
Cointegration Regression Results: Wage Growth, Unemployment Rate and Inflation, Barbados 1975–1996

Variable	Coefficient	Standard Error	*t* Statistic	Prob.
Engle–Granger Procedure				
C	18.487	4.717	3.919	0.0010
UN	–0.336	0.234	–1.436	0.1683
π	–0.006	0.208	–0.028	0.9782
Trend	–0.631	0.167	–3.784	0.0014
R^2	0.712	Mean dependent variable		6.00484
Log likelihood	–55.116	DW statistic		2.936
Johansen Procedure				
C	18.721			
UN	–0.189	0.082	–2.305	
π	0.173	0.057	3.035	
Trend	–0.630	0.037	–17.027	

Note: *UN:* unemployment rate (%); π: inflation (%).

TABLE 6.14
Engle–Granger Test Results, 1975–1996

Variable	Coefficient	Standard Error	*t* Statistic	Prob.
$\hat{u}_{t-1}$	–1.473	0.195780	–7.523	0.0000
R^2	0.739	Mean dependent variable		0.070
Log likelihood	–50.308	DW statistic		2.395

Note: The regression of interest is $\Delta\hat{u}_{t-1} = a\hat{u}_{t-1} + e_t$.

6.4 SUPPLEMENTARY EXERCISES

Question 6.23 Testing for cointegration using the Engle–Granger procedure no longer attracts researchers. Why? (Adapted from UWI, EC36D, final examination May 2003.)

Question 6.24 Write a careful note on fully modified OLS in the context of cointegration. (See Phillips and Hansen, 1990 and Mamingi, 1997.)

Question 6.25 Reexamine, in light of cointegration, the relationship between the consumer price index and the import price index for Jamaica such as dealt with in Question 1.14. Use data from Question 1.14.

Question 6.25 Granger causality distortions in unrestricted VAR in first differences due to an omission of the error correcting term are now well documented. Using a

TABLE 6.15
Data for Wage Model: Barbados 1975–1996

Year	*wi* (%)	*UN* (%)	π (%)	Productivity
1975	9.474537	22.40000	18.68333	7.093785
1976	9.170843	16.20000	4.710447	7.480594
1977	18.46099	17.00000	8.098610	7.702948
1978	10.17827	12.20000	9.054121	8.023649
1979	7.096941	13.40000	15.63631	8.090526
1980	18.39228	12.90000	13.32551	7.999003
1981	9.984533	10.80000	13.71515	7.721295
1982	10.71688	13.70000	9.791295	7.743271
1983	5.611903	15.20000	5.140797	7.855799
1984	8.752367	17.20000	4.543010	8.361976
1985	4.744788	18.70000	4.012779	8.543974
1986	4.143967	18.40000	0.995033	8.605619
1987	1.661380	18.00000	3.438548	8.062738
1988	7.093437	17.90000	4.611409	8.102493
1989	2.679252	17.70000	6.141245	8.138765
1990	4.933736	17.60000	2.990350	7.759047
1991	0.871465	17.20000	6.091886	7.887955
1992	−1.805795	23.00000	5.890027	7.828909
1993	1.598476	24.30000	1.127739	7.997012
1994	−1.653709	21.70000	0.097466	7.904356
1995	0.000000	19.60000	1.210375	7.801090
1996	0.000000	15.80000	2.330664	7.898601

Note: *wi*: Log(wage)-Log(wage(−1)); *UN*: unemployment rate in %; π: inflation: Log(cpi)-Log(cpi(−1)); *wi* and π have been multiplied by 100. Productivity is the ratio of GDP in 1974 Bds$ millions to labour employment.

Sources: Central Bank of Barbados, *Annual Statistical Digest*, 1998; Downes, A. and McLean, W. *The Estimation of Missing Values of Employment in Barbados*, Research Paper 13, Centre of Statistics of Trinidad and Tobago (1988, 115–116).

bivariate framework, point out and explain intuitively the determining factors of Granger causality distortions in the above context. (See Lahiri and Mamingi, 1996.)

Question 6.26 Using data from Table 6.15, conduct a full cointegration analysis of the relationship between wage growth, unemployment, inflation and productivity for Barbados for the period 1975–1996. Compare the results obtained here with those from Question 6.22.

CHAPTER 7

Aggregation Over Time

7.1 INTRODUCTION

Most decisions made by policy makers, as well as empirical studies undertaken by economists, are based on temporally aggregated data, particularly in developing countries. In general, the prohibitive cost of frequently collecting and processing (new) data explains this situation. In other words, in many instances aggregated data are the only time series observations available to researchers and policy makers. Yet, a gap often exists between the agent's time decision interval and the data sampling interval. Hence, this gives rise to the issue of aggregation over time (or temporal aggregation) (Mamingi, 1992).

Aggregation over time basically arises in two ways. On the one hand, it is a shift from continuous time to discrete time. In this respect, one can define temporal aggregation as well as systematic sampling. Suppose one has a process $y(t)$ defined over an interval $-\ell < t < \ell$. Then, temporal aggregation of $y(t)$ is the average or the integral of the process over the interval $[-\ell,\ell]$: e.g., average:

$$\bar{y}_t = \int_{-\ell}^{\ell} y(t-\tau)\,d\tau / 2\ell \tag{7.1.1}$$

That is, $Y_T = \bar{y}_t$ for $t = 0, \pm 1, \pm 2, \ldots$ is the sample average and T is some aggregate time unit. Similarly, systematic sampling is the sampling point in time for a continuous process:

$$Y_T = y(t) \tag{7.1.2}$$

with $t = 0, \pm 1, \pm 2, \ldots$ and T is some aggregate time unit.

On the other hand, and most interestingly, aggregation over time can also be a shift from a small discrete unit to a large discrete unit. Thus, temporal aggregation of y_t with $t = 0, \pm 1, \pm 2, \ldots$ is either a sum of lagged values of y_t or an average of the latter, for example, as a sum:

$$Y_T = \sum_{i=0}^{k-1} y_{kT-i} \tag{7.1.3}$$

where k is the sampling interval frequency. In economics, the variables temporally aggregated are flow variables (for example, income, consumption and saving). Systematic sampling (or skip sampling or point-in-time sampling) picks up the kth element of y_t:

$$Y_T = y_{kT} \tag{7.1.4}$$

The stock variables undergo this type of aggregation. Examples include capital stock at a given instant of time (Mamingi, 1992).

Aggregation over time can lead generally to (a) a lower precision of estimation and prediction; (b) lower power of test; (c) inability to make short-run forecasts; (d) Granger causality distortion; (e) exogeneity distortion; (f) changes in seasonal unit roots; (g) change in impulse response functions and (h) change in trend-cycle decomposition (see, for example, Zellner and Montmarquette, 1971; Mamingi, 1992, 1993, 1996; Marcellino, 1999).

On the positive side, aggregation over time is invariant to cointegration and unit roots (see, for example, Stock, 1987b; Mamingi, 1992, 1993).

The exercises in this chapter reflect on some of the issues of aggregation over time understood here as a shift from small discrete units to large discrete units.

7.2 QUESTIONS

7.2.1 Theoretical Exercises

Question 7.1 Consider the following process:

$$y_t \sim ARIMA(0,1,0) \tag{Q7.1.1}$$

a) Suggest another name for this process.
b) Write down the process.
c) Suppose that Y_T is the aggregated counterpart of y_t with k as the sampling interval and T as some aggregate time unit.
   i) Show, using a formula, the process that Y_T follows under temporal aggregation with $k = 3$;
   ii) Show, using a formula, the process that Y_T follows under systematic sampling with $k = 3$;
   iii) Suppose you are interested in testing for unit root in the disaggregated and aggregated series. Using results from (i) and (ii), indicate the type of aggregation over time which more likely distorts the result obtained in the disaggregated framework and explain why. (UWI, EC36D, final examination May 2001)

Question 7.2 Consider the following model:

$$y_t = a + bx_t + u_t \tag{Q7.2.1}$$

where $t = 1, 2, \ldots, n$, $y_t \sim I(1)$, $x_t \sim I(1)$ and u_t is the error term.

a) Fill in the blanks in the following sentences and explain your answers:

   i) If $u_t \sim I(1)$, then the basic regression is said to be…
   ii) If $u_t \sim I(0)$, then the variables are said to be …

b) Show that if $u_t \sim I(1)$, then its systematically sampled counterpart is also $I(1)$. (UWI, EC36D, final examination May 1997)

Question 7.3 Consider the following disaggregated model:

$$y_t = c + ax_t + u_t \tag{Q7.3.1}$$

where $y_t \sim I(1)$, $x_t \sim I(1)$ and u_t is the error term. Prove that if u_t follows a random walk process, then:

a) its systematically sampled counterpart U_T follows a random walk process;
b) its temporally aggregated counterpart U_T follows an $IMA(1, 1)$ process;
c) its mixed aggregated counterpart U_T follows an $IMA(1)$ process. (See Mamingi, 1993.)

7.2.2 Empirical Exercises

Question 7.4 Using a Monte Carlo investigation, Mamingi (1996) documented Granger causality distortion in error correction models under aggregation over time. He used two DGPs to do so. One of them, a variant of the well-known DGP used by Engle and Granger (1987) is:

$$\Delta y_t = \delta u_{t-1} + e_{1t} \tag{Q7.4.1}$$

$$\Delta x_t = -\delta u_{t-1} + e_{2t} \tag{Q7.4.2}$$

where
$u_t = \rho u_{t-1} + w_t$ = the error correcting term;
w_t = white noise;
$\delta = 1 - \rho$, $0 \leq \rho \leq 1$ = the degree of cointegration;
Δ = the first difference;

$$\text{var}(e_{it}) = \text{var}(e_{1t}, e_{2t})' \sim iid\begin{pmatrix} 1 & 0 \\ 0 & 1 \end{pmatrix} \quad \text{and} \quad t = 1, 2, \ldots N.$$

The number of observations in the disaggregated model is also the data span, $S = N$. Equations (Q7.4.1) and (Q7.4.2) reveal feedback between y_t and x_t. Using Monte

TABLE 7.1
Monte Carlo Simulations (1000 replications): Causality Distortions (in %) in Temporally Aggregated ECMs

$S = N$	M	ρ	FD	NOD	FA	NOA	$DISTO$
150	50	0.0	100.0	0.0	92.6	0.0	7.4
		0.6	100.0	0.0	58.0	0.1	42.0
		0.9	83.2	0.0	1.1	19.8	98.7
300	50	0.0	100.0	0.0	66.1	0.0	33.9
		0.6	100.0	0.0	24.3	0.0	75.7
		0.9	98.0	0.0	0.3	4.7	99.7
600	50	0.0	100.0	0.0	41.1	0.0	58.9
		0.6	100.0	0.0	14.3	59.3	85.7
		0.9	100.0	0.0	0.9	0.2	99.1
300	100	0.0	100.0	0.0	99.8	0.0	0.2
		0.6	100.0	0.0	94.1	0.0	5.9
		0.9	98.0	0.0	9.5	2.1	90.3
600	100	0.0	100.0	0.0	91.4	0.0	8.6
		0.6	100.0	0.0	49.6	0.0	50.4
		0.9	100.0	0.0	1.7	0.0	98.3
600	200	0.0	100.0	0.0	100.0	0.0	0.0
		0.6	100.0	0.0	100.0	0.0	0.0
		0.9	100.0	0.0	69.1	0.0	30.9

Notes: Equations (Q7.4.1) and (Q7.4.2) and their aggregated counterpart are of interest here. $S = N$ where S is the data span and N is the number of observations in the disaggregated ECMs. ρ = the degree of cointegration in the disaggregated ECMs; M = the number of observations in the aggregated ECMs ($M = S/k$ where k is the sampling interval); FD = the percentage of feedback relationships in the disaggregated ECMs; FA = the percentage of feedback relationships in the aggregated ECMs; NOD = the percentage of noncausality in the disaggregated ECMs; NOA = the percentage of noncausality in the aggregated ECMs; $DISTO$ = the percentage of changes in the true relationship; that is, the percentage of feedback detected in the disaggregated model that changes into another type of causality in the aggregated ECMs. Note that the Granger causality pattern is derived from the t statistics of error correction terms.

Source: Mamingi (1996).

Carlo simulations with 1000 replications, temporally aggregating and systematically sampling the above models give the results shown in Tables 7.1 and 7.2. Carefully interpret the results of the study.

Question 7.5 Consider the data shown in Table 7.3 on money supply and price in Barbados from January 1995 to December 1998. Consider systematically sampling the data using a sampling interval of three and also temporally averaging the series using the same sampling interval.

TABLE 7.2
Monte Carlo Simulations (1000 replications): Causality Distortions (in %) in Systematically Sampled ECMs

S = N	M	ρ	FD	NOD	FA	NOA	DISTO
150	50	0.0	100.0	0.0	100.0	0.0	0.0
		0.6	100.0	0.0	91.2	0.4	8.8
		0.9	83.2	0.0	22.9	19.8	60.3
300	50	0.0	100.0	0.0	100.0	0.0	0.0
		0.6	100.0	0.0	92.0	0.3	8.0
		0.9	98.0	0.0	23.9	26.4	74.1
600	50	0.0	100.0	0.0	100.0	0.0	0.0
		0.6	100.0	0.0	92.2	0.2	7.8
		0.9	100.0	0.0	21.4	27.4	78.6
300	100	0.0	100.0	0.0	100.0	0.0	0.0
		0.6	100.0	0.0	99.9	0.0	0.1
		0.9	98.0	0.0	54.1	5.7	43.6
600	100	0.0	100.0	0.0	100.0	0.0	0.0
		0.6	100.0	0.0	99.8	0.0	0.2
		0.9	100.0	0.0	53.1	7.2	46.9
600	200	0.0	100.0	0.0	100.0	0.0	0.0
		0.6	100.0	0.0	100.0	0.0	0.0
		0.9	100.0	0.0	89.1	0.5	10.9

Note: $S = N$ where S is the data span and N is the number of observations in the disaggregated ECMs. ρ = the degree of cointegration in the disaggregated ECMs; M = the number of observations in the aggregated ECMs ($M = S/k$ where k is the sampling interval); *FD* = the percentage of feedback relationships in the disaggregated ECMs; *FA* = the percentage of feedback relationships in the aggregated ECMs; *NOD* = the percentage of noncausality in the disaggregated ECMs; *NOA* = the percentage of noncausality in the aggregated ECMs; *DISTO* = the percentage of changes in the true relationship; that is, the percentage of feedback detected in the disaggregated model that changes into another type of causality in the aggregated ECMs. Note that the Granger causality pattern is derived from the t statistics of error correction terms

Source: Mamingi (1996).

a) Comment on temporally aggregating money supply.
b) Conduct a detailed study on the time series properties (unit root/stationarity) of the disaggregated series (*M*), its systematically sampled analogue (*MS*) and its temporally aggregated analogue (*MT*) using graphs, correlograms and unit root tests.
c) Comment on the impulse response functions of the disaggregated series and the aggregated series.
d) Examine whether there are Granger causality distortions in aggregated series between money supply and price.

TABLE 7.3
Money (Bds$ '000) and Price (CPI): Barbados 1995:01–1998:12

Year	M	P	Year	M	P
1995:01	718,408	101.4	1997:01	987,675	114.4
1995:02	747,503	102.0	1997:02	1,005,614	113.8
1995:03	754,802	101.4	1997:03	1,005,991	113.2
1995:04	762,599	100.8	1997:04	1,041,991	113.3
1995:05	799,063	101.3	1997:05	1,102,028	114.3
1995:06	761,378	102.3	1997:06	1,113,937	114.8
1995:07	781,678	103.5	1997:07	1,170,360	115.5
1995:08	749,717	104.2	1997:08	1,147,188	115.5
1995:09	765,136	104.5	1997:09	1,115,268	115.5
1995:10	767,582	104.8	1997:10	1,095,275	110.8
1995:11	783,374	105.0	1997:11	1,144,971	111.5
1995:12	899,174	105.1	1997:12	1,263,776	110.8
1996:01	831,570	104.3	1998:01	1,101,336	111.0
1996:02	798,874	104.5	1998:02	1,136,086	111.0
1996:03	822,145	104.4	1998:03	1,205,521	111.3
1996:04	902,105	104.7	1998:04	1,277,647	112.0
1996:05	837,718	105.6	1998:05	1,260,285	112.8
1996:06	846,724	105.1	1998:06	1,232,075	112.6
1996:07	863,322	105.4	1998:07	1,245,539	112.0
1996:08	906,840	105.6	1998:08	1,307,289	112.1
1996:09	885,004	105.8	1998:09	1,270,958	112.7
1996:10	874,524	106.5	1998:10	1,258,502	112.8
1996:11	905,078	106.9	1998:11	1,258,036	113.1
1996:12	1,036,746	107.0	1998:12	1,317,394	112.7

Source: Various issues of *Economic and Financial Statistics* (Central Bank of Barbados).

7.3 ANSWERS

Answer 7.1

a) This is a random walk process.
b) $y_t = y_{t-1} + e_t$ where e_t is a white noise process.
c) i) Stram and Wei (1986) showed that temporal aggregation of a process y_t ~ $ARIMA(p, d, q)$ gives rise, in the absence of hidden periodicity, to another process, Y_T ~ $ARIMA(p, d, q*)$, where p is the order of the autoregressive part, d is the degree of integration,

$$q* = \left[p + d + 1 + \frac{q - p - d - 1}{k} \right]$$

is the order of the moving average part (the integer part of the expression in brackets), and k is the sampling interval. In this particular exercise k = 3, and y_t ~ $ARIMA(0, 1, 0)$. Applying the above formula with $k = 3$ gives $q* = [1.334] = 1$. That is, Y_T ~ $ARIMA(0, 1, 0)$ or Y_T ~ $IMA(1, 1)$.

ii) Similarly, the systematically sampled counterpart of $y_t \sim ARIMA(p, d, q)$ is $Y_T \sim ARIMA(p, d, q^*)$ where (see Wei, 1982):

$$q^* = \left[p + d + \frac{q - p - d}{k} \right]$$

In our particular case, with $k = 3$, $q^* = [0.667] = 0$, $Y_T \sim ARIMA(0, 1, 0)$ or Y_T is a random walk.

iii) Most likely temporal aggregation, as in theory it alters the structure of the time series. Recall the usual ADF test stipulates a random walk as the null hypothesis. Since with temporal aggregation the process has become an $IMA(1,1)$ process most likely there is a distortion of the size of the test due to the presence of a moving average process.

Answer 7.2

a) i) If u_t is $I(1)$, then the basic regression is said to be *spurious*, in the sense that the regression is not valid (it indicates a relationship that does not really exist).

ii) If u_t is $I(0)$, then the variables are said to be *cointegrated*. That is, x_t and y_t have a long-run equilibrium. Although x_t and y_t are individually $I(1)$, their linear combination is of low order, $I(0)$; that is, stationary.

b) Recall, we have the following model:

$$y_t = a + bx_t + u_t \quad \text{(A7.2.1)}$$

We assume that the variables of interest are integrated of order one at the zero frequency and rule out the case examined by Granger and Sicklos (1995) in which one variable is integrated of order one at the zero frequency and the other is integrated of order one at another frequency. Without loss of generality, let us define the variables of interest as follows:

$$\begin{aligned} y_t &= \delta_1 z_{1t} + e_{1t} \\ x_t &= \delta_2 z_{2t} + e_{2t} \end{aligned} \quad \text{(A7.2.2)}$$

where the *e*s are white noise series and the *z*s are two random walks with drifts:

$$\begin{aligned} z_{1t} &= c + z_{1,t-1} + \eta_{1t} \\ z_{2t} &= c + z_{2,t-1} + \eta_{2t} \end{aligned} \quad \text{(A7.2.3)}$$

Use Equation (A7.2.2) in Equation (A7.2.1) to derive u_t.

$$u_t = \delta_1 z_{1t} - b\delta_2 z_{2t} - a + e_{1t} - be_{2t} \quad \text{(A7.2.4)}$$

Use Equation (A7.2.3) in Equation (A7.2.4):

$$u_t = c + \delta_1 z_{1,t-1} - b\delta_2 z_{2,t-1} + \delta_1 \eta_{1t} - b\delta_2 \eta_{2t} + e_{1t} - be_{2t} \quad \text{(A7.2.5)}$$

where c here represents all the constant terms. The right-hand side of Equation (A7.2.5) is a combination of integrated processes (random walks) and white noise series. As the equation reveals, the two random walks (nonstationary processes) do not cancel out, even with $b = \delta_1/\delta_2$. Since a linear combination of $I(1)$ series with a stationary series is an $I(1)$ process, u_t is $I(1)$.

Now let us systematically sample variables in Equation (A7.2.1) and derive the aggregate variable equation:

$$Y_T = ka + bX_T + U_T \quad \text{(A7.2.6)}$$

where $Y_T = y_{kT}$; $X_T = x_{kT}$; $U_T = u_{kT}$, k is the sampling interval and T is some time index in the aggregate framework.

Redefining analogously Equations (A7.2.2) and (A7.2.3) with aggregated variables, the aggregate counterpart of Equation (A7.2.5) using Equation (A7.2.6) becomes:

$$U_T = d + \delta_1^k Z_{1,T-1} - (b\delta_2)^k Z_{2,T-1} + \delta_1 N_{1T} - b\delta_2 N_{2T} + E_{1T} - bE_{2T} \quad \text{(A7.2.7)}$$

where d represents all constant terms.

We know that Z_{1T} and Z_{2T}, the aggregate counterparts of z_{1t} and z_{2t}, respectively, remain $I(1)$ (see Answer 7.1) and E_{1T} and E_{2T}, the aggregate counterparts of e_{1t} and e_{2t}, respectively, remain stationary. Since the Zs do not cancel out and the linear combination of $I(1)$ process and stationary process is an $I(1)$, U_T is thus $I(1)$.

Answer 7.3

This proof is along the lines of Stram and Wei (1986), Wei (1981) and Weiss (1984). It has been developed in Mamingi (1993, appendix). Under the null hypothesis of no cointegration, the basic equation is:

$$y_t = c + ax_t + u_t \quad \text{(A7.3.1)}$$

where:

$$(1-B)u_t = e_t \quad \text{(A7.3.2)}$$

B is the backward shift operator in the disaggregated model and e_t is a white noise series.

a) Systematic sampling. Define the following filter:

$$S(B) = \frac{(1-B^k)}{(1-B)} \quad \text{(A7.3.3)}$$

where k is the sampling interval or order of aggregation. Multiply both sides of Equation (A7.3.2) by $S(B)$:

$$S(B)(1-B)u_t = S(B)e_t \tag{A7.3.4}$$

or:

$$\left(1-B^k\right)u_t = S(B)e_t \tag{A7.3.5}$$

Systematically sampling the variables leads to: $U_T = u_{kT}$, and $E_T = e_{kT}$ with T as the time index of aggregated variables. Thus, Equation (A7.3.5) reads:

$$(1-L)U_T = \left(1-B^k\right)u_{kT} = S(B)e_{kT} \tag{A7.3.6}$$

where L is the backward shift operator in the aggregated model, that is,

$$(1-L)U_T = U_T - U_{T-1} \tag{A7.3.7}$$

We can write Equation (A7.3.6) as:

$$(1-L)U_T = S(B)e_{kT} = c_{kT} \tag{A7.3.8}$$

Since:

$$E\left(c_{kT}\ c_{kT-k}\right) = \mathrm{E}\left[\left(1+B+\ldots+B^{k-1}\right)e_{kT}\left(1+B+\ldots+B^{k-1}\right)e_{kT-k}\right] = 0$$

and $c_{kT} = \Delta U_T$ is white noise, then U_T is a random walk process. QED

b) Temporal aggregation. Define the following filter:

$$T(B) = S(B)S(B) \tag{A7.3.9}$$

where *S(B)* is defined as in Equation (A7.3.3). Multiplying both sides of Equation (A7.3.2) by Equation (A7.3.9) gives:

$$T(B)(1-B)\,u_t = T(B)e_t \tag{A7.3.10}$$

or

$$S(B)\left(1-B^k\right)u_t = T(B)e_t \tag{A7.3.11}$$

Applying the aggregate index to Equation (A7.3.11) leads to:

$$S(B)\left(1-B^{k}\right)u_{kT}=T(B)\,e_{kT} \qquad \text{(A7.3.12)}$$

where:

$$S(B)u_{kT}=\left(1+B+B^{2}+\ldots+B^{k-1}\right)u_{kT}=U_{T}$$

Define:

$$D_{T}=d_{kT}=\left(1-L\right)U_{T}=T(B)\,e_{kT} \qquad \text{(A7.3.13)}$$

That is:

$$D_{T}=\left(1+B+B^{2}+\ldots+B^{k-1}\right)^{2}e_{kT}$$

or

$$D_{T}=d_{kT}=e_{kT}+\ldots+e_{kT-2(k-1)}$$

Similarly:

$$D_{T-j}=d_{kT-jk}=e_{kT-jk}+\ldots+e_{kT-jk-2(k-1)}$$

Clearly:

$$\mathrm{E}\left(D_{T}\,D_{T-j}\right)\neq 0$$

if

$jk=2\left(k-1\right)$ or $j=2-\dfrac{2}{k}=1$ [the integer part] with $k > 1$.

This translates into $D_T \sim MA(1)$ or $U_T \sim IMA(1,1)$. QED

c) Mixed aggregation. The proof proceeds along the lines of the two previous cases. Let the filter be:

$$M(B)=\left(T(B),S(B)\right) \qquad \text{(A7.3.14)}$$

where $S(B)$ and $T(B)$ are defined as in Equations (A7.3.3) and (A7.3.9), respectively. Multiplying both sides of Equation (A7.3.2) by $M(B)$ yields:

$$M(B)(1-B)u_t = M(B)\,e_t \qquad \text{(A7.3.15)}$$

Using the aggregation index, Equation (A7.3.15) becomes:

$$M(B)(1-B)\,u_{kT} = M(B)\,e_{kT} \qquad \text{(A7.3.16)}$$

Writing u_{kT} as a vector $\left(u_{kT}, u'_{kT}\right)'$ and e_{kT} as $\left(e_{kT}, e'_{kT}\right)'$, Equation (A7.3.16) becomes:

$$T(B)(1-B)\,u_{kT} + S(B)(1-B)\,u_{kT} = T(B)\,e_{kT} + S(B)\,e_{kT} \qquad \text{(A7.3.17)}$$

The left-hand side of Equation (A7.3.17) is simply $U_T - U_{T-1}$ where U is composed of temporally aggregated and systematically sampled parts, $T(B)u_{kT}$ and $S(B)u_{kT}$, respectively. The exercise under (a) reveals that $S(B)e_{kT}$ is white noise. With (b), it is known that $T(B)e_{kT}$ is an $MA(1)$ process. The sum of the two components is an $MA(1)$ process (see, for example, Granger and Morris, 1976). Hence, the mixed aggregated counterpart of u_t as in Equation (A7.3.1) follows an $IMA(1, 1)$ process.

Answer 7.4

The results of the exercise indicate overall there are Granger causality distortions in ECMs due to aggregation over time. Distortions depend on:

1. The type of aggregation; indeed, while systematic sampling gives rise to few distortions except when ρ is a local alternative, temporal aggregation seriously distorts Granger causality in ECMs.
2. The degree of cointegration; indeed, the lower the degree of cointegration (higher value of ρ), the bigger the size of the distortions. For example, with $S = 300$ and $M = 50$ and $\rho = 0.9$, 99.7 percent of ECMs undergo Granger causality pattern changes under temporal aggregations (74.1 percent under systematic sampling).
3. The size of the sample with a fixed data span; indeed, keeping the data span fixed and increasing the sample size helps reduce Granger causality distortion. For example, with a data span of 300, increasing the sample size from 50 to 100 helps reduce Granger causality distortion by 99.41 percent when ρ = 0 under temporal aggregation.
4. The size of the data span with a fixed sample size; that is, with fixed sample size and degree of cointegration, the larger the data span, the larger the size of the distortion. For example, under temporal aggregation, with ρ = 0.6 and $M = 50$, an increase in the data span from 300 to 600 raises the size of Granger causality distortion by 13.2 percent.

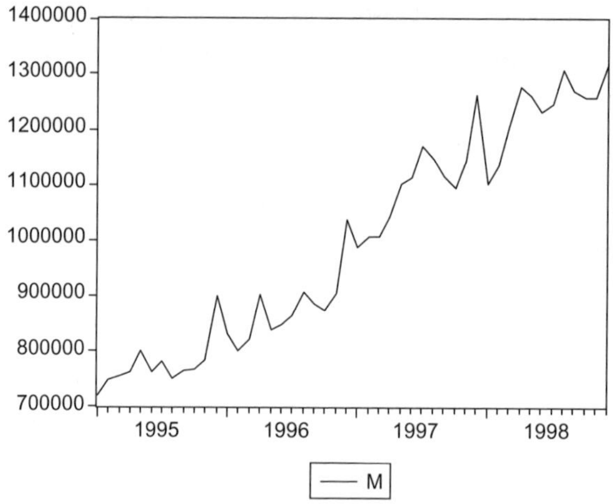

FIGURE 7.1
Barbados money supply (*M*): 1995:01–1998:12

5. The sample size and the data span; indeed, increasing both sample size and data span leads to a reduction in the size of the Granger causality distortion.

Perhaps, the most surprising result is (5). Indeed, while elsewhere (e.g., Lahiri and Mamingi, 1995) it has been shown that data span is more important than the number of observations in terms of the power of tests, here the reverse seems to prevail. This needs further investigation.

Answer 7.5

a) Since money is a stock variable, temporally averaging it is not conceptually appropriate. However, here, it is done just for the sake of illustrating the effects of aggregation over time.

b) Recall, *M* and *P* are the disaggregated monthly series, *MS* and *PS* are the systematically sampled (quarterly) series and *MT* and *PT* are the temporally averaged (quarterly) series. Figures 7.1, 7.2 and 7.3 are the graphs for *M*, *MS* and *MT*. The three figures show that the three series are trending up. This is an indication of nonstationarity of the series. Moreover, this confirms the theoretical aggregation over time results, according to which a nonstationary series remains nonstationary after aggregation over time. It can also be noticed that the temporally aggregated series is smoother than the two other series. For the sake of space the graphs of the first differences of series are not presented.

   Figures 7.4, 7.5 and 7.6 are the correlograms of the three series in levels. While the correlogram of the disagrregated series seems to point out a clear case of nonstationarity, those for the aggregated series (*MT* and *MS*) seem to underline stationarity. Yet, the graphs of the three series clearly indicate nonstationarity.

   The formal unit root test results are presented in Table 7.4. It can be inferred that the level of each series is integrated of order one, at least at

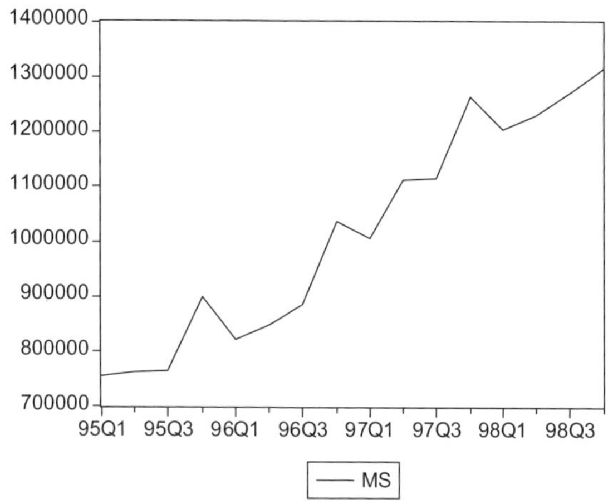

FIGURE 7.2
Quarterly sampled money supply (*MS*): Barbados 1995:1–1998:4

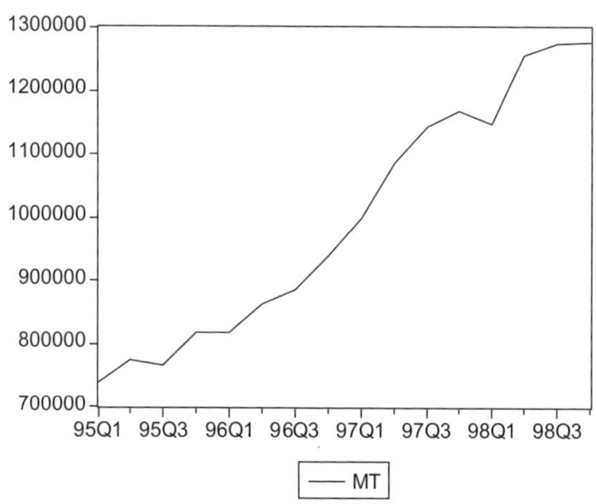

FIGURE 7.3
Quarterly temporally aggregated money supply (*MT*) Barbados 1995:1–1998:4

the 5 percent or 10 percent level of significance. Overall, the three series (disaggregated and aggregated) are each integrated of order one.

c) Recall that the impulse response functions (IRFs) concern the relationship between money and price at the disaggregate level as well as at the aggregated levels. Since the series money and price are integrated of order one (check for price for yourself), the question is whether VAR in levels, or VAR in first differences or ECM should be used to derive the IRFs. The Johansen procedure applied to the two series at different levels of aggregation indicates that they are not cointegrated (check it for yourself). The lack of cointegration between variables implies that VAR in first differences should be used to derive the IRFs. We use a VAR in the first differences with two lags. Theoretically the lag structure may change when aggregating

Autocorrelation	Partial Correlation		AC	PAC	Q	Prob
. |*******|	. |*******|	1	0.865	0.865	38.193	0.000
. |****** |	. |*. |	2	0.766	0.072	68.808	0.000
. |***** |	. | . |	3	0.682	0.019	93.589	0.000
. |***** |	. | . |	4	0.611	0.020	113.95	0.000
. |**** |	.*| . |	5	0.518	-0.113	128.94	0.000
. |*** |	. | . |	6	0.453	0.039	140.67	0.000
. |*** |	. | . |	7	0.383	-0.049	149.25	0.000
. |** |	. | . |	8	0.325	0.002	155.59	0.000
. |** |	.*| . |	9	0.244	-0.118	159.24	0.000
. |*. |	. | . |	10	0.183	-0.004	161.36	0.000
. |*. |	. |*. |	11	0.149	0.072	162.79	0.000
. |*. |	. |*. |	12	0.137	0.074	164.04	0.000

FIGURE 7.4
Correlogram: the case of the disaggregated money supply, Barbados 1995:01–1998:12
Note: AC, autocorrelation coefficients; PAC, partial autocorrelation coefficients; Q, Ljung–Box test for autocorrelation; Prob, p value of the Q statistic.

Autocorrelation	Partial Correlation		AC	PAC	Q-Stat	Prob
. |***** |	. |***** |	1	0.673	0.673	8.6852	0.003
. |**** |	. | . |	2	0.468	0.029	13.195	0.001
. |** . |	. *| . |	3	0.235	-0.166	14.415	0.002
. |* . |	. |* . |	4	0.172	0.121	15.123	0.004
. |* . |	. *| . |	5	0.067	-0.084	15.241	0.009
. | . |	. | . |	6	0.036	0.003	15.279	0.018
. | . |	. | . |	7	-0.003	0.005	15.279	0.033
. | . |	. | . |	8	0.000	0.001	15.279	0.054
. | . |	. | . |	9	0.000	0.018	15.279	0.084
. | . |	. | . |	10	0.000	-0.017	15.279	0.122
. | . |	. | . |	11	0.000	0.007	15.279	0.170
. | . |	. | . |	12	0.000	-0.000	15.279	0.227

FIGURE 7.5
Correlogram of (quarterly) systematically sampled money: Barbados 1995:1–1998:4

models (see the literature on the effects of aggregation on distributed lag models). However, from a practical point of view, it is better to use the same lag structure. Another remark is that we use the generalized IRFs in

```
                      Partial
Autocorrelation     Correlation         AC      PAC    Q-Stat    Prob

   .  |*****  |    .  |*****  |    1   0.705   0.705   9.5513   0.002
   .  |****   |    .  |   .   |    2   0.472  -0.051   14.131   0.001
   .  |**  .  |    .  *|   .  |    3   0.250  -0.127   15.518   0.001
   .  |*   .  |    .  |   .   |    4   0.129   0.029   15.917   0.003
   .  |   .   |    .  |   .   |    5   0.065   0.017   16.026   0.007
   .  |   .   |    .  |   .   |    6   0.044   0.017   16.082   0.013
   .  |   .   |    .  |   .   |    7   0.025  -0.019   16.102   0.024
   .  |   .   |    .  |   .   |    8   0.000  -0.031   16.102   0.041
   .  |   .   |    .  |   .   |    9   0.000   0.033   16.102   0.065
   .  |   .   |    .  |   .   |   10   0.000   0.001   16.102   0.097
   .  |   .   |    .  |   .   |   11   0.000  -0.011   16.102   0.137
   .  |   .   |    .  |   .   |   12   0.000   0.001   16.102   0.187
```

FIGURE 7.6
Correlogram of (quarterly) temporally aggregated money supply: Barbados 1995:1–1998:4

TABLE 7.4
Unit Root Tests for Money Supply in Barbados:
Disaggregate, Skip Sample and Temporal Aggregate Models

ADF (Level)	ADF (First Difference)	KPSS (Level)	KPSS (First Difference)
M			
0.140 (3) (0.965)	–7.861(2) (0.000)	0.890	0.163
MS			
–0.188(1) (0.920)	–3.355(1) (0.034)	0.507	0.098
MT			
–0.079(0) (0.935)	–4.119(0) (0.008)	0.505	0.141

Note: Numbers in parentheses beside the ADF values are the optimal lags for the ADF regressions; numbers in parenthesis beneath the ADF statistics are the associated p values. The critical values for the KPSS are 0.739, 0.463 and 0.347 for the 1 percent, 5 percent, and 10 percent levels of significance, respectively. *M*, *MS* and *MT* are defined as above. The regressions contain a constant term.

the manner of Pesaran–Shin, which solves the problems generated by the Chowleski decomposition. The results of the exercise are presented in Figures 7.7, 7.8 and 7.9.

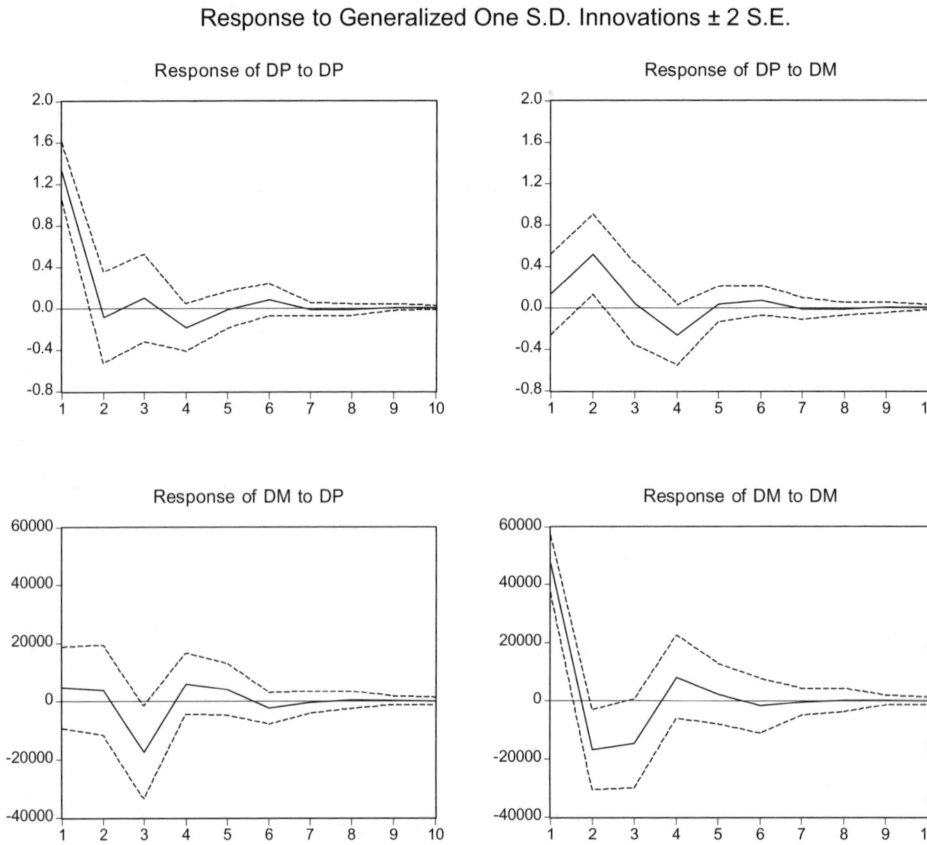

FIGURE 7.7
Impulse response functions in the disaggregated model
Note: $DM = M_t - M_{t-1}$: change in money supply; $DP = P_t - P_{t-1}$: change in price.

Concerning the disaggregated level, Figure 7.7 reveals that a one standard deviation (SD) to price change innovation increases price change by just about 1.2 points in the first month, decreases it in the second month before leveling off at the seventh month and onwards. The same innovation shock only significantly decreases money change after three months. The decrease is in the order of Bds \$20,000.00. The impact runs off after seven months. A one SD shock to money change innovation increases price change by almost 0.2 point by the first month, increases it further after two months, decreases it after three and four months before leveling off. The same innovation shock brings about a substantial increase in money change after just one month (in the order of Bds \$50,000.00) before decreasing and leveling off after seven months.

As far as the systematically sampled model is concerned (see Figure 7.8), a one standard deviation shock to price change innovation increases price change by just above two points in the first quarter and decreases until it levels off after six quarters. This innovation shock only decreases money change after the first quarter by almost Bds \$20,000.00, increases

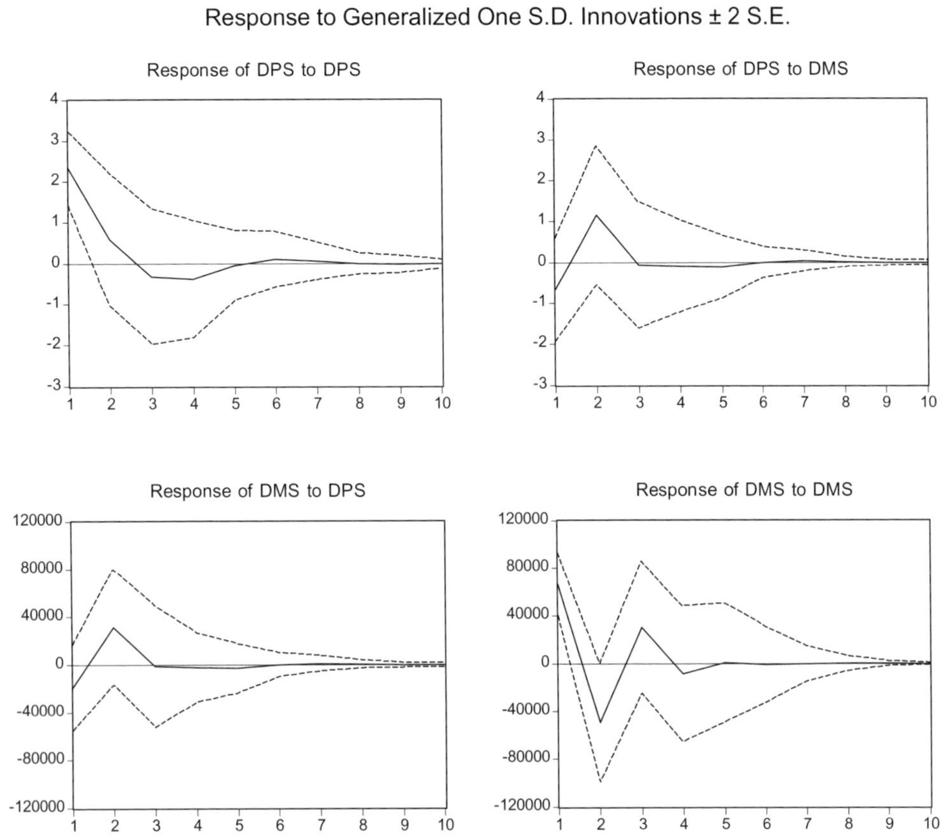

FIGURE 7.8
Impulse response functions under systematic sampling
Note: *DMS* = $MS_t - MS_{t-1}$: change in money supply; *DPS* = $PS_t - PS_{t-1}$: change in price.

it by almost Bds \$30,000.00 by the second quarter, then decreases it and levels off by the third quarter. A one SD shock to money change innovation decreases price change in the first quarter then increases in the second quarter before leveling off in the third quarter. The response of money change to a SD shock to money change innovation is erratic before leveling off at the fifth quarter.

Regarding the temporally aggregated model (see Figure 7.9), a one SD to price change innovation increases price change by just below three points in the first quarter and decreases it until it levels off after six quarters. This innovation shock increases money change by approximately Bds \$20,000.00 by the second quarter, and decreases the change before leveling off after seven quarters. A one SD shock to money change innovation increases price change in the first quarter by just about one point, then decreases it in the second quarter before leveling off by the sixth quarter. The response of money change to a SD shock to money change innovation is similar to the impact of the shock on price change.

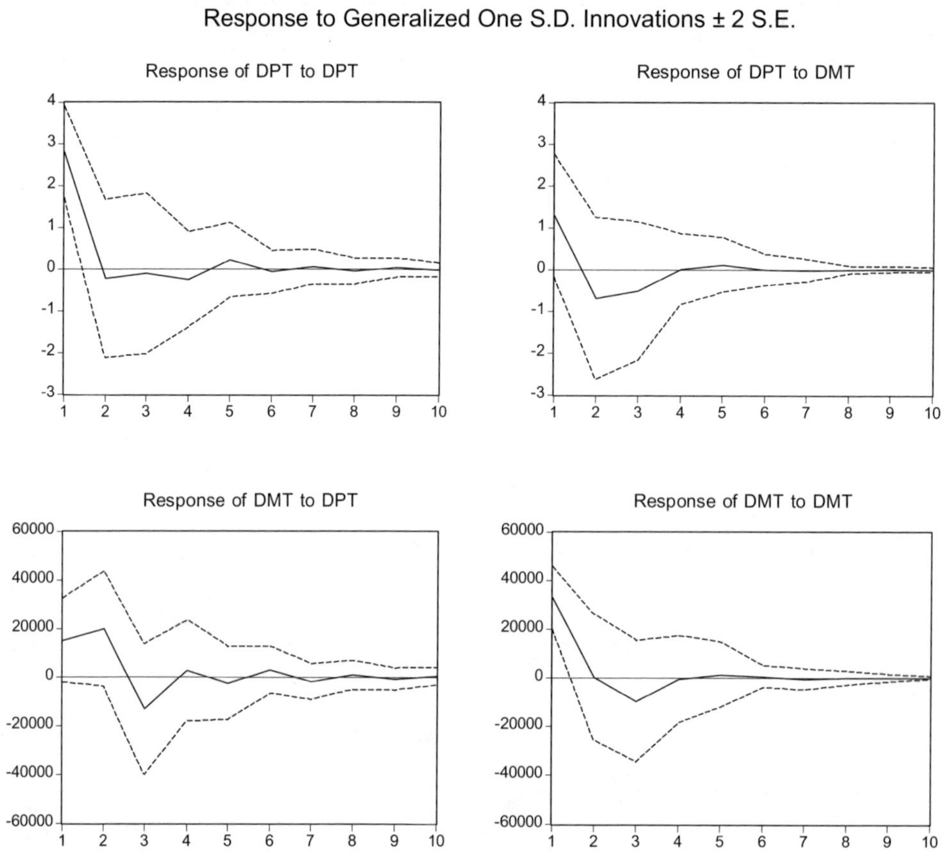

FIGURE 7.9
Impulse response functions under temporal aggregation
Note: $DMT = MT_t - MT_{t-1}$: change in money supply; $DPT = PT_t - PT_{t-1}$: change in price.

A careful look at the three sets of figures indicates that they are different even after adjusting for frequency differences (monthly shocks versus quarterly shocks). To some extent, IRFs from the systematically sampled model mimic better the IRFs from the disaggregated model than the IRFs from the temporally aggregated model. This also means the IRFs from the systematically sampled model are, in general, different from those from the temporally aggregated model. This result is robust to changes in the lag structure. This means that the empirical results mimic well the theoretical results.

d) Table 7.5 is concerned with Granger causality patterns in the relationship between money change and price change at the three levels of aggregation (disaggregated, systematically sampled and temporally aggregated). Granger causality is derived from the VAR in first differences as above. The *F* test statistic is the test of interest here. The lag issue is an important one. It is worth pointing out that owing to model selection the theoretical

TABLE 7.5
Granger Causality Patterns in DS, SS and TA Models

Lag	H_0	DS Model	SS Model	TA Model
1	$DM \nrightarrow DP$	6.79650*	1.14327	0.11587
		(0.01250)	(0.30787)	(0.73997)
1	$DP \nrightarrow DM$	0.04882	1.53844	6.95502*
		(0.82617)	(0.24066)	(0.02311)
2	$DM \nrightarrow DP$	4.49546*	1.63561	0.51336
		(0.01733)	(0.25379)	(0.61694)
2	$DP \nrightarrow DM$	2.36053	0.76981	2.68794
		(0.10739)	(0.49458)	(0.12796)
3	$DM \nrightarrow DP$	2.92601*	0.97214	0.23856
		(0.04642)	(0.47506)	(0.86613)
3	$DP \nrightarrow DM$	1.35902	0.67303	1.75334
		(0.27305)	(0.60453)	(0.27187)
4	$DM \nrightarrow DP$	2.10756	1.69080	0.76822
		(0.10137)	(0.40437)	(0.63307)
4	$DP \nrightarrow DM$	1.11859	3.59251	15.8549**
		(0.36392)	(0.22942)	(0.06021)
>4	$DM \nrightarrow DP$	H_0 not rejected	H_0 not rejected	H_0 not rejected
>4	$DP \nrightarrow DM$	H_0 not rejected	H_0 not rejected	H_0 not rejected

Note: DS model: disaggregated model; SS model: systematically sampled model; TA model: temporally aggregated model; $DM \nrightarrow DP$: money change does not Granger cause price change; (…) are p values attached to the F test statistics; lag: number of lags in the VAR in first differences of the original variables; (*) significant at the 5 percent level; (**) significant at the 10 percent level.

lag structure is not necessarily the empirical lag structure. As far as the aggregated models are concerned, with few observations the room for manoeuvre is rather limited. Two or three lags are enough. In any case, the reader can pursue this matter by finding the optimal lag for himself or herself. The objective of the exercise is to show what can happen in general, in terms of Granger causality, to a model that has undergone aggregation over time.

With one lag in the VAR, Table 7.5 reveals that a one way causality from money change to price change has changed into no causality in the systematically sampled model as well as the temporally aggregated model. At the same time, a lack of causality from price change to money change has turned into causality under temporal aggregation. With two and three lags, a one way causality from money change to price change has changed to no causality in both aggregated models. With four lags, no causality between the two variables in the disaggregated model becomes a one way causality from price change to money change. It is only with more than four lags that there is no Granger causality distortions in the three models.

7.4 SUPPLEMENTARY EXERCISES

Question 7.6 Consider the following disaggregated model:

$$y_t = \alpha y_{t-1} + e_t \tag{Q7.6.1}$$

where $t = 1, 2, 3, \ldots, N$ and e_t is a white noise error term.

a) Equation (Q7.6.1) can give rise to several models, depending on the values taken by the parameter α. Provide and explain three models derived from Equation (Q7.6.1).
b) Suppose that $|\alpha| < 1$, show the process that the aggregate counterpart Y_T follows (i) under temporal aggregation and (ii) under systematic sampling.
c) What happens to Y_T under systematic sampling if the sampling interval, k, becomes very large.

Question 7.7 Consider a country Z and its partner X. Test for time aggregation effect on Z's purchasing power parity. Justify your results. Hint: use three levels of exchange rates: disaggregate level, average and end-of-period. Data can be found in *International Financial Statistics* of the International Monetary Fund.

Question 7.8 In terms of aggregation over time and perhaps aggregation in general, there is often a gap between theoretical results and empirical results. Carefully explain the reasons for such a gap (see also Granger, 1990.)

PART FOUR

Other Topics

Among the many topics that could have been dealt with in this last part of the book, we have chosen two: forecasting and panel data models. Thus, this part consists of two chapters. Chapter 8 has exercises on forecasting using the quantitative approach (time series methods and causal methods). Chapter 9 presents exercises dealing with panel data models at a very elementary level.

CHAPTER 8

Forecasting

8.1 INTRODUCTION

One of the objectives of econometrics is to predict or forecast future values or paths of (economic) dependent variables. There are basically two reasons for forecasts. First, forecasts help "internalize" the uncertainty that plagues the future. Second, forecasts are an acknowledgment of the existence of a lag between the time a decision is taken and the time the full impact is felt. It is thus expected that accurate predictions of the future are important for the decision making process, as they improve the efficiency of the latter (Holden et al., 1990, 3). Not surprisingly, forecasts are sought by various entities, such as governments, the private sector and individuals. Paradoxical as it may appear, forecasts may also concern the present or the past (in-sample forecasts or simulations) rather than the future. Put differently, beyond predictive purposes, forecasts are also useful for sensibility analysis and policy analysis (see Pindyck and Rubinfeld, 1998).

Forecasts can arise from quantitative as well as qualitative models, or from a mixture of both. Quantitative methods are based on quantitative or numerical data and assume that the past pattern affects the present and the future (continuity assumption). They are divided into time series methods and causal methods. The time series approach is concerned mainly with the extrapolation of components of time series (trend, cycle and seasonal elements). However, for economists, time series methods are equated with the Box–Jenkins, or ARIMA, approach to forecasting, which views the variable of interest as a reflection of its own past and/or present and past errors. The causal approach to forecasting includes regression models (single equation and simultaneous equations models) as well as VAR types of model (although some consider the latter as time series models). The key emphasis in the causal model is the link between the dependent variable (the object of the forecast) and the explanatory variables.

Qualitative or technological forecast methods rely on judgment, intuition and accumulated knowledge to conduct forecasts. Without totally dismissing qualitative forecast methods, econometrics is mainly interested in the quantitative approach to forecasting.

At the outset of the forecasting process, there is a need to define clearly the object(s) of the forecast. Forecasts are distinguished according to time horizon (short-run, medium-range and long-run) as well as according to whether the actual values of the variables are known or not known or partially known: in-sample forecasts, out-of-sample forecasts, ex-post forecasts and ex-ante forecasts. More important, there is the issue of accuracy of forecast models. This requires some statistical measures. Among the standard statistical measures, perhaps the most popular one is the mean square error (MSE) or its square root (RMSE). Although less popular than the MSE, a superior measure of forecast accuracy is Theil's U statistic.

The exercises below deal with selected aspects of forecasting. In any event, they emphasize theoretical as well as empirical aspects of forecasting.

8.2 QUESTIONS

8.2.1 Theoretical Exercises

Question 8.1 Consider the following model:

$$y_t = \beta_0 + \beta_1 x_t + u_t \qquad \text{(Q8.1.1)}$$

where y_t and x_t are the variables of interest and u_t is the error term. Provide and explain four sources of forecast errors.

Question 8.2 Explain why point forecasts are in practice more popular than interval forecasts and density forecasts (see Diebold, 2001).

Question 8.3. Explain the following concepts:

a) In-sample forecasts;
b) Out-of-sample forecasts;
c) Ex-post forecasts;
d) Ex-ante forecasts.

Question 8.4 The mean square error (MSE) is a popular statistic for forecast accuracy. Name and explain four drawbacks of this accuracy measure. What is (are) the way(s) out?

Question 8.5 Explain the following concepts:

a) Optimal forecast;
b) Forecast encompassing;
c) Forecast combination.

Question 8.6 Find the predicted Y_t for the following models:

a) Log-lin: $$Log(Y_t) = \beta_0 + \beta_1 X_t + u_t \qquad \text{(Q8.6.1)}$$

b) Double Log: $$Log(Y_t) = \beta_0 + \beta_1 Log(X_t) + u_t \qquad \text{(Q8.6.2)}$$

c) Logistic: $$Log(Y_t/(1-Y_t)) = \beta_0 + \beta_1 X_t + u_t \qquad \text{(Q8.6.3)}$$

Question 8.7 Suppose you have data on consumption for the period 1935 to 1995 for country X and you are interested in obtaining the ex-post forecasts for consumption

TABLE 8.1
Contributions (in Bds$ '000) in Barbados 1969–2002

Year	Contributions	Year	Contributions
1969	5,803	1986	105,685
1970	6,500	1987	115,765
1971	8,226	1988	122,113
1972	8,358	1989	137,941
1973	9,626	1990	133,866
1974	13,069	1991	142,600
1975	14,225	1992	134,506
1976	15,863	1993	128,935
1977	18,320	1994	169,238
1978	25,458	1995	182,572
1979	31,382	1996	201,820
1980	34,057	1997	218,567
1981	41,287	1998	250,686
1982	67,573	1999	276,734
1983	83,006	2000	295,268
1984	91,916	2001	307,350
1985	96,615	2002	293,543

Source: *Economic and Financial Statistics*, Central Bank of Barbados, March 2003.

for the period 1990 to 1995. Explain how you are going to obtain those forecasts using the Box–Jenkins approach. (UWI, EC36D, final examination May 2001)

8.2.2 Empirical Questions

Question 8.8 Table 8.1 presents contributions to national insurance schemes in Barbados in the period 1969 to 2002. The variable is in Bds$ '000.

a) Check for the stationarity/nonstationarity of the series.
b) If the series is nonstationary, make it stationary.
c) Given the shapes of the correlogram and the partial correlogram, choose and estimate an appropriate ARIMA (or ARMA) model for the variable "contributions". Use a diagnostic check to accept or reject the particular fit.
d) Forecast the values of "contributions" for 2001 and 2002 using dynamic and static forecasts.
d) Provide the name of the methodology implemented in (a), (b), (c) and (d). (UWI, EC36D, tutorial 1997)

Question 8.9 Consider the variables shown in Table 8.2, loan rate (LRA) in percent and discount rate (DR) in percent, for South Africa in the period 1970 to 1999:

a) Fit a linear trend model for loan rate using the estimation period 1970–1997, and obtain the summary statistics for in-sample forecasts.
b) Estimate the following regression model:

TABLE 8.2
Loan Rates and Discount Rates:
South Africa 1970–1999

Year	LRA	DR	Year	LRA	DR
1970	8.17	5.50	1985	21.50	13.00
1971	8.83	6.50	1986	14.33	9.50
1972	8.79	6.00	1987	12.50	9.50
1973	8.00	3.78	1988	15.33	14.50
1974	10.17	6.48	1989	19.83	18.00
1975	11.79	7.42	1990	21.00	18.00
1976	12.25	8.28	1991	20.31	17.00
1977	12.50	8.41	1992	18.91	14.00
1978	12.13	7.87	1993	16.16	12.00
1979	10.00	4.70	1994	15.58	13.00
1980	9.50	6.54	1995	17.90	15.00
1981	14.00	14.54	1996	19.52	17.00
1982	19.33	14.35	1997	20.00	16.00
1983	16.67	17.75	1998	21.79	19.32
1984	22.23	20.75	1999	18.00	12.00

Note: LRA: loan rate in percent; DR: discount rate in percent.

Source: *International Financial Statistics*, International Monetary Fund, Washington, D.C., 2000.

$$LRA_t = c + b\,DR_t + u_t \qquad \text{(Q8.9.1)}$$

where t = 1970, 1971, …, 1997, and obtain the summary statistics of in-sample forecasts.

c) Compare the two in-sample forecasts.
d) Generate the ex-post forecast values for LRA in the period 1998 to 1999 using the two previous models and compare their summary statistics.
e) Study the optimality of the two ex-post forecasts.
f) Does one forecast encompass the other?
g) Implement forecast combination.

Question 8.10 Table 8.3 shows monthly data for Barbados for two variables: money supply in Bds$ '000 captured by m_t and consumer price index captured by p_t. The period of interest is January 1995 to December 1998. From the raw data, define money growth as $Dm_t = (m_t - m_{t-1}) / m_{t-1}$ and price change (inflation) as $Dp_t = (p_t - p_{t-1}) / p_{t-1}$.

a) Fit an ARIMA model for inflation for the period 1995:02–1997:12. Obtain the summary statistics of ex-post forecasts for the period 1998:01–1998:12.
b) Estimate the following regression model:

$$Dp_t = c + b\,Dm_t + u_t \qquad \text{(Q8.10.1)}$$

TABLE 8.3
Money Supply and Price: Barbados 1995:01–1998:12

Period	M	P	Period	M	P
1995:01	718,408.00	101.4	1997:01	987,675.00	114.4
1995:02	747,503.00	102.0	1997:02	1,005,614.00	113.8
1995:03	754,802.00	101.4	1997:03	1,005,991.00	113.2
1995:04	762,599.00	100.8	1997:04	1,041,991.00	113.3
1995:05	799,063.00	101.3	1997:05	1,102,028.00	114.3
1995:06	761,378.00	102.3	1997:06	1,113,937.00	114.8
1995:07	781,678.00	103.5	1997:07	1,170,360.00	115.5
1995:08	749,717.00	104.2	1997:08	1,147,188.00	115.5
1995:09	765,136.00	104.5	1997:09	1,115,268.00	115.5
1995:10	767,582.00	104.8	1997:10	1,095,275.00	110.8
1995:11	783,374.00	105.0	1997:11	1,144,971.00	111.5
1995:12	899,174.00	105.1	1997:12	1,263,776.00	110.8
1996:01	831,570.00	104.3	1998:01	1,101,336.00	111.0
1996:02	798,874.00	104.5	1998:02	1,136,086.00	111.0
1996:03	822,145.00	104.4	1998:03	1,205,521.00	111.3
1996:04	902,105.00	104.7	1998:04	1,277,647.00	112.0
1996:05	837,718.00	105.6	1998:05	1,260,285.00	112.8
1996:06	846,724.00	105.1	1998:06	1,232,075.00	112.6
1996:07	863,322.00	105.4	1998:07	1,245,539.00	112.0
1996:08	906,840.00	105.6	1998:08	1,307,289.00	112.1
1996:09	885,004.00	105.8	1998:09	1,270,958.00	112.7
1996:10	874,524.00	106.5	1998:10	1,258,502.00	112.8
1996:11	905,078.00	106.9	1998:11	1,258,036.00	113.1
1996:12	1,036,746.00	107.0	1998:12	1,317,394.00	112.7

Note: *M* stands for money supply in BDS$ '000 and *P* is consumer price index.

Source: *Barbados Statistical Digest*, various issues.

for the period 1995:02–1997:12. Is the regression a valid one?

c) From the regression above, obtain the summary statistics for the ex-post forecast of *Dp* for the period 1998:01–1998:12.
d) Fit a VAR or ECM to the data for the period 1995:02–1997:12. Also obtain the summary statistics for the ex-post forecasts of inflation for the period 1998:01–1998:12.
e) Comment on the ex-post forecasts summary statistics of the three models.

8.3 ANSWERS

Answer 8.1

The first source of forecast error is specification error. The latter can be traced back to at least three sources. First, the workable model is usually a parsimonious model; that is, a simple model that is assumed to be the most appropriate. Yet, the simplification may introduce errors. For example, we may have omitted some important variables despite our care. Second, it may also be the case that the functional form is incorrect.

Third, the parameters may be varying instead of being constant. These types of errors, called *specification errors*, are a component of forecast errors. Note, however, that although we acknowledge their existence, they are not taken into account when the confidence interval for forecast is built.

The second source of forecast errors (residuals) is error (or residual) uncertainty. This source of error exists because future errors are unknown at the time forecasts are made. Put differently, since the residual (the difference between the actual value and the predicted value) at a given point in time or space is not zero, although its expected value is zero, we expect large variation in individual errors to give rise to non-negligible overall errors in the forecasts.

The third source of forecast errors is parameter (coefficient) uncertainty. Because parameters are unknown quantities, we resort to estimators (estimates). The latter, being random variables, are subject to sampling variability, which introduces uncertainty or risk. The variance or the standard error of estimate of the parameter measures that uncertainty of the estimate. The lesser the deviation between the exogenous variables and their means, the smaller the forecast uncertainty.

The fourth source is related to the exogenous variable(s) on which the forecast is based or conditioned. Indeed, there is a possibility that the exogenous variable, which, from time to time, needs itself to be forecast, contains errors. This affects the forecast of the dependent variable and consequently, the forecast errors.

Answer 8.2

The answer is adapted from Diebold (2001, 39–42). Recall, a point forecast is a single number which is the best guess of the future value. For example, the projected rate of failure in Econometrics I will be 2 percent in 2060. The interval forecast represents a set of values within which the forecast is expected to fall with some probability. For example, the 90 percent interval forecast for failure rate in Econometrics I in 2060 will be between 1 percent and 4 percent; that is, the interval forecast is the interval [1%, 4%] with a probability of 90 percent. The density represents "the entire probability distribution of the future value of the series of interest". For example, we might say that the probability distribution for failure rate in Econometrics I in the year 2060 will be normally distributed with mean 2.5 percent and variance 3 percent.

In terms of information gains, if we assume the more the better, then density forecast is better than interval forecast, which is superior to point forecast. Despite this ranking, point forecast is still more popular than the two other measurements, for the following reasons. First, the additional information required to derive the two other forecasts may be too costly to obtain. Second, quite a number of assumptions (some incorrect most likely) are needed to derive interval and density forecasts. Note, however, in some situations the point forecast is not of interest but rather a set of forecasts. The following example, inspired by Granger and Newbold (1977, 146), illustrates the point. For a buyer of tea, it is useful to have forecasts of future tea prices over some period so he or she may decide when to buy tea on the commodity market.

Answer 8.3

To explain the different concepts, let us use the diagram shown in Figure 8.1 (see, for example, Ramanathan, 1998, 565).

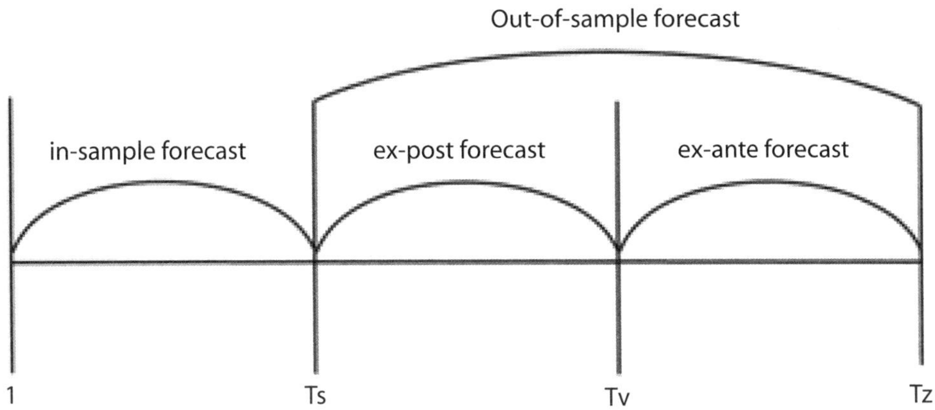

FIGURE 8.1
Forecast types

a) In-sample forecasts. They represent the fitted values of the forecast object or variable in the estimation period; that is, the period 1 to T_s in Figure 8.1. They basically serve two purposes. First, the original data can be compared with the simulated data and these forecasts become a barometer of the validity of the model. Second, they are useful for policy analysis.
b) Out-of-sample forecasts. These are the fitted values of the forecast object in the period beyond the estimation period, with the particularity that actual values of variables may or may not exist for all variables. In our case, the period of interest is T_{s+1} to T_z.
c) Ex-post forecasts. These are out-of-sample forecasts for which the dependent variable (forecast object) and independent variables (if they exist) are known. In our case, they represent forecasts for the period T_{s+1} to T_v. These types of forecasts help gauge the accuracy of the model.
d) Ex-ante forecasts. These are out-of-sample forecasts for which we do not, in general, possess information for all variables. In Figure 8.1, forecasts related to the period T_{v+1} to T_z are ex-ante forecasts. Note that in general when we advocate forecasts we really mean ex-ante forecasts.

Answer 8.4

a) MSE suffers from the same problem as the R^2 and RSS to the extent that an increase in the number of variables artificially decreases the MSE, because the degrees of freedom are not taken into account by the statistic. This means that a lower MSE does not necessarily mean a good forecast model, to the extent that out-of-sample forecast performance may be poor. Put differently, in-sample overfitting and data mining are not sound for out-of-sample forecast performance.
b) MSE results from calibrating a model with historical data. A lower MSE can be obtained by inflating the polynomial degree of the model. This of course does not necessarily imply that the forecast is good.
c) Different methods apply different algorithms in the fitting phase. Hence, comparison of MSE becomes dubious.

d) The fact that MSE uses squares makes this statistic difficult to interpret intuitively.

Queries (a) and (b) are answered by supplementing MSE with other measures of model accuracy that take the degrees of freedom into account, e.g., the Akaike information criterion (AIC) and the Schwarz information criterion (SIC). Query (d) is addressed by using the root mean square error (RMSE). (Elements of these answers were adapted from Makridakis et al., 1983, 45–46.)

Answer 8.5

a) Optimal forecast. The optimal forecast is essentially the best forecast that can be made in a given circumstance. It is known by some as the rational expectation forecast. That is, it is characterized by the use of all available information at the time the forecast is made. In other words, the optimal forecast is unbiased and efficient. In many instances, unbiasedness is sufficient to qualify a forecast as optimal. In any event, unbiasedness means that on average the forecast values are equal to the actual values. That is, although discrepancies between forecast values and actual values do exist, on average they cancel out. To check for unbiasedness one regresses the actual values on a constant and the forecast values, as in

$$z_{t+h} = c + \beta z^{F}_{t+h,t} + u_{t+h} \qquad \text{(A8.5.1)}$$

where the superscript F stands for forecast. In Equation (A8.5.1) the forecast is unbiased if $c = 0$ and $\beta = 1$. This is the Mincer–Zarnowitz regression, which has been criticized by Granger and Newbold (1977).

Note the existence of autocorrelation in a several-steps-ahead forecast because of overlap. Thus, the rule for unbiasedness for an h-steps-ahead forecast needs to be changed. Indeed, there is a need to include a moving average error of order $h - 1$. It means that if autocorrelation persists at order h, $MA(h)$, then the forecast cannot be optimal even if $c = 0$ and $\beta = 1$. This joint null hypothesis can also serve as a test of efficiency.

b) Forecast encompassing. Forecast encompassing refers to the situation where one forecast contains all information on the competing forecasts. Consider two forecast techniques giving rise to forecasts "a" and "b", such that:

$$z_{t+h} = \gamma z^{a}_{t+h,t} + \delta z^{b}_{t+h,t} + u_{t+h,t} \qquad \text{(A8.5.2)}$$

Forecast "a" encompasses "b" if $\gamma = 1$ and $\delta = 0$. Conversely, forecast "b" encompasses "a" if $\gamma = 0$ and $\delta = 1$. If neither one encompasses the other then the two forecasts are suboptimal.

c) Forecast combination. It has been shown by some authors that if no forecast is optimal then a combination of suboptimal forecasts can give rise to an improved forecast. The question of which weight to use to form a combined forecast is of interest here. Variance-covariance methods and regression-based methods can be used to answer the question. Precisely, in terms of regression we run the following type of regression:

$$z_{t+h} = \alpha + \gamma z^{a}_{t+h,t} + \delta z^{b}_{t+h,t} + u_{t+h,t} \qquad \text{(A8.5.3)}$$

Diebold (2001) points out that the inclusion of a constant term allows for bias correction, as well as for the forecast bias to be combined.

Answer 8.6

a) Log-lin model. We know that:

$$e^{Log(y_t)} = y_t = e^{\beta_0 + \beta_1 x_t + u_t}$$

Taking the expected value of the above leads to:

$$E(y_t) = E[e^{\beta_0 + \beta_1 x_t + u_t}] = E[e^{\beta_0} e^{\beta_1 x_t} e^{u_t}] = e^{\beta_0} e^{\beta_1 x_t} E(e^{u_t})$$

assuming that x_t is fixed. But:

$$E(y_t) = e^{\beta_0} e^{\beta_1 x_t} E(e^{u_t}) \neq e^{\beta_0} e^{\beta_1 x_t}$$

since $E(u_t) = 0$ does not imply that $E(e^{u_t}) = 1$. It is known that if $u_t \sim N(0, \sigma^2)$ then:

$$E(e^{u_t}) = e^{\sigma^2/2}$$

Using an estimate of σ^2 which is $\hat{\sigma}^2$, the above becomes:

$$\hat{y}_t = e^{\hat{\beta}_0 + \hat{\beta}_1 x_t + \hat{\sigma}^2/2}$$

b) Log-log model. We know that:

$$y_t = e^{\beta_0} x_t^{\beta_1} e^{\sigma^2/2}$$

That is,

$$\hat{y}_t = e^{\hat{\beta}_0} x_t^{\hat{\beta}_1} e^{\hat{\sigma}^2/2}$$

b) Logistic model. We know that:

$$e^{Log(y_t/(1-y_t))} = y_t / (1 - y_t) = e^{\beta_0 + \beta_1 x_t + u_t}$$

That is,

$$y_t = (1 - y_t)e^A$$

where:

$$A = \beta_0 + \beta_1 x_t + u_t$$

That is,

$$y_t = \frac{1}{1 + e^{-A}}$$

Similarly to (a) or (b),

$$\hat{y}_t = \frac{1}{1 + e^{-(\hat{\beta}_0 + \hat{\beta}_1 x_t + \hat{\sigma}^2/2)}}$$

Answer 8.7

a) Identification. Suppose consumption is captured by *Cons*. Identification refers to the determination of the autoregressive order (AR), p, the level of integration, d, and the moving average (MA) order, q, of the process. To do so, we start investigating the order of integration of *Cons* by using graphs, correlograms and unit root tests. In particular, correlogram and unit root tests (ADF test, PP test, etc.) will help determine the order d (an integer here). If $d > 0$, the series needs to be differenced d times to become stationary. To recall, a series that needs to be differenced once to become stationary is integrated of order one; that is, $d = 1$. A process that needs to be differenced twice to become stationary is integrated of order two; that is, $d = 2$. Most economic variables are $I(1)$ or, rarely, $I(2)$. After making the series stationary if it is not, then one examines the order of the process. Correlograms will help determine the AR and MA orders of *Cons*. Note that the AR process has an autocorrelation function dying out exponentially and a partial autocorrelation function cutting off after a certain number of lags. The MA process is the reverse of the AR process in terms of the behaviour of the two autocorrelation functions. The ARMA will be a mixture of the above. An important point is that the empirical shape does not necessarily exactly match the theoretical shape. This is one of the reasons the Box–Jenkins approach is really an art. Summing up, this stage enables us to derive one or more than one tentative model(s) for *Cons*.

b) Estimation. Once a model or models has (have) been chosen, we estimate it (them) using the period 1935–1989. Usually nonlinear or maximum likelihood estimations are of interest (for a pure AR model, OLS is appropriate).

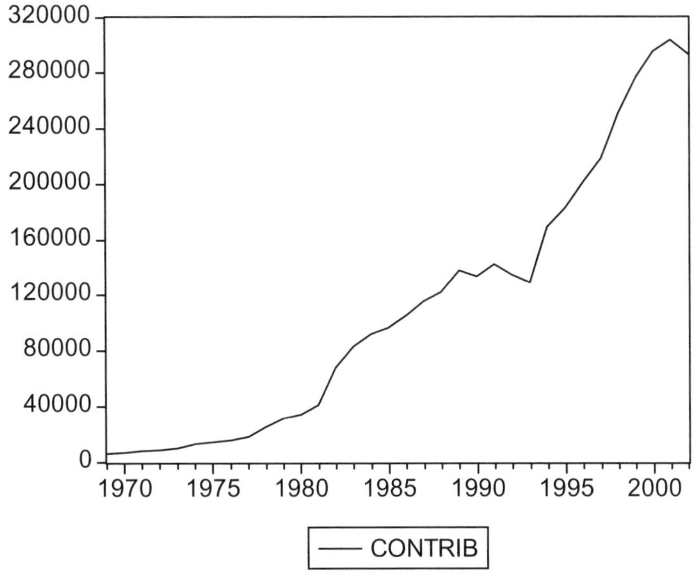

FIGURE 8.2
Contributions in Barbados 1969–2002

c) Diagnostic checking. Identification and estimation have given rise to an estimated (or some estimated) ARIMA model(s) for *Cons*. The next stage is to see whether the model(s) passes the diagnostic checking tests. In this connection, one set of tests can be applied to the estimated coefficients of a given model. That is, we may test the significance of an included variable or a subset of such variables. The most important diagnostic checking is, however, the test for randomness of residuals. The LM and Ljung–Box tests are among the appropriate tests for autocorrelation here. If residuals are not white noise then the model is rejected. In such a case, if there is no other model that fulfils that condition, we return to the identification stage.
d) Forecasting. If the modelling is satisfactory, then we forecast *Cons* in the period 1990–1995. Static or dynamic forecasts can be used. Generally forecasters prefer dynamic forecasts. To know how good ex-post forecasts are, we compute some accuracy statistics such as Theil's *U*.

Answer 8.8

a) We check for stationarity/nonstationarity using graphical methods, correlograms and unit root tests. Figure 8.2 shows the graph of "contributions" in levels. The variable is trending up. This is a clear indication of nonstationarity.

   Figure 8.3 is the graph of contributions in first differences. With respect to the levels, the shape has undergone a drastic change. The first difference is most likely stationary as the series seems to be reverting to its mean. We tentatively say that the contributions variable is an integrated process of order one.

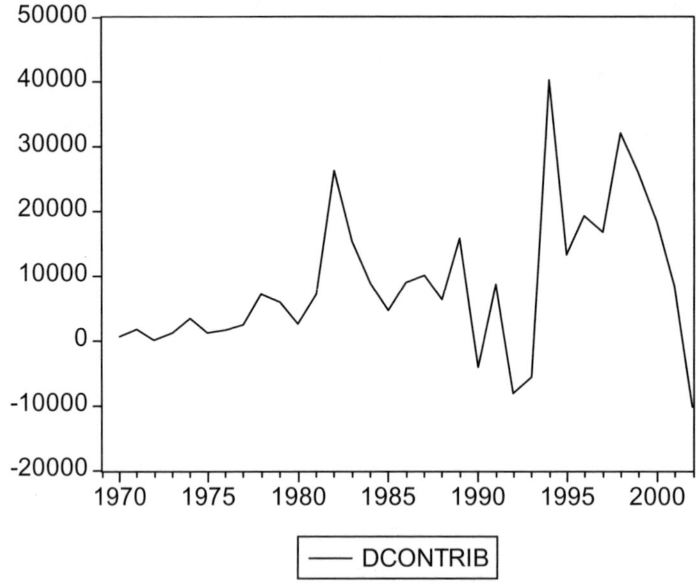

FIGURE 8.3
First difference of contributions

<table>
<tr><th>Autocorrelation</th><th>Partial Correlation</th><th></th><th>AC</th><th>PAC</th><th>Q-Stat</th><th>Prob</th></tr>
<tr><td>. |****** |</td><td>. |****** |</td><td>1</td><td>0.797</td><td>0.797</td><td>23.584</td><td>0.000</td></tr>
<tr><td>. |***** |</td><td>.*| . |</td><td>2</td><td>0.592</td><td>-0.120</td><td>36.995</td><td>0.000</td></tr>
<tr><td>. |*** |</td><td>. | . |</td><td>3</td><td>0.446</td><td>0.037</td><td>44.865</td><td>0.000</td></tr>
<tr><td>. |*** |</td><td>. | . |</td><td>4</td><td>0.347</td><td>0.022</td><td>49.791</td><td>0.000</td></tr>
<tr><td>. |**. |</td><td>. | . |</td><td>5</td><td>0.290</td><td>0.050</td><td>53.350</td><td>0.000</td></tr>
<tr><td>. |**. |</td><td>. | . |</td><td>6</td><td>0.243</td><td>-0.005</td><td>55.940</td><td>0.000</td></tr>
<tr><td>. |* . |</td><td>. | . |</td><td>7</td><td>0.197</td><td>-0.012</td><td>57.691</td><td>0.000</td></tr>
<tr><td>. |* . |</td><td>. | . |</td><td>8</td><td>0.156</td><td>-0.000</td><td>58.835</td><td>0.000</td></tr>
<tr><td>. |* . |</td><td>. | . |</td><td>9</td><td>0.121</td><td>-0.006</td><td>59.553</td><td>0.000</td></tr>
<tr><td>. |* . |</td><td>. | . |</td><td>10</td><td>0.089</td><td>-0.016</td><td>59.953</td><td>0.000</td></tr>
<tr><td>. | . |</td><td>. | . |</td><td>11</td><td>0.063</td><td>-0.003</td><td>60.166</td><td>0.000</td></tr>
<tr><td>. | . |</td><td>. | . |</td><td>12</td><td>0.044</td><td>-0.005</td><td>60.272</td><td>0.000</td></tr>
</table>

FIGURE 8.4
Correlogram of contributions for Barbados 1969–2002

Figure 8.4 is the correlogram of "contributions". The figure indicates the autocorrelation function is dying out slowly. Indeed, at lag 1, the autocorrelation is 0.797; at lag 2, it is 0.592; at lag 3, it is 0.446. This is an indication of a nonstationary process.

<table>
<tr><th>Autocorrelation</th><th>Partial Correlation</th><th></th><th>AC</th><th>PAC</th><th>Q-Stat</th><th>Prob</th></tr>
<tr><td>. |**. |</td><td>. |**. |</td><td>1</td><td>0.295</td><td>0.295</td><td>3.1517</td><td>0.076</td></tr>
<tr><td>. |**. |</td><td>. |* . |</td><td>2</td><td>0.201</td><td>0.125</td><td>4.6641</td><td>0.097</td></tr>
<tr><td>. |* . |</td><td>. | . |</td><td>3</td><td>0.127</td><td>0.043</td><td>5.2899</td><td>0.152</td></tr>
<tr><td>. | . |</td><td>. | . |</td><td>4</td><td>0.049</td><td>-0.021</td><td>5.3857</td><td>0.250</td></tr>
<tr><td>. | . |</td><td>. | . |</td><td>5</td><td>0.060</td><td>0.033</td><td>5.5339</td><td>0.354</td></tr>
<tr><td>. | . |</td><td>. *| . |</td><td>6</td><td>-0.043</td><td>-0.082</td><td>5.6124</td><td>0.468</td></tr>
<tr><td>. | . |</td><td>. | . |</td><td>7</td><td>0.022</td><td>0.044</td><td>5.6332</td><td>0.583</td></tr>
<tr><td>. | . |</td><td>. | . |</td><td>8</td><td>-0.044</td><td>-0.053</td><td>5.7221</td><td>0.678</td></tr>
<tr><td>. | . |</td><td>. | . |</td><td>9</td><td>-0.047</td><td>-0.025</td><td>5.8298</td><td>0.757</td></tr>
<tr><td>. *| . |</td><td>. *| . |</td><td>10</td><td>-0.085</td><td>-0.068</td><td>6.1939</td><td>0.799</td></tr>
<tr><td>. | . |</td><td>. | . |</td><td>11</td><td>-0.029</td><td>0.036</td><td>6.2380</td><td>0.857</td></tr>
<tr><td>. | . |</td><td>. | . |</td><td>12</td><td>-0.043</td><td>-0.029</td><td>6.3380</td><td>0.898</td></tr>
</table>

FIGURE 8.5
Correlogram of contributions in first differences: Barbados 1969–2002

TABLE 8.4
ADF Test for Contributions: Barbados 1969–2002

ADF	Value	*p* Value
Level	–1.665(0,c,t)	0.7442
First difference	–3.704(0,c)	0.0088

Note: In parentheses, 0 represents the optimal number of lags, *c* stands for the presence of a constant term in the ADF regression and *t* that of a deterministic trend.

Figure 8.5 shows the correlogram of contributions in first differences. As can be seen the autocorrelation coefficients and the partial autocorrelation coefficients seem to be within the two standard deviation. There does not seem to be autocorrelation, although there is some doubt for the first and second autocorrelation coefficients at the 10 percent level (and not at the 5 percent level). In any event, the first difference of contributions is clearly stationary. As above, tentatively, we conclude that the contributions series has a unit root.

To confirm the conjectures of graphical methods and correlograms, we resort to unit root tests. We use the ADF test. Table 8.4 clearly indicates that the level of contributions is nonstationary since the *p* value of the statistic is greater than any standard level of significance and the first

TABLE 8.5
Regression of *Dcontributions* on a Constant Term: Barbados 1970–2002

Variable	Coefficient	Standard Error	t Statistic	Prob.
C	8719.394	1994.692	4.371299	0.0001
R^2	0.000000	Mean dependent variable		8719.394
Adjusted R^2	0.000000	SD dependent variable		11458.63
SE of regression	11458.63	Akaike information criterion		21.56071
RSS	4.20E+09	Schwarz criterion		21.60606
Log likelihood	–354.7517	DW statistic		1.308971
Breusch–Godfrey Serial Correlation LM Test with One Lag				
F statistic	2.988648	Probability		0.093799
Obs*R^2	2.901716	Probability		0.088485

difference of contributions is stationary. In other words, the level of contributions is integrated of order one, $I(1)$.

b) To make the series stationary we difference it once (series are not reported here, to save space).

c) We reexamine the shape of the correlogram (see Figure 8.5) of the first difference of contributions. The autocorrelation coefficients as well as the partial autocorrelation coefficients are inside the two standard deviations. Since there is some doubt whether there is autocorrelation for the two first lags, we can conjecture that the model (contributions in first differences) is either a white noise process, or an $AR(1)$, $MA(1)$, $MA(2)$ or $ARMA(1,1)$ process.

After some search, tentatively the two best models are the following. The first one corresponds to a random walk with a drift in the level of contributions; that is, the one for which contributions in first differences (*Dcontributions*) is regressed on a constant term. The second one is an $AR(1)$ model.

Tables 8.5 and 8.6 contain the results of estimation for the two models. Table 8.5 indicates that the constant term is statistically different from zero. This means if this model is chosen, then the level of contributions follows a random walk with a drift process. Note, however, the Breusch–Godfrey LM test signals the presence of some autocorrelation at the 10 percent level of significance. Table 8.6 indicates the constant term and the $AR(1)$ coefficient are statistically significant at the 10 percent level. Moreover, there is no autocorrelation, as the LM test indicates. Thus, we retain the latter model.

d) The forecast values for static and dynamic scenarios are presented in Table 8.7. We use an estimation period of 1969–2000. The dynamic approach uses the forecast values for the lagged dependent variable or the ARMA term if available. The static approach uses the actual values of the dependent variables if available.

e) This is the Box–Jenkins approach to forecasting.

TABLE 8.6
An *AR*(1) Model for *Dcontributions*: Barbados 1971–2002

Variable	Coefficient	Standard Error	*t* Statistic	Prob.
C	8761.270	2899.949	3.021181	0.0051
AR(1)	0.315409	0.184819	1.706583	0.0982

R^2	0.088490	Mean dependent variable	8970.094
Adjusted R^2	0.058106	SD dependent variable	11549.66
SE of regression	11209.09	Akaike information criterion	21.54730
RSS	3.77E+09	Schwarz criterion	21.63891
Log likelihood	–342.7568	*F* statistic	2.912425
DW statistic	1.914672	Prob(*F* statistic)	0.098232

Breusch–Godfrey Serial Correlation LM Test with One Lag

F statistic	0.341538	Probability	0.563462
Obs*R^2	0.372482	Probability	0.541654

TABLE 8.7
Actual Values, Ex-Post Dynamic Forecast Values and Ex-Post Static Forecast Values for Contributions (in Bds$ '000)

Year	Contrib[a]	Confdy[b]	Confsta[c]
2001	303,750.0	308,075.97	308,075.97
2002	293,543.0	318,966.64	318,723.28

Notes:

[a] Contrib: actual values of contributions.
[b] Confdy: ex-post forecast for contributions using the dynamic approach.
[c] Confsta: ex-post forecast contributions using the static approach.

Answer 8.9

a) The OLS results of the linear trend model are presented in Table 8.8. The model has been corrected for autocorrelation and heteroscedasticity using the Newey–West HAC standard error and covariances. The significance of the *p* value from the F statistic allows us to assert that 61 percent of the variation in loan rate in South Africa is explained by the trend. The loan rate increases at the instantaneous rate of 0.43 percent per year.

The summary statistics of the in-sample forecasts of the model are presented in Table 8.9. The root mean square error and the mean absolute error are absolute measures of accuracy (they are scale dependent). They are useful in comparing forecasts for the same variable across different models, the rule being the smaller the value of the statistic the better the forecast. The mean absolute percentage error and the Theil inequality coefficient are scale invariant. The Theil inequality coefficient with a value of zero captures a perfect forecast. The Theil inequality coefficient can be

TABLE 8.8
Linear Trend Model for Loan Rate: South Africa 1970–1997, with Newey–West HAC Standard Errors

Variable	Coefficient	Standard Error	*t* Statistic	Prob.
C	8.595476	0.960066	8.953008	0.0000
Trend	0.434869	0.061702	7.047836	0.0000
R^2	0.611358	Mean of dependent variable		14.90107
Adjusted R^2	0.596410	SD of dependent variable		4.575070
SE of regression	2.906485	Akaike information criterion		5.040515
RSS	219.6390	Schwarz criterion		5.135672
Log likelihood	–68.56721	*F* statistic		40.89956
DW statistic	0.903976	Prob(*F* statistic)		0.000001

TABLE 8.9
Summary Statistics of In-Sample Forecasts of LRA: The Trend Model, South Africa 1970–1997

Forecast: LRAFTREND1
Actual: LRA
Forecast sample: 1970 1997
Included observations: 28

Root mean squared error	2.800759
Mean absolute error	2.157324
Mean absolute percentage error	14.53041
Theil inequality coefficient	0.090718
Bias proportion	0.000000
Variance proportion	0.122401
Covariance proportion	0.877599

decomposed into bias proportion, variance proportion and the covariance proportion. The bias proportion measures the distance between the mean of the actual series and the mean of the forecast. The variance proportion informs on the gap between the variability of the actual series and that of the forecast. The covariance proportion is a measure of the remaining unsystematic forecasting errors. Ideally, one targets small values for bias and variance proportions. A value of at least 0.10 for variance proportion is alarming.

Table 8.9 indicates the Theil inequality coefficient is acceptable. However, the variance proportion is a little alarming. This is expected to the extent that the model is only explained by the trend.

b) The OLS estimation results of Equation (Q8.9.1) are given in Table 8.10. The results indicate the absence of autocorrelation and heteroscedasticity. The fit is very good: 86 percent of the variation in loan rate is explained by the discount rate (*DR*). Given the results, we expect this model to fare very well for in-sample forecasts.

TABLE 8.10
Loan Rate Regression Model Results: South Africa 1970–1997

Variable	Coefficient	Standard Error	*t* Statistic	Prob.
C	4.827835	0.876819	5.506080	0.0000
DR	0.866861	0.069751	12.42794	0.0000
R^2	0.855919	Mean dependent variable		14.90107
Adjusted R^2	0.850377	SD dependent variable		4.575070
SE of regression	1.769689	Akaike information criterion		4.048233
RSS	81.42675	Schwarz criterion		4.143391
Log likelihood	–54.67527	*F* statistic		154.4536
DW statistic	1.869504	Prob(*F* statistic)		0.000000
Breusch–Godfrey Serial Correlation LM Test (2 Lags)				
F statistic	0.691956	Probability		0.510308
Obs*R^2	1.526539	Probability		0.466140
White Heteroscedasticity Test				
F statistic	1.316823	Probability		0.285939
Obs*R^2	2.668561	Probability		0.263348

TABLE 8.11
Summary Statistics for In-Sample Forecasts of LRA: The Regression Model, South Africa 1970–1997

Forecast: LRAFREG1
Actual: LRA
Forecast sample: 1970 1997

Root mean squared error	1.705315
Mean absolute error	1.216341
Mean absolute percentage error	8.427389
Theil inequality coefficient	0.054951
Bias proportion	0.000000
Variance proportion	0.038875
Covariance proportion	0.961125

Table 8.11 presents the results of in-sample forecasts for the model. As predicted, the Theil inequality coefficient is almost zero, the bias proportion is zero and the variance proportion is below the limit. This is not a surprise, as in-sample forecasts are based on measure of goodness of fit.

c) The comparison of the in-sample forecast statistics for the two models indicates that the regression model gives better in-sample forecasts than the trend model. This is well illustrated in Figure 8.6.

d) Table 8.12 contains the summary statistics of ex-post forecasts for the two models. Using the regular accuracy measures (RMSE, MAE, MAPE, Theil's *U*), it can be seen that the regression model dominates the trend

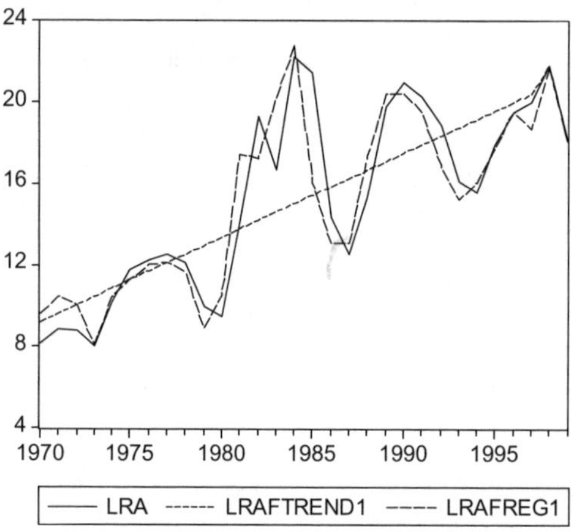

FIGURE 8.6
Loan rate (LRA) and its forecasts: LRAFTREND1 (trend model) and LRAFREG1 (regression model)

TABLE 8.12
Summary Statistics of Ex-Post Forecasts of LRA: Trend Model (LRAFTREND2) and Regression Model (LRAFREG2), South Africa 1998–1999

Forecast:	LRAFTREND2	LRAFREG2
Actual: LRA		
Forecast sample: 1998 1999		
Included observations: 2		
Root mean squared error	2.607782	1.964425
Mean absolute error	2.112434	1.492119
Mean absolute percentage error	11.45391	8.185961
Theil inequality coefficient	0.062974	0.050814
Bias proportion	0.343819	0.576947
Variance proportion	0.413825	0.423053
Covariance proportion	0.242356	0.000000

model. However, the bias and variance proportions convey the reverse message, hinting that a model with a very good fit does not necessarily perform well out of samples.

e) Optimality. The optimality of the two ex-post forecasts can be studied from the bias or efficiency point of view. We regress the actual value of loan rate on each forecast and a constant term using the full period, 1970–1999. (Why?) Since this is a two-steps-ahead forecast we expect autocorrelation to be at most of $MA(1)$ order. The forecast is optimal if the constant term is statistically zero and the coefficient of the forecast is 1. Tables 8.13 and 8.14 show the results of the exercise for the two models of interest. As can be seen autocorrelation is still present in the form of $MA(2)$ in both models. It means that the two forecasts are not optimal.

TABLE 8.13
Optimality of Ex-Post Forecasts for the Trend Model: South Africa 1970–1999

Variable	Coefficient	Standard Error	t Statistic	Prob.
C	0.149694	0.130912	1.143468	0.2633
LRAFTR2	0.988660	0.007806	126.6471	0.0000
MA(1)	−1.437882	0.030135	−47.71533	0.0000
MA(2)	0.917264	0.040101	22.87404	0.0000
R^2	0.987779	Mean dependent variable		15.23400
Adjusted R^2	0.986369	SD dependent variable		4.619597
SE of regression	0.539355	Akaike information criterion		1.726679
RSS	7.563490	Schwarz criterion		1.913505
Log likelihood	−21.90019	*F* statistic		700.4801
DW statistic	1.474299	Prob(*F* statistic)		0.000000
Inverted *MA* roots	.72–.63i	.72+.63i		

Note: LRAFTR2: forecast values of LRA, 1970–1999.

TABLE 8.14
Optimality of Ex-Post Forecasts for the Regression Model: South Africa 1970–1999

Variable	Coefficient	Standard Error	t Statistic	Prob.
C	0.648064	0.429101	1.510282	0.1430
LRAFRG2	0.979265	0.019657	49.81872	0.0000
MA(1)	1.822493	0.040897	44.56266	0.0000
MA(2)	0.916014	0.040999	22.34253	0.0000
R^2	0.991543	Mean dependent variable		15.23400
Adjusted R^2	0.990568	SD dependent variable		4.619597
SE of regression	0.448656	Akaike information criterion		1.358443
RSS	5.233588	Schwarz criterion		1.545270
Log likelihood	−16.37665	*F* statistic		1016.180
DW statistic	0.973469	Prob(*F* statistic)		0.000000
Inverted *MA* roots	−.91 −.29i	−.91+.29i		

Note: LRAFRG2: forecast values of LRA, 1970–1999.

f) Forecast encompassing. We check for forecast encompassing by running a regression of actual values of loan rate on predicted values in the two models and a constant term. If one forecast variable has coefficient one and the other zero, then the former encompasses the other. Table 8.15 shows the results of the exercise. As can be seen, no forecast encompasses the other.

g) Forecast combination. Since no forecast encompasses the other, we combine them. Table 8.16 shows the summary statistics of forecast combination. As can be seen the combination is really successful to the extent that the Theil's inequality is almost zero (perfect forecast) and the bias and the variance proportions are each zero.

TABLE 8.15
Forecast Encompassing: Trend and Regression Models, South Africa 1970–1999

Variable	Coefficient	Standard Error	t Statistic	Prob.
C	–0.046191	0.043553	–1.060577	0.2983
LRAFRG2	0.577078	0.011050	52.22368	0.0000
LRAFTR2	0.426866	0.010733	39.77230	0.0000
R^2	0.999799	Mean dependent variable		15.23400
Adjusted R^2	0.999784	SD dependent variable		4.619597
SE of regression	0.067896	Akaike information criterion		–2.447026
RSS	0.124468	Schwarz criterion		–2.306906
Log likelihood	39.70539	F statistic		67111.11
DW statistic	1.891050	Prob(F statistic)		0.000000

TABLE 8.16
Forecast Combination: Trend and Regression Models, South Africa 1970–1999

Forecast: LRAFCOMB
Actual: LRA
Forecast sample: 1970 1999
Included observations: 30

Root mean squared error	0.064412
Mean absolute error	0.028347
Mean absolute percentage error	0.157874
Theil inequality coefficient	0.002026
Bias proportion	0.000000
Variance proportion	0.000050
Covariance proportion	0.999950

Answer 8.10

a) ARIMA model and ex-post forecast. Figure 8.7 represents the correlogram of inflation (Dp) for the period January 1995 to December 1997. As can be seen the series is stationary. This is also confirmed by the associated p value (0.000) of the ADF test value (–6.047) with a constant term and zero as the optimal lag. Going back to the correlogram (acf and pacf), we notice that there is a spike at lag 9, a hint for an $AR(9)$ process or an $MA(9)$ process, or a combination of both. A search indicated that the best model is an $MA(9)$ process. Table 8.17 shows the result of the estimation of the model. The model passes the autocorrelation test, the most important diagnostic test for the ARIMA model. Table 8.18 shows the ex-post forecast of inflation for the period January to December 1998. Static forecasts are better than dynamic forecasts using any one of the accuracy measures.

Autocorrelation	Partial Correlation		AC	PAC	Q-Stat	Prob
.*| . |	.*| . |	1	-0.071	-0.071	0.1915	0.662
. | . |	. | . |	2	-0.002	-0.007	0.1917	0.909
. | . |	. | . |	3	-0.024	-0.024	0.2141	0.975
. | . |	. | . |	4	0.006	0.003	0.2157	0.995
. | . |	. | . |	5	-0.036	-0.035	0.2704	0.998
. | . |	. | . |	6	0.043	0.038	0.3525	0.999
.*| . |	. | . |	7	-0.062	-0.057	0.5297	0.999
. |*. |	. |*. |	8	0.081	0.073	0.8456	0.999
***| . |	***| . |	9	-0.384	-0.379	8.1932	0.515
. | . |	. | . |	10	0.026	-0.017	8.2285	0.607
.*| . |	.*| . |	11	-0.104	-0.135	8.8130	0.639
.*| . |	.*| . |	12	-0.110	-0.164	9.4923	0.660
. | . |	. | . |	13	-0.012	-0.041	9.5002	0.734
. | . |	.*| . |	14	0.011	-0.061	9.5072	0.797
. | . |	. | . |	15	0.022	0.046	9.5376	0.848
. | . |	. | . |	16	0.037	-0.031	9.6329	0.885

FIGURE 8.7
Correlogram for inflation (*Dp*): Barbados 1995:01–1997:12

TABLE 8.17
Inflation as an *MA*(9) Process

Variable	Coefficient	Standard Error	*t* Statistic	Prob.
C	0.002495	0.001409	1.771103	0.085800
MA(9)	–0.941359	0.043129	–21.82681	0.000000
R^2	0.446404	Mean dependent variable		0.002636
Adjusted R^2	0.429628	SD dependent variable		0.014489
SE of regression	0.010942	Akaike information criterion		–6.136890
RSS	0.003951	Schwarz criterion		–6.048013
Log likelihood	109.3956	*F* statistic		26.61026
DW statistic	2.119110	Prob(*F* statistic)		0.000012

TABLE 8.18
Summary Statistics for Barbados ARMA Ex-Post Inflation Forecasts: Static and Dynamic, 1998:01–1998:12

Forecast	Dpsta	Dpdy
Actual: *Dp* (Inflation)		
Forecast sample: 1998:01 1998:12		
Included observations: 12		
Root mean squared error	0.002362	0.003375
Mean absolute error	0.001843	0.002647
Mean absolute percentage error	62.18603	91.98534
Theil inequality coefficient	0.294776	0.453561
Bias proportion	0.030320	0.150915
Variance proportion	0.000437	0.167102
Covariance proportion	0.969243	0.681983

Note: Dpsta: static forecast; Dpdy: dynamic forecast.

TABLE 8.19
Inflation–Money Growth Regression Results: Barbados, 1995:01–1997:12

Variable	Coefficient	Standard Error	*t* Statistic	Prob.
C	0.003232	0.002605	1.240309	0.2236
Dm	–0.033917	0.047716	–0.710810	0.4822

R^2	0.015080	Mean dependent variable	0.002636
Adjusted R^2	–0.014766	SD dependent variable	0.014489
SE of regression	0.014595	Akaike information criterion	–5.560764
RSS	0.007030	Schwarz criterion	–5.471887
Log likelihood	99.31337	*F* statistic	0.505251
DW statistic	2.054839	Prob(*F* statistic)	0.482196

b) Table 8.19 shows the results of the estimation of Equation (Q8.10.1) for the period January 1995 to December 1997. There is no autocorrelation. Moreover, the White's test (not reported here) indicates the absence of heteroscedasticity. It seems that there is no relationship between inflation and money growth. The regression is valid, because the two variables are stationary; that is, the case of spurious regression is excluded.

c) Table 8.20 shows the accuracy measurements of ex-post inflation forecasts in the period January to December 1998.

d) The following *VAR*(2) has been fitted to the data of interest. Table 8.21 shows the results of the estimation of the model.

$$Dp_t = \alpha_0 + \alpha_1 Dp_{t-1} + \alpha_2 Dp_{t-2} + \alpha_3 Dm_{t-1} + \alpha_4 Dm_{t-2} + u_{1t}$$

$$Dm_t = \beta_0 + \beta_1 Dp_{t-1} + \beta_2 Dp_{t-2} + \beta_3 Dm_{t-1} + \beta_4 Dm_{t-2} + u_{2t}$$

TABLE 8.20
Summary Statistics of Barbados Ex-Post Regression Inflation Forecasts: 1998:01–1998:12

Forecast: DPFREGR
Actual: *Dp*
Forecast sample: 1998:01 1998:12

Root mean squared error	0.004229
Mean absolute error	0.003521
Mean absolute percentage error	129.2530
Theil inequality coefficient	0.570135
Bias proportion	0.151103
Variance proportion	0.203688
Covariance proportion	0.645210

TABLE 8.21
Vector Autoregressions Results: Inflation and Money Growth, Barbados 1995:04–1997:12

	Dp	Dm
Dp(–1)	–0.130644	0.275463
	[–0.71416]	[0.40796]
Dp(–2)	0.041680	–0.887481
	[0.24951]	[–1.43934]
Dm(–1)	0.138506	–0.339937
	[2.79783]	[–1.86038]
Dm(–2)	0.077143	–0.401097
	[1.41330]	[–1.99084]
C	–1.72E-05	0.029311
	[–0.00629]	[2.89953]
R^2	0.233655	0.207890
SE equation	0.013894	0.051284
F statistic	2.134261	1.837162
Log likelihood	97.00347	53.90846
Akaike information criterion	–5.575968	–2.964149
Schwarz criterion	–5.349224	–2.737406
Determinant residual covariance		5.06E-07
Log likelihood (df adjusted)		145.5419
Akaike information criterion		–8.214658
Schwarz criterion		–7.761171

Note: *t* statistics in [ ].

Table 8.22 shows the accuracy measures for the ex-post forecast of inflation in the period January to December 1998. Both dynamic and static forecasts are presented. The two forecasts are comparable.

TABLE 8.22
Summary Statistics for Barbados VAR Ex-Post Inflation Forecasts, Static and Dynamic: Barbados 1998:01–1998:12

Actual: *Dp*		
Forecast sample: 1998:01–1998:12	Forecast:	
Included observations: 12	Dpfvastat	Dpfvady
Root mean squared error	0.006941	0.007002
Mean absolute error	0.005257	0.005212
Mean absolute percentage error	183.9659	177.8224
Theil inequality coefficient	0.565475	0.566750
Bias proportion	0.013708	0.012584
Variance proportion	0.409294	0.418726
Covariance proportion	0.576998	0.568690

Note: Dpvastat: static forecast; Dpfvady: dynamic forecast.

e) A comparison of Tables 8.18, 8.20 and 8.22 indicates that, overall, the ARMA model dominates the two other models (the regression model and the VAR model) in terms of the major accuracy measures (e.g., RMSE and Theil's *U*). This confirms the point often made that a simple model can outperform a more sophisticated model.

8.4 SUPPLEMENTARY EXERCISES

Question 8.11 Write an essay on the accuracy measures of forecasts.

Question 8.12 Explain the concept of simulation.

Question 8.13 Some years ago, while he was a student at the State University of New York at Albany, a friend of mine met a professor of atmospheric science of the same university. When the professor asked what he was studying, my friend replied, "Economics". The professor responded: "We have one thing in common: we don't know how to forecast." Assess the professor's statement.

Question 8.14 Using the data in Question 4.15, forecast (or simulate) the demand for labour using an ARIMA model, a vector autoregression (or an error correction model) and a simultaneous equations model. Comment on the results.

CHAPTER 9

Panel Data Models

9.1 INTRODUCTION

Data in econometrics arise mainly in the form of time series, or cross section or panel data. As already pointed out, time series data are data ordered in time for a given entity or unit. Cross section data are data related to units (e.g., individuals, firms, nations, or regions) at a given point in time. Panel data or longitudinal data combine time series and cross section features; that is, they deal with a set of units observed (and recorded) over time.

This chapter is concerned with panel data models. At the outset, the question of interest is whether panel data offer advantages compared to other data configurations. There seems to be a consensus that panel data do indeed offer some advantages (see, for example, Hsiao, 1986; Klevmarken, 1989; Baltagi, 1995). Panel data models improve the efficiency of econometric estimators by increasing the sample size (more data points), increasing the degrees of freedom, increasing the variability in explanatory variables and decreasing the extent of multicollinearity among explanatory variables. In some circumstances, panel data can help address questions that other data configurations cannot deal with. Moreover, panel data models control adequately for individual heterogeneity; hence, heterogeneity biases are avoided. Finally, panel data models are suitable to trace the dynamics of adjustment.

On the negative side, panel data configurations have some limitations (see Baltagi, 1995, 6–7). Indeed, since panel data most often come from surveys, they are in general affected by design and data collection, errors of measurement distortions, the selectivity problem and most often shortness of time series dimension.

In terms of estimation and properties of estimators, above all perhaps there is the question of "poolability" of data that needs to be raised in every applied panel data exercise. Although advances have been made in terms of tests of poolability (parametric as well as nonparametric: see, for example, Baltagi, 1995; Baltagi et al., 1996;Vashid, 1999), most empirical work still ignores the issue. Fixed effects models and random effects models are the key panel data models. Recently, advances in the panel data framework have been made in several directions. First, dynamic models have gained their place in panel data models. Second, semiparametric estimation techniques have timidly penetrated panel data models. Third, generalized method of moments (GMM) estimation has been found very appropriate in panel data estimation (e.g., Dasgupta et al., 2001; Wang et al., 2003). Fourth, limited dependent variables estimation in the context of panel data has enriched the latter. Fifth, unit root and cointegration previously thought only appropriate for time series are now present in panel data (see, for example, Kao, 1997; Levin and Lin, 1993; Breitung, 1994; Im et al., 1996; McCoskey and Kao, 1998: Pedroni, 1995; Phillips and Moon, 2000). The exercises in this chapter cover a selected set of panel data issues. TSP 4.4 was used for empirical exercises.

9.2 QUESTIONS

9.2.1 Theoretical Exercises

Question 9.1 Write an essay on the issue of "poolability" in panel data models.

Question 9.2 Write a note on the choice between a fixed effects model and a random effects model.

Question 9.3 Consider the model:

$$Y_{it} = \beta X_{it} + \gamma V_i + \alpha_i + u_{it} \tag{Q9.3.1}$$

where

u_{it} = a random disturbance
i = 1, 2, …, N = units or individuals
t = 1, 2, …, T = time
Y_{it}, X_{it} and V_i = variables of interest.

a) Explain the use of the constant α_i.
b) In the model, the variable V_i does not have a subscript "t". What does it mean? Give a concrete example of V_i. Compare and contrast V_i and α_i.
c) Suppose α_i is uncorrelated (in the limit) with X_{it} and V_i. Explain how to obtain efficient estimators for β and γ.
d) Suggest a test procedure to check the assumed independence of X_{it} and V_i with α_1 as in (c). (UWI, EC36D, tutorial, March 2004).

Question 9.4 Consider the following model:

$$y_{it} = \beta_i y_{i,t-1} + \gamma_i x_{it} + e_{it} \tag{Q9.4.1}$$

where

$\beta_i \sim IID(\beta, \sigma^2_\beta)$
$\gamma_i \sim IID(\gamma, \sigma^2_\gamma)$
$E(\beta_i x_{is}) = 0$
$E(\beta_i e_{is}) = 0$
$E(\gamma_i y_{is}) = 0$
$E(\gamma_i x_{is}) = 0$
$E(\gamma_i e_{is}) = 0$
$i = 1, 2, \ldots, N$
$t = 1, 2, \ldots, T$.

a) Assume that the interest centres on getting the mean values of the β_i and the γ_i. Describe briefly four different classical procedures that can enable you to obtain such mean values.
b) Briefly explain why all four methods yield inconsistent mean values if T is small.
c) Which estimation technique yields a consistent estimate of the two mean values when T and N are large? (Adapted from Pesaran and Smith, 1995.)

Question 9.5 Consider the following general model:

$$y_{it} = A_i + B_i x_{it} + u_{it} \tag{Q9.5.1}$$

where

i = 1, 2, …, N = units or individuals
t = 1, 2, …, T = time
y_{it} and x_{it} = some quantitative variables
u_{it} = the usual error term

Equation (Q9.5.1) can give rise to several models. Several tests can be devised to study the validity of the models. The software package programme TSP includes quite a number of them.

a) Explain the following null hypotheses that TSP provides:
   i) $A, B = A_i, B_i$;
   ii) $A_i, B = A_i, B_i$;
   iii) $A, B = A_i, B$.
b) In each of the scenarios above provide the F test of interest, including the relevant degrees of freedom.

9.2.2 Empirical Exercises

Question 9.6 Chuhan, Claessens and Mamingi (1998) examined the factors that impacted the large capital flows to Latin America and Asia in the late 1980s and early 1990s. The flows of interest were equity flows and bond flows. They used a panel data framework to conduct the study. The models of interest are:

$$Y_{it} = \alpha_i + \beta_1 PCS_{it} + \beta_2 PI_{it} + \delta_1 T + e_{it} \tag{Q9.6.1}$$

$$Y_{it} = \alpha_i + \gamma_2 PCS_{it} + \gamma_2 PI_{it} + \gamma_3 \mathrm{Re}t_{it} + \gamma_4 PE_{it} + \delta_2 T + e_{it} \tag{Q9.6.2}$$

where

i = 1, 2, …, N = the country index
t = 1, 2, …, T = the time index
PCS_{it} = the first principal component of credit ratings and secondary market debt prices

PI_{it} = the first principal component of five types of US interest rates (US Treasury bill rate, certificate of deposit rate, long-term rate [10-year], Libor [3-month] and medium term [3-year]) and industrial activity (deviation of industrial production index from a time trend)
Ret_{it} = the rate of return of a stock
PE_{it} = price-earnings ratios
T = trend
Y_{it} = the capital flow (either equity or bond)
e_{it} = the usual error term

In this exercise we concentrate on Latin America. Equation (Q9.6.2) is the appropriate model. Unfortunately, it could only be run for six Latin American countries, as three others lacked data in one or another variable. Equation (Q9.6.1), a nested version of Equation (Q9.6.2), uses all nine Latin American countries of interest (see note to Table 9.1). The results of the estimations of the two models for Latin America are presented in Table 9.1.

TABLE 9.1
Panel Data Estimates: Bond Flows, Latin America 1988:01–1992:09

Method	GLS	GLS	GLS	GLS
PCS	4.288**	7.564*	8.662**	12.854**
	(2.432)	(2.118)	(3.605)	(3.299)
PI	–9.825*	–2.300	–14.340*	–3.196
	(3.588)	(3.299)	(5.259)	(4.761)
Ret			–0.047	–0.065
			(0.136)	(0.138)
PE			–0.944**	–0.782**
			(0.412)	(0.415)
T	0.227****	0.498*	0.419***	0.816*
	(0.185)	(0.198)	(0.259)	(0.294)
Adjusted R^2	0.982	0.982	0.984	0.983
m	0.153	3.602	0.173	2.790
	(0.999)	(0.703)	(1.000)	(0.904)
Nobs	513	513	342	342

Note: Equations (Q9.6.1) and (Q9.6.2) are of interest: columns 2 and 4 use nominal interest rates; columns 3 and 5 use real interest rates. Equation (Q9.6.1): countries of interest are Argentina, Brazil, Chile, Colombia, Mexico, Venezuela, Ecuador, Jamaica and Uruguay. Equation (Q9.6.2): countries of interest are all of the above except Ecuador, Jamaica and Uruguay (missing data). Period of investigation: 1988:01–1992:09. GLS: generalized least squares. Figures in parentheses are standard errors except for the Hausman statistic ($m \sim \chi^2$) for which they represent the p values. Some dummies have been included in the model to capture the Brady Plan. (*), (**), (***), and (****) mean significant at the 1, 5, 10 and 15 percent level, respectively.

Source: Chuhan, Claessens and Mamingi (1998, Tables 4 and 6).

a) Provide and explain the expected signs in the two models.
b) It has been argued that one of the virtues of panel data models is to decrease the extent of multicollinearity. In the present models, explain why PCS_{it} and PI_{it} were used.
c) Using the results from the above table, do you accept or reject the random effects model? Explain.
d) Interpret the results of the study.
e) Some advances have been pointed out in the introductory part of the chapter; among them, which one could you pick up to reexamine the study. Why?

Question 9.7 Table 9.2 shows data on gross domestic product (GDP) growth and share of gross domestic investment to GDP for four African countries (Botswana, Burkina Fasso, Gabon and Mauritius) in the period 1988–1997. The exercise assesses the relationship between GDP growth and gross domestic investment share to GDP in the African context using the four named countries. Consider the following general model:

$$Y_{it} = \alpha_i + \beta_i X_{it} + u_{it} \qquad \text{(Q9.7.1)}$$

where
Y_{it} = GDP growth
X_{it} = share of gross domestic investment to GDP
i = 1, 2, 3, 4 = country
t = 1988, …, 1997 = year of interest

TABLE 9.2
GDP Growth and Gross Domestic Investment Share to GDP in Four African Countries (Botswana, Burkina Fasso, Gabon and Mauritius)

Year	gdbo	gibo	gdbf	gibf	gdga	giga	gdma	gima
1988	15.3	26.7	6.6	19.8	12.8	37.5	6.8	31
1989	13.1	29.0	0.9	21.6	8.5	26.3	4.5	31.1
1990	5.6	31.8	–1.5	20.6	5.2	21.7	7.2	30.9
1991	8.7	31.6	10	20.6	6.1	26.5	4.3	28.7
1992	6.3	29.4	2.5	21.3	–3.3	22.4	6.2	29.3
1993	–0.1	27.9	–0.8	19.8	2.4	22.4	5.4	30.7
1994	4.1	24.6	1.2	19.3	3.4	21.9	4.1	32.3
1995	3.1	24.4	3.8	22.5	7	22.7	4.7	25.7
1996	7	24.1	6.2	25.4	3.8	23.3	5.4	25.1
1997	7	26.1	6.6	24.9	4.1	26.3	5	27.6

Note: gdbo, gdbf, gdga, and gdma represent GDP growth for Botswana, Burkina Fasso, Gabon and Mauritius, respectively; gibo, gibf, giga, and gima represent share of gross domestic investment to GDP for Botswana, Burkina Fasso, Gabon and Mauritius, respectively. Variables are in percent.

Source: *African Development Indicators*, World Bank, Washington, D.C., 1998.

a) Derive the pooled regression and obtain the estimates of interest.
b) Derive the between regression and obtain the estimates of interest.
c) Derive the within regression and obtain the estimates of interest.
d) Derive the variance components model and obtain the estimates of interest.
e) Conduct a thorough discussion on the validity of the different results.

Question 9.8 Consider the relationship between inflation (Y) and money supply growth (X) for eighteen sub-Saharan African countries for the period 1999–2002. The general model is written as follows:

$$Y_{it} = \alpha_i + \beta_i X_{it} + u_{it} \qquad \text{(Q9.8.1)}$$

where the variables are as above, $i = 1, 2, \ldots, N$ stands for country, $t = 1, 2, \ldots, T$ is time, and u_{it} is the error term. Using the data in Table 9.3, conduct a thorough investigation on the relationship between the two variables using a panel data framework.

9.3 ANSWERS

Answer 9.1

The issue of "poolability" or the question of "to pool or not to pool", is the question of whether cross section regressions pertaining to different points in time can be regrouped (stacked) to give rise to a single regression or whether data from time series and cross section regressions can be combined (stacked). To explain better, consider the following model

$$y_{it} = \alpha_i + \beta_i x_{it} + u_{it} \qquad \forall i = 1,2,3,\cdots,N \qquad t = 1,2,\cdots,T \qquad \text{(A9.1.1)}$$

The question of "poolability" in the strict sense is the question of whether Equation (A9.1.1) can be rewritten as:

$$y_{it} = \alpha + \beta x_{it} + u_{it} \qquad \text{(A9.1.2)}$$

In other words, it is the question of whether the following null hypothesis is not rejected:

$$H_0 : \begin{cases} \alpha_1 = \alpha_2 = \cdots = \alpha_N = \alpha \\ \beta_1 = \beta_2 = \cdots = \beta_N = \beta \end{cases} \qquad \text{(A9.1.3)}$$

If it is not rejected, then Equation (A9.1.2) should be used instead of Equation (A9.1.1), in which case data are poolable. If it is rejected, then it is worth analysing what it means, because the alternative hypothesis to (A9.1.3) can take several forms. If the α_is are different and the β_is common, then a case of weaker poolability is established. In fact, this is what we really mean by poolability, as we do not expect, for example, the individual effects, α_i, to be the same across units. If the α_is are different across different

TABLE 9.3
Inflation and Money Supply Growth in Eighteen Sub-Saharan African Countries 1999–2002

Country	Year	Inflation	Money	Country	Year	Inflation	Money
Benin	1999	0.30	46.90	Ghana	1999	12.40	15.80
Benin	2000	4.20	35.00	Ghana	2000	25.20	38.20
Benin	2001	4.00	10.00	Ghana	2001	32.90	46.30
Benin	2002	2.50	–8.60	Ghana	2002	14.80	59.90
Botswana	1999	7.70	17.30	G.Bissau	1999	–2.00	22.40
Botswana	2000	8.60	6.90	G.Bissau	2000	8.50	63.70
Botswana	2001	6.60	23.90	G.Bissau	2001	3.20	7.80
Botswana	2002	8.10	7.40	G.Bissau	2002	0.90	22.30
Burk. Fasso	1999	–1.10	–1.90	Kenya	1999	5.70	16.40
Burk. Fasso	2000	–0.30	5.30	Kenya	2000	10.00	8.60
Burk.Fasso	2001	5.00	–3.00	Kenya	2001	5.70	6.20
Burk. Fasso	2002	2.20	–7.10	Kenya	2002	2.00	18.50
Cameroon	1999	1.50	10.80	Lesotho	1999	8.00	–2.60
Cameroon	2000	–2.10	17.40	Lesotho	2000	6.10	8.20
Cameroon	2001	4.50	12.80	Lesotho	2001	–9.60	24.70
Cameroon	2002	2.80	14.30	Lesotho	2002	33.80	11.50
CAR	1999	–1.40	12.60	Madagascar	1999	9.90	20.20
CAR	2000	3.20	3.20	Madagascar	2000	12.00	13.20
CAR	2001	3.40	–2.60	Madagascar	2001	6.90	30.30
CAR	2002	3.40	–4.40	Madagascar	2002	15.90	7.50
Chad	1999	–6.80	–3.10	Malawi	1999	44.80	33.10
Chad	2000	3.80	17.70	Malawi	2000	29.60	37.20
Chad	2001	12.40	21.80	Malawi	2001	27.20	8.90
Chad	2002	5.20	27.30	Malawi	2002	14.70	27.20
Congo	1999	5.40	27.80	Mali	1999	–1.20	–0.60
Congo	2000	–0.90	68.20	Mali	2000	–0.70	9.40
Congo	2001	0.10	–23.1	Mali	2001	5.20	29.60
Congo	2002	4.40	13.90	Mali	2002	5.00	28.90
C. d'Ivoire	1999	0.80	–1.70	Mauritius	1999	6.90	3.60
C. d'Ivoire	2000	2.50	–3.70	Mauritius	2000	4.20	10.80
C. d'Ivoire	2001	4.30	14.80	Mauritius	2001	5.40	16.20
C. d'Ivoire	2002	3.10	32.10	Mauritius	2002	6.70	17.50
Ethiopia	1999	7.90	12.30	Nigeria	1999	4.80	22.50
Ethiopia	2000	0.70	11.10	Nigeria	2000	14.50	62.10
Ethiopia	2001	–8.10	4.30	Nigeria	2001	13.00	25.70
Ethiopia	2002	1.60	14.80	Nigeria	2002	12.90	15.90

Note: Burk. Fasso: Burkina Fasso; C. d'Ivoire: Côte d'Ivoire; CAR: Central African Republic. Inflation and money supply growth are expressed in percent.

Source: *International Financial Statistics,* August 2003, International Monetary Fund, Washington, D.C.

units and so are the β_is, then poolability is rejected. Note that in the latter case, it is possible to search for poolability of subsets of cross sections; that is, it is possible to establish partial poolability (see, for example, Vashid, 1999).

In terms of tests of poolability, as the above regressions implicitly indicate, some type of Chow test (restricted versus unrestricted) is recommended. Several remarks are, however, worth making. First, since the variance of errors is most likely not constant, the Chow test needs to be modified to take variability of errors into consideration. This is particularly true for error components models (see Baltagi, 1995). Second, as pointed out by Maddala (1991, 256) and ignored by most econometrics practitioners, the Theil's $\bar{R}^2$ rule implies choosing the null hypothesis (restricted model or pooled model) if the F ratio is greater than one. This means that the relevant significance level is 50 percent instead of the usual 5 percent. Third, since the rejection of the null hypothesis can be due to functional misspecification, nonparametric tests are welcome (see, for example, Baltagi et al., 1996).

Although "poolability" gives some credibility (validity) to a pooled regression, the question of whether the pooled estimator $\hat{\beta}_p$ is superior to $\hat{\beta}_i$ coming from other scenarios remains important. Using forecast properties, some researchers have found that the Stein-rule estimator and the Bayesian estimator perform better than the pooled estimator or the individual $\hat{\beta}_i$ (see Maddala, 1991; Zeimer and Wetzstein, 1983).

Answer 9.2

This discussion is based largely on Hsiao (1986, 41–43). The question of choice between the fixed effects and random effects models is inevitable. To proceed, let us concentrate on the individual effects, α_i. The question turns out to be whether these are fixed or random. The issue is particularly important when the time dimension (T) is small and the unit dimension (N) is large. This is so because in this scenario the two models usually give rise to different results.

At the outset let us point out that the individual effects capture the omitted variables that we have no knowledge of for one reason or another. Basically, this reflects our ignorance (the researcher's ignorance). If α_i can be considered as a random variable with some distribution then it can be assimilated to an error term. This means that it seems as if the sample of individuals that we are dealing with has been drawn from a certain population. In other words, the inference we make from the results will concern the entire population (unconditional or marginal inferences with respect to the population of all effects). In this situation α_i represents the random effects and the associated model is the random effects or variance components or error components model. On the contrary, α_i can remain constant for a given unit (no variation over time). In that sense, it is fixed. This scenario basically reflects the case where we want to make inference conditional on the effects that are in the sample. That is, our inference only concerns the sample we are dealing with and not the population per se. In this situation the appropriate model is the fixed effects model. Naturally, the way the data are gathered (randomly or not) as well as the environment affect the outcomes concerning the nature of α_i.

At the purely statistical or econometric level, the distinction between fixed effects and random effects boils down to whether there are correlations between the explanatory variables and the individual effects or whether it is reasonable to posit that, for example, $\alpha_i \sim iid(0,\sigma_\alpha^2)$. If they are correlated then GLS as well as LS estimators are similar to omitted variable misspecification and the GLS estimator is biased and inconsistent. However, the within estimator (least square dummy variable [LSDV] estimator, covariance [CV] estimator or fixed effects [FE] estimator) is BLUE. It seems plausible to use a variance components model if $\alpha_i \sim iid(0,\sigma_\alpha^2)$ and N is sufficiently large for reliable estimation of σ_α^2. Put differently, if the explanatory variables and the individual effects are correlated or N is small, a fixed effects model would be suitable. Note that the choice between the two models may be aided by the Hausman test. Indeed, if the null hypothesis of lack of correlation between the explanatory variables and the individual effects is not rejected using the Hausman test, then the random effects model would not be rejected; otherwise it is rejected. Moreover, when N is fixed and $T \to \infty, \beta_{FE} \to \beta_{GLS}$.

Answer 9.3

a) As said above, the α_i are the individual specific effects. They capture omitted variables that the researcher is ignorant about. They may be fixed; that is, they are constant over time in a given unit and vary across units. In that case, they are correlated with other explanatory variables. On the other hand, they may be random; that is, uncorrelated with explanatory variables.

b) V_i is a time-invariant characteristic variable. Demographic characteristics such as race, sex and DNA fall in this category. V_i and α_i are both time-invariant, individually specific variables. While V_i is observed (a time-invariant, observable random variable), α_i is unobserved (a latent individual effect).

c) The solution is based on Hausman and Taylor (1981). Let us introduce two important idempotent matrices or transformations:

$$P_S = \left[I_N \otimes \frac{1}{T} l_T l_T' \right] \tag{A9.3.1}$$

and

$$Q_S = I_{NT} - P_S \tag{A9.3.2}$$

where l is a vector of ones with dimension T and $\otimes$ is the Kronecker product. If α_i is uncorrelated with the explanatory variables then the efficient estimator can be obtained using GLS. The following regression model is of interest:

$$\Omega^{-1/2} Y_{it} = \Omega^{-1/2} X_{it}\beta + \Omega^{-1/2} V_i \gamma + \Omega^{-1/2}\alpha_i + \Omega^{-1/2} e_{it} \tag{A9.3.3}$$

or

$$Y_{it} - (1-\lambda)\bar{Y}_i = [X_{it} - (1-\lambda)\bar{X}_i]\beta + \lambda V_i \gamma + \lambda \alpha_i + [e_{it} - (1-\lambda)\bar{e}_i] \tag{A9.3.4}$$

where

$$\lambda = \left[\frac{\sigma_e^2}{\sigma_e^2 + T\sigma_\alpha^2} \right]^{1/2}$$

and

$$\Omega^{\frac{1}{2}} = I_{TN} - (1-\lambda) P_S.$$

d) The Hausman test is of interest here. It is a test of random effects against fixed effects; that is, it tests the null hypothesis $H_0 : E(\alpha_i / x_{it}, V_i) = 0$ versus the alternative hypothesis $H_0 : E(\alpha_i / x_{it}, V_i) \neq 0$. The test statistic is computed as $m = \hat{q}V^{-1}\hat{q}$, where $\hat{q} = \hat{\beta}_W - \hat{\beta}_{GLS}$, $\hat{\beta}_W$ and $\hat{\beta}_{GLS}$ are within and GLS estimators, respectively, $V = \text{var}(\hat{\beta}_w) - \text{var}(\hat{\beta}_{GLS})$ and *df* is the number of degrees of freedom. The *m* test follows a χ^2 distribution, with *df* being the number of explanatory variables, excluding the constant term. If $m > \chi^2_{df}$ (or the *p* value is less than the nominal level of significance) one rejects the null hypothesis; otherwise, one does not reject it.

Answer 9.4

a) The four procedures are the following:

i) aggregate time series regressions of group averages;
ii) cross section regressions of averages over time;
iii) pooled regressions with fixed or random intercepts, and
iv) separate regressions for each group with coefficient estimates averaged over the groups (Baltagi, 1995, 196).

The first method averages data over groups and estimates the aggregate time series. The second method is the cross section regression; that is, at each instant of time cross section regressions are run and averages are obtained as means of the coefficients from the regressions. The third procedure is the pooled regression, which combines the data to impose common slopes and different intercepts (fixed or random intercepts). The fourth method consists simply in running regular regression on each group and averaging the estimates.

b) All four methods yield inconsistent estimates if *T* is small. Baltagi (1995, 196–197) summarizes well the reasons put forward by Pesaran and Smith (1995). It can be noted that Equation (Q9.4.1) can be rewritten as:

$$y_{it} = \beta y_{i,t-1} + \gamma x_{it} + v_{it} \tag{A9.4.1}$$

where

$$v_{it} = e_{it} + (\beta_i - \beta) y_{i,t-1} + (\gamma_i - \gamma) x_{it}$$

Expanding Equation (A9.4.1) using continual substitution of $y_{i,t-1-s}$ reveals that the error v_{it} is correlated with $y_{i,t-1-s}$ and $x_{i,t-s}, \forall s \geq 0$. This implies that the OLS estimator is inconsistent and, furthermore, given the type of correlation lagged $y_{i,t-1}$ and x_{it} are not valid instruments.

c) The cross section procedure, which gives rise to long-run estimates, can yield consistent estimates when T is large, because the individual parameters can be consistently estimated each using T observations for each individual i. The averaging will give rise to consistent estimates.

Answer 9.5

a) The null hypotheses are explained below.

i) The null hypothesis A, B = A_i, B_i is relevant for testing for common intercept and common slope. This is a strong version of the "poolability" hypothesis. It is a stringent version of "poolability", as few people believe that at the same time intercepts are the same across individuals (units) and so are the slopes.

ii) The null hypothesis A_i, B = A_i, B_i is adequate for testing for common slope. This is the null hypothesis one should contemplate, particularly once the null hypothesis of the poolability in (i) has been rejected. If the current null is not rejected then we have another case of "poolability". In fact, as noted in Answer 9.1, this is really what most econometricians mean by pooling data ("to pool or not to pool").

iii) The null hypothesis A, B = A_i, B means that the intercepts are common given that the slopes are the same. It is a conditional hypothesis. In fact, it is a null hypothesis leading to the test for group effects.

b) The tests associated to the above null hypotheses are presented below. We use the F test statistic throughout, although we acknowledge the existence of other tests. The F test of interest is the one for restricted versus unrestricted regression:

$$F = \frac{(\text{RRSS} - \text{URSS}) / df1}{\text{URSS} / df} \qquad \text{(A9.5.1)}$$

where RRSS is the restricted residual sum of squares, URSS is the unrestricted residual sum of squares, df is the number of degrees of freedom of the denominator, that is URSS, $df1$ is the number of degrees of freedom of the numerator, that is the difference of the degrees of freedom of RRSS and URSS.

i) To construct the F test statistic to test the null hypothesis A, B = A_i, B_i, we need two regressions: the unrestricted regression and the restricted one. The unrestricted regression is:

$$y_{it} = A_i + B_i x_{it} + u_{it} \quad \forall i,\ i = 1,2,3,\cdots,N \ \ t = 1,2,\cdots,T \qquad \text{(A9.5.2)}$$

The unrestricted residual sum of squares (RSS1) is the sum of individual residual sum of squares. The restricted residual sum of squares (RSS2) comes from the following pooled (OLS) regression:

$$y_{it} = A + Bx_{it} + u_{it} \qquad i = 1,2,3,\cdots,N,\ t = 1,2,\cdots,T \tag{A9.5.3}$$

The F test of interest is thus:

$$F = \frac{(\text{RSS2} - \text{RSS1})/[N(k+1)-(k+1)]}{\text{RSS1}/[NT - N(k+1)]} \tag{A9.5.4}$$

where k is the number of explanatory variables in the model excluding the constant term(s). If the F calculated is greater than the F from the table, one rejects the null hypothesis of "poolability"; otherwise, one accepts it. Equivalently, one can use the p value of the F test statistic. If the p value is less than the nominal level of significance, one rejects the null hypothesis; otherwise, one does not reject it.

ii) As above, to construct the F test statistic to test the null hypothesis A_i, $B = A_i$, B_i, we need two regressions: the unrestricted regression and the restricted one. The unrestricted regression is Equation (A9.5.2) with RSS1 as the relevant residual sum of squares. The restricted regression is as follows:

$$y_{it} = A_i + Bx_{it} + u_{it} \qquad i = 1,2,3,\cdots,N,\ t = 1,2,\cdots,T \tag{A9.5.5}$$

This regression acknowledges the existence of individual effects. Let us call the resulting residual sum of squares, RSS3. Thus, the F test statistic of interest is:

$$F = \frac{(\text{RSS3} - \text{RSS1})/k(N-1)}{\text{RSS1}/[NT - N(k+1)]} \tag{A9.5.6}$$

If the p value associated with the F test statistic is smaller than the nominal level of significance, one rejects the null hypothesis; otherwise, one accepts it ("poolability").

iii) Recall, the null hypothesis in this scenario is A, $B = A_i$, B. The elements to construct the relevant F test have been presented above. The F test statistic is:

$$F = \frac{(\text{RSS2} - \text{RSS3})/(N-1)}{\text{RSS3}/[NT - (N+k)]} \tag{A9.5.7}$$

The usual conclusion about nonrejection or rejection of the null hypothesis applies here.

Answer 9.6

a) We expect the following: Credit ratings and secondary market prices (or their principal components measurement) to positively impact on capital inflows. Indeed, both are measurements of a country's creditworthiness. An increase in creditworthiness attracts capital. The rate of return on the domestic stock market (relative to the US) is expected to have a positive impact on capital inflows. Indeed, an increase in the return rate attracts capital as the pay-off increases. Price-earnings ratio is expected to negatively impact on capital inflows. Indeed, an increase in the ratio means that price is greater than earnings; hence, it is a deterrent for attractiveness of capital. An increase in US interest means that it is more profitable to leave the capital in the US than to shift it to the region of interest as the capital becomes more rewarding in the US than elsewhere. An increase in US production activity means that the climate in the US is more favourable to investment than elsewhere; hence, it has a negative impact on capital inflows in the regions of interest. This also means that the principal components of the US interest rates and US industrial activity will exert a negative impact on capital inflows. The trend captures omitted variables. It can have any sign depending on the impact of the dominant missing variable.

b) The use of PCS is justified to the extent that credit ratings and secondary market prices are both measures of creditworthiness of a country. It means a high correlation is expected between the two in each individual country. This implicitly means using the two variables at the same time will not really help reduce multicollinearity. The use of PI is highly justified to the extent it is dominated by the interest rates, which are highly correlated. Moreover, all the countries face the same US interest rate and industrial production activity. Thus, in this particular case there is zero scope for reducing multicollinearity. Note that although pairwise high correlation can be misleading in the context of multiple regression, in the particular case of interest rates there is no doubt on multicollinearity.

c) Note that the null hypothesis of randomness of the individual effects is tested here using the Hausman m test. As said above, the m test statistic follows a chi-squared distribution. We do not reject the null hypothesis of the randomness of the individual effects as the p value of the test statistic (m) is far greater than any common level of significance. Indeed, if the test statistic is less than the critical value (or its associated p value is greater than the level of significance), one does not reject the null hypothesis, meaning the individual effects are random; otherwise, one rejects it and concludes that the individual effects are fixed.

d) The values of adjusted R^2 are incredibly high. This is simply due to the presence of some dummy variables to capture the Brady plan. In fact, without those dummies, the statistic reduces to 0.16. Credit ratings and secondary market prices through their first principal components have a positive impact on capital inflows. As predicted, US interest rates and US industrial activity, through their first principal components, negatively affect capital inflows in the Latin America countries. Return does not have an impact on capital inflows. As predicted, price-earnings ratio negatively affects capital inflows. A one-unit increase in the ratio reduces capital inflows by \$0.944 million (\$944,000.00), at least in the model with nominal interest rates. There seems to be some missing values which positively affect capital inflows. Note that we cannot compare directly the magnitudes of these coefficients as they are derived using different units of measurement. A computation of elasticity is in order. Yet, the existence of principal components brings a formidable problem of interpretation.

e) Most likely panel data unit root and cointegration issues should be looked at. This is so since most economic variables are not stationary.

Answer 9.7

a) Assuming that in Equation (Q9.7.1) $\alpha_1 = \alpha_2 = \ldots = \alpha_N = \alpha$ and $\beta_1 = \beta_2 = \ldots \beta_N = \beta$, then the pooled regression model is:

$$Y_{it} = \alpha + \beta X_{it} + u_{it} \qquad \text{(A9.7.1)}$$

where Y_{it} is panel data growth rate, X_{it} is panel data share of gross domestic investment to GDP and u_{it} is the error term. The OLS estimation of the model gives the results shown in Table 9.4.

b) The between regression model is the regression model using the group averages. That is, Equation (Q9.7.1) is transformed into:

$$\overline{Y}_i = \alpha + \beta \overline{X}_i + \overline{u}_i \qquad \text{(A9.7.2)}$$

The results are presented in Table 9.5.

TABLE 9.4
Pooled Growth Rate Regression Model Results: Four African Countries 1988–1997

Variable	Coefficient	Standard Error	t Statistic	Prob.
C	–5.489466	3.285004	–1.671068	0.1029
X_{it}	0.414359	0.125346	3.305720	0.0021
R^2	0.223345	Mean dependent variable		5.23000
Adjusted R^2	0.202907	RSS		419.7229
SE of regression	3.323453	LM(hetero.)		0.212406
DW statistic	1.412860	Prob(F statistic)		0.645000

TABLE 9.5
Between Growth Rate Regression Model Results: Four African Countries 1988–1997

Variable	Coefficient	Standard Error	t Statistic	Prob.
C	–3.206840	5.07871	–.631429	0.5920
$\overline{X}_i$	0.326125	195110	1.67149	0.2370
R^2	0.582801	Mean dependent variable		5.23000
Adjusted R^2	0.374202	RSS		2.52847
SE of regression	1.124380	LM(hetero.)		2.24246
		Prob(LM statistic)		0.13400

TABLE 9.6
Within Growth Rate Regression Model Results: Four African Countries 1988–1997

Variable	Coefficient	Standard Error	*t* Statistic	Prob.
X_{it}	0.493362	0.173225	2.84810	0.00700
R^2	0.279200	Mean dependent variable		5.23000
Adjusted R^2	0.196823	RSS		389.538
SE of regression	3.336110	LM(hetero.)		0.020963
DW statistic	1.554641	Prob(LM statistic)		0.885000

TABLE 9.7
Variance Components Growth Rate Regression Model Results: Four African Countries 1988–1997

Variable	Coefficient	Standard Error	*t* Statistic	Prob.
C	–6.82570	3.48023	–1.74775	0.0810
X_{it}	.437285	.132106	3.41011	0.0010
R^2	0.223345	Mean dependent variable		5.23000
Adjusted R^2	0.202907	RSS		420.09200
SE of regression	3.324920	LM(hetero.)		0.217901
DW statistic	1.417120	Prob(LM statistic)		0.641000

c) The fixed effects model is obtained by letting the individual effects in Equation (Q9.7.1) be fixed; that is:

$$Y_{it} = \alpha_i + \beta X_{it} + u_{it} \qquad \text{(A9.7.3)}$$

We use, however, the within version of Equation (A9.7.3); that is:

$$(Y_{it} - \bar{Y}_i) = \beta\,(X_{it} - \overline{X}_i) + (u_{it} - \bar{u}_i) \qquad \text{(A9.7.4)}$$

Table 9.6. shows the results of the exercise.

c) Error components models are derived under the condition that the individual effects are random. The model of interest reads as follows:

$$(Y_{it} - (1-\lambda)\overline{Y}_i) = \beta\,(X_{it} - (1-\lambda)\overline{X}_i) + (v_{it} - (1-\lambda)\bar{v}_i) \qquad \text{(A9.7.5)}$$

where:

$$\lambda = \left[\frac{\sigma_u^2}{\sigma_u^2 + T\sigma_\alpha^2}\right]^{1/2} \qquad \text{(A9.7.6)}$$

and $\qquad v_{it} = \alpha_i + u_{it}.$

As can be see if $\lambda = 0$ then GLS = within and if $\lambda = 1$ then GLS = OLS. Note that a constant term is usually added to Equation (A9.7.5). The results of the estimation of Equation (A9.7.5) are presented in Table 9.7.

d) The models are really comparable, at least the pooled (OLS) model, the within regression (fixed effects, FE) model and the random effects (RE or GLS) model. To throw more light on the results, we discuss some test results. The first question is whether the "poolability" condition is satisfied. The null hypothesis $\alpha, \beta = \alpha_i, \beta_i$ is not rejected. Indeed, the associated $F(6,32)$ with a value of 0.72023 and a p value of 0.6363 largely confirms it even at the 50 percent level of significance, as suggested by Maddala (1991, 256). The pooled model also indicates an absence of autocorrelation as well as a lack of heteroscedasticity. The nonrejection of the above null hypothesis means that the following two null hypotheses must not be rejected: $\alpha_i, \beta = \alpha_i, \beta_i$ and $\alpha, \beta = \alpha_i, \beta$. Indeed, the null hypothesis $\alpha_i, \beta = \alpha_i, \beta_i$ is not rejected, as the F test statistic value, $F(3,32) = 0.56976$, with an associated p value of 0.6390, indicates it. The other null hypothesis, $\alpha, \beta = \alpha_i, \beta$, is not rejected either, since the associated F test statistic with a value of $F(3,35) = 0.90405$ and a p value of 0.4490 confirms it. Overall, the pooled (OLS) results indicate that in the African context a 1 percent increase in the share of gross domestic investment to GDP brings about a 0.41 percent increase in GDP growth.

Note that a second look at the results indicates that $\beta_{GLS} \rightarrow \beta_{OLS}$. This can be justified in two ways. First, the random effects model supplants the fixed effects model in this exercise. Indeed, the Hausman m test whose null hypothesis is random effects and alternative hypothesis is fixed effects, with a value of 0.25047 and a p value of 0.6167, indicates that the random effects model is the adequate model. Second, and more important, the value taken by the weight factor as in Equation (A9.7.6) indicates that the GLS estimator goes to the OLS estimator. Indeed:

$$\lambda = \left[\frac{\sigma_u^2}{\sigma_u^2 + T\sigma_\alpha^2}\right]^{1/2} = \left[\frac{9.7384}{9.7384 + (10 * 0.75463)}\right]^{1/2} = 0.750607$$

that is, $\lambda \rightarrow 1$ as in Equation (A9.7.5) , hence $\beta_{GLS} \rightarrow \beta_{OLS}$.

Answer 9.8

Following the scheme developed in Answer 9.7 we first start examining the issue of "poolability". The null hypothesis of full poolability, that is, $\alpha, \beta = \alpha_i, \beta_i$, is rejected since the associated $F(34,36)$ with a value of 2.2768 has a p value of 0.0083, which is lower than any standard nominal level of significance. It means OLS results are invalid. The rejection of overall poolability allows us to consider the null hypothesis $\alpha_i, \beta = \alpha_i, \beta_i$. With an $F(17,36)$ value of 0.65342 associated with a p value of 0.8249 this null hypothesis is not rejected. This acknowledges the existence of country-specific effects and the commonality of money supply growth impact on inflation (common slope or elasticity). That is, the data pass the weaker form of poolability. The next concern is whether the country-specific effects are fixed or random. To answer this

TABLE 9.8
Within Inflation Regression Model Results:
Eighteen African Countries 1999–2002

Variable	Coefficient	Standard Error	t Statistic	Prob.
X_{it}	0.042427	0.055838	0.759834	0.45100
R^2	0.627381	Mean dependent variable		6.87222
Adjusted R^2	0.500831	RSS		2334.83
SE of regression	6.637270	LM(hetero.)		5.720640
DW statistic	1.821100	Prob(LM statistic)		0.017000

question, as above we recourse to the Hausman m test statistic, which has a value of 5.2151 and a p value of 0.0224. At the 5 percent or the 10 percent level of significance, the hypothesis of random effects is rejected in favour of fixed effects. The results are presented in Table 9.8.

The t test statistic value of the coefficient of money supply growth indicates an absence of relationship between money growth and inflation in the seventeen countries studied. A further look at the results leads to the conclusion that the latter are most likely not spurious given the size of the DW test statistic value. Indeed, it is well known that a white noise series is stationary (the reverse is not true). Perhaps the only worry is the size of the LM test statistic for heteroscedasticity. Indeed, there is the presence of heteroscedasticity at the 5 and 10 percent levels and not at the 1 percent level. The reader is invited to correct for heteroscedasticity and check whether the conclusion of the lack of relationship between money growth and inflation still holds.

9.4 SUPPLEMENTARY EXERCISES

Question 9.9 Consider the following model:

$$Y_{it} = \alpha_i + \beta X_{it} + u_{it} \tag{Q9.9.1}$$

where α_i is fixed. If one is only interested in the parameter β one can use either the first difference estimation or the within estimation. Carefully explain why the latter is better than the former. What happens if the time dimension is 2?

Question 9.10 The word "unbalanced" is met from time to time in econometrics. Explain two meanings of the concept, including the one in the panel data context.

Question 9.11 Using the data in Question 9.8 obtain the individual specific effects in the FE model.

Question 9.12 Consider the following model:

$$Y_{it} = \alpha_i + \lambda_t + \beta X_{it} + \gamma V_i + \delta W_t + u_{it} \tag{Q9.12.1}$$

where $i = 1, 2, 3, \ldots, N$ stands for individual, $t = 1, 2, 3, \ldots, T$ stands for time, u_{it} is the usual error term.

a) Explain the following: α_i, λ_t, V_i and W_t. When necessary provide examples.
b) Suppose that Equation (Q9.12.1) is a fixed effects model.
   i) Can you estimate the model as it stands? Why or why not? If not, provide the solution.
   ii) Suppose you decide to estimate the model using the within estimation. Indicate whether you can obtain all parameter estimators. Why or why not?
   iii) In any case, provide the within estimators of α_i and λ_t.
c) Suppose that Equation (Q9.12.1) is a random effects model.
   i) The model can be called a "two-way error components model". Explain.
   ii) Can you estimate all the parameters of the model? Why or why not? If not, provide the solution.

References

Ai, C. and E.C. Norton (2003), "Interaction terms in logit and probit models", *Economics Letters* 80:123–129.

Ando, A., F.M. Fisher, and H.A. Simon (1963), *Essays on the Structure of Social Science Models*, Cambridge: MIT Press.

Baltagi, B.H., J. Hidalgo, and Q. Li (1996), "A non parametric test for poolability using panel data", *Journal of Econometrics* 75:345–367.

Baltagi, B.H. (1995), *Econometric Analysis of Panel Data*, Chichester: John Wiley & Sons.

Banerjee, A., D.F. Hendry, and G.W. Smith (1986), "Exploring equilibrium relationships in econometrics through static models: Some Monte Carlo evidence", *Oxford Bulletin of Economics and Statistics* 51:345–350.

Banerjee, A., J. Dolado, J.W. Galbraith, and D.F. Hendry (1993), *Co-Integration, Error Correction, and the Econometric Analysis of Non-Stationary Data*, Oxford: Oxford University Press.

Breitung, J. (1994), "Testing for unit roots in panel data: Are wages on different bargaining levels cointegrated?", *Applied Economics* 26:353–361.

Cameron, S. (1993), "Why is the R-squared adjusted reported?", *Journal of Quantitative Economics* 9:183–186.

Chuhan, P., S. Claessens, and N. Mamingi (1998), "Equity and bond flows to Latin America and Asia: The role of global and country factors", *Journal of Development Economics* 55:439–463.

Dasgupta, S., B. Laplante, N. Mamingi, and H. Wang (2001), "Inspections, pollution prices, and environmental performance: Evidence from China", *Ecological Economics* 36:487–498.

Diebold, F.X. (2001), *Elements of Forecasting*, Cincinnati: South-Western.

Downes, A.S. and W. McLean (1988), The estimation of missing values of employment in Barbados", Research Paper 13, Centre of Statistics of Trinidad and Tobago, 115–136.

Downes, A.S., N. Mamingi, and R.M. Antoine (2004), "Labour market regulation and employment in the Caribbean", in J. Heckman and C. Pagès (eds.), *Law and Employment from Latin America and the Caribbean*, Chicago: Chicago University Press, 517–551.

Engle, R.F. and C.W.J. Granger (1987), "Co-integration and error correction: Representation, estimation and testing", *Econometrica* 55:251–276.

Engle, R.F. and B.S. Yoo (1987), "Forecasting and testing in cointegrated systems", *Journal of Econometrics* 535:143–159.

Engle, R.F., D.F. Hendry, and J.F. Richard (1983), "Exogeneity", *Econometrica* 55:277–304.

Ericsson, N.R. (1997), "Distributed lags" , in D. Glasner (ed.), *Business Cycles and Depressions: An Encyclopedia.* New York: Garland Publishing, 168–173.

Ghosh, S.K. (1991), *Econometrics: Theory and Applications*, Englewood Cliffs: Prentice Hall.

Granger, C.W.J. (1969), "Investigating relations by econometric models and cross spectral methods", *Econometrica* 37:428–438.

Granger, C.W.J. (1983), "Co-integrated variables and error correcting models", Discussion Paper 83-13a, University of California, San Diego.

Granger, C.W.J. (1990), "Aggregation of time series variables: A survey", in T. Baker and M.H. Pesaran (eds.), *Disaggregation in Econometric Modelling*, London: Routledge, 17–34.

Granger, C.W.J. and A.J. Morris (1976), "Time series modelling and interpretation", *Journal of the Royal Statistical Society Ser. A* 139(Pt 2):246–257.

Granger, C.W.J. and P. Newbold (1974), "Spurious regressions in econometrics", *Journal of Econometrics* 2:111–120.

Granger, C.W.J. and P. Newbold (1977), *Forecasting Economic Time Series*, New York: Academic Press.

Granger, C.W.J. and P.L. Siklos (1995), "Systematic sampling, temporal aggregation, seasonal adjustment, and cointegration: Theory and evidence", *Journal of Econometrics* 66:357–369.

Greene, W.H. (2003), *Econometric Analysis,* 5th ed., Englewood Cliffs: Prentice Hall.

Gujarati, D.N. (1995), *Basic Econometrics*, 3rd ed., New York: McGraw-Hill.

Halvorsen, R. and R. Palmquist (1980), "The interpretation of dummy variables in semilogarithmic equations", *American Economic Review* 70:474–475.

Hamilton, J.D. (1994), *Time Series Analysis*, Princeton: Princeton University Press.

Hardy, M.A. (1993), *Regression with Dummy Variables*, Newbury Park: Sage Publications.

Hausman, J.A. and W.E. Taylor (1981), "Panel data and unobserved individual effects", *Econometrica* 49:1377–1398.

Hendry, D.F. (1995), *Dynamic Econometrics*, Oxford: Oxford University Press.

Holden, K., D.A. Peel, and J.L. Thompson (1990), *Economic Forecasting: An Introduction*, Cambridge: Cambridge University Press.

Howard, M. and N. Mamingi (2001), "The monetary approach to the balance of payments: An application to Barbados", unpublished manuscript.

Howard, M. and N. Mamingi (2002), "The monetary approach to the balance of payments: An application to Barbados", *Singapore Economic Review* 47:213–228.

Hsiao, C. (1986), *Analysis of Panel Data*, Cambridge: Cambridge University Press.

Im, K.S., M.H. Pesaran, and Y. Shin (1996), "Testing for unit roots in heterogenous panels", Discussion Papers, Cambridge: University of Cambridge.

Johansen, S. (1988), "Statistical analysis of cointegration vectors", *Journal of Economic Dynamics and Control* 12:231–254.

Johnston, J. (1984), *Econometric Methods*, 3rd ed., New York: McGraw-Hill.

Johnston, J. and J. DiNardo (1997), *Econometric Methods*, 4th ed., New York: McGraw-Hill.

Judge, G.G., W.E. Griffiths, R.C. Hill, H. Lütkepohl, and T.C. Lee (1985), *The Theory and Practice of Econometrics*, 2nd ed., New York: John Wiley & Sons.

Kao, C. (1997), "Spurious regression and residual based tests for cointegration in panel data", *Journal of Econometrics* 90:1–44.

Kennedy, P. (1992), *A Guide to Econometrics,* 3rd ed., Cambridge: MIT Press.

Kennedy, P.E. (1981), "Estimation with correctly interpreted dummy variables in semilogarithmic equations", *American Economic Review* 71:801.

Klevmarken, N.A. (1989), "Panel studies: What can we learn from them?", *European Economic Review* 33:523–529.

Koop, G. (2000), *Analysis of Economic Data*, Chichester: John Wiley & Sons.

Koutsoyiannis, A. (1977), *Theory of Econometrics*, 2nd ed., Hampshire: MacMillan Press.

Lahiri, K. and N. Mamingi (1995), "Testing for cointegration: Power versus frequency of observation: another view", *Economic Letters* 49:121–124.

Lahiri, K. and N. Mamingi (1996), "Granger causality and misspecified vector autoregressions", in A. Banerjee and B. Chatterjee (eds.), *Economic Theory, Trade and Quantitative Economics: Essays in Honour of Professor P.N. Roy*, Calcutta: University of Calcutta, 315–329.

Lahiri, K. and P. Schmidt (1978), "On the estimation of triangular systems", *Econometrica* 46:1217–1221.

Levin, A. and C.F. Lin (1993), "Unit root test in panel data: New results", Economics Working Paper Series, University of California at San Diego, 93–56.

Lewis, D. and N. Mamingi (2003), "Valuing Barbados Harrison's Cave: A contingent valuation approach", *Journal of Eastern Caribbean Studies* 28:30–56.

Litterman, R.B. (1979), "Techniques of forecasting using vector autoregressions", Federal Working Paper, Reserve Bank of Minneapolis, 15.

Maddala, G. S. (1977), *Econometrics*, New York: McGraw-Hill.

Maddala, G. S. (1983), *Limited Dependent and Qualitative Variables in Econometrics*, Cambridge: Cambridge University Press.

Maddala, G. S. (1991), "To pool or not to pool: That is the question", *Journal of Quantitative Economics* 7:255–264.

Maddala, G.S. (1992), *Introduction to Econometrics*, 2nd ed., Englewood Cliffs: Prentice Hall.

Maddala, G.S. and In.-M. Kim (1998), *Unit Roots Cointegration and Structural Change*, Cambridge: Cambridge University Press.

Makridakis, S., S.C. Wheelwright, and V.E. McGee (1983), *Forecasting: Methods and Applications*, New York: John Wiley & Sons.

Mamingi, N. (1984), "The causal relationship between money supply and inflation in Zaire, 1965–1982: A time series approach", Research Paper, Institute of Social Sciences, The Hague.

Mamingi, N. (1992), "Essays on the effects of misspecified dynamics and temporal aggregation on cointegrated relationships", unpublished PhD thesis, Department of Economics, State University of New York at Albany.

Mamingi, N. (1993), "Residual based tests for cointegration: Their actual size under aggregation over time", Albany Discussion Papers 93-09, Department of Economics, State University of New York at Albany.

Mamingi, N. (1996), "Aggregation over time, error correction models and Granger causality: A Monte Carlo investigation", *Economics Letters* 52:7–14.

Mamingi, N. (1997), "Saving-investment correlations and capital mobility: The experience of developing countries", *Journal of Policy Modeling* 19:605–626.

Mamingi, N. (1999), "Testing for convergence and common features in international output: The case of the Eastern Caribbean countries", *Journal of Eastern Caribbean Studies* 24:15–40.

Mamingi, N., K.M. Chomitz, D.A. Gray, and E. Lambin (1996), "Spatial patterns of deforestation in Cameroon and Zaire", Poverty-Growth-Environment Working Paper No. 8, Washington, D.C.: World Bank.

Marcellino, M. (1999), "Some consequences of temporal aggregation in empirical analysis", *Journal of Business and Economic Statistics* 17:129–136.

McCoskey, S. and C. Kao (1998), "A residual based test of the null of cointegration in panel data", *Econometric Reviews* 17:57–84.

Mizon, G.E. (1995), "A simple message for autocorrelation correctors: Don't", *Journal of Econometrics* 69:267–288.

Mukherjee, C., H. White, and M. Wuyts (1998), *Econometrics and Data Analysis for Developing Countries*, London: Routledge.

Pedroni, P. (1995), "Panel cointegration: Asymptotic and finite sample properties of pooled time series tests with an application to the PPP hypothesis", Indiana University Working Papers in Economics, No. 95–013, June.

Pesaran, M.H. and Y. Shin (1998), "Generalized impulse response analysis in linear multivariate models", *Economics Letters* 58:17–29.

Pesaran, M.H. and R.P. Smith (1995), "Estimating long-run relationships from dynamic heterogenous panels", *Journal of Econometrics* 68:79–113.

Phillips, A.W. (1954), "Stabilization policy in a closed economy", *Economic Journal* 64:290–323.

Phillips, P.C.B. (1986), "Understanding spurious regressions in econometrics", *Journal of Econometrics* 33: 311–340.

Phillips, P.C.B. and B. Hansen (1990), "Statistical inference in instrumental variables regression with *I*(1) process, *Review of Economics and Statistics* 57:99–125.

Phillips, P.C.B. and H.R. Moon (2000), "Nonstationary panel data analysis: An overview of some recent developments", *Econometric Reviews* 19:263–286.

Philips, P.C.B. and H.R. Wickens (1978a), *Exercises in Econometrics,* Vol. I, Oxford: Philip Allan/Ballinger Publishing.

Philips, P.C.B. and H.R. Wickens (1978b), *Exercises in Econometrics,* Vol. II, Oxford: Philip Allan/Ballinger Publishing.

Pindyck, R.S. and D.L. Rubinfeld (1981), *Econometric Models and Economic Forecasts*, 2nd ed., New York: McGraw-Hill.

Pindyck, R.S. and D.L. Rubinfeld (1998), *Econometric Models and Economic Forecasts,* 5th edition, New York: McGraw-Hill/Irwin.

Ramanathan, R. (1998), *Introductory Econometrics with Applications*, 4th ed., Fort Worth: Dryden Press.

Rao, P. and R.L. Miller (1971), *Applied Econometrics*, Belmont: Wadworth Publishing.

Sargan, J. D. (1964), "Wages and prices in the United Kingdom: A study in econometric methodology", in P.E. Hart and J.K. Whitaker (eds.), *Econometric Analysis for National Planning*, London: Butterworths.

Sims, C.A. (1980), "Macroeconomics and reality", *Econometrica* 48:1–48.

Stock, J.H. (1987a), "Asymptotic properties of least squares estimators of co-integrated vectors", *Econometrica* 55:1035–1056.

Stock, J.H. (1987b), "Temporal aggregation and structural inference in macroeconomics: A comment", *Carnegie Rochester Series on Public Policy* 26:131–140.

Stock, J.H. and M.W. Watson (1988a), "Variable trends in economic time series", *Journal of Economic Perspectives* 83:1097–1107.

Stock, J.H. and M.W. Watson (1988b), "Testing for common trends", *Journal of the American Statistical Association* 83:1097–1107.

Stock, J.H. and M.W. Watson (2001), "Vector autoregressions", *Journal of Economic Perspectives*, 15:101–115.

Stram, D.O. and W.W.S. Wei (1986), "Temporal aggregation in the ARIMA process", *Journal of Time Series Analysis* 7:279–292.

Van Garderen, K.J. and C. Shah (2002), "Exact interpretation of dummy variables in semilogarithmic equations", *Econometrics Journal* 5:149–159.

Vashid, F. (1999), "Partial pooling: A possible answer to 'To Pool or not to Pool'", in R.F. Engle and H. White (eds.), *Cointegration, Causality and Forecasting*, New York: Oxford University Press, 410–428.

Veall, M.R. and K.F. Zimmermann (1994), "Goodness of fit measures in the Tobit model", *Oxford Bulletin of Economics and Statistics* 56:485–499.

Wang, H., N. Mamingi, B. Laplante, and S. Dasgupta (2003), "Incomplete enforcement of pollution regulation: Bargaining power of Chinese factories", *Environmental and Resource Economics* 24:245–262.

Watson, P.K. and S.S. Teelucksingh (2002), *A Practical Introduction to Econometric Methods: Classical and Modern*, Kingston: University of the West Indies Press.

Wei, W.W.S. (1981), "The effect of systematic sampling and temporal aggregation on causality: A cautionary note", *Journal of the American Statistical Association* 378:316–319.

Wei, W.W.S. (1982), "Effect of systematic sampling on ARIMA models", *Communication in Statistics, Theory, and Math* A10:2389–2398.

Weiss, A.A. (1984), "Systematic sampling and temporal aggregation in time series models", *Journal of Econometrics* 26:271–281.

Woolridge, J.M. (2000), *Introductory Econometrics: A Modern Approach*, Australia: South-Western College Publishing.

Zeimer, R.F. and M.E. Wetzstein (1983), "A Stein-rule method for pooling data", *Economics Letters* 11:137–143.

Zellner, A. and C. Montmarquette (1971), "A study of some aspects of temporal aggregation problems in econometric analyses", *Review of Economics and Statistics* 53:335–342.

Index